LOST AT SEA

Also by the Authors

Michael Goss

The Evidence For Phantom Hitchhikers (1984)
The Halifax Slasher (1987)
Poltergeists: An Annotated Bibliography, 1882–1979 (1980)

George Behe

Titanic: *Psychic Forewarnings of a Tragedy* (1988)
The Launching of the Titanic*'s Lifeboats: A New Chronology* (1992)
Titanic: *Safety, Speed and Sacrifice* (1994)

LOST AT SEA

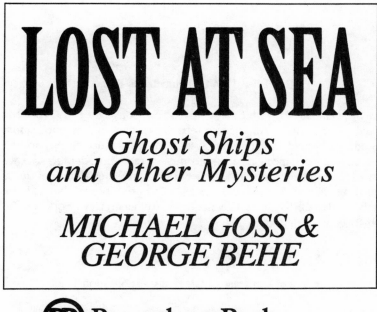

Ghost Ships and Other Mysteries

MICHAEL GOSS &
GEORGE BEHE

59 John Glenn Drive
Amherst, NewYork 14228-2197

Published 1994 by Prometheus Books

98 97 96 95 94 5 4 3 2 1

Library of Congress Cataloging-in-Publication Data

Goss, Michael.
Lost at sea : ghost ships and other mysteries / Michael Goss and George Behe.
p. cm.
Includes bibliographical references.
ISBN 0-87975-913-5 (acid-free)
1. Shipwrecks. 2. Sea stories. 3. Supernatural. I. Behe, George. II. Title.
G525.G67 1994
904—dc20 94-20990
CIP

Printed in the United States of America on acid-free paper.

To our parents,
Henry and Ivy Goss
and
Paul and Helen Behe,
with love

Contents

II. Mysteries Under the Sea

III. Lost Liners

IV. Assorted Tales

Acknowledgments

Source material for a book such as this one is seldom acquired without the authors asking for help from many diverse sources. We would like to thank the following individuals and institutions for their generous assistance during the research phase of this book.

Mike Dash provided extensive help and advice on our chapter dealing with submarines, for which we are very grateful. Les Cozens, Sean Tudor, George Goldsmith Carter, and the Deal Public Library were all of great help during our search for information on the Goodwins Ghost Ship. Ed and Karen Kamuda (president and secretary respectively of the Titanic Historical Society) kindly provided us with manuscript material detailing the Frank Goldsmith *Titanic* case. Don Lynch (THS historian and author of Titanic: *An Illustrated History*) generously made his own *Titanic* files available for our perusal and use. Kalman Tanito put forth great effort to provide us with translations of *Titanic*-related material from Finland. Geoff Whitfield (secretary of the British Titanic Society) kindly put us onto the track of the case involving Tyrone Power and the last voyage of the *President.* Roland Hauser's generous and unhesitating assistance was absolutely crucial to our discovery of the truth about the "haunted" UB-65. Also, we are grateful to the Bundesarchiv-Militararchiv in Freiburg, Germany, for providing us with photocopies of the UB-65's log and war daybook, with further thanks to R. M. Coppock of the Ministry of Defence Directorate of Naval Staff Duties (Foreign Documents Section) for making it possible for us to scrutinize documents relevant to this chapter.

We are especially grateful to the National Archives, the U.S. Navy, and the Peninsular and Oriental Steam Navigation Company, for providing photographs depicting ships and events discussed in this book.

To all of the above, our sincere thanks.

Introduction

> This is no fairy tale, and I've not done yet; and I think this yarn should prove to you that some mighty strange things do happen at sea, and always will while the world lasts. It's the home of all the mysteries; for it's the one place that is really difficult for humans to investigate. Now just listen. . . .
>
> Duprey, hero of
> William Hope Hodgson's *The Stone Ship* (1914)

Without further ado, then, we enter Duprey's watery world. You will not find any stone ships in the next few pages, but you will find the mysteries he speaks of: you will also find the authors grimly confronting his aphorism that the sea, and more pertinently the mysteries it breeds, are entities "really difficult for humans to investigate."

Perhaps the authors will not prove that some mighty strange things happen at sea. Perhaps we only manage to prove that there are some people who *say* mighty strange things happen at sea. There is an important distinction here, but the reader will discover that a study of that distinction itself is truly fascinating.

"Second sight"—the term is an ancient one and is widely accepted as meaning that certain gifted people are sometimes "permitted" to catch a fleeting glimpse of events that have not yet occurred. There is no way of predicting just *when* such a glimpse will be vouchsafed to the individual in question, but it is surprising how often such psychic experiences are connected with approaching misfortune or tragedy. And, in the vast litany of such experiences, none are more dramatic than those associated with the sea, with ships, and with the men who sail them.

A mother pleads with her son not to sail on a certain steamer because she has dreamt—three times in a row—that the vessel will never reach her destination. Modern-day observers watch in awe as an old windjammer—blazing from bow to stern—dutifully reenacts a two-hundred-year-old tragedy that the observers' fathers and grandfathers also watched reenacted with the same sense of awe. A crewman walks past a solitary figure seated in the ship's restaurant only to turn a moment later and find the restaurant empty. A red glow appears in the darkness ahead of a modern warship, and the faint outline of an old galleon, her sails in tatters, is seen approaching against the wind—only to vanish a moment later before the startled eyes of fascinated observers.

Such things have been reported for centuries and are being reported to this very day. The witnesses are, for the most part, sober and responsible human beings. They are people like you and me.

And yet the experiences these people claim to have undergone are so extraordinary that we often do not know what to make of them. The accounts in question are greeted with incredulity by some and, often, with credulity by others. In other words, each listener's personal belief system must be called into play to help process and digest the narrative in question; this is a necessary step if the listener wishes to come to comfortable terms with *any* kind of extraordinary information.

However, when stories of remarkable true experiences are being related to rapt listeners, the listeners themselves are at a disadvantage: they often do not know if *all* the pertinent facts are being relayed to them. The narrator may inadvertently leave out details which to him seem unimportant or trivial but which, to a listener with wider experience in those areas, might suggest a rational explanation for the narrator's extraordinary adventure.

Down through the centuries countless mariners have undergone unusual experiences at sea—experiences that they cannot readily explain. Many of those experiences will remain forever unexplained, "hidden" in the trackless waste of the briny deep. The sea is a place that has her own way of hiding what she doesn't want known.

But if we hope to understand *any* of these strange events and determine the truth about them, we first have to comprehend the facts as they are known and then determine what, if any, rational explanation is possible. This, then, is what the present authors have attempted to do in this book; the success or failure of our efforts must be determined by the reader himself.

One way or another, port or starboard . . . welcome aboard.

I

Ghost Ships

1

The Ghost Ship of the Goodwins Meets the *Flying Dutchman*

It is the night of the thirteenth of February, a night governed by a ferocious wind that blows across the English Channel driving ships before it and the good people of the Kentish coastal towns home to their firesides.

But you—you will not see your fireside for many a long hour yet. You are a seaman. You are on watch. The merciless wind has edged your small ship uncomfortably close to a stretch of water that it is traditional for seamen to hate: the notorious Goodwin Sands.

You do not hate the Goodwins, however. You respect them, but you do not fear them. True, the sands have taken hundreds, perhaps thousands of ships, but it is not inevitable that they will take yours, not even with this gale blowing on a night obscured by dark clouds and driving rain. And you are not superstitious. Perhaps you are too familiar with the real signs and dangers of the sea to worry about those conjured up in tales told in the night watches, tales of phantom ships bathed in eerie light, for example.

So when a strange sailing vessel sweeps across your bow as if materialized from the blackest portions of the night, you are not thinking of ghosts. She looks too real and solid to be a ghost. The shock comes from the suddenness, and only moments later do you find yourself troubled by the incongruity of her: by the obsolete three-mast design or the fact that she has taken in no sail . . . by the blaze of lights which seems to come from below her decks or—least credible of all—the sounds of laughter, music, and gay abandon you hear despite the roar of the waves and wind. Then a sense of alarm as you realize that no one on her, not even the shadowy, upright form at her helm, seems aware of the dangers as the ship is impelled toward the unseen water-wastes of the sands somewhere up ahead. Perhaps you utter something that brings other members of your crew to your elbow. Perhaps, then, you are not alone as you watch the ship churning toward terrible catastrophe on a course so direct that it seems preordained.

Then over the sounds of wind and waves comes the muffled roar of a hull ramming itself into the embrace of the Goodwins. Other noises, too, which seem to defy the acoustical competition of the elements: the snap of spars, the tortured groan of timbers parting and, like a record suddenly played at a wrong and faster speed, laughter turning into screams of terror. Then the lights of the ship vanish. There is only wind, water, impenetrable dark.

Do not send up a distress flare; do not reach for your radio. What you saw, what you heard, were real . . . but neither Coast Guard nor the lifeboatmen of Deal or Ramsgate will want to know. There is nothing for them to search for, nobody to rescue. Down the centuries they have searched many times before, always on the night of February the thirteenth and always in vain. They know all about the ghost ship of the Goodwins. Now you know of her, too.

Eight miles or so seaward from the Kentish town of Deal on England's southern coast, the Goodwin Sands sprawl across one of the busiest shipping areas in the world in the shape of a giant lobster. Pierced by clear-water channels or "swatches" varying in depth from a few feet to fathoms and pitted with shallow pools known locally as "fox-falls," the sands present a desolate enough picture at low tide, but it is when high tide steals in, covering even the highest (northerly) parts beneath at least eight feet of water that they revert to the menace sailors have feared for centuries. In the phrase penned by William Lambarde in 1570, this ten-by-four-mile shoal is notorious as "a great gulf and ship swallower": perhaps the worst hazard of its kind anywhere on the globe.

Writers habitually glamorize the Goodwins, talking of them as "treacherous" and "fatal." No doubt on occasions—upon too many occasions—they have proven to be both, but viewed at low water they are less than spectacular or dramatic. A prospect of monotonous, dreary mud archipelagos greets the eye, but, to be honest, the magic of the Goodwins has little to do with their physical appearance. It is the imagination that transforms them into an uncanny realm whose name cannot fail to evoke images of storm, shipwreck, and tragedy. There would be something very wrong if the Goodwins lacked at least one supernatural story and it would be just as odd if that narrative did not feature a ghost of some former casualty.

Logically enough, just such a story exists, a story of a ghost ship lit with eerie, phosphorescent light, a spectral record of a long-past tragedy born of homicidal jealousy that doomed the vessel to hoist sail when the anniversary of that evil deed should come round. Again and again and again the baffled lifeboatmen look on as she rushes unheeding into the grim lips of those treacherous, fatal quicksands—

The Goodwins are not quicksands in the common sense of the word. They are a great sandbank roughly aligned north to south, lat. 51° 9′ 35″ by 51° 19′ 23″, whose dimensions and outline vary according to weather and tidal movements, as do the swatches that dissect them, although the larger and deeper ones like "Ramsgate Man's Bight," the quarter-to-three-quarter mile channel leading into "Trinity Bay," are reasonably constant. It is to Treanor, chaplain at the Mission to Seamen, Deal and the Downs, that we owe the idea that the Goodwins are "not unlike a great lobster, with his back to the east, and his claws, legs and feelers extending westwards towards Deal and the shipping in the Downs." Ironically in view of their ferocious reputation, the Goodwins act as a natural breakwater from easterly gales, and the deepwater Downs has been honored as a refuge for shipping from earliest times. The Goodwins are clear sand and resting on blue clay to depths estimated at anything from fifteen to ninety feet. At low water many parts become dry and almost as hard to the step as stone, although the southern sections—scenes of numerous nineteenth-century wrecks like the *Ganges, Leda,* and *Sorrento*—are barely uncovered at low tide and are noticeably more yielding beneath a walker's feet. During the last century, when there appears to have been a vogue for confronting the menace of the sands, visitors with more than their share of bravado staged picnics, cricket matches, and once (on August 31, 1855) a one-mile cycle race against this lonely vista broken only by spars and ribs of lost vessels. What a grandly Victorian image is conjured up by the idea of cricket on the Goodwins! Titillated by the notion of flirting with death the players certainly were, but they were safe enough until the tide turned. The worst inconvenience of the 1824 match was that fielding (unsurprisingly!) was rather awkward; the problems about the 1839 game, when the players had to be rescued by lugger, have been variously attributed to a change in the wind or to the suspicion the participants had imbibed too freely of alcohol.

That normally sensible folk should go to all the trouble and cost involved merely to be able to say they'd picnicked and frolicked on the Goodwins is an oblique compliment to the doom-laden reputation of the sands. As we have implied, they exert a spell over the human imagination vastly disproportionate to their physical appearance. Men have found them a place to be buried, not only by accident, but by choice, which is a still greater compliment. An eighty-four-year-old man named Granville was interred there in accordance with his will in April 1705. The *London Evening Post* of May 16, 1751, reported that a coffin bearing the embalmed corpse of Francis Humphry Merrydith, lately recovered off North Foreland by the Hamburg-bound *Johannes,* had also been buried in the Goodwins, and again as set down in the deceased's will. Some mystery revolves around why these two eighteenth-century gents (neither of whom appears to have had any close connection with the sea, let alone the Goodwins) should have elected to be laid to rest in a cemetery of so many ships. But perhaps that was the reason.

For that, all else apart, is what the Goodwin Sands mean to most of us. Those spars and ribs we just mentioned are the skeletal tokens of the Goodwins' unenviable record as a ship devourer. Not for nothing did Shakespeare have Salarino talk about them as "a very dangerous flat and fatal, where the carcass of many a tall ship lie buried"; contemporary audiences of *The Merchant of Venice* would have caught the allusion at once and probably felt that there were few likelier places for Antonio's "ship of rich lading" to founder. As late as 1859 Board of Trade statistics showed that on average a dozen British ships came to grief on the Goodwins every year. Early and primitive attempts at beacons proved impractical for want of firm foundations and it was only the advent of a lightship system beginning in 1809 that bilked the sands of their regular annual tribute.

Many folk still harbor the false belief that any ship driven onto the Goodwins by a gale is irrevocably doomed to be sucked down in an instant. In fact, the process is usually more leisurely but no less destructive. A vessel *may* vanish immediately if it chances to strike the east or southeast slopes of the sands, recoiling back and heeling over into the fifty-fathom depths of the outer edges, but a more frequent and greater peril is that it will be helplessly grounded and demolished piecemeal by the remorseless waves, the remains being slowly covered by the constantly shifting, realigning sands. The Goodwins, declared George Byng Gattie in his 1890 *Memorials,* are "little more than one vast Golgotha, the grave indeed of thousands of brave and gallant hearts, who have hurried to their doom with a rapidity and certainty alike appalling."

The only things more attracted to the Goodwins than helpless ships and seagulls are legends. The earliest dwelt upon the supposed origins of this maritime mortuary. They told how the sands were once the "low, fertile island of Lomea" (to quote John Twyne in *De Rebus Albonicis Britannicus,* 1590), part of the estates held by Earl Goodwin, the Saxon warrior-patriot who oversaw the south coast defenses. They were "very fruitful and had much pasture," but for one reason or another they "sank suddenly into the sea." The connection between the hero-patriot earl and the sands that bear his name may be a piece of folk legend; some writers have suggested that monkish and perhaps Norman scribes hoped to discredit Goodwin by associating him with the terrible ship-engulfer. Although Lomea may have been known to Roman cartographers as Infera Insulum, and certainly to Canterbury schoolmaster John Twyne, whom we just cited, geological and archaeological evidence of it is slender, while Lambarde's assertion that the land was inundated by the same sea action that flooded Flanders in 1099 has been ruled out no matter how often other cartographers have repeated it.

A more endearing tale blames the submersion on ecclesiastical malpractice. The story as sermonized by Bishop Latimer in 1550 goes that in the reign of Henry VIII "an old man with a white beard" told Sir Thomas More that a church at "Tenterden was the cause of Goodwin Sands." His reasoning seemed hard to follow, but it drew on the folk tradition that the abbot of Rochester supposedly subverted the funds set aside for maintenance of the sea-wall for building an impressive new church at nearby Tenterden, with the result that the defenses were breached and the land drowned by sudden incursion of high seas.

> Well then (quoth Maister Moore) how say you in this matter? What think ye to be the cause of these shelves and flats that stoppe up Sandwich haven? Forsooth sir (quoth he) I am an old man, I thinke that Tenterton steeple is the cause of Goodwin Sands. For I am an old man, Sir . . . and I may remember when there was no steeple at all there. And before that Tenterton steeple was in building, there was no manner of speaking any flats or sands that stopped the haven, and therefore I think that Tenterton's steeple is the cause of the destroying and decay of Sandwich haven.

Since the Goodwins existed long before any sizable church at Tenterden the explanation is more than slightly dubious, but the proverbial phrase "Goodwin Sands and Tenterden Steeple" lived on for many years as an expression for any illogical answer or non sequitur piece of reasoning.

These folk tales aroused the curiosity of scholars throughout the nineteenth-century, but the Goodwins legend still being told today is of a different caliber. As we have suggested already, few places deserve to be haunted more than this nautical graveyard with its sorry catalogue of wrecked vessels. What better venue than the Goodwins for a retelling of that classic sea mystery, the "Phantom Ship"? And the Goodwins have no shortage of tragic candidates for the role of phantom-ship-in-residence: from the thirteen men-of-war lost there with twelve hundred men on November 26, 1703, virtually up until the present. Yet the Ghost Ship of the Goodwins is none of the famous casualties. The craft that ghost-loving visitors are told to expect one certain day once every fifty years, when it allegedly celebrates the anniversary of its destruction upon the Sands, is the *Lady Luvibund.*

Or *Lady Lovibond*; as you may have guessed, this is a story with variations of detail, the implications of which we will deal with later. If you are the kind of reader who is prone to expect this type of narrative flexibility, the chances are that you are able to appreciate the difference between a told-as-true ghost story which is actually legendary (that is, not literally or 100 percent true, though the narrator assures us that it is) and an authenticated one (that is, a story which presents evidence in support of its authenticity, and, moreover, evidence which somebody has looked into and approved). The former is folklore, the latter—for want of a prettier phrase—parapsychological.

And if you are the kind of reader who has studied parapsychology's century-plus records of authenticated apparitions, you may feel vaguely uneasy about any ghost that keeps regular anniversaries. Frankly, the ones in the parapsychological records are boringly irregular in their appearances; the majority are seen once and gone forever. Folklore ghosts often if not always manifest on cue to celebrate their last moment on the physical plane. But enough of that for now.

Far more regular than the phantom craft's cyclical reappearances on the Goodwins is her recurrence in anthologies of amazing-but-true maritime mysteries. This explains why the *Lady Luvibund* not only ranks alongside the *Flying Dutchman* as one of the classic ghost stories of the sea (albeit on a minor scale), it also explains those variations in the telling on which we just remarked. What follows is taken from *The Goodwin Sands* (1953) by George Goldsmith Carter, former lightship-man and local historian. His was definitely not the earliest printed version, but (as will be discussed) it proved one of the most influential inasmuch as it placed the anniversary-observing spectral vessel at the disposal of later writers, particularly those whose approach to ghost stories was eclectic rather than discriminating.

Tempestuous passions, love, and homicide are key ingredients of many a traditional ghost story. The *Lady Luvibund* adventure has them aplenty, but a cast of only three main players: the vessel's just-married captain, Simon Reed, and his "young and beautiful bride," who are using a general cargo run to Oporto as their honeymoon trip, and the obligatory villain, John Rivers. The ship sailed from London on February 13, 1748, with Reed unaware that Rivers, best man at his wedding and now first mate on the *Lady Luvibund,* had been in love with the bride and was nursing a jealous hatred for the man who took her from him. This may never have been known at all save for the fact that at an inquiry sometime later Rivers's mother testified that her son had vowed to be revenged on the captain even if it cost him his life.

The Thames was cleared and the vessel on its way past the Kentish coast. Down below in the cabin the lights blazed on linen and silverware; laughter rang out as toasts were drunk to the happy couple by the bride's relatives and friends. On deck Rivers fanned his obsessive jealousy until, goaded by these festive sounds, he took up a belaying pin and slipped silently behind the helmsman. Shattering the man's skull with one ferocious blow, the mate seized the helm and jerked the *Lady Luvibund* deep into the treacherous Goodwins. Mast and timbers crashed down, trapping the revellers while over the din of tortured wood and pounding waves echoed "the hideous cacophony of a madman's laughter." By next morning the sands had lived up to their reputation; every trace of the *Lady Luvibund* and those on board her had been swallowed forever. Or so it seemed.

Fifty years later to the fatal February 13, Captain James Westlake of the *Edenbridge* was forced to swing his helm violently to avoid a three-masted schooner that bore down on him without warning, all sails set and with sounds of "female voices and gaiety coming from below." So incensed was he at this dangerous lack of seamanship that he reported the incident when he got ashore and was perhaps surprised to learn that the crew of a fishing vessel had seen the schooner go onto the Goodwins where she started to break up—only to have vanished without hint of spar or canvas by the time they arrived to help. A similar phantom wreck—breaking up on the Goodwins one minute, gone the next—baffled some Deal residents. A century later an American vessel on February 13, 1848, witnessed exactly the same phenomenon, as did a group of watchers on shore a half-century thereafter.

"So through all eternity," ends Carter, "every fifty years and on the thirteenth of February, a madman's deed of violence and treachery is reenacted and the phantom schooner is doomed to wreckage on the same spot. Real ghosts are far from being the shadowy, insubstantial things of popular belief."

We have selected George Carter's version of this story not with a view to deriding or criticizing it, but simply because so many later writers appear to have been indebted to it. A selective sample of them appears in the bibliography to this chapter. One inevitable feature of the borrowing process is that certain details are altered—for instance, Simon Reed becomes Simon Reid or even Simon Peel—without affecting the main fabric of the story. As we point out later, it is reasonably certain that

Carter himself was retelling something from an older source (in which the date of the incident was not 1748, but 1724).

All that established, it is apparent that there are a few problems with the *Lady Luvibund* story as just outlined. The remark about real ghosts and popular belief may arouse in some readers the objection that Carter's narrative resembles nothing in the records of modern parapsychology. Perhaps we could gloss over the cavil that authenticated apparitional material collected during the past hundred years since ghost-hunting "went scientific" suggests that hauntings indisputably referable to known historical tragedies are the exception rather than the rule or that ghosts scrupulous enough to observe set anniversaries are even rarer, but the extreme literary flavor of the tale is still suspicious. The plot is too neat. Can we really accept that Rivers's mother could have reconstructed the last hours of the ship (including the felling of the helmsman) so accurately even though nobody on the ship survived to tell the tale? And there are too many concrete details. It is uncommon to find an authentic ghost story with named participants and specific dates; we could anticipate hearing that the *Lady Luvibund* may be seen on nights when a gale blows from the east (or something equally general), but assurances that she is available every fifty years, regular as clockwork, on February 13, is the sort of touch that belongs to a fiction writer. Or someone telling a folk tale.

Even so, the *Lady Luvibund* has the look of a fine and antique sea mystery rooted in local tradition and sanctioned by generations of storytellers. This isn't the same as saying it is authenticated, but of course the argument runs that so many wouldn't have taken it as such for so long unless at least a part of it was true. Unfortunately there is little evidence that the *Lady Luvibund* story *is* an old one: all the signs are that it is relatively modern.

This was the suspicion of "G. H. W.," a correspondent of the magazine *Notes & Queries,* whose interest had been alerted by a paragraph in the *Daily Chronicle* for February 14, 1924, which announced "The anniversary of the ghostly visitation of the *Lady Luvibund* sunk in the Goodwins in 1724, was marked last night by a terrific gale. There was at least one wreck, but from enquiries . . . the legendary apparition due every fifty years at midnight on Feb. 13 was not seen."

Despite the variations in the spelling of the name and dating of the wreck, this is plainly the same tale as the one told by George Carter. G. H. W. was slightly puzzled to find no one at Deal who seemed to have heard of this purportedly famous local apparition; just as bewildering was the fact that none of the Goodwins' many chroniclers seemed aware of it, either. Nowhere in the thirteen exhaustive books published between

1864 and 1917 on the history and legends of the Goodwin Sands consulted by G. H. W. was there any space for the *Lady Luvibund* as a Goodwins wreck, let alone for its supernatural renaissance in 1874, or at any other time. "The story," concluded G. H. W., "would appear to be of modern origin. Did it first appear in some work of fiction, and if so what is the title and by whom was it written? As no local historian mentions the legend, perhaps its author may be known to some . . . readers." Evidently not, since none of *N&Q*'s numerous and eruditely curious correspondents appears to have replied to G. H. W.'s appeal for information.

In consulting the residents of Deal about the ghost ship, G. H. W. was unwittingly duplicating the research efforts of that anonymous *Daily Chronicle* special correspondent whose article had first aroused his curiosity. The journalist appears to have gone to Deal specifically to check up on the *Lady Luvibund* story. Having arrived as close to what he calls the "haunted scene of a jealous lover's crime" as he could come without getting his boots wet, he briefly ran through the story—"The *Lady Luvibund* is supposed to have sunk with fifty persons on board, through the jealousy of a Deal man named Rivers, who, to spite Simon Peel, the skipper, when he was celebrating his marriage to a pretty girl, got the ship steered on the treacherous Sands."

Compare this with the version we just set forth. Acknowledging the tangle over dates and ignoring such superficial details as the destination of the ship, the braining of the helmsman, and the inquest—later additions, surely?—this sounds unmistakably like the story that George Carter was to publish almost thirty years later. Then, not unreasonably, our journalist set out in pursuit of someone who had actually *seen* the ghost ship, or, failing that, somebody who knew a bit about it.

The chase led the correspondent to a sector of Deal's oldest seafarers, who presented themselves in ascending scale of age. At eighty-years-plus John May told stirring tales of wrecks and rescues he'd known or heard of in "this graveyard of the sea"—but knew nothing of any Goodwins ghost. Much-experienced rescue man Richard Roberts (eighty-five) was equally negative. He'd never seen any ghost out on the Goodwins, he said: "Seals and porpoises, yes . . . plenty of them, but nothing in the shape of a spook." Feeling perhaps that he'd let the visitor down, Roberts suggested that the *Chronicle* talk to someone even older than he was, namely James Sneller, ninety-six years old and still nimble. The writer duly went. "Challenged on the ghost question, the oracle declared on oath that . . . no ghost had been seen by him on the Goodwin Sands." It was a small compensation for the journalist to learn that Sneller could, however, testify to having seen the (living) Duke of Wellington—not on the sands, but on Deal's Admiralty Pier.

The *Chronicle* man's failure to locate anyone who had seen the ghost ship of the Goodwins may make the equally unfruitful outcome of G. H. W.'s inquiries among his Deal friends less incomprehensible.

The questions G. H. W. posed as to the *Lady Luvibund*'s provenance remain unanswered today. In researching this phenomenon we trod much the same path as the *N&Q* searcher and with little more luck. First there was the obligatory blitz on the libraries to check the titles G. H. W. had consulted plus quite a few others he hadn't. And the newspapers, of course, with a preference for the local ones like the *Deal*, the *Walmer*, the *Dover and Kentish Telegram*, the *Dover Express*, the *Dover Standard*, and so forth, concentrating mainly on years especially significant to the story: those allegedly marking the ghost ship's anniversary schedule (e.g., 1874, 1924, 1948). Newspapers awash with the minutiae of Kentish coastal life—and not lacking detailed reports of the latest Goodwins dramas—were resoundingly silent about the *Lady Luvibund*. All told, the results of our newspaper check were spectacularly negative. We do not rule out the chance that we looked in the wrong newspapers for the wrong years, but there have to be limits as to how long you will spend on a story. In the case of one whose historical basis became increasingly suspect, we felt we'd reached it.

While conducting what we hoped would be a thoroughgoing literature search, we sought the advice of a few people who might have inside knowledge of the story. Local historian Les Cozens confirmed that the tale "has been going around Deal for years," but even his extensive records of shipwrecks and other inquiries have been unable to pin down its print debut. George Goldsmith Carter told us quite frankly that *he* couldn't recall when or where he first heard it. All we were left with is the fact that the story exists—and is believed—and that the only real quibble concerns the date of the accident. G. H. W.'s source (the *Daily Chronicle*) introduces the interesting variation wherein the year of the wreck is switched from 1748 to 1724, necessitating a recalibration of the ghost ship's anniversary manifestations to 1774, 1824, 1874 and so on, but most recent authors follow Carter's version, including Kentish journalists, who have lifted it from his book wholesale whenever a local ghostly yarn is required. Repetition has had the important result of making the story of the *Lady Luvibund* seem well-established and as factual as any ghost story can ever hope to be. Its authenticity seemed strong enough for maritime disaster authority Richard Larn to include it on a map of Goodwins wrecks in 1977, where he confidently assigns the site at which it took place to an ESE section of the sands. (This detail puzzled Les Cozens slightly. What would an outward-bound ship be doing in the ESE vicinity of the sands?) Set beside the map's record of so many indisputably historical Goodwins victims, the *Lady Luvibund* has thus become part of history.

But is it? Accepting that it is usually impossible to pinpoint the original or "Ur" version of a legend when tracking down ghostly classics, it is always advisable to begin at the beginning: that is, to establish who first told the story and when. This, as we just heard, was precisely what G. H. W. wanted to do, and couldn't. On the face of things, the *Lady Luvibund*'s dating (1724/1748) suggests that it must have been promoted sometime in the eighteenth century, yet surveys of notable wrecks for that period contain no reference to it. Nor does *The Gentleman's Magazine,* an otherwise excellent by-the-month chronicler of contemporary accidents, no matter how trivial, which is curious indeed.

At least one of the thorough and highly legend-conscious authors checked by G. H. W. *ought* to have been conversant with the *Lady Luvibund,* if only to poke fun at it as a quaint superstition . . . but apparently none were. To the titles thrown up by G. H. W.'s literature search (covering a period of nearly fifty years, and a generation of writers with voracious appetites for the flimsiest legend or supernatural rumor) can be added Charles Harper's *The Kentish Coast* (1914). As Harper had been the author of a book on haunted houses published only seven years before, the idea of him passing up a good phantom isn't very credible, no more so than T. F. Thiselton Dyer's purposely omitting it from his chapter on spectral craft in *The Ghost World* (1893). Yet neither breathe a word of it, while Fletcher Bassett's colossal *Legends and Superstitions of the Sea and Sailors* (1893) only echoes their silence. Surely these aficionados of weird tales didn't mention the *Lady Luvibund* because they had never heard of it—neither as ship nor ghost—and that this may be explained by the probability that the story had yet to be invented.

But the fact that G. H. W. saw the story in the *Daily Chronicle* of February 15, 1924 (where it is set forth as if it was an old, familiar story), proves that a version existed long before George Carter's book on the Goodwins gave it some publicity. This source also predates all the other (briefer) versions you may inspect in our bibliography. Finally, there is in this "primary source" the hint that the date of the alleged wreck was 1724, not 1748.

But *is* it the primary source? We just said that the fluency, the confidence of the *Daily Chronicle*'s special correspondent makes his tale seem old and familiar. That doesn't at all preclude the possibility that he or she fabricated the whole thing—invented the *Lady Luvibund* on the spot, as it were, and cleverly passed it off as a traditional tale that required no more than a sketchy outline to refresh readers' memories.

After all, it would certainly not be the first time that a journalist fabricated a ghost story out of nothing. That theory would explain why we have found no version of the *Lady Luvibund* earlier than the *Daily Chronicle*'s.

Maybe our years of sifting ghostly mysteries and the like have made us unreasonably suspicious, but we cannot imagine why the *Chronicle* would send a special correspondent to Deal if not to cover hard news; despite the evidence that the paper was fond of ghost stories in general, we can't quite imagine them sending a reporter down to Deal to cover *this* one: a story not mentioned in any of the local papers we've seen, a story which by that reporter's own admission and G. H. W.'s own inquiries seems to have been unknown at Deal until the *Chronicle* published it. Was the "special correspondent" what we nowadays call a "stringer"? Did he/she live in Deal and feed the London papers tidbits like these and, if so, did he/she compose them specifically for the purpose?

All this may be grossly unfair to the special correspondent, or to the true author of the legend. The Goodwins Ghost Ship may have been an obscure story in some magazine or newspaper. Its author could have been a professional writer (though not, we fancy, a well-known one—we have gone through a checklist of some dozen "possibles" without finding anything) or an amateur; the folksy ballad style could belong to either class. Or again, it might have been a film: a quite superficial scan of cinema bills up to 1924 could be rewarding, but we have to confess that none of the information agencies we approached could help out here. In fact, we've not done any better than G. H. W. managed to do.

It is not impossible that an oral version of the *Lady Luvibund* may have circulated during the nineteenth century, though given the Victorian enthusiasm for getting folk tales into print its escape from the ever-avid collectors seems little short of miraculous. As it stands today, however, the yarn is consciously modern in style. Our guess is that the Ghost Ship of the Goodwins sailed into view between 1914 and 1924 and that the insistence on February 13 as the day of its anniversary appearance is no accident. What more appropriate time could there have been to bring forth a ghost story based on a tragic love affair than the eve of St. Valentine's Day? Or conversely, what better way of filling the need for a St. Valentine's Day story than a ghostly legend based on a tragic love affair?

It has been said that few things are harder to invent than a truly original ghost story. Whoever was responsible for the *Lady Luvibund* could only hope for a variation on a theme—specifically, the phantom ship theme—yet he or she deserves credit for managing the job quite well by improvising with several standard motifs. If this was to be a supernatural tale for St. Valentine's Day, the idea of a wrecked bridal party was a sound one. Several writers have noticed similarities between the Goodwins story and Allan Cunningham's *Traditional Tales of the English and Scottish Peasantry* (1822 etc.), a somewhat tedious collection in which the humble narrators display an amazing talent for decorative speech. The miniseries of tales devoted to the Haunted Hulks of the Solway catches the eye, but none of the stories contained there has more than a general application; much closer to the *Lady Luvibund* plot is "The Last Lord of Helvellyn," in which a wedding barge is sunk by a paranormal whirlwind to fulfill an ancient prophecy of doom on the noble hero's house. We could imagine a subsequent writer mulling this over and finding it much too stagy for twentieth-century tastes. Better substitute a human villain and strengthen the love-interest motif by having him consumed with insane jealousy, then transfer the action from the Solway to a place where wreck tragedies were too familiar to sound incredible. The note of criminal passion lent itself to the folk belief that ghosts are salutory judgments on wrongdoers—shades forced to reenact the crimes that bound them to the physical world for all time. This sense of karmic justice was already part of maritime folklore: if the blasphemy of the *Flying Dutchman*'s skipper caused his ship to wander the seaways for eternity, the treachery of Rivers would assuredly bind the *Lady Luvibund* to the Goodwins.

Denigrating the *Lady Luvibund* as a false ghost story and fabricated phantom may seem unnecessarily harsh: after all, what does it matter if it never really existed, when its purpose was obviously to entertain? We could object that the trouble with pseudotraditions like this is that, however enjoyable they may be, they tend to obscure the possibility that the sea holds genuine mysteries—and perhaps genuine phantom ships among them.

It would be quite simple to deride the notion of phantom ships purely because stories of the *Lady Luvibund* kind prove on close inspection so tenuously related to hard fact. When pressed for substantiating materials, the Goodwins Ghost Ship sinks faster and deeper than she was supposed to have done in 1748 (or 1724) and it would be easy to assume that the hundreds of parallel stories around the world are just as porous. But looking at these accounts, several factors suggest that the reduction-to-absurdity process is too scathing.

For what remains of this chapter and throughout the next, we want to pursue the topic of phantom ships: undeniably a worldwide legend-motif, but arguably a worldwide paranormal phenomenon as well. As a matter of course we will be looking at the ominous *Flying Dutchman,* poeticized by Leyden as "The Spectre-Ship, in livid glimpsing light/Glares baleful in the shuddering watch of night." North America's eastern shores are especially rich in phantom craft, from Block Island's *Palatine* and the fire ship of Bay Chaleur to the *Packet Light* which rises like a ball of flame and sinks back into the Gulf of the St. Lawrence, or the full-rigged three-master whose fiery doom used to attract crowds of spectators to the Nova Scotia village of Merigonish each autumnal equinox. All these might indicate nothing more than the universal popularity of certain folklore themes, but the next considerations take us deeper into what may lie behind the motif.

Despite a near-universal insistence that tries to rationalize phantom ship sightings by recourse to some questionable tale of tragedy (usually related in turn to high-seas crime and passions out of control) the descriptions themselves reveal a prosaic consistency: enough for us to consider that the witness truly saw something. If we can put the supernumerary "explanations" to one side as stories which evolved to help the witnesses make sense of what they have observed, we find that "something" appears as a kind of luminescence or radiance out at sea which, with the aid of only a little imagination and a lot from cultural preconception, suggests to these observers a weirdly illuminated ship, or a ship on fire.

"Phantom" and "fire ship" theorists have roamed freely from speculations about "a peculiar modification of electricity" and "inflammation of phlogogistous gas" to seabed petroleum deposits ignited by lightning and St. Elmo's fire. It is possible that yarns like the *Palatine* or *Flying Dutchman* began with sightings of a peculiar light out to sea which not unnaturally was interpreted as coming from a ship: the eerie nature of the light in turn suggesting a vessel not of this earth. The tale "explaining" the phenomenon could not help following the established traditional themes wherein hauntings are always the products of tragedy and unbridled passions and in some cases it was logical enough to suppose that the tragedy associated with the (supposed) ship had something to do with arson, hence a fiery phantom. Even if these phantasmal vessel narratives derive from phenomena more meteorological than paranormal, they seem to encapsulate a genuine anomaly, which is more than can be said for the *Lady Luvibund* saga.

Yet we may have been too dismissive of the Goodwins Ghost Ship. It may also be that the Goodwins have their ghost ship after all and George Carter believes he saw it when serving on the North Goodwin Light. Through a swirling blizzard on February 1, 1947, he and other crewmen observed a steamer heading for the sands, followed soon after by distress signals that prompted them to summon the Ramsgate lifeboat. Had any vessel been on the Goodwins, *some* sign of her would have been visible, but the terse comment made by the lifeboat's commander on his return was that they "couldn't find a thing."

It is a matter of historical record that in 1857 the Ostend-Dover packet *Violet* was lost on the sands with all on board despite warning rockets from a lightship and that the next day only a life raft with three bodies lashed to it marked her going. The accident occurred on an identical snow-squalling night, although—disappointingly if you feel ghosts should keep strict anniversaries—the date was February 5, not February 1. Carter has said that he thinks he witnessed the end of the *Violet* ninety years after it took place and concurred with my opinion that it was a more convincing story than the *Lady Luvibund*: "Yes, I told *that* as a legend, but I saw that other spectre. I know what I saw and I know what others saw."

Strange things undoubtedly happen on or around the Goodwins, then. Les Cozens has examined the records of the North Deal lifeboat and professes himself "amazed in reading their call-outs in answer to guns being fired from light vessels and visible sightings from the shore of ships going onto the Goodwins and disappearing." He calculates that between 1865 and 1890 these phantasmal vessels-in-trouble accounted for nearly one in every four of the call-outs, a disturbingly high ratio.

In this respect the *Lady Luvibund* story may not be so exceptional. At all events it, and every ghost-ship story of the same ilk—is an essentially harmless, romantic response to an evocative landscape and to a sense of historical tradition. Folklore is sacrosanct: no amount of skeptical cold water can remove tales of this kind from people's hearts. The odds are that when the next *Lady Luvibund* anniversary rolls around in 1998, the esplanades of Deal and Walmer will be crowded with watchers, eyes straining out toward the Goodwin Sands (or in 2024, if you prefer the alternative dating of the story).

* * *

> I became aware of a dull, sullen glare of red light which streamed down the sides of the vast chasm where we lay, and threw a fitful brilliancy upon our deck. Casting my eyes upwards, I beheld a spectacle which froze the current of my blood . . . a gigantic ship, of perhaps four thousand tons . . . her apparent size . . . exceeded that of any ship of the line or East Indiaman in existence. Her huge hull was of a deep dingy black, unrelieved by any of the customary carvings of a ship. A single row of brass cannon protruded from her open ports, and dashed from their polished surfaces the fires of innumerable battle-lanterns which swung to and fro about her rigging. But what mainly

inspired us with horror and astonishment, was that she bore up under a press of sail in the very teeth of that supernatural sea, and of that ungovernable hurricane.

This account, as compelling as it is melodramatic, belongs to a man who is describing an encounter with the premier of all sea mysteries, the Phantom Ship. Some readers may not need the additional information that it also belongs to fiction and more specifically to Edgar Allan Poe's "MS Found In A Bottle," a wonderful tale performed in the author's favorite first-person-narrator mode. But now consider the following.

The writer is Rear Admiral Gordon Campbell, VC, DSO, and the account is taken from his well-known personal record of the WWI "Q" or "mystery" ships that set out to decoy the U-boats into attacking them. Having won his Victoria Cross for antisubmarine actions on the *Farnborough* /Q5 before a brief spell on the *Pargust,* to which another such cross was awarded, Campbell transferred to the *Dunraven,* a three-thousand-ton "mystery ship" sunk by a U-boat on its first sortie. Recalling the shipboard conversations on the night of August 7, 1917—less than twenty-four hours before the *Dunraven* successfully enticed but could not overcome the submarine that destroyed her—the author tells how the men discussed a white, three-masted schooner that had appeared that same afternoon before disappearing suddenly in the fog:

> "I expect we will strike a tin fish [nickname for torpedo] and pretty quick, too," chipped in one of the old salts. "I've heard of the Phantom Ship in the Bay of Biscay before, but I never believed it till I and several others saw it this afternoon. There she was on our starboard beam, when suddenly she vanished. Bad sign—something happens to a ship that sights her, so I'm told."
>
> Someone started to ridicule the idea. "Coming events cast their shadow," another replied. "Don't you remember how the birds used to fly into the skipper's cabin? And when we said it was a good omen you laughed then."
>
> One of the wireless ratings [enlisted men who operated the wireless] who had been standing at the door said, "Well, it is funny you should be talking like this, because I've had a feeling all day that I am going to be wounded, and I've gone out of my way to have a good bath, so as to be nice and clean if anything happens."
>
> As he was saying it, another wireless rating entered and said, "That's funny, 'cos I've just had a bath for the same reason."

Rear Admiral Campbell was not a man given to superstition, maritime or otherwise; in an earlier part of his book he mentions the inconvenience of having a couple of men requesting transfers because their wives had suffered "ominous" dreams of disaster. But here he merely remarks, "No wonder sailors are superstitious, as by a strange coincidence, or whatever you like to call it, the man who made the remark about 'coming events' was mortally wounded the following day, and the two wireless ratings were both seriously wounded."

And of course the *Dunraven* was sunk. Whether we ought to blame that on the Phantom Ship of the Bay of Biscay ("or whatever you like to call it") is an open question.

There is an intrinsic difference between an orally transmitted story and a printed one upon the same theme, perhaps a whole series of intrinsic differences. Despite this, there is considerable interplay between the two kinds of medium. Oral folk narratives have been constantly written down, tidied up, dressed up to suit the demands of larger and perhaps more cosmopolitan audiences; what the original oral version loses in immediacy is compensated for by the fact that it reaches those larger audiences and, in a sense, enjoys a longer lease on life as a result. Subsequently these printed versions may provide easily available sources of inspiration for a new generation of oral narrators. The principle can be seen to operate everywhere; you may have heard at a party some ostensibly real-life, personal experience of the teller that you recognize as a pared-down version of a plot to a television movie you saw eight months ago.

Late Victorian folklorists were considerably exercised and perhaps threatened by the idea that the purity of folk narratives had been corrupted by literary influences. They desired to segregate authentic, orally told, orally presented material from simulcra either generated directly from literature or (more common still) the kind that had adapted features from literature so that what began as an "authentic" story was remodeled to incorporate details from the narrator's experience of literary forms. They also found it extremely difficult to achieve that state of affairs. The feedback from literature was and is practically impossible to eliminate as long as there are books, magazines, and people able to read them.

The Goodwins Ghost Ship appears (as far as we can see) a fairly modern and most probably a literary legend, not one that a nineteenth-century folklorist would recognize as an authentic and suitably ancient legend indigenous to the Kentish shoreline. But of course, folklore doesn't stand still and it doesn't observe historical cutoff points. Today the Goodwins Ghost Ship *is* genuine Kentish folklore, regardless of its literary origin. It has filtered back via printed repetition into the realms of folk narrative and folk belief. A similar repackaging has applied itself to the best-known of *all* ghost-ship stories—the one whose name is synonymous with all ghost-ship stories. For talk of the *Lady Luvibund,* or the *Palatine,* or any one of a dozen others and you will be understood to be talking of the world-famous *Flying Dutchman.*

The *Flying Dutchman* is one of those legends whose name is self-definitive—a classic ghost story, a classic legend, almost a classic myth: an eponym. Everybody "knows" the *Flying Dutchman,* even if when challenged they prove slightly vague on the specifics of the story. Although factually just a variant on the kind of legend that folklorists log as the "Phantom Ship," it is so universally known as to stand for any phantom ship (a sobriquet not infrequently appended as a subtitle to stories headed, "The *Flying Dutchman*"). As such, it subsumes a small folkloric library of otherwise unconnected ghost-ship legends (not all of them from Western tradition) with a danger that all ghost-ship stories will be mistaken as variants on the *Flying Dutchman* instead of vice versa. More to our purpose here, it can be seen to have been heavily influenced by literature and literary artifice.

It could be argued that despite non- and perhaps preliterary prototypes (Nordic, European, Hindu, and Japanese—more on the latter later) the *Flying Dutchman* as most of us know it is a purely literary legend and not a particularly ancient one at that. So it seemed to J. G. Lockhart, who gallantly pursued the evidence for some historical core of the story and concluded by saying it was "so modern that while three hundred years ago the *Flying Dutchman* was as yet unknown, less than a century ago he was still almost an article of faith among mariners."

A century (or for us, let's say a century and a half) is nonetheless a credible record of existence, yet the fact remains that the legend as it survives nowadays owes a mighty debt to printed page and stage. And that it continues to survive is manifested in the way writers continued to draw and improvise upon the theme, vying to inject some new life into the spectral carcass. For example, Peter Haining's recent anthology of *Flying Dutchman* tales peaks with Malcolm Jameson's "Train for Flushing" (from a 1940 issue of *Weird Tales*) wherein the mad and deathless Captain Vanderdecken is liberated from the sea and commandeers a New York train, which then becomes a *Flying Dutchman* on rails, racing backwards through time with an on-board narrator regressing simultaneously toward childhood.

Vanderdecken, a near-nonsense name, literally "On the Deck," is what the *Flying Dutchman*'s captain and evil genius is *usually* called, but according to the version you are hearing (or more frequently, reading) it may be Van Demien or Van Straaten. All are, or sound, conspicuously Dutch, strengthening for some researchers the theory that the legend arose in grudging testimony to the way that nation dominated the seventeenth-century naval world. It could, however, be the German Falkenberg, who was condemned to wander the seas for murdering his brother and that brother's bride in a fit of jealousy, having wanted her for himself. (The similarity between this legend and that of Reeves and the *Lady Luvibund* is temptingly obvious.)

Among those who provided this version was Benjamin Thorpe (*Northern Mythology,* 1852) and in that version he gives the eternal voyage of the *Flying Limbourger* (the result of a penance imposed by a hermit) as having lasted six hundred years while two inhuman forms in black and white respectively throw dice for Reginald Falkenberg's soul. If the fabulous captain is *not* Falkenberg, though, he may be Bernard Fokke, a daring and indisputably real seventeenth-century captain whose spectacularly rapid voyages led to rumors. He was said to have equipped his ship with iron masts (or masts encased in iron), he always crammed on every inch of sail, and he owed his success to the help of the devil. When Fokke at last failed to come home from a voyage, everyone took his nonappearance as confirmation that the devil claims his own eventually (even if he lets them loose in phantom ships afterwards).

The contribution of Washington Irving in his *Chronicles of Wolfert's Roost* (1855), is the identification of the Dutchman as "Ramhout Van Dam of graceless memory," who drunkenly ignored warnings against rowing on a Sabbath to his eternal damnation.

The *Flying Dutchman* herself is subject to vagaries of description. In popular iconography she is virtually any kind of antique sailing vessel, especially one with a high poop deck, and more often than not she is veiled in an eerie, phosphorescent light. The *Flying Dutchman* is often associated with storms and she sails independent of or contrary to wind and tide, which is the more remarkable if you consider that her sails and rigging are customarily described as ragged and mildewed. So also is the garb of her crew: a set of phantoms or corpses or antiquely clad automatons seemingly fossilized in time past like flies in amber. To see the *Flying Dutchman* is taken (usually, but not always) as an omen of doom since she is "the harbinger of wreck and woe," as Scott writes in canto 2 of *Rokeby.* Were that not enough, it is terribly dangerous to accept letters from her—a recall of the old nautical custom whereby one ship would act as courier for another's letters intended for ports on her course. The *Dutchman* was devious, too; in some versions she stole up on the otherwise wary by changing her shape so that she wasn't immediately recognizable as the *Flying Dutchman.*

This was the composite legend that evolved throughout the nineteenth century. Fletcher Bassett's *Legends and Superstitions of the Sea and of Sailors* (1885) which, acknowledged or not, is usually the researcher's first port of call for aid in tracing the history of the *Flying Dutchman,* cites a dozen Victorian writers, British and American, who took the theme and employed it with greater or lesser success. The Phantom Ship was especially popular with narrative poets: Scott, his friend Leyden, Victor Hugo, Longfellow, O'Reilly, and Hood; on a higher literary level there is Coleridge's *Rime of the Ancient Mariner,* with its spectre ship and life-in-death theme—possibly inspired by an article on the *Flying Dutchman* in *Chambers's Encyclopedia.*

Following Bassett it has become the norm to begin the discussion by naming Auguste Jal and his *Scenes de la Vie Maritime* (1832) as if he were the first to exploit the yarn, whereas a glance at the extensive bibliography shows at once that he wasn't. He was preempted by John Howison in *Vanderdecken's Message Home; or The Tenacity of Natural Affection,* published in the May 1821 issue of *Blackwood's Edinburgh Magazine.* This contains all the essential elements of the legend as it came to be known to Victorian writers. The eternally damned captain is unambiguously called Vanderdecken; the narrator's vessel meets the phantom ship in a storm and narrowly avoids accepting the fatal letters that would betray her, despite piteous appeals for them to take these tokens of "natural affection" addressed to Amsterdammers who have been in the churchyard for scores of years. *Vanderdecken's Message Home* is quite a touching story in the way the accursed Dutchmen cannot or will not believe that they have outlived everyone whom they knew when they left port; more importantly, it reveals that the author had at his fingertips a ready-made legend complete in all its narrative details, from which we might deduce that it was already old when he came upon it.

The aforementioned Washington Irving, whose fondness for returning to the phantom ship motif was exceeded only by that of his countryman John Greenleaf Whittier, made an early sortie with "The Storm Ship," a kind of American *Flying Dutchman* which formed part of his popular *Bracebridge Hall* (1822), some four years before Edward Fitzball's *The* Flying Dutchman, *or The Phantom Ship,* "a nautical drama in three acts," sailed the boards of the Adelphi Theater in London.

What Jal appears to have done, however, was to give the legend a sort of publicity and standard format, one that advertised the obvious melodrama and pathos of the story. It is true that he was somewhat cavalier about the historical accuracy of the story and the real identity of its hero—in fact, he announces early on that the central character was "said to have been a Dutchman, but I do not know, nor does it greatly matter from which town he came." What he *is* interested in, however, is ferocious action and incident. The hero/villain is depicted trying to round the Cape of Good Hope in the teeth of headwinds, being mad, drunk, or both. He refuses pleas to return to port and at a critical juncture hurls one dissident over the ship's side. The Dutchman blasphemes in his stubbornness. Cautioned by a heavenly form who descends to the deck, he repeats his defiance of God and fires his pistol at the celestial boarder—whereupon he is condemned to an eternity of sailing the seas, his only food is red-hot iron, his only drink is gall, and his only crew the cabin boy who, for good measure, would grow horns, a tiger's muzzle, and the skin of a dogfish. (Why? What had *he* done to deserve all that?) By way of consolation to the fiendlike captain, the ship is destined to become "the evil spirit of the sea and . . . bring misfortune to all who sight it."

While it would be foolish to credit or blame Jal for all the *Dutchman* material that followed, it seems evident that his story did a great deal to popularize the legend among other writers, who, however, quite possibly drew upon other ghost-ship sources in offering their variations. Heinrich Heine's *The Memoirs of Herr Von Schnabelwopsky* (1836), the outpourings of a garrulous and sensual-sounding traveler, contains a clever twist; the *Flying Dutchman* story is actually an account of the plot of a play bearing that name which Herr von S. claims to have seen in Amsterdam. Heine's tale may have influenced Wagner's opera *Der Fliegende Hollander* (1843), which allows Vanderdecken to be almost redeemed from his curse by love (but not quite). In between there appeared Captain Frederick Marryatt's full-length novel *The Phantom Ship* (1839), which is probably afforded the status of "classic" without actually being read. Undeniably, though, Marryatt gave further popularity to the legend.

To recapitulate: the legend of the *Flying Dutchman* may well have been an orally transmitted story predating all of these sources. The chances are heavily in favor of the belief that it was and did; it is rare that so potent an image as Vanderdecken springs fully armed from a writer's cranium, and on the evidence of the 1821 *Blackwood*'s story we might guess that this particular version had been around long enough to assume its distinctive outline. At the same time, we cannot be absolutely sure it did not. In the final analysis, it seems safe to assume that while the legend drew upon any number of oral tales about ghost ships doomed to wander the seas as punishment for some heinous crime (and to bring misfortune on all who met them), literature, by settling on the Vanderdecken/Cape of Good Hope version, gave that legend a more standard form and a much wider audience.

Attempts to tie the legend to any historical sea captain usually founder, whether the proposed original be Bernard Fokke or, as some have suggested, Bartolomeo Diaz, who authentically made the first European rounding of the oft-mentioned Cape of Good Hope and was biographized by one writer in a way that made him sound almost as supernatural a personage as Vanderdecken. Against this, there are any number of prototype stories that lent themselves to the legend as it finally evolved and that arguably prepared the audience for the superior plot structure to follow. T. Percy Armstrong's historical survey of these "contributory" legends in *Notes and Queries* for May 23, 1931, is not exhaustive, but it is typical. He brings in tales of phantom vessels crewed by ominous black men rumored to enter harbors as precursors of plague in Justinian's reign, as well as tales from Nordic sea-burial rites, stories from Cornwall, the Solway Firth, the Maine coast, and the Gulf of St. Lawrence (to which we will return in a later chapter). None of these shows the kind of sustained narrative development we find in Jal et al., but they may have acted as a matrix from which the more polished literary version(s) evolved.

In any case, the latter phase of what is ostensibly a sailor's legend has a strange melodramatic appeal that enchants landlubbers. Perhaps some of that strangeness is the intrinsic mystery of the sea itself, but, as in the story of the Wandering Jew with whom he is to be compared, the center of the legend is a human one. Despite his alien nature, Vanderdecken is a strongly sympathetic figure. The enduring portrait of the blasphemous captain raging against both contrary winds and God and being damned to sail till the last apocalyptic day arouses a dual response. It is hubris perfected—overwhelming pride—and we know it is to be shunned; part of us is delighted when the overreaching captain is condemned by a righteous God. But the other part of us respects any human who defies limits imposed upon him. We know and accept that he will be punished, but we applaud that human desire to rebel against divine constraint. On this level, the legend's core is perfectly intelligible to all cultures and all cultures appear to have responded to it.

Calling the *Flying Dutchman* a universal sea legend is really another way of saying that there is within it something that all cultures can recognize. It may appear a loosely "regional" story, in that the details about the Cape of Good Hope and the Dutch nationality of the hero occur so frequently in versions told from the nineteenth century onwards; it may well be that Vanderdecken and the Cape were features of just one phantom ship legend, one that achieved unusual prominence through literature until it subsumed all the rest in the fashion already outlined. But none of this worked against the "new" ghost ship being identified by and associated with older material from other cultures. A good case in point is the way that Kumagusu Minikata, a *Notes & Queries* correspondent from Tanabe, Japan, instantly recognized familial features in Washington Irving's "The Storm Ship" from *Bracebridge Hall* (which, as we noticed, was a story set on the Hudson River, not off the Cape):

> Formerly, the seafaring folks of Japan held in great dread the so-called ship ghosts [*funa-yurei*]—the unredeemed souls of those who had lost their lives in maritime disasters. Very envious of the living, and exasperated with never-ending despair, these evil-minded spirits are supposed to be ever ready to make full display of their crafty artifices, wherewith to augment their malcontent troop by fatally misleading and drowning any unfortunate seaman who might fall in with them. Thus, for example, in the dark, tempestuous night they are said to make a show of several tens of vessels all under sail; and, should a real vessel follow their course, her calamitous ruin would be the immediate effect. This ship-like apparition, it is popularly said, is so deceptively mimetic, even in details, that, notwithstanding the distance and darkness, one could distinctly perceive the lines and patterns on the clothes of its ghostly inmates; the only point of distinction being that, whereas the ordinary vessels progress leeward, the diabolic ones invariably sail against the wind. Such is the account of the Japanese ship ghosts I could gather from the mouth of many old sailors as well as Yamazaki's *Seiji Hyakudan,* written early in the last century.

The dissimilarities between this and the "Europeanized" *Flying Dutchman* legend are less important than the similarities: the "deceptively mimetic" power of the ghost ship, the ability to sail against the wind, the crew of "unredeemed souls." It lacks only a single, strong central character (Vanderdecken) in place of an indeterminate host of *funa-yurei* to bring it more firmly into line still. Paring down drastically, we could conclude that around the seagoing world we can locate stories with common elements: spectral ships manned by the souls or bodies of sailors condemned for crimes in the past or perhaps victims of wreck and drowning doomed to sail to the Judgment Day (or equivalent) and almost always regarded as omens of misfortune to their beholders.

The *Flying Dutchman* is the Wandering Jew of the seas; it may have owed some of its narrative development to that far older legend and a few folklorists may care to class it as a subtype of the latter, with more specifically maritime features from original "non-*Dutchman*" stories being remodeled according to external influences. In this paradigm, the example of the Wandering Jew led storytellers to place the Phantom Ship in the care of a remarkable captain whose name, given due process of time and the influence of the literati, came to be written "Vanderdecken." The etiology may have been far more complicated than that. Bassett (p. 363) draws attention to folk traditions about itinerant heroes, some of whom—Cain, the Wild Huntsman, the Jew—were subject to the eternal curse of wandering, each variant working into the others to form what he calls "a network of legends." It would be entirely natural, after all, for sailors to take their landlocked legends to sea with them and to invent a uniquely marine equivalent of them.

Researchers enough have attempted to see the legend as an imaginative response to unusual maritime atmospheric effects, to encounters with derelicts, or to other natural sources honestly or willfully misunderstood. More of this in a moment. Far more interesting is what the legend stood for, what values it encapsulated that made it so popular. Hubris and the human dual response to it we have already mentioned; the metaphysical impact of the deathless punishment motif and expiating of sin demands more room than we can afford here. We will content ourselves by quoting how Richard Wagner saw and interpreted the story in his *A Communication to My Friends*:

> The figure of the *Flying Dutchman* is a mythical creation of the folk: a primal trait of human nature speaks out from it with heart-enthralling force. This trait, in its most universal meaning, is the longing after rest from amid the storms of life. In the blithe world of Greece we meet with it in the wanderings of Ulysses and his longing after home, house, hearth and wife: the attainable, and at last attained, reward of the city-loving son of ancient Hellas. The Christian, without a home on earth, embodied this trait in the figure of the Wandering Jew: for that wanderer, forever doomed to a long-since out-lived life, without an aim, without a joy, there bloomed no earthly ransom; death was the sole remaining goal of all his strivings; his only hope, the laying down of being.

The writer, like Vanderdecken, has the prerogative of moving on when and where he will. So rather than answer those questions, we will raise a couple of others. Has anyone ever and seriously claimed to have met the *Flying Dutchman*—anyone, that is, who, despite the tradition of doom that goes along with such an event, came home to port and was able to boast about it? Are there accounts which assert that the *Flying Dutchman* is more than a legend of the sea and of pen—a rare but veritable fact of marine life?

There are indeed. If one accepted everything that the chroniclers of sea mysteries have put forth as "authenticated" cases of the *Flying Dutchman,* the effect would probably demonstrate that too much of the wrong sort of evidence works against corroboration instead of for it. Admitting that you may find other material in other books to support the casually made assertion that the *Dutchman* has been recorded dozens, hundreds or countless times down through history—which is what certain writers have implied—we opted to select a handful of accounts that appear of better-than-average credibility in terms of detail, narrators' standing, and other evidential factors.

Our first case is important because its author (or editor) doesn't settle for merely retelling a story culled from an antique source. He is patently interested by the inferences arising from what he has written; he attempts some theoretical analysis of how this *Flying Dutchman* might be explained, thus introducing a highly useful line of inquiry into how other episodes might be explained—and how the legend(s) could have arisen in the first instance, perhaps. Since referring to the original source reveals that our commentator, J. G. Lockhart, has transcribed a few factual errors, the version that follows has been corrected against Captain William Fitz William's original account in his *Narrative of Voyages to Explore the Shores of Africa, Arabia and Madagascar,* a two-volume work published in 1833.

Commissioned by the Admiralty for an extensive survey-expedition that would take them round the Cape of Good Hope, along the Mozambique coast, and so on up to the Arabian Gulf, HMS *Leven* and *Barracouta* left England in January 1822. The survey work, intermingled with various shore trips, proceeded routinely, the vessels plying back and forth around the Cape and giving Captain Owen, master of the *Leven,* leisure to observe such facets of African life as hippopotamus hunting, the differences of Portuguese settlements, and tropical fevers (the latter threatening to decimate the expedition's crews).

On the evening of April 6, 1823, Owen's vessel was off the ominously named Port Danger. The *Leven* had already experienced more than enough of the gales that made the Cape of Good Hope notorious; the small squadron of ships that had accompanied her out of Algoa Bay on March 16 for the next phase of the surveying operation had been dispersed and, having lately reprovisioned, the *Leven* was headed for Simon's Town to rendezvous. Now Owen was pleased to see HMS *Barracouta* appear two miles to leeward, though he was simultaneously puzzled at the speed with which the ten-gun brig had caught up. There was no doubt in his mind that the ship he saw *was* the *Barracouta*; he recognized the peculiarities of her rigging, "and other circumstances convinced us that we were not mistaken. Nay, so distinctly was she seen that many well-known faces could be observed on deck, looking towards our ship." The *Barracouta* surprised them, though, by standing off, and *Leven* proceeded ahead to port, but not before noticing that at sunset the other ship had lowered a boat as though to collect someone who had fallen overboard.

Leven duly anchored in Simon's Bay, expecting *Barracouta* to join her at any moment. A week went by, but the other ship was notable by her absence. In fact, she did not arrive until the fourteenth. To abbreviate, it transpired that on the evening of April 6 *Barracouta* had been no nearer *Leven* than a sizable gap of three hundred miles. Despite Owen's certainty-beyond-mistake, she had not been the vessel he and his crew had sighted two miles to leeward; for that matter, no known ship matching *Barracouta* had been in the vicinity.

You may be wondering what this story, odd though it is, has to do with the *Flying Dutchman.* You may even suspect that attribution to have come solely from Lockhart, who seizes on the fact that the episode took place in a locality, the Cape of Good Hope, which is, he says, "just right": just right as far as the *Flying Dutchman*'s infamous connection with the Cape of Good Hope goes. Rather less cogently, Lockhart suggests that the pseudo-*Barracouta*'s tactic of standing off—and maybe the lowering of a boat—are reminiscent of the phantom ship's deceptive machinations. And if the *Dutchman* can disguise itself in any way it wishes, why not as the *Barracouta*?

In fact, Lockhart suggests little if anything more than Owen suggested in his original account. It is he who talks about the incident in terms of the *Flying Dutchman*; he makes a point of prefacing his account in that fashion:

> For many years, the *Flying Dutchman* has been a popular superstition and source of terror to mariners. Few have often passed the Cape but can tell their tale of what they saw, or what others have told them of this mischievous phantom-ship. Old seamen still while away the tedious night-watch in repeating to their young and marvel-loving comrades stories of this water-sprite; and many a stout heart has quailed, as with anxious ears they have listened to the freaks of this airy terror. The following circumstances happened to us during this voyage, which called forth many an almost forgotten record of the *Flying Dutchman.*

This confirms for us the hallowed place that the legend held among Cape seamen around the start of the nineteenth century; Owen's remarks make it sound like a kind of "occupational lore," an oral tradition passed from elders to initiates and neophytes like a secret of the ocean that marked them off from outsiders. At the end of this segment of his text, he adds:

> This is not told in order to authenticate the stories of fear and fancy, or to add to the visionary terrors of superstition, but it is recorded as a strange and at present unaccountable fact, doubtless attributable to natural and probably simple causes. Time or accident may solve them; but until then, the imagination of those who delight in unaccount-

> able things may picture the phantom ship as an apparition of dreadful and supernatural mystery. The popular sequel of the *Flying Dutchman*'s history is, that he always visits those ships off the Cape to whom misfortune is threatened: sometimes, it is said, he sends a boat on board with letters, which, if received, seal the fate of that vessel, and she must be wrecked, and every soul perish. For the credit of this nautical goblin, it ought to be believed, that every ship lost in these seas has been so visited, which, if as required, all are drowned, either may or may not be true, as there can be none to contradict it. The boat never reached us; and although if in a future stage of this expedition he made another attempt to allure us to a communication, the malicious fiend was contented with a smaller sacrifice, and allowed us to return and tell the tale.

It is quite clear that Owen is familiar with every detail of the legend. He omits only the key name, "Vanderdecken"; in other particulars he is perfect, almost as if his reading matter before he left England had included the *Blackwood*'s issue that carried "Vanderdecken's Message Home" but not registered the hero's denominate. It is intriguing to see him half-sneering at the credulity of "those who delight in unaccountable things," only to interpret the episode of the quasi-*Barracouta*'s lowering a boat in the light of the *Dutchman*'s ploy of asking the victim to accept and deliver letters on her behalf. Rationality sweeps in again; Owen playfully comments on the logical impossibility of confirming a story whose narrative demands no one survives to be able to confirm it, yet immediately dwells on the fact that although *Leven* lived to tell of the encounter, the brig *Delight*—also laying up in Simon's Bay—was lost some time after in a hurricane so that "the malicious fiend" had his sacrifice after all.

Despite his not-altogether-consistently skeptical stance, Owen stood by what he had written: it was "a strange and at present unaccountable fact," not a piece of superstition. To his verdict that the phenomenon was "doubtless attributable to natural and probably simple causes" there appears an asterisk leading to a confident footnote, perhaps from Owen himself, but more likely introduced by his editor, Heaton Bowstead Robinson: "Such effects may be produced by refraction." Lockhart was inclined to agree. In fact, among writers who are prepared to think that the *Flying Dutchman* could conceivably be more than a legend there exists a broad consensus that the answer could lie in the region of nautical mirages.

The author of the Owen account's footnote might well have read the sixth of Sir David Brewster's *Letters on Natural Magic addressed to Sir Walter Scott* (1842), wherein such optical phantasmagoria as the

Brocken Spectre, armies in the sky, *and* phantom ships were firmly put down to unequal refraction caused by layers of cool and warm air. Writing with the zeal of one who believes science has a duty to deflate the pretensions of the supernatural, Brewster paraded a number of illustrative cases wherein the images of ships were seen in the air across a distance of many miles; he is particularly fond of inverted images of ships as witnessed by the Greenland traveller Captain Scoresby in 1820 and 1822. Brewster certainly does enough to prove that his examples are far from isolated. (As a point of interest, HMS *Archer* sighted a fleet of nineteen British warships during her Baltic service of 1854; the fleet was proven to have been thirty miles off at this time). According to this scientist's thinking, unequal refraction had "no doubt given rise in early times to those superstitions which have prevailed in different countries respecting 'phantom ships' . . . which always sail in the eye of the wind, and plough their way through the smooth sea, where there is not a breath of wind upon its surface."

It is possible to overreact to the smug certainty of science and scientists. It is also time to say that Brewster's reconstruction of how the mirage works (accompanied in his book by diagrams and plenty of "Let ABCD be a glass trough . . . let a small ship be placed at S . . .") is beyond dispute. But turning back to Owen's narrative, we beg leave to wonder about the applicability of the theory in all its respects. The fact that the image of the *Barracouta* was not inverted nor in the air need not bother us; Brewster stipulates that these phantom-ship mirages need be neither. Yet to be wholly certain of the matter we would need to know far more of the weather conditions up to and during the incident than Owen tells us, so that the hypothetical refractive strata of air over the ocean could be shown to fit Brewster's model. Taking the witness's statement that the *Barracouta* was three hundred miles off at the time to be true, we might ask whether the distance was too great to fit that model; Brewster's cases feature ships still beneath the horizon from the observer's viewpoint, but not at that gulf of sea miles. Finally, it would be instructive to know whether, as in the *Leven*'s sighting, the *Barracouta* indeed *had* lowered away a boat as her supposed image was seen to do.

Perhaps the Cape of Good Hope and other places have some peculiar refractive quality to the air above their waters that may have contributed to a tradition of spectral ships haunting such locales. Certainly the mirage hypothesis sounds more convincing than T. Percy Armstrong's suspicion (*Notes & Queries*) that the *Flying Dutchman* arose as a story told by older sailors to motivate younger ones to perform their duty, the unpleasantness of which was plainly preferable to the unremitting eternal drudgery they'd know if carried off by Vanderdecken. And it is more universally applicable than the lesson related by T. C. Bridges in his *Book of the Sea* (1927), where he discusses "the mystery of the well-known phantom ship" reportedly seen by many vessels rounding the Cape—*not* the Cape of Good Hope this time, but Cape Horn, and by those bound in an east-to-west direction.

The Cape Horn phantom appeared as a large ship, decks awash and drifting dangerously under the dark cliffs of the Straits of Le Maire. Like many before her, the *Crown of Italy* had hastened to the rescue; like many before her (reportedly) she was promptly wrecked upon a reef. In 1907 the Argentine government responded to a request from the United States by sending a steamer to investigate; the phantom craft proved to be a large white rock which loomed out of the black cliffs surrounding it in the passable guise of a sailing ship.

We can imagine that white rocks—or dark ones artfully decorated with sea-birds' droppings—might pass for phantom vessels under some conditions. Yet the hypothesis seems too restricted to apply to *all* cases—as, let it be said, is the mirage explanation. This is particularly true, we feel, when the ghost ship is observed to move with a freedom not known of rocks and mirages; we also feel unsatisfied by the Brewsteresque explanation's failure to take into account the fact that the majority of phantom ship stories take place, not in the daylight, but at night. Perhaps our knowledge of optics is at fault. Are there nocturnal mirages, too? Anyway, we will have a mobile and nocturnal version of the *Flying Dutchman* for our next case.

"We had been in dirty weather for several days," declares our informant, "and to begin the afternoon I commanded [commended?] after-dinner narratives to the French officers and passengers about the *Flying Dutchman.*" So far, so good—this is to be a first-person account, then, and they always count for more in the long run. He takes up the story when (having got the after-dinner narratives out of the way) the assembled gathering stepped out on deck into the stiff gale that had been developing for some hours. Dark, heavy clouds raced across a bright moon "whose lustre is so peculiar in the southern hemisphere"—bright enough to illuminate as far as the horizon some eight to ten miles distant. And then:

> Suddenly the second officer, a fine Marseilles sailor, who had been among the foremost in the cabin in laughing at and ridiculing the story of the *Flying Dutchman,* ascended the weather rigging and exclaimed: "Voila le volant Hollandais!" The captain sent for his night-glass and soon observed: "It is very strange, but there is a ship bearing down on us with *all sail set,* while we dare scarcely show a pocket-handkerchief to the breeze."

> In a few minutes the stranger was visible to all on deck, her rig plainly discernible, and people on her poop; she seemed to near us with the rapidity of lightning, and apparently wished to pass under our quarter for the purpose of speaking. The captain, a resolute Bordeaux mariner, said it was quite incomprehensible and sent for the trumpet to hail an answer, when in an instant, and while we were all on the *qui vive* ["alert," literally "who goes there"], the stranger totally disappeared, and was seen no more.

Yes, first-person accounts always count for more, but only when we know who the "first person" is. The extract just quoted may look like a piece of firsthand testimony, but hardly deserves to be called one. We found it in R. L. Hadfield's *The Phantom Ship* (1937), a superior sea-mysteries book whose title neatly predicates its contents; he footnotes his source for the story as Wilbur Bassett's *Wanderships.* When a writer informs you he has such-and-such a story on the authority of some earlier writer, it is a good idea to get hold of that prior source and check that the account is as per the second writer's summary; there may be more to be added which, for one reason or another, he has left out. Sad to relate, we have so far failed to get hold of a copy of Bassett's *Wanderships,* so what follows is inevitably compromised by that fact.

Hadfield affirms that the story was "taken from a log written in 1835." That's not very helpful. We would like to be told *who* wrote the log—not the captain, evidently, since he is spoken of as a separate person; we'd like to know which ship the log belonged to (but are only told she was officered by Frenchmen) and where she was at the time of the incident (apart from the southern hemisphere). The writer, whoever he is, possesses a style rather more flamboyant than is usual for a ship's log—does this mean that the log was a private journal? Notice, for example, how the story's token skeptic, that "fine Marseilles sailor," is singled out for reproof and correction by events! Yet beyond stressing that the putative *Flying Dutchman* wore full sail despite the ferocious winds, the phantom ship is scarcely described at all. The main point of the piece is that she "totally disappeared." If we can overcome the feeling that we'd need to know a bit (or a lot) more before taking this tale at face value, there is the suspicion that a kind of expectancy or suggestion was operative here and that those "after-dinner narratives . . . about the *Flying Dutchman,*" in concert with the kind of meteorological conditions traditional to its appearance, conjured up some kind of hallucination, illusion, or delusion that captivated each man of the unspecified number who trooped up on deck to survey the stormy, moonlit sea.

Nearly half a century later, another by no means unschooled writer took up his private log or journal to write: "July 11th. At 4 a.m. the *Flying Dutchman* crossed our bows." That flat, prosaic statement plunges us into one of the most frequently repeated true-life narratives of the Seven Seas' most celebrated phantom: a story routinely pulled forth to counter any impression that the *Dutchman* is a disreputable legend and no fact at all.

Part of its status rests in the identity of the witnesses—no ancient and obscure sea-dogs, but heirs-presumptive to the British throne. The events that brought together the *Flying Dutchman* (or something like her), and Edward, Duke of Clarence (elder son of Edward VII and expected to be England's next king), and Edward's brother George (who actually became that next king) began in 1879 with the commissioning of the cruiser-rigged steamship *Bacchante.* Already entered into their naval cadetships, the two princes were dispatched on a three-year, character-building cruise on this vessel, and with them (somewhat reluctantly) went their tutor John Neill Dalton. It was a crammed itinerary that took in the Mediterranean, the West Indies, and Argentina before the *Bacchante* and her escorts bore east to visit Britain's colonial possessions in South Africa and so on to Australia, a cruise in which the princes' duties as midshipmen and royal dignitaries still left time for cricket matches and games of prisoners' base. Their minds were, no doubt, as fully expanded as the planners of their future could have wished.

Soon after their return the experiences of the young royals—Eddie was seventeen, George sixteen—appeared in a two-volume book based on the private journals, notebooks, and letters they had religiously written each day, subedited and pedantically annotated throughout by Dalton who, however, insists that most of what appears in those pages was all their own work.

The incident that interests us—some would say it is the only truly interesting incident in an overlong book—occurred during the princes' visit to Australia. It is worth mentioning that at the time (July 1881) they were not on board *Bacchante,* but on HMS *Inconstant*; the *Bacchante* was laid up in Hobson's Bay, having damaged her rudder during the crossing from South Africa and the princes were not able to join her again until the following August. The royal record (packed with observations as ever) follows the passage of *Inconstant* from Melbourne through the Bass Straits towards Sydney. Thanks to the "seamless" editing, we cannot tell whether the writer was Edward (to whom the book is formally accredited) or George. In full, the entry reads:

> July 11th.—At 4 a.m. the *Flying Dutchman* crossed our bows. A strange red light as of a phantom ship all aglow, in the midst of which the

masts, spars, and sails of a brig 200 yards distant stood out in strong relief as she came up on the port bow. The look-out man on the forecastle reported her as close on the port bow, where also the officer of the watch from the bridge clearly saw her, as did also the quarterdeck midshipman, who was sent forward at once to the forecastle; but on arriving there no vestige nor any sign whatever of any material ship was to be seen either near or right away to the horizon, the night being clear and the sea calm. Thirteen persons altogether saw her, but whether it was *Van Diemen* or the *Flying Dutchman* or who else must remain unknown.

> Traft ihr das Schiff im Meere an
> Blutroth sie Segel, schwarz der Mast? Auf
> hohem Bord der bleiche Mann
> Des Schiffes Herr, wacht ohne Rast.
> Hui!—Wie Sauft der Wind!—Johohe! Hui!—
> Wie pfeift's im Tau!—Johohe! Hui!—Wie ein
> Pfeil fliegt er hin, Ohne Ziel, ohne Rast,
> ohne Ruh!"*

The *Tourmaline* and *Cleopatra,* who were sailing on our starboard bow, flashed to ask whether we had seen the strange red light. At 6:15 a.m. observed land (Mount Diana) to the north-east. At 10:45 a.m. the ordinary seaman who had this morning reported the *Flying Dutchman* fell from the foretopmast crosstrees on to the topgallant forecastle and was smashed to atoms. At 4:15 p.m. after quarters we hove to with the headyards aback, and he was buried in the sea. He was a smart royal yardman, and one of the most promising young hands in the ship, and every one feels quite sad at his loss. (At the next port we came to the Admiral also was smitten down.) The midshipman's half-yearly examination began to-day with the Algebra paper.

We already commented on the remarkably factual-sounding opening of this passage—"At 4 a.m. the *Flying Dutchman* crossed our bows"—and the ending is no less so: an abrupt switch from the supernatural

---

*Have you encountered the ship at sea,
blood-red her sails, black the mast?
High on board the pale man
the ship's master, on duty without rest.
Oh, how savage the wind. God! Oh!
How it whistles in the ropes. God! Like an
arrow she flies yonder, without time,
without rest, without peace!

world to the mundane one of midshipman's exams, as if there were no qualitative difference between algebra and a phantom ship. There is a good deal else to notice besides. First of all, the writer is describing "A strange red light, as of a phantom ship all aglow"—in other words, a strange red light that might be compared with a phantom ship; the inference is that the light *suggested* such a ship (to one who had heard previously of such a phenomenon). It did not *literally* resemble a spectral vessel until the observer (primed by his initial impression to interpret what he saw along the same lines?) adds that "masts, spars and sails . . . stood up in strong relief." At the estimated distance of two hundred yards, the witness's accuracy seems reasonable.

Another thing to dwell upon is that the sighting was made by several additional persons ("The look-out man . . . the officer of the watch . . . the quarterdeck midshipman": it would be interesting to have their testimonies as well, but unluckily we have to make do without them) and the spectacle ended abruptly. The fact that accompanying vessels to starboard signalled in a way that proves they had also seen the strange red light adds a touch of valuable corroboration, which is seemingly what the royal writer wanted to convey; the remarks about the fact that "thirteen people altogether" and not including those on the *Tourmaline* and *Cleopatra* hints that he is anxious to show evidence that he is not inventing anything—anxious to be believed, perhaps.

It is equally apparent that our narrator had some prior awareness or information that helped him to interpret what he saw. The strange red light is unequivocally and immediately described as "the *Flying Dutchman*" and only subsequent to this is it qualified ("A strange red light as of . . ."). Later, almost apologetically, the narrator half-suggests that it may have been Van Diemen (i.e., Van Demien—revealing an acquaintanceship with the legend) and detaches himself at once from the idea with the disclaiming, "or who else must remain unknown."

But straight away the legend reasserts itself. The writer does not blatantly attribute the death of the smart and promising royal yardsman's death to the misfortune that traditionally attends seeing the *Flying Dutchman*, but that is the implication of his words, as is the somewhat joking reference to the way that at the next port "the Admiral was also smitten down." The tone of the piece—an uneasy balance of excitement, belief, and nervous skepticism—compares closely with that of Captain Owen's account.

The seriousness of the writer is slightly impugned by the bursting into poetry in the middle of the account—a passage usually and conveniently edited out when this narrative is reproduced in discussions of the *Flying Dutchman*'s reality. Some readers may feel it also impugns the writer's credibility. Why would anyone putting down a personal testimony of so bizarre an event lapse into poetics (always assuming he or she had the sort of memory that trotted out eight lines of German verse on demand)? At the very least the passage strongly suggests a delay or addition: either the prince wrote his account long enough after the event for him to be able to consult his Wagner libretto—for that proves to be where the lines are from: see Senta's ballad in the armchair, act 2 scene 1—or he (or someone else? John Dalton?) later added it to the original journal entry as a literary flourish.

Dalton's preface to *The Cruise of H.M.S.* Bacchante disclaims any literary pretensions; he presents it as a genuine record of the princes' experiences in their own words (with the editor's own contributions and clarifications clearly shown as such by parentheses). We might query this, of course, but the fact remains that, on the strength of his notebooks and journals, at least, the princely writer was patently a very literate young man and we cannot rule out the idea that not only had he the ability to memorize substantial quantities of poetry, but also the disposition to quote appositely in his writing. The snatch of German versification at this point in the record does not stand alone. Amidst a welter of topographical, anthropological, economico-commercial, and other data, the published record reveals sporadic Latin tags, Browning, Byron, Tennyson, Shakespeare (the writer being especially enamored of *Henry V,* it seems). It is pretty obvious that the prince or princes went to sea fully prepared; like any dedicated tourist, he or they read up on the places they were to visit and quoted accordingly—as when a visit to the Bermudas unleashed a stream of allusions to *The Tempest,* for instance. They almost certainly had a private library along with them and it would not be remarkable if it included some Wagner. "It is evident that a large and well-chosen library was included in the furniture of the *Bacchante*" remarked the *Athenaeum* in a cautiously respectful if not overenthusiastic review of the royal tome, "and that, as each place of interest was approached, reached or passed, Canon Dalton called his pupil's attention to what had been said about it."

The report, we have to say, gains by the status of its author—but it remains unsupported by independent testimony. A crown prince can be as mistaken—or lie—as well as any commoner, no doubt. Nonetheless, our own response to the account is of a writer honestly setting down his impressions, enthusiastically, of course, and with a desire to be believed, stressing his own objectivity and then moving on to other, quite unrelated matters. There is a tendency to present those impressions in terms of a legend he has read about, but this does not mean that the phenomenon itself was less credible.

Internal evidence here is not easily challenged. It's worth repeating that of the "thirteen persons altogether" who saw the phantom ship phenomenon, only one appears to have left a written record of it: the royal writer just quoted. The incident is not described among the bulletins issued regularly on the princes' progress and published in the British newspapers as a matter of course. (For example, the *Illustrated London News,* which had a correspondent on the *Bacchante* and received from him an exciting report of the rudder damage sustained by the ship in a squall, is silent on this incident. Perhaps the journalist did not transfer to the *Inconstant* along with the princes, however). At one stage we were unsettled by the way the narrator doesn't bother to name the unfortunate yardman who crashed to his death within hours of having seen the phantom ship; on reflection, there is no reason to suppose that he ever knew it. The forematter of the book scrupulously lists the deaths that occurred during the *Bacchante*'s commission, including that of William Foster who "fell from aloft" on November 30, 1880, and ending five months prior to the *Flying Dutchman* adventure with the demise of sailmaker George Dunn from "brain-softening" (February 12, 1881).

But the princes were not on the *Bacchante* at this particular juncture, but on *Inconstant,* and may not have known her crew as well. Out of interest, the seaman lost overboard from the flagship on April 30 is not named, either.

How one reacts to the story depends upon temperament. William Clark Russell, a prolific author of sea stories and saltwater memories, plainly felt ill at ease with the *Bacchante* (i.e., *Inconstant*) account and tried it out on an elderly sailor whose objection was not to the incredibility of the tale per se, but to its departure from type and tradition:

> Certainly the appearance looked uncommonly like the *Flying Dutchman*, and for his part he was willing enough to believe it was; if he had a misgiving, it lay in the smallness of the trouble that followed. "The fallin' of a young seaman from the masthead and the sarcumstance of a hadmiral being took wuss wasn't consequences sufficient if that there wessel wur the genuine Phantom. The *Baykant* . . . herself oughter ha' got lost. That's what would have happened when I wus fust goin' to sea; but there's bin a good many changes since then, and who's a-goin' to say that that their curse ain't growed weak like physic wot's kept too long?"

Or who's a'goin to say that changes and passing years may not bring alterations to a legend's narrative structure? Or that while a phenomenon does not change, men's interpretations of it—and hence the ending of a story derived from it—may not alter, too?

All told, there is no cause to suspect fabrication—rather, it might well have been an adolescent's desire to brighten up his fairly unspectacular journal, say, or an older subeditor's desire to spice up a fairly unspectacular book. If such allegations have been made (and supported), we have not heard of them. Nor have we ever heard anyone blame Albert Edward's premature death from typhoid in 1892 on his having met the *Flying Dutchman.*

We can accept the account as it stands, then: as a firsthand testimony to the reality of, not the *Flying Dutchman* per se, but a curious nautical light phenomenon whose nature tends to be confused by the habit of interpreting it according to that talismanic name.

We wish we could be so positive about our next case study. The story comes from the captain of a tug working on the salvage of the steamship *Hannah Regan* (not from the captain of the *Hannah Regan* herself, as stated in one recent retelling) which had been lost off Okinawa in 1899 with around a million dollars of gold bullion on board. (The *Hannah Regan* was not lost after meeting the *Flying Dutchman,* though; the steamer lost her propellor and succumbed to heavy gales, as a written record found in an open boat alongside the bodies of the captain, first mate, and four crew explains). The wreck was located in ten fathoms by a San Francisco tug, and it was on a fine, calm, clear night following a hard day's salvage operations that the alleged incident took place. With the tug anchored close to the marker buoys, the captain's attention was drawn to what at first he took to be "a peculiar shadow" some half a mile distant. As he watched it closely

> the shadow assumed the shape and appearance of a sailing vessel, clearly distinguishable but of a type which had not sailed the seas for at least two hundred years. There could be no mistaking it. She was headed in our direction, and driving along as if in the grip of violent winds, yet she carried no sail. I stood spellbound. She rolled heavily at times though the seas were flat calm; and she looked to be sinking by the stern. I was about to shout, to summon help, for it looked as if she could not help running us down, but then it flashed into my mind that this was a phantom vessel and no material vessel.

The captain goes on to say that he did not give way to his initial impulse to call out for fear of spreading general alarm, but also ("if my imagination were in control of my senses") lest he be met with a scornful response.

> The spectral ship came on, her starboard quarter almost awash with masses of heavy water pouring over her. She came right alongside, and then I doubted my own shocked senses, for I could see right through her, though every detail of her deck work and her rigging stood out clearly. Two of her boats were hanging from their falls and dragged alongside; so she passed us by, still lower at the stern, and in such a way *disappeared beneath the sea!*

The narrator goes on to give what we might expect as the inevitable sequel: the next day two divers were drowned while working on the submerged *Hannah Regan.* Eventually the salvage attempt was abandoned and the tug returned to San Francisco.

Are we being too cynical in discerning a rather literary flavor to all this? The skipper's observations do not read like a straightforward record of facts. They contain the kind of suspense-builders and artificial coloring which are the fictioneer's tools: "I stood spellbound . . . then it flashed into my mind. . . . The spectral vessel came on" and the special emphasis of that last, climactic stage in the description. While we can't rule out the possibility that the account refers to an authentic experience (albeit polished up to make for better audience impact), we would like to know a good deal more of how the story came to be written, by whom and where.

What we *can* say is that this is a story that has had a respectable run throughout the pages of sea-mystery books; it's not the fault of the tale itself that it has never enjoyed the kind of popularity which has kept the *Mary Celeste,* Flannan Isle, Haunted UB-65, and all the other classics going. It appears in both Raymond Lamont Brown's *Phantoms of the Sea* (1972) and Warren Armstrong's *Sea Phantoms* (1963); those writers seem to have borrowed it from a still-earlier source that we have not been able to identify.

The fact that we have not managed to do so may not matter, because there is a better than strong possibility that the story originated yet again in R. L. Hadfield's *The Phantom Ship* (1937), the writer who gave us the 1835 account mentioned several pages ago. Hadfield says that he received the narrative from the captain of the unlucky salvage ship itself, whom he met in San Francisco in 1906. It is an account heavy in the discreet, disguising initials traditional to the nineteenth-century ghost story. Out of consideration for the ship's owners and the relatives of the lost, footnotes Hadfield, the *Hannah Regan* becomes the steamer *H—— R——* sunk in 1889 off the South Pacific island of O——. (To be geographically correct, by the way, Okinawa is part of the Ryukyu Islands, which trail southwest of Japan and by no stretch of the imagination is it in the

South Pacific). Hadfield reduces the amount of bullion to 150,000 pounds sterling but of course that's still a sum worth having.

So thought Captain M—— evidently. After a small steamer bent on its salvage had been lost on an uncharted reef and another venture (a syndicate) failed, M—— took his ship to the southern Pacific and located the sunken *H—— R——* much as we've already heard. Now, after a string of minor differences with the foregoing story, we run into some major ones. Not least of all, it is the *H—— R——* (*not* the *Flying Dutchman*) that is the phantom ship, and it is her ghost that rises to dog the would-be salvagers with misfortune. At first, Captain M——'s version à la Hadfield corresponds with what we have already seen, until we find him confronted by the sight, *not* of a two-hundred-year-old sailing vessel, but a spectral steamer (which the *H—— R——* was, you remember, though she evidently has sails as most steamers did at the time). She is still going down by the stern, still awash; the captain can still see through her despite her gear, et cetera, but in Hadfield he notices much more. Her boats aren't merely hanging from their davits but are being lowered away; there are men busy on the bridge where "a forlorn figure" clutches the handrail. Moreover, she sinks abruptly as before and next day, "true to her reputation as foreteller of disaster" the two divers are drowned.

As we said, Hadfield presents this story as a memorate—something he was told in person by a leading actor (the only witness!) in the affair. As such, it can hardly be corroborated. After the tale left his hands, it was considerably confused by the additions of various writers, not least of whom was the unknown author who (for reasons of narrative efficiency, we presume) filled in the gaps left by the initials. Somewhere along the line the steamer *H—— R——* became the antique sailing vessel *Hannah Regan*—a ship closer in type to the *Flying Dutchman*—which Hadfield never said she was; in fact, his book gives the *Flying Dutchman* a separate chapter to itself. It is one of those oft-repeated, purportedly true accounts which go to show that ghost stories are more often tracked down in libraries than in haunted houses.

Our point here is that, as in the case of the Goodwins Ghost Ship, the story has been repeated without anybody troubling to check its credentials. But that may be too severe a judgment. Granted that no one seems to have gone back to Hadfield and noted the discrepancies between his original version and later ones that remodeled it (drastically!). And yet what guarantee was there that Hadfield was telling the real story? He had this highly flavored tale from a solitary witness whom he does not name. Always assuming that he had grounds for accepting what he was told, could Hadfield have cross-examined Captain M——

about it even if he'd wanted to? In the last analysis, first-person ghost stories are virtually beyond objective proof or disproof. We have to settle for the doubtful alternative of saying the witness *seemed* credible—that he did not strike us as a liar, a mere raconteur, a legend-teller.

The same applies to yet another of Hadfield's *Flying Dutchman* canon. The account appeared (he writes) in "the *Daily News* some years ago" and he was impressed by its being a rare example of the *Dutchman* being reported far from her usual haunting grounds, the Capes of Good Hope and/or Horn, that is, or else in southerly waters. This incident takes us to a patch of sea about five miles off Reykjavik, Iceland. We join the narrator, a second mate, and the captain on the bridge of the large whaling cruiser *Orkney Belle* one evening in January 1911. The ship has just passed through a belt of all-obscuring mist and visibility has returned—only, to their mutual horror and surprise, for them to see a sailing vessel looming up and practically head on:

> I rammed the helm hard aport and we seemed to escape collision by a hair's breadth.
>
> Meantime, the captain signalled dead slow to the engine room. Then with startling suddenness old Anderson, the carpenter, bawled out: "The *Flying Dutchman*!"
>
> The captain and I scoffed at him, for we thought that oft-fabled ship existed in the minds of only superstitious sailors.
>
> As the strange vessel slowly slid alongside within a stone's throw, we noticed with amazement that her sails were billowing, yet *there was no wind at all.* She was a replica of a barque I once saw in a naval museum—high poop and carved stern—but we could not observe her name.
>
> Meantime, practically all the crew rushed to the ship's side, some in terror, but unable to resist their curiosity. Not a soul was to be seen aboard this strange vessel, not a ripple did her bows make.
>
> Then, like a silver bell, so sweet was the tone, three bells sounded, as if from the bowels of the phantom ship, and as if in answer to a signal, the craft heeled to starboard and disappeared into the fog which was returning.
>
> I sailed with the old *Orkney Belle* several times, but never saw the queer old ship again. If any of my old shipmates on the *Orkney Belle* are still alive, I am sure they would corroborate my statement.

Were they? Did they? This highly unusual account certainly seems to have cried out for corroboration. For a good idea of how a practiced psychical researcher might have responded to the challenge, let's turn to our next case.

We can see at once that the compiler, Sir Ernest Bennett, is not interested in unauthenticated stories. The present one is given as case 104 in his *Apparitions and Haunted Houses* (1939), a collection of recent firsthand ghost stories elicited in response to the author's 1934 radio broadcast. Here, as throughout the rest of the book, the researcher has done his best to obtain independent corroboration of what the informant is saying.

The forwarder of case 104—one of Sir Ernest's few accounts to feature the ghost of an inanimate object—was N. K. Stone, the assistant bursar of Stowe School, but formerly fourth officer of the *P&O Barrabool* (Australia-London). His letter relates how he had taken up the midnight watch on January 26, 1923, shortly after the ship left Capetown, along with Second Officer "C. C. W." and with a cadet and the helmsman in attendance. At 12:15 on that dark, moonless night they sighted a strange light two or three miles off the port bow and trained binoculars and the ship's telescope upon it. The light appeared to be the luminous hull of a sailing vessel "with two distinct masts carrying bare yards, also luminous," as was the space between the masts; no sails were visible, nor any navigation lights. The strange spectacle seemed to approach the *Barrabool* at a speed similar to her own, but quite suddenly and with only half a mile separating them, she vanished.

"Good God, Stone," said the second officer, "it's a ghost ship."

That said everything there was to say. Stone subsequently made a sketch of what they had seen and, as he told Sir Ernest, many people who saw it "wonder if it was the *Flying Dutchman* we saw that night."

The psychical researcher was impressed by Stone's account, but saw an obvious and highly necessary way to corroborate it; he obtained the full name and whereabouts of 2nd Officer C. C. W. and contacted him. C. C. W. was willing and able to confirm Stone's narrative in all details, though he added that their first reaction had been to conclude the ship was a derelict, a theory summarily abandoned when she vanished. "I wondered at the time if some form of mirage could be responsible for the phenomenon," he concluded. Sir Ernest, for reasons left uncertain, was quite convinced that this explanation was not appropriate.

We have here an account as fully corroborated as any of its type can hope to be. Sir Ernest could not secure the testimony of the other two witnesses (the cadet and the helmsman) but for all practical purposes we have more than enough here. A pair of trained seamen observe for an appreciable length of time a mysterious light that closely resembles a sailing ship endowed with a strange luminosity through which the distinctive features of such a vessel appear—masts and yards; the witnesses' description corresponds well with that of the writer describing the glowing apparition with "masts, spars and sails . . . in strong relief" seen from HMS *Inconstant* some forty years before. (The discrepancy of the *Barrabool*'s visitor not having sails seems inconsequential.) In both cases, the "phantom ships" vanished abruptly, inexplicably.

The other point in common is the writer's failure to resist a temptation of interpreting or naming the phenomenon after the legendary *Flying Dutchman.* As we just saw, it was not H. K. Stone but viewers of his sketch who offered that piece of identification, yet the very fact he mentions that detail is significant. It is hardly a damning clause. One may as well label the phenomenon a "*Flying Dutchman*" as anything else, perhaps. It is very possible that Stone had the legend at the back of his mind when he wrote the letter; it would not be inconceivable that he thought of it around the time that the *Barrabool* encountered the spectral light, the more so as they were in the very cape waters famous for Vanderdecken's activities. Notice, though, that unlike the royal witness of *The Cruise of H.M.S.* Bacchante, he makes no effort to make the episode conform more closely to tradition by grafting on a sequel of mishaps. If it *was* the *Dutchman* that the *Barrabool* saw off the Cape in 1923, she failed to live up to her reputation of spelling doom to all beholders.

So we began this survey with a (presumed) mirage off the Cape of Good Hope in 1823 and finish a century later with an odd luminosity reported from the same area. Backtracking further, there are traditions, not necessarily based on actual sightings, of phantasmal vessels from other waters, meaning that the legend (and perhaps the actual phenomenon behind it, if there is one) is not confined to the Cape after all. The legend, contrary to Bassett's valedictory in 1885, did not die with the age of tall ships and wind-driven sailing. One of the latest and possibly overquoted pieces of testimony came from Admiral Karl Doenitz in 1944: "Certain of my U-boat crews claimed that they saw the *Flying Dutchman* or some other so-called phantom ship on their tours of duty east of Suez. When they returned to their base, the men said they preferred facing the combined strength of the Allied warships in the North Atlantic than know the terror a second time of being confronted by a phantom vessel!"

"The *Flying Dutchman* or some other so-called phantom ship": we began by looking at this subject as a nautical legend of modest vintage that became heavily influenced in later tellings by literature. Hopefully we have also indicated that besides acting as a species or generic name for a whole gamut of supernatural sea legends, the "*Flying Dutchman*" also codifies a range of uncommon marine experiences. That is, over a period of, say, one hundred years the legend lent itself readily as a name for certain uncommon marine events, the origins of which may have resided in optical anomalistics, but which more reasonably can be sought in a little-understood maritime phenomenon in which an eerie light of indeterminate origin impresses onlookers as nothing more or less than an old-time sailing ship. We have no accepted term for such a phenomenon. Therefore we label it a phantom ship . . . a *Flying Dutchman.*

The investigation into what this luminescent mystery might be continues in the next chapter.

References

On the Goodwin Sands: Historical, Topographical, etc.

George Byng Gattie, *Memorials of the Goodwin Sands and their surroundings, legendary and historical* (London: W. H. Allen, 1890).

Charles G. Harper, *The Kentish Coast* (London: Chapman & Hall, 1914), especially pp. 228–39.

Notes & Queries, 2nd series IX, March 24, 1860, p. 220; XI, February 23, 1861, p. 151; 6th series IX, January 5, 1884, p. 15; January 26, 1884, p. 73; February 23 1884, p. 158; March 29 1884, p. 259; 7th series V, April 14, 1888, p. 288; May 12, 1888, p. 369–70; 13th series 155, October 27, 1928, p. 289; 160, March 14, 1931, p. 181; June 6. 1931, p. 397; 179, no date, p. 163.

Thomas Stanley, Treanor, *Heroes of the Goodwin Sands* (n.d.—1905?).

*On the Goodwins Ghost Ships [*Lady Luvibund *and* Violet*]: Main items with a sample of secondary sources.*

Warren Armstrong, *Sea Phantoms* (1963), pp. 39–49.

Tony Arnold, "Ghost Ship on the Goodwins," *East Kent Mercury,* December 30, 1971, p. 2 (reprinted December 21, 1983).

Alan Bignell, *Kent Lore: A Heritage of Fact and Fable* (1983), pp. 61–64.

Raymond Lamont Brown, *Phantoms of the Sea* (1972), pp. 73–75.

George Goldsmith Carter, *The Goodwin Sands* (1953), pp. 137–40.

Anthony D. Hippisley Cox, *Haunted Britain* (1975), p. 74.

"Ghost Ship on the Goodwins," *Daily Chronicle,* February 15, 1924, pp. 1, 7.

R. L. Hadfield, *The Ghost Ship and Other Ghost Stories of the Sea* (1937), p. 53.

Jack Hallam, *The Ghost Tour* (1967), pp. 52–53.

Mollie Hardwick, *The World's Greatest Sea Mysteries* (1967).
Christina Hole, *Haunted England* (1940), p. 77.
Richard Larn, *Goodwins Sands Shipwrecks* (1977). See map.
Frank Madigan, "Ghost Ship on the Goodwin Sands," *Fate* (June 1955): 27–30.
"G. H. W.," "Ghost Ship of the Goodwins," *Notes & Queries* 157 (December 21, 1929): 443.

Personal information from Les Cozens and George Carter

On the Flying Dutchman *and ghost ships in general:*

Warren Armstrong, *Sea Phantoms.*
Fletcher S. Bassett, *Legends and Superstitions of the Sea and of Sailors in all Lands and at all Times* (1885), especially pp. 343–63.
Paul Begg, "Phantom of the High Seas," *The Unexplained* 10, no. 109 (1982): 2168–71.
Sir David Brewster, *Letters on Natural Magic addressed to Sir Walter Scott* (London: John Murray, 5th ed., 1842), especially letter 6.
Raymond Lamont Brown, *Phantoms of the Sea.*
Admiral von Doenitz, in R. L. Brown, *Phantoms of the Sea,* p. 24. He footnotes H. Lotzke and H. S. Brather's *Ubersicht uber die Bestande der Deutschen Zentralarchivs Postdam* (Berlin, 1957).
T. F. Thistelton Dyer, *The Ghost World* (1893), pp. 284–302.
Peter Haining, *The Ghost Ship: Stories of the Phantom* Flying Dutchman (1985).
J. G. Lockhart, *Mysteries of the Sea* (1924), chapter entitled "The *Flying Dutchman.*"
Notes & Queries, selected items in 8th series IX (June 6, 1896): 448, and X (July 18, 1896): 60.
"Phantom Ships," *Man, Myth and Magic,* issue 9 (1970), ("Frontiers of Belief" series running on inside and back covers).
William Clark Russell, *A Book for the Hammock* (1887), "Who Is Vanderdecken?" pp. 294–302.
"Spectres of the Sea," *Chambers's Journal* 7, no. 332 (May 10, 1890): 300–303.

On Flying Dutchman *cases discussed in the text:*

1835 "log": see R. L. Hadfield, *The Ghost Ship and Other Ghost Stories,* pp. 17–18. Hadfield cites Wilbur Bassett's *Wanderships: Folk Stories of the Sea* (Chicago: Open Court, 1917) as his source.

Bacchante (i.e., *Inconstant*) case, 1881: Albert Victor, Duke of Clarence, *The Cruise of Her Majesty's Ship* Bacchante, *1879–1882* (1886), vol. 1, p. 551, discussed in Michael Harrison's *Clarence: The Life of H.R.H. the Duke of Clarence and Avondale* (1972). For a typical review of the book see the *Athenaeum* 3058 (June 5, 1886): 739.

Barrabool case, 1923: Sir Ernest Bennett, *Apparitions and Haunted Houses* (1939), pp. 368–70.

Barracouta case, 1823: Captain W. F. W. Owen, R.N., *Narrative of Voyages to Explore the Shores of Africa, Arabia and Madagascar performed in H.M. Ships* Leven *and* Barracouta . . . (1883), vol. 1, pp. 241–43. (n.b., this case is summarized in Lockhart, *Mysteries of the Sea,* where he misnames HMS *Leven* as "*Severn*").

Dunraven case, 1917: *My Mystery Ships.* (London: Hodder & Stoughton, 1928). See Cheaper Edition (*sic*) September 1929, pp. 251–52.

Hannah Regan or *H—— R——* case, 1889 (1899?): W. Armstrong, *Sea Phantoms;* Raymond Lamont Brown, *Phantoms of the Sea;* R. L. Hadfield, *The Ghost Ship and Other Ghost Stories,* pp. 142–48.

Orkney Belle case, 1911: R. L. Hadfield, *The Ghost Ship and Other Ghost Stories,* pp. 19–20.

2

The *Palatine* and Other Flaming Wrecks

The ghost-haunted Goodwins, the storm-stressed Cape of Good Hope are far behind us. Now we are on Block Island, just a few miles seaward of the New England coast. The narrator is a Mrs. Rose, descended from some of the allegedly unsavory characters from the island's legendary past. What she has to say is no legend, though it relates strongly to one. Standing on her verandah some years ago, her attention was drawn to a peculiar phenomenon:

> The house windows shining as though a great bonfire was reflected on them. I turned toward the ocean and . . . I saw a great ship come sailing out from behind Clay Head to the north and glide swiftly over the sea in the direction of Newport. I was surprised to see that she had every sail set, and was bending under her canvas as though driven before a strong wind, while there was apparently no wind elsewhere on the sound. I was still more astonished that she appeared to be all on fire from the water's edge to her highest sail, and that the flames seemed to leap upward toward the gray sky. The sea around her was lit up with the radiance and it was the reflection from the burning ship that shone on the windows of my house and the roofs of the village at the basin. The strangest thing was that the flames appeared to have no effect on the ship, and though she was in sight for nearly fifteen minutes her sails were not consumed. The vessel glided swiftly eastward and disappeared. First the flames died slowly out, the hull became gray and misty, and finally she vanished or dissolved in the air.

Truly a sight to make any observer stand rooted to the spot with his (or her) eyes glued seaward. Indeed, this very sight, or one closely resembling it, has transfixed shorebound viewers on Block Island for generations.

But before we examine this phenomenon in more detail, there are three more characters we must meet. Moving back in time and sideways (more or less) in geographical space, we arrive at a picturesque salt meadow somewhere close to Hampton on the long, sandy shoreline of New Hampshire; there is a white tent on the beach and inside it are three male visitors holidaying from the strenuous demands of their everyday lives.

The first is a literary man who, despite an all-too-common pattern, has never allowed all his years of close textual study to kill his love of great literature. The next is a dreamy poet who is giving his visionary soul a chance to refresh itself; the third is a tanned traveler who has been practically everywhere and who in consequence has seen a good deal. As we join them, we find the trio engaged in the kind of mutual entertainment to which folk were prone in the simple days that preceded the invention of portable televisions, radios, and personal cassette players. They are telling stories, of course.

Or rather, each man taking turn, they are swapping "quaint traditions and legends strange." Many of these relate to the surrounding countryside. The narrators give us the witch Goody Cole and how she caused the Rivermouth wreck; they encompass Abraham Davenport and his legendarily calm reaction to the terror of May 19, 1780, when New England was invested with phenomenal darkness and men feared that the end of the world was at hand. Then, not long before the close of the tale-telling session, one of them chips in with "The Dead Ship of Harpswell," which puts the group on an eerie nautical tack. Tall and white, her name and history are known only to the oldest men who walk the Isle of Orr. This "ghost of what was once a ship" is both "a wonder and a sign." Steered by no crew other than the Angel of Death, she hovers outside the small Maine port. She never enters harbor, but puts down a boat that bears off the souls of those who are destined to die.

> ". . . I'm glad to see
> Your flying Yankee beats the Dutch"

remarks one when the story is finished and he promptly sets out to cap it with something he caught in Narragansett Bay in lieu of the fish he was after. *His* story concerns the flaming wreck of the *Palatine.*

Our three storytellers have an odd propensity to speak in rhyme. But that is only natural: the tent on the beach and the three men who fill it with their versified legends were almost the inventions of the Quaker and abolitionist poet John Greenleaf Whittier of East Haverhill, Massachusetts, whose eponymous work this is. "Almost," because in point of fact he did not create his poetic threesome out of thin air; they were confessedly modelled on his friends Fields ("the lettered magnate"), Taylor ("the free cosmopolite") and Whittier himself. Still less did he invent the harrowing tale of the *Palatine*.

Today, Whittier's place in American letters is that of an interesting and moderately important figure for his time (1807–1892) and place (New England) whose work suffers by comparison with that of his contemporaries. It offers none of the sable depths and complexities of Hawthorne, say, or the verbal pyrotechnics of Whitman, nor even the transcendental grandeur of Ralph Waldo Emerson: it is, put crudely, minor stuff. But then (and sadly) no purely literary evaluation does justice to Whittier's achievement in turning folklore, oral or published, into narrative verse, transforming oft-obscure local tales into the semblance of high drama. True it is that the mannered language and tacked-on moralizing robbed the material of some freshness and vitality; the compensation was that it reached and was accepted by larger audiences who might have sneered at the originals. If his literaricized versions supplanted in people's minds those original sources—if Whittier created "standardized" versions of legends that drew energy from their flexibility or their amenability to alteration with each telling—we might even say the process was inevitable.

In his own times, which were those of a creative artist, Whittier was a great admirer of his native traditions and tales. Folklorist Richard M. Dorson has said that rarely has a writer left clearer evidence of indebtedness to popular sources; Whittier for his part acknowledged that the potential of the field was vast and that he'd only partially explored it. He began to exploit that fictive potential at the age of twenty-four with his first book, *Legends of New England in Prose and Verse,* and throughout a career of almost seven decades he seldom strayed from it for long. Around 1867 he chalked up a literary success that neither he nor his admirers could have foreseen: he promoted to the status of one of America's most famous ghost stories a legend known until then only among the small seaboard communities of Rhode Island. There, in the five-mile stretch of water between Montauk and Gay Head and roughly opposite the town of Point Judith, sailed the ghost wreck of the *Palatine*.

Just twelve miles off Rhode Island is a globular, tree-less, windswept clay bank that trails off northwards in the recurving hook of Sandy Point. The original inhabitants, the Narragansett Indians, had called this eight-mile expanse Manisses: "the isle of the little god." By Whittier's day those aboriginals were long gone, exterminated or otherwise displaced by uncongenial white Puritan neighbors from whom the present farmers and fishermen were descended. The island was given a new name—Block Island—commemorating a Dutch sailor. Its chief claim to celebrity was that it represented something of a shipping hazard. Samuel Adams Drake's *A Book of New England Legends and Folklore* (1884) provides it with a point in common with the notorious Goodwin Sands of our last chapter. Like them, the island was "planted . . . right athwart the highway of a vast and interesting commerce . . . a veritable stumbling-block in the way of the anxious navigator." Cliché or not, Block Island won itself the sobriquet, "Graveyard of the North Atlantic."

And if New England popular parlance spoke true, the terrors of Block Island were not entirely nature's responsibility. A slander-like tradition affirmed that the residents of Block Island weren't adverse to adding to the unease of "the anxious navigator" by erecting false beacons that lured vessels onto the rocks and shoals; worse yet, no one who survived the rocks and the waves was likely to do so when the islanders came upon them.

It is hard to assess the truth of such "wrecker" stories. For certain, Block Island could be made to sound a small, primitive community, insular in both literal and figurative senses and peculiarly vulnerable to accusations of inbred degeneracy and the vilest forms of criminality. Its folk possessed either a strong sense of their own separateness or a distrust of outsiders; as late as 1960, when the *Saturday Evening Post*'s John Kobler visited them, they were referring to nonislanders as "foreigners." So while charitable souls like Drake appear to have dismissed the predatory rumors, some mariners allegedly took the opposite view and averred that they would sooner be wrecked anywhere in the world than upon Block Island.

Once again we are looking at a place infertile in the normal agrarian sense yet decidedly fertile for the cultivation of legends. Block Island has its dire quota of ghost stories; like many parts of the New England littoral, it has its Captain Kidd tales. More pertinent to us and preeminent over all rival legends, it also had the flaming wreck of the *Palatine*.

As the story came to be known in the late nineteenth century (and mainly thanks to Whittier), the *Palatine* was a ship laden with emigrants which sailed from Holland to America over a hundred years before. The usual date of the story is 1719 or 1720; one version puts it at 1752. Irrespective of this detail, the *Palatine* came hardly closer to her destination than Block Island and was fated to become immortally connected with it by virtue of what happened to her there.

Trouble broke out weeks before the New World was sighted. There was, or so the legend ran, a mutiny; the captain was murdered and with supplies running low the crew ruthlessly charged her passengers extortionate prices for water and biscuits. Soon the *Palatine* sprang a leak. The crew abandoned her (though not before transferring what remained of her stores into the lifeboats) and left the ship drifting helplessly, "a floating hell," in Drake's graphic description, "tenanted only by maniacs or the unburied corpses of those who had died from famine or disease." So the *Palatine* drifted—or, in some versions, was betrayed by the false lights of the wreckers—until she grounded on Block Island. There the wolfish islanders fell upon her, mercilessly slaughtering all but one demented woman who was either overlooked or else refused to leave the looted vessel as, set on fire by the Block Island devils, it was whisked seaward in a sudden gale. While the blazing *Palatine* moved out into open water, the wild screams of the madwoman floated back toward the shore in a ghastly aria.

That, or something like it, furnished Whittier with the unsavory yet impactful theme of what is probably his best-remembered poem. Perhaps we ought to recall that he was working in a period when oral traditions were regarded as legitimate new material; folklore, with its emphasis on recording accurately and respecting the sanctity of the text-as-told, was in its infancy and the writer felt quite free to alter and adapt as he or she saw fit, especially if alteration and adaption looked likely to improve the story somehow. Whittier's declared intention was to "present in interesting form some popular legends and traditions of New England"; he had great respect for his sources, oral or written, but not so much as to rule out artistic rearrangement. In the case of "The *Palatine*" as elsewhere, the final treatment was all his own.

Unlike many of his revised New England legends, this one came from a strictly oral source: Joseph P. Hazard of Newport, Rhode Island, who gave it to Whittier in about 1865. The poet owned to some unease about his "little ballad" before permitting it to take a prominent place in his collection *The Tent on the Beach* two years later. Perhaps he had qualms about how the violent subject matter might affect his more genteel readers, but despite the verdict of the "Book-man" that it is "a fitter tale to scream than sing," his version shows a good deal of restraint; nasty details like the villainous crew's maltreatment of the passengers are omitted and others, like the wreckers' even worse treatment of the same sufferers, are deleted. Even the demented lady who ought to go down with the burning ship is dismissed from the action (though not from an editorial note that prefaces most editions of the poem, and even there her sex and dementia aren't given). It may be that Whittier deemed these too strong for Victorian-Bostonian tastes; in all events, what interests him more is the central image of the spectral fire ship as an enduring judgment on "the hands that fed / The false lights over the rocky Head."

Whittier doesn't dwell too forcefully on the massacre of the defenseless emigrants beyond the necessary observation that

> Down swooped the wreckers, like birds of prey
> Tearing the heart of the ship away
> And the dead had never a word to say.

The culprits count on the fact there are no witnesses to their crime— " 'The sea and the rocks are dumb,' they said / 'There'll be no reckoning with the dead.' " But as the original Flying Dutchman learned to his cost and as the somber morality of folk tradition never tires of repeating, the crimes of humanity are overseen and judged by a Higher Authority, who has a way of inflicting punishment on whatever is hidden from earthly tribunals. Far from fading into oblivion, speculates the poet, the *Palatine* may have been recorded "On Nature's infinite negative," manifesting henceforth annually as a grim, ghostly, incandescent reminder of the wreckers' collective guilt and secondarily as a warning to wise skippers to reef their sails.

And, of course, every year on the anniversary of the wreck and of a crime too gross for expiation, the terrible scene is replayed:

> Behold! again with shimmer and shine,
> Over the rocks and the seething brine,
> The flaming wreck of the *Palatine*!

Whittier invents very little; he edits. Patently, what he gives us is a literary version of an authentic New England ghost-ship story as he received it from Joseph Hazard, who in turn was handing on a legend he shared with countless other narrators from that part of New England. It may have been well known to the Hazard clan, who figure large as informants or participants in the traditional tales of Narragansett recorded by Thomas Robinson Hazard, sheepraiser, textile manufacturer, Quaker, spiritualist, and, above all, folklore collector whose "Jonny Cake Letters" originally appeared in the *Providence Journal* in 1879 and 1880. Drawing on his fifty years in the southwestern corner of Rhode Island, but also upon experiences of older men dating back to the early 1800s and perhaps a little before, "Shepherd Tom" reproduced not only the fabric of the stories but the rambling oral style in which they were told. A fair taste of this Narragansettese can be had in his appropriately titled *Recollections of Olden Times* (1879), where, venturing for once beyond the boundaries of his native parish, he gives a short version of the *Palatine* legend, presumably one of several or many known to Rhode Islanders.

Thus there was no need for Whittier to invent anything. Even the moralistic core of the tale was presented to him ready-made; all he had to do was to emphasize it, elegantly and distinctly. We can discern the same, if undeveloped, moral thinking in a letter the poet received in 1869 from a Benjamin Corydon of Napoli, New York, which introduces a few more variations of the story:

> The *Palatine* was a ship that was driven upon Block Island, in a storm, more than a hundred years ago. Her people had just got ashore, and were on their knees thanking God for saving them from drowning, when the islanders rushed upon them and murdered them all. That was a little more than the Almighty could stand, so He sent the Fire or Phantom Ship to let them know He had not forgotten their wickedness. She was seen once a year, on the same night of the year on which the murders occurred, as long as any of the wreckers were living; but never after all were dead.

We can see at once that, give or take a few subsidiary details, the legend is remarkably consistent, most especially as regards the idea of the fire/phantom ship acting as an agent of heavenly punishment on the murderous criminals with strict cyclical accuracy. But besides demonstrating the fixity of folk belief that underlies oral legends, particularly ones featuring ghostly apparitions, the Corydon letter affirms that the story is told in connection with a genuine phenomenon, one which acts as a popular, quasihistorical explanation of it. We can believe the *Palatine* legend because there are witnesses, actual witnesses, who testify to having seen the fiery spectre of which the story is told. Benjamin Corydon claimed to have been one of them:

> I must have seen her eight or ten times—perhaps more—in my early days. It is seventy years or more since she was last seen. My father lived right opposite Block Island, on the mainland, so we had a fair view of her as she passed down by the island; then she would disappear. She resembled a full-rigged ship, with her sails all set and all ablaze. It was the grandest sight I ever saw in my life. I know of only two living who ever saw her—Benjamin L. Knowles, of Rhode Island, now ninety-four years old, and myself, now in my ninety-second year.

Let's first address the troublesome question of oral tradition and factuality: in other words, whether a folk version of history can stand wholly or in part for authentic or "real" history. Obviously there are problems in suggesting that it can, but experience suggests that on a popular level it frequently *does.* Legend could be called "unfounded history"—in fact, that was exactly what R. C. Temple called it in "The Science of Folk-Lore" in the *Folk-Lore Record* for 1886; the difficulty, as his contemporary Charlotte Burne said, was how much dependence could be placed on tradition (*Folk-Lore* 1, 1890). Sticking with that near-synonym, tradition can be either something that professes to fill up the gaps of history (Lach-Szyrma, *Folk-Lore Record* 3, 1881) or "a collection of venerable and romantic blunders" (Andrew Lang, *Morning Post,* November 2, 1906). In the instance of the *Palatine*—and for the present ignoring its supernatural component—where does actual history end and gap-filling, romantic but accepted blunder, begin?

First and with due deference to Elizabeth Dickens (longtime Block Island resident) and to other New England historians who took a great deal of trouble to establish the facts, we can say that there never was any such vessel named *Palatine,* or rather, that no ship of that name was ever wrecked on Block Island. That admission doesn't alter the truism that America's most celebrated sea phantom is far from being a complete fabrication or a fantasy. The ship commemorated in the legend is almost certainly the 220-ton *Princess Augusta,* which left Rotterdam in August 1738 under Captain George Long carrying 350 emigrants from the Upper and Lower Palatinates of Germany: the first of 3,000 potential New World settlers from these states bound (according to the *Gentleman's Magazine*) for a German landowner's property on the James River, Virginia. This immediately and satisfactorily explains the confusion over the ship's name. For the sake of colloquial convenience, the settlers would have been known as "Palatines" and their vessel as the "Palatine (ship)," which is how she is designated in the official depositions of her officers as reprinted in 1939.

In all events, the ship *was* wrecked on Block Island, though not under the circumstances the legend insists upon. The initial cause of *Princess Augusta*'s troubles was not mutiny or murder, but a debilitating run of bad luck that commenced when the ship's casks of drinking water were found to be contaminated. Following the death of Captain Long and seven of his fourteen crewmen—as well as over two hundred passengers—command passed to the first mate, Andrew Brook. Severe gales drove the ship northwards, where she struggled for three excruciating months with stocks of edibles and water diminishing. Here reality begins to meld with legend as, for reasons not readily understood but readily condemned, Brook and his crew began to force the emigrants to pay for such meagre supplies as remained.

Brook seems to have tried to reach Rhode Island, where his distress signals attracted no attention. In consequence and presumably in desperation, he elected to make the long run down to Philadelphia, but was frustrated by the weather: the merciless winds refused to let the ship escape, pushing her instead back toward the "graveyard of the North Atlantic."

At 2 p.m. on December 27, the now-leaking *Princess Augusta* ploughed through a heavy snowstorm onto Sandy Point, the northernmost extremity of Block Island. Even allowing for the details that water had entered her hold and the ship's bottom damaged, it remains hard to defend Brook's decision to order the hundred-or-so surviving emigrants to stay on board the battered vessel while he and the crew rowed ashore; charitably minded folk may care to suppose he was reconnoitering what he may have felt was hostile or otherwise dangerous country. But that hypothesis scarcely explains why it was necessary for *all* the crew to go, nor why Brook ensured that when the emigrants were permitted to disembark the next day their possessions were left behind on the ship. It was left to the latterly maligned Block Islanders to eventually salvage some twenty chests from the crippled vessel and to direct them to their proper owners. They also buried the score of passengers who died soon after landing; the memorial marker placed by the Block Island Historical Society in 1947 testifies to that.

The penultimate stages of the story are slightly confused. There may have been a general agreement that the *Princess Augusta* was beyond saving; her anchor cable was severed to allow her to float away and sink in deep water, which she managed to do after striking a rock to the west of the island. It may or may not have been the case that islanders tried to expedite matters by putting her to the torch, though (taking up a point that one octogenarian made to John Kobler in 1960) it seems curious that anybody living on treeless Block Island should be so spendthrift with that much free timber. And, though it seems hard to believe, in the melee a woman sometimes named as the wealthy Mary Van Der Line, who had been driven insane by her recent suffering and who refused to leave the ship, was overlooked and went down with it. More certain is the claim that Brook and his crew succeeded in evading any misconduct charges brought against them and vanished not long after they reached the mainland, as did all but two of the surviving passengers. This exceptional pair settled on Block Island, where one is credited with playing an instrumental role in the evolution of the colorful ghost-ship legend.

However, most of the blame for that fell on Whittier, "a character-assassin," as an island man called him in Kobler's hearing. Often as they concede that the *Palatine* has become a useful, revenue-generating tourist attraction, Block Islanders have long resented being portrayed as human hyenas and they were defended by local pastor and historian the Rev. Samuel Livermore, whose *A History of Block Island* (1877) spoke of "a little population of as pure morals as ever adorned Puritan New England." Being a Block Islander himself, the reverend may have been subject to a permissible bias, but ironically the many who took up his version of the *Palatine* story tended to ignore his strictures on the innocence of his flock's forebears.

Research by recent chroniclers go some way toward upholding them. Elizabeth Dickens offers a reevaluation of the "wrecking" tradition; in actuality, it was salvage operations fully condoned by nautical practice and carried out with the shipowners' knowledge. Pirates and, yes, wreckers of the unsanctioned variety, *may* have used Block Island as a temporary base, but never as a permanent one, she notes. Contrary to the usual run of the tale, there is no evidence that the Palatine ship was led astray by the wreckers' "false lights on the beacon's head." Despite the deaths of two elderly women on the beach, there are no grounds for talking of pillage and slaughter when the islanders clearly did all that was in their power to help. Oddly enough, the harrowing tale of premeditated wreckage and casual slaughter may not have been Whittier's original inspiration. Instead, we may have to blame a disenchanted local resident.

"Long Kattern," one of the two Palatine survivors to settle on Block Island, is said to have married a former black slave named "New Port," acquiring with time three children and a reputation as a sorceress. Kobler found the islanders of 1960 clannish; how much more so must they have been two hundred years before! It is easy to imagine Kattern, ostracized from the tightly knit community, passing down to her offspring the blood-curdling yarn of the homicidal, raptorial wreckers still heard today. If this genesis is not another example of folk history in action, perhaps it represents an outsider's durable revenge on a society that excluded her.

So much for the reconstructed history of the misnamed "*Palatine*." That of her spectral, incandescent image, the ghostly fire ship, is another problem. When was it first seen, and by whom?

According to Kobler's "The Mysterious Palatine Light" in the *Saturday Evening Post* of June 11, 1960, the retributive apparition celebrated the first anniversary of the wreck by deluding the captain of the trader *Somerset,* who was "so distressed by the sight that we followed the burning ship to her watery grave, but failed to find any survivors or flotsam." By its very nature, this anecdote is beyond a researcher's power to check properly. Then there is ninety-two-year-old Ben Corydon's claim to have sighted her ("eight or nine times—perhaps more") and from the dating he attaches in his letter it seems that the ghost ship continued on view throughout the dying years of the eighteenth century. This confirms that she had become an article of belief or tradition along the Rhode Island shoreline long before Whittier happened on the legend courtesy of Joseph Hazard.

We may as well add here that his poeticized effusion was postdated by a small shelf of books written due to the burgeoning interest of the late 1800s in local history and folklore, each routinely giving further impetus to the *Palatine* story: W. P. Sheffield's *An Historical Sketch of Block Island* (1876); Livermore's previously cited, similarly titled work (1877); Thomas Hazard's *Recollections of Olden Times* (1879), where the *Palatine* is a brief excursion beyond the writer's native district; Edward E. Pettee's *Block Island Illustrated* (1884); and Drake's *Book of New England Legends and Folklore* (1884). This sudden concentration of interest in what had formerly been treated as a highly obscure corner of New England may have been a token of writers' consciousness of the place they lived in; less doubtfully the legend-history of the *Palatine* was one of those dramatic episodes that serve as a stamp of distinction. In a suggestive fashion it came to typify the ancient mystery that was Block Island.

Used cautiously, Corydon's alleged sightings ("seventy years or more" since the *Palatine* was last seen, he reckoned) place the phenomenon in the late eighteenth century. Bringing the log closer to our own times, Kobler quotes two Block Island witnesses. Temperance hotel owner Sam Mott claimed to have seen the ghost ship three times (but, the journalist pointed out, "Alert listeners . . . sometimes detect a certain lack of conviction in his recital"). Milkman Clarence Lewis saw the light "mebbe fifty years ago" (1910?) followed by a sou'easter. To come upon a more vivid eyewitness account we have to retreat still further to a travel feature on "Block Island Legends: Folklore of the 'Lazy Man's Paradise' " in the *New York Times* for October 19, 1884.

The *Palatine,* the article said, had been seen as recently as February 9, 1880—its first appearance for half a century, despite the cyclical annual tradition—and by Mrs. Rose, whose account we heard at the start of this chapter, as well as by fifty others on different parts of the island who shared with her the distinction of being descended from the "early wreckers."

Switching back to Kobler's 1960 article, it is worth mentioning that regardless of how they felt about Whittier's imputations on their character, few islanders would disagree that the *Palatine* was an excellent tourist attraction. The anonymous *New York Times* piece has all the hallmarks of wanting to encourage readers to visit the Lazy Man's Paradise of Block Island; could Mrs. Rose's spectacular account have been specially selected for the way it lent itself to that purpose? What emerges more strongly from it is the unmistakable element of traditional or "folkloric thinking" contained in her closing remarks: "As soon as I saw the *Palatine,* I knew something dreadful was going to happen, and I told my neighbors so. And sure enough, only four days later a party of young Block Islanders, descendants of those who wrecked the old ship, were drowned in Newport harbor."

This reinforces what appears to have been an intriguing motif within the *Palatine* legend, to which Ben Corydon also referred, which confined the ship's apparitional appearances to the original guilty parties. Thus it is visible only to descendants of the wreckers *or* only during the lifetimes of the eighteenth-century wreckers; besides strengthening the retributive factor, the motif seems to allude to the universal ghost-vessel type in which the ghost ship appears in order to convey the souls of the moribund to the beyond, which (as we just heard) Whittier used for his "Dead Ship of Harpswell." The ominous quality of the *Palatine* that restricts its significance to relatively few Block Islanders—those descended from the "birds of prey" who wrecked her—had little appeal for later audiences, however. This refinement of the legend was superseded by the more general motif or observation that the ship is the harbinger of gales and storms, particular sou'easters.

Corydon had spoken of the *Palatine* ghost as a thing of the past—erroneously, perhaps, and with mistaken pride in being one of only two people who could boast of having seen it. A highly quotable account published long before his letter to Whittier suggests there was a large contingent who could have made the same claim. When he provided the first carefully written description of the phenomenon as far back as 1811, Dr. Aaron C. Willey had affirmed that,

> The light is actually seen, sometimes one-half mile from shore, where it lights up the walls of a gentleman's room through the windows. The people here are so familiarized with the sight they never think of giving notice to those who do not happen to be present or even mentioning it afterwards, unless they hear some particular enquiries have been made.

This is an instructive piece of prose. It fixes the *Palatine* as a phenomenon widely known locally—so much so as to be deemed unworthy of special remark—yet we can't fail to notice that it is not specifically described as a *ship,* but only as a light that may have suggested a ship to observers. This is an important distinction to which we will return.

For the moment we can muse on the paradox that although the

"Palatine light" or ghost ship seems to have conferred a sort of uniqueness on this small corner of New England, there was little which could truly be called unique about it at all. For the *Palatine* is not the only maritime wraith to haunt the coastal waters of northeastern America, nor yet the only one to assume the form of a fire ship. Ralph De S. Childs of the New York Folklore Society logged over a dozen phantom-vessel legends from this part of the country and his estimate may err on the conservative side. More recently (and extending the survey's scope from California round to Nova Scotia and Canada, not omitting the Great Lakes, and including such humble classes of spectral shipping as Indian canoes) Mark A. Hall and Loren Coleman list thirty-eight sites associated with the supernatural effect.

Sticking with the northeast, we find more than enough apparitional vessels to suit the needs of this chapter. There is the *Dash* of Casco Bay, Maine, which vanished in 1812 with sixty on board and which now reappears during August fogs complete with crew and sails set. And there's the schooner *White Rover,* which foundered a century ago at Isle of Shoals, New Hampshire. Out by Cape Cod (Massachusetts) an incandescent ship is to be seen after a storm; to the north, the Bay of Fundy near St. Martin's, New Brunswick, in September or October are the place and time to encounter an alternative ship in flames. Others, not unlike the *Palatine,* become local eponyms: the aptly named "Teazer Light" of Mahone Bay, Nova Scotia, for instance, or the "Packet Light" of Prince Edward Island in the Gulf of St. Lawrence, a fireball that rises and sways over the water, resolving itself into the semblance of a burning ship only to sink again. Usually it is taken to be a portent of a coming storm, a meteorological motif we will meet several times and in several places during this review of the northeast's fiery sea phantoms.

Apart from providing material for Whittier and his writer-contemporaries, this superabundance of conflagrant vessels has been of publicity value to several hitherto secluded fishing ports. Phantom craft can be tourist attractions, especially when they are on fire, as an Associated Press report for December 8, 1953, suggests. Hundreds of people were said to have observed the nightly performances of a ghost ship alleged to patrol the Northumberland Strait between Prince Edward Island and Nova Scotia; the chief doubt here is which one they were looking at, for Northumberland Strait claims no less than three. The ship off Richibucto is another lambent promise of a storm; off Cape St. John (Nova Scotia) the correct season for phantom-spotting is December. Marking the autumnal equinox, the more frequently described full-rigged three-master off Merigomish sails to her doom annually, northeastward and at a respectable 20 knots, attracting crowds of spectators along the shore. If the moon shines, they are likely to see the gleam of her copper keel; if fog prevails, she is outlined in eerie phosphorescence. The display is nothing if not spectacular: a sudden lurch as if the ship had gone aground, flames leap up and dim figures are seen in the act of throwing themselves overboard as rigging and mast collapse and the blackened hull slides beneath the waves. It seems remarkable that if the molten wreck has been performing like this for three generations, which is what some sources tell us, her identity remains unknown.

There is, of course, the possibility that the three "burning ships" of Northumberland Strait are actually one and the same. Such an idea occurred to Edward D. Ives, who heard the stories while researching a quite unrelated topic in the Lot Seven Shore area of Prince Edward Island. A subsequent letter to the local paper introduced him to "some fifteen" people who claimed to have seen the ship. One, a Glengarry (Prince Edward Island) man whose wife had drawn his attention to a strange light on the strait, described what he saw as a full-rigged ship in flames sailing northward "at an impossible speed"; both had watched it for half an hour until it disappeared from view. A Burton woman had surveyed it through her window for twice as long "and she not only saw the rigging in flames but could see people running around on the deck."

Aware of a certain monotony in reproducing eyewitness accounts that differ only in minor detail, Ives attempted to generalize. The burning ship defied his initial assumption that it was confined to the waters of the West End area from Ebbsfleet to West Point (and particularly off Richibucto) whence came half of the sightings; it was also reported from the central South Shore (Albany to Canoe Cove) and further east around Murray Harbor. It had "evidently been seen all through the Northumberland Strait," he concluded. It was described as full-rigged, but not always as the three-masted square rigger of some written versions; a DeSable informant who had seen it forty or more years before called the ship a top-sail schooner "of much more ancient rig than I had ever seen" and two Argyle Shore witnesses spoke of her as a large steamer with brilliantly lit decks.

Some witnesses, it appears, discerned more than others. A few gave highly detailed descriptions of the flames, with or without the running figures mentioned by the Burton lady. Most agreed the ship headed north or northwest up the strait (but two said east—others that she was not moving at all) and typically at great speed: no less than thirty to thirty-five miles in only ten minutes, offered one informant, while a Campbellton fisherman who met her on the water had not been able to overhaul her. At some time varying between ten minutes and two hours the ship would either sail out of visibility or sink. This phenomenal event could take place at all seasons (including winter, when the strait was filled with ice) and usually prior to midnight, although one Murray Harbor incident took place in daytime. Some informants associated the fire ship with an approaching storm, but others do not seem to have attached any meteorological significance to it.

Ives felt sure that the Northumberland Strait phenomenon was "closely related" to other fire ships of the northeast American coast. Two of his informants were obviously aware of Bay Chaleur's analogous story cycle; at least, when invited to explain what the thing signified, they responded with legendary pseudohistories that seemed to have been borrowed from that source. Ives also felt it possible that the "Packet Light" of Prince Edward Island lore was none other than an alternative name for the fire ship he had been studying. Three fire ships in the same stretch of seaway seem to verge on having too much of a good thing.

Could Ives or his informants attach a name to the Burning Ship of Northumberland Strait? They could not. By contrast, up at Cap d'Espoir on the St. Lawrence they seem fairly confident about what their fire ship represents. It is a memorial of a disastrous debacle that dates from 1711, when England had serious designs on French Canada. These included a naval sortie up the St. Lawrence to undefended Quebec, but the fleet of nine ships of the line, two smaller war vessels, and sixty miscellaneous craft under Admiral Hovenden Walter came to ignominious grief in a thick fog (conjured up, some say, by the noted Isle of Orleans sorcerer Jean Pierre Lavallee) and drifted onto the northern shore of the seaway with a loss of a fifth of its forces. Walter abandoned the attack on Quebec and returned to England and ample recriminations. So today at Cap d'Espoir (or so we're told) the discomfiture of the English is commemorated by a strange light presaging a storm; an olden-day sailing craft crowded with red-coated soldiers appears and if your luck is in and your eyesight is good you may see an officer-like figure on the bowsprit, one hand pointing at the shore, the other clasping a white-clad lady. But the light dims, a crash resounds, echoed by a fearful shriek—and the unlucky ship vanishes.

In comparison, the fire-phantom ship of the Bay of Chaleur (Baie des Chaleurs) in the Gaspé Peninsula is a relatively sober affair, though it too attracts its share of attention. And it is worth remarking that, once again, we appear to be dealing with more than a quaint local legend; a Galena (Illinois) woman who initially knew the story from her reading told *Fate* for February 1964 that the fluorescent phenomenon had once been vivid and credible enough to have five hundred Catholics returning from a midnight mass rushing to the rescue. In response to her inquiries a South Gaspean—"a responsible woman who, I am sure, is not given to fantasy"—said she'd seen the apparition many times. To which *Fate*'s editor (citing a filler article in the June 1958 issue) confirmed that reportedly hundreds had done so for at least a century; the apparition was described as a sailing ship or galleon, its rigging and upper works engulfed in flames, and some witnesses spoke of figures scurrying aloft.

There is a notable gap between popular journalistic treatments of the Bay Chaleur story with their casual estimates of "hundreds" of witnesses and graphic details including dimly perceived figures and what one critical researcher learned when he investigated the case in the early 1900s. Edward Ives, too, found that when he sought an explanation of the Northumberland Strait's burning vessel his oral informants were of little assistance; to fill that gap he had to go to popular literature—to books, particularly to Roland H. Sherwood's *Story Parade,* or to tourist guides evidently reliant upon it. Thus the ship was a pleasure craft accidentally burned when a lamp was overturned in the captain's cabin—some said *Captain Kidd*'s cabin—during a drunken brawl, or else a Quebec-bound immigrant ship blown off course, struck by lightning, consumed with all hands lost. At Pictou, Nova Scotia, she was said to be the ghost of a ship that vanished after sailing for Scotland—a tale reminiscent of the lost *Dash* of Maine, perhaps—and New Brunswickers named her the "John Craig Light" after the boat wrecked off Shippigan Island. Finally, on Pictou Island the ship was weirdly placed as the third in a series of supernatural events that began with an apparitional woman in white striding into the sea, bounding up as a fireball, and then transforming into a phantom vessel.

The writers were free in their invention; by and large, Ives's informants were not. "Most of them were quite certain that what they saw was, or looked like, a ship on fire, and yet at the same time they seemed to feel that there was some perfectly rational explanation." Observation and explanatory legend were two different things, then. Leaving that aspect for the present, we can say that the occurrence of so many similar-sounding fire-ship stories around the northeastern coastline of America is more significant than the hint that there is little to choose between them as far as melodrama goes. Folklorists know that the world's oral traditions are repetitive in the sense that they fall into set narrative patterns ("types" or "motifs") and variants upon them; it is as if there was nothing so hard for a folk narrator as to invent a truly original storyline.

Northeastern America's fire ships demonstrate a consistent pattern as regards narrative development. A blazing vessel (usually if not always a sailing vessel) is discerned out to sea; she may or may not be equipped with figures suggestive of a crew, she is not static but moves, and she vanishes abruptly. The event may presage or follow a storm, normally the former. The event is said to occur annually or cyclically and to have done so for a century or more, during which period "hundreds" of people have reputedly witnessed it. Not infrequently, the texts refer to a *light* rather than to a ship as such, but most justify the co-identification by adding that at various times people have been so thoroughly convinced as to put out to rescue what they could only assume was a real ship in real, fiery trouble. This we could call the "observational" or "phenomenal" phase. In the more dramatic and perhaps "mature" instances, the phenomenal phase is accompanied by a story which *accounts* for the light; we get (as at Block Island and Cap d'Espoir) a narrative that presents the story behind the supernatural manifestation.

To invoke the lessons of folklore again, such a noteworthy concentration of fire-ship legends around the northeastern shores of America might argue a common response to a shared environment—the adoption of stories appropriate to a particular nautical setting—if not the actual borrowing and relocation of those narratives from one locality to another. Nothing would be easier than to take, let us say, the Merigomish three-master and transpose it to a setting in Casco Bay, Maine; given the nautical heritage of the two places, the legend seems equally appropriate to both. But returning to our "observational" or "phenomenal" phase, it is equally cogent to suggest that at various points around this extended coastline there occurs a strange phenomenon to which people have reacted via the same quasi-explanatory stories: those of the "narrative" phase. "The *fons et origo* of all Folk-Lore is apparently the instinct of man to account for the facts that he observes about him," pointed out R. C. Temple. In other words, legends are attempts (however naive) to impress meaning on the unknown phenomena that surround us. The legends and/or inferences may be dramatizations and literal fallacies, but they have their own internal significance.

We tend to lose sight of this if we mistakenly believe the "Palatine Light" to be unique. Yet there's no gainsaying that none of America's ghostly fire flotilla has managed to capture the imagination in the way the Block Island phenomenon—thanks partly to Whittier et al.—has managed to do. Denying that would be an act of iconoclasm. "Hundreds have claimed to have seen the apparition," wrote journalist Edwin C. Hill enthusiastically, and the "Palatine Light" is a well-known phenomenon along the New England coast. There is, apparently, "some kind of light—strange, mysterious, inexplicable—which is seen far out to sea at certain times. . . . [T]here are people living to this day on Block Island who will tell you . . . that they have gazed seaward in the blackness of the night, startled by a bright radiance at sea, and have watched with straining eyes, while the *Palatine,* blazing from truck to keelson, swept along the horizon. . . ."

Stirring words indeed—an example of what one reviewer likes to call "gee-whiz rhetoric," and perhaps a little too lively to be wholly convincing. But then, austere critics are likely to find the secondary, narrative component of the *Palatine* case the weaker part. To repeat what we said of the *Lady Luvibund* in chapter 1, researchers tend to look askance at ghosts that behave too much like their counterparts in folklore and fiction. The *Palatine* as a possible actual event seems contaminated by an overlay of "creative history" intended to consolidate it.

Popular belief asserts that apparitions are some kind of enduring record of past events, especially of tragic ones redolent of savage violence, betrayal, and other heightened emotions. Parapsychologists generally find that authenticated apparitions have no discernible or overt connection with memorably bloody events; they merely arrive inexplicably and depart unidentifiably. In suggesting that,

> . . . pictures of all ages live
> On Nature's infinite negative,
>
> Which, half in sport, in malice half, She shows
> at times, with shudder or laugh,
> Phantom and shadow in photograph. . . .

Whittier anticipates a widespread theory that ghosts are visual prerecordings impressed (somehow) on the atmosphere. It is a somewhat mechanical metaphor, but one that has appealed to a fair number of metaphysicians. It is a hypothesis that parapsychology has still to corroborate. And in any case, do the eyewitness descriptions make the "Palatine Light" sound like some spectacular visual display minus any visible apparatus to account for it? Do they talk *specifically* of the light as a ship, or merely of a light?

Old Benjamin Corydon was fairly unambiguous on the subject: he'd seen something that "resembled a full-rigged ship, with her sails all set and all ablaze" and it was "the grandest sight I ever saw in my life." But, aside from any doubts about how much reliance can be placed on the accuracy of a ninety-two-year-old recalling something from his "early days," there is the query as to what he meant by "resembled." Did the phenomenon look *exactly* like a ship on fire, or did it suggest (perhaps in its dimensions, outline, or configuration) something more like a blazing vessel than anything else that came to mind? In Willey's earlier description (1811), the phenomenon is a light that "beams with various magnitudes. Sometimes it is small, resembling the light through a distant window, at others expanding to the highness of a ship with all her canvas spread. The blaze actually emits luminous rays." Elsewhere he says it is "pyramidal, or in three streamers like a ship, flickering and reappearing, but not lasting longer than three minutes. It is seen before easterly and southerly storms, and at all seasons."

Again the conclusion is that the light takes a shape highly suggestive of a ship but perhaps not literally representing one. As the Rev. Livermore argued, the "Palatine Light" consists of two parts: fact and fiction, or observation and imaginative construction arising from it. Put another way, the phenomenon is well-attested and quite credible even if inexplicable, but the ghost-ship identity legend ostensibly integral to it may be an unnecessary luxury. We can admit the one without having to believe in the other.

The *Palatine* legend is an attempt to explain, however sensationally, a truly curious effect. As a rule, people are not content to let perplexing events pass without attaching to them some form of narrative which, if it doesn't explain them, gives the impression that they are not without a certain rationality. From creation myth to local legend, the story tries to accommodate a lack of genuine knowledge. The results may draw upon some popular hypothesis or conventionally unconventional idea that goes beyond what science can back up. Folk tradition has its own unwritten (or rather, uncorroborated) "laws" and "theories," particularly where the supernatural is concerned. As we've already noticed, ghosts are supposed to walk as a result of past crimes, past tragedies, past injustices. Ghost ships sail, usually on the anniversary of those events, for the same reasons. If a person has seen a ghost, or a ghost ship, it can only mean that somewhere in the past lies a crime, a tragedy, or an injustice to account for it.

At some indeterminate time in the eighteenth century people along the Rhode Island coastline became aware of a strange radiance out to sea. It vaguely resembled a ship—since it appeared out to sea it could hardly be anything else!—and the brightness implied that the mystery vessel must surely be on fire. The fact of its sudden disappearance and the absence of wreckage strongly suggested it could be no mortal, earthly ship. But if a ghost, *whose* ghost? What unhappy craft and tragic tale was responsible for the weird illumination?

A universally spread oral tradition of ghost ships in which the *Flying Dutchman* figured as a leading component went only part way toward a solution. The memorability of ghost stories depends on them attaching themselves to a specific locality—in their becoming part of local history. The historical facts concerning the wreck of a Palatine ship (the *Princess Augusta*) on Block Island seemed to answer many of the questions about the anomalous light. And why should she be in flames—what foul crime did her appearance betoken? Block Island was a self-contained community, one little understood by outsiders; there were the wrecker rumors. These made it comparatively easy to believe in a story that combined the known and the conjectured, the historical and the traditional, as did the version attributed (rightly or wrongly) to Long Kattern.

The *Palatine* legend as it came to be told in the nineteenth century was a logical product of New England's maritime heritage, not the least constituent of which was an emphasis on ghost-ship lore. Every culture interprets unexplained phenomena according to time-honored interpretive processes. Here the first person to observe the "Palatine Light" automatically thought in terms of ghostly vessels. A rural community (as opposed to a maritime one) might have spoken of will o' the wisp or corpse candles; today the "Palatine Light" might pass for some kind of UFO, perhaps one of Ivan Sanderson's submersible varieties. But, of course, there could have been no culturally contoured explanation of any species without the phenomenon to provoke it in the first place. So, assuming that the light came first and the legend afterwards, we can look more closely at the phenomenal phase of the operation. If we have to wave the ghost-ship explanation goodbye, just how *can* the "Palatine Light" be explained?

With great difficulty, as a review of the theories put forward to account for several of New England's fiery ghost ships proves. There have been intermittent attempts to assign them to freakish yet mundane causes, meteorological or geological ones, for example; unfortunately, few have been more than superficially convincing and none of them absolutely corroborated.

If the popular theorizing of folklore tends to exceed what science is prepared to support, then popular science—or people's versions of scientific thinking—has a way of obscuring ignorance behind a cloud of near-meaningless jargon, predictably the kind fashionable at the time. To Willey in 1811, the "Palatine Light" was "a curious subject for philosophical speculation" and in his case such cerebral exercise took the form of suggesting the light was a "peculiar modification of electricity" or "the inflammation of phlogogistous gas." Sixty or more years after him, the Rev. Livermore pondered ingeniously about the possible effects of lightning igniting seabed deposits of petroleum. He had been intrigued by recollections of the so-called "Burning Brook" of Canandaigua, New York, where petroleum or otherwise inflammable gas bubbled to the surface, and guessed that a similar curiosity of nature might occur at Block Island.

The problem in reconciling the phenomena to specific physical causes lies in persuading readers to accept things for which no empirical evidence exists. There was *no* evidence of Willey's phlogogistous gas; nowadays, we don't believe in phlogiston at all. There was no concrete evidence of Livermore's offshore petroleum deposits, which may have been no great loss; the reverend was clearly troubled by the fact that even in his Canandaigua analogy, where some form of flammable gas *did* arise, it still required a person to apply a match before the Burning Brook would burn. The best he could offer was that Block Island's conjectured oil reservoirs were susceptible to seasonal and fortuitously accurate lightning strikes.

It is facile to deride these attempts to apply scientific thinking to the paranormal or (perhaps more aptly) the unexplained. But when he is forced by a much-reported phenomenon that claims to lie beyond the parameters of science, what more constructive thing is there for a person to do than to approach that phenomenon in terms of what science has already established? Are we justified in mocking Rhode Island historian Welcome A. Greene because one day in September 1880 he returned from a fishing trip convinced that the "Palatine Light" was nothing more than the glow cast by a huge shoal of menhaden? Now, menhaden are oily fish and vaguely phosphorescent. The folly lies in insisting that the hypothesis *must* be right, that the mystery *is* solved, if only because any refusal to admit that formula puts us back where we started.

Neither Willey nor Livermore insisted absolutely that they had cracked the mystery of the "Palatine Light" and in retrospect they were right to be cautious. W. F. Ganong had little to advance beyond their propositions when he investigated New Brunswick's rival of the "Palatine Light": the celebrated Fire or Phantom Ship of Bay Chaleur.

Apparently described by rough consensus as resembling the hull of a vessel on fire, the spectacle was recorded at least as early as 1801 (in the *Colonial Times* of Miramichi for November 2 of that year) and by the time the researcher came to deal with it in his paper for the *Bulletin of the Natural History Society of New Brunswick* in 1906 it had already entered the realms of fiction, with consequent distortion of an authentically mysterious effect, Ganong believed. Initially prejudiced by these literary treatments with their "banshees, pirates or picturesque historical personages," he started out a skeptic, but was open-minded enough to revise his opinion. "One cannot be long in the Bay Chaleur country, especially in the eastern part, without hearing of the fire (or phantom) ship, said so often to be seen on the bay," he wrote. What you heard wasn't necessarily as exciting as what you read, however. Some writers had come up with a trivial tale in which the ship was a turn-of-the-century trader boarded by pirates who murdered all on board and were themselves drowned during a northwest gale; others, like E. B. Chase, in her unpromisingly titled *Quest of the Quaint* (1902), preferred to have the craft set ablaze by Indians. There was little here to enthrall a serious-minded investigator and Ganong had been unimpressed until one or two visits to the area and some conversations with its inhabitants encouraged him to pause, then to alter his opinion, until: "I now believe there is really some natural phenomenon in that region which manifests itself in such a way as to be imaginable as a vessel on fire."

One written account of which Ganong approved was that of A. M. Belding in the *St. John Sun* of some years before. The named witnesses quoted there included Robert Young of Caraquet, who told the journalist that the "ship" was frequently to be seen at night before a storm, that is, a large light would appear, winter or summer, on the bay's surface and in no predictable quarter, sometimes brighter than at other times and occasionally so much so that it cast a reflection on the houses at Grand Anse. The Rev. Father Allard had seen it several times; indeed, Belding had the impression that it was quite common. One didn't need to take notice of the theatrical subjoined tales of pirates or Indians to concede that "sometimes the mysterious light emits rays that shoot into and athwart the gloom and might by a particularly well-nourished imagination be likened to the flame-lit rigging of a ship."

When Ganong visited Bay Chaleur, he found an impressively numerous band of witnesses to back up what Belding had said. Captain Turner of Riverside, Albert County, "a clear-headed sea-captain," let's note, had seen the phantom ship four years before; there was a lady who had been sufficiently convinced that the light came from a burning vessel as to fear the loss of one of her husband's schooners. James Harper of Miscou had spotted it on the icebound waters off Clifton and at a range of perhaps ten miles; it had risen and fallen away, dying to a scarcely visible flame and then building slowly to a thirty-foot-tall column. Harper added that, contrary to tradition, the spectacle had not preceded a storm and he would not necessarily have described what he saw as a ship, although other people told him that was what it was.

Two other Miscou residents who may or may not have been relations expanded Ganong's knowledge of the Bay Chaleur apparition. Robert Wilson had seen the burning ship, as he called it, several times, the last as recently as autumn 1905; the nearest he ever came to it was eleven years before, off Caraquet on a very dark night. "It was somewhat the shape of a half-moon resting on the water, flatside down," he testified, "or like a vessel on the water with a bowsprit but no masts, etc., and all glowing like a hot coal." In fact, he had encountered the phenomenon enough times to become blasé and now paid it little attention. "Sometimes it looked like a ship, sometimes not"; usually it danced or vibrated. It might appear as a single tall light that rose in three "streamers." He found that it occasionally vanished if you kept looking at it.

The sum of evidence revealed that the phenomenon might be described as a boat *or* as a light. The second Wilson qualified that what he had seen resembled a whaleboat (a rowing vessel) rather than a ship; McConnell, keeper of the Miscou Gulley light, said that from two miles off it did not look like a ship, "but more like a bonfire." Other, unnamed witnesses alleged that it could be called a "flaming ship" *or* a round light; all agreed that it preceded a storm. Finally, some Miscou folks who sailed the bay regularly deponed that they had never seen the phantom light and didn't believe in it.

On the strength of all this, Ganong was prepared to make a series of conclusive statements about the Bay Chaleur phenomenon, not least of which was a repetition of his affirmation that it was genuine. It was, he wrote, a physical light to be seen frequently on the bay and its immediate vicinity, in all seasons (winter and summer alike) and preceding a storm. It was roughly hemispherical in shape, resting with its flat side on the water, sometimes constant, but rising at others in slender columns that gave "an appearance capable of interpretation as the flaming rigging of a ship, its vibrating and dancing movements increasing the illusion." But Ganong ran into difficulties when, as he felt obliged to do, he attempted to assign the Bay Chaleur Light Ship to some probable and known physical agency.

The best he could do was to suggest the effect was "probably electrical." Dr. J. Orne Green, a professor at Harvard Medical School, had also visited Miscou and actually had the fire ship pointed out to him (though he said that without external help as to its identity he might have taken it to be a fire in the neighboring backdrop of woods). Also like Ganong, the professor had been intrigued enough to investigate more closely and, like the New Brunswick naturalist again, he came to accept that behind popular exaggeration and distortion lurked a strange but not unnatural effect "of the general nature of 'St. Elmo's Fire.' " Ganong claimed to have reached the same conclusion independently and echoed it when qualifying that the "probably electrical" quality of the Bay Chaleur Light was "very likely a phase of that phenomenon known to sailors as St. Elmo's Fire."

Given the marine setting, it was a logical rather than an adventurous hypothesis, and it is worth our while to dwell briefly on the idea even if we eventually discard it. St. Elmo's fire is a nautical will o' the wisp also known by the names "corposant," "corpusant," "cormozant," and "furole" as well as by various derivations from St. Elmo (St. Elme, Santelmo, St. Helm, St. Ermyn, St. Hermes, plus other, apparently unconnected saints); Christian association of the phenomenon with the body of Christ was preceded by Greek mythical ones that invoked the Dioscuri (Castor and Pollux). For many early seamen these names were more or less literal identifications of one or more spectral lights which shone, sometimes with blinding brilliance, on or above the upper spars, rigging, and yardarms during the atmosphere that preceded or accompanied a storm. Normally static but on occasion mobile, St. Elmo's fire was an uncommon yet well-attested meteorological event known from the days of classical authors such as Horace, Xenophanes, Ovid, and Lucian, at least by report.

In fact, the description in Pliny's *Natural History*—and claimed by him *not* as a secondhand report, but as an eyewitness observation—may be as good as any other: "a luminous appearance, like a star . . . producing a kind of vocal sound like that of birds fluttering about." Few other writers mention any such aural accompaniment, though Forbin (ca. 1700) says that at close quarters the fire hissed like damp gunpowder put to the match; their alternative versions compare it in size and strength with glowworms or candles (large and small).

Pliny is often criticized for his ingenuous blend of hard fact with outright fancy. Typically, his eyewitness impression includes the remark that while as a single manifestation St. Elmo's fire was dreaded as an omen of misfortune, a double ball was highly auspicious; however, the fact that Erasmus also mentions the same belief proves the earlier writer had picked up a genuine sailors' tradition. It seems to have been widely accepted that multiple outbreaks of St. Elmo's fire were tokens of protection and, Pliny notwithstanding, even a solitary fire might be interpreted as a sign of a lull in the storm. Columbus, who encountered the phenomenon on his second New World voyage as a bright body and "seven lighted candles," confirmed the reassuring effect the fire had on his crew. In 1519 Magellan often saw it or them during stormy weather: once "like a brilliant flambeau on the summit of the mainmast . . . which was a matter of great consolation to us" and again as three "holy bodies," which his men credited with an immediate abatement in the rough weather. Perhaps it is not surprising that in some quarters they were called "the Peaceable Fires."

There can be no doubt that St. Elmo's fire was an unusual but absolutely natural atmospheric electrical phenomenon, nor that it was of a caliber to inspire imaginative, not entirely specious inferences that connected the appearance during a lull in any storm with supernatural guardianship. The nexus may have been valid as far as the correlation between the outbreak of the fires and the end of the storm goes; less certain is the link between this class of marine luminescence and the phantom fire ships of northeastern America.

In "The Tradition of the St. Elmo's Fire," George C. Carey assumes that the difference between the two is only a matter of dimensions. The fire ships, he writes in *American Neptune* for January 1963, are simply "large editions" of the main topic of his paper. He makes the useful point that both the Palatine and Teazer Lights are associated, like the corposant, with foul weather. As we just heard, W. F. Ganong in 1906 was hypothesizing along the same lines. On consulting an expert on St. Elmo's fire—Professor R. De C. Ward, assistant professor of climatology at Harvard University—he ran into an objection that does the fire-ship-equals-corposant notion very few favors. St. Elmo's fire is consistently described as a normally bright but relatively small affair.

Allowing for the possibility that atmospheric distortion might magnify what a shore-based observer might see, and also that not all descriptions of the Bay Chaleur light uniformly agree that it is significantly large, was it feasible that an outburst of "free-ranging" St. Elmo's fire could be mistaken at a distance for a ship in flames? Could a ball of light as stipulated in all recognized accounts pass itself off as the half-moon hemisphere or mastless vessel that Robert Wilson claimed to have seen at a range of no more than a hundred yards?

The size discrepancy may seem awkward; the question of whether St. Elmo's fire has ever been observed outside the usual context (as anything other than a shipboard phenomenon, that is) must be seen as relevant since in the Bay Chaleur case there is no suggestion of the light manifesting itself on an actual boat. As it turned out, Professor Ward met Ganong's inquiry about whether he knew of any instance of St. Elmo's fire behaving as spectacularly (and untypically) as it would have to do to match the Bay Chaleur data. He didn't. Though he did not forthrightly abandon his "phase of . . . St. Elmo's Fire" theory, Ganong looked at alternatives: topographical, geographical, geological.

One fresh angle led him to G. L. Ellis, a lecturer in geology at Newnham College, Cambridge (England), who held it possible that the Bay Chaleur fire ship might be marsh gas, generated on marshy ground yet capable of moving over water and which "frequently assumes the most curious forms." Throughout the nineteenth century writers had been triumphing over the credulity of their forebears who evidently did not know that the elusive, delusive will o' the wisp famed for terrifying and misleading benighted travelers was merely a gaseous emanation from boggy areas; the hypothesis that it could wander out to sea and assume the look and magnitude of a flaming vessel seemed tempting. To his credit, however, Ganong did not conceal the problem that the Bay Chaleur region was not noted for marshes or bogs. Exploring yet another avenue of thought, he looked at the idea that the same coastline included oil-bearing slates and shales—only to concede that the predominant formation was neither of these, but sandstone. It might be that oil deposits existed in submerged strata, but without trying to explain how (if so) these came to be ignited periodically—and without bringing Livermore's fortuitous lightning strikes into it—Ganong had to rule that as there was no actual evidence of such oil reserves the thing became another piece of hopeful conjecture. All he could say for certain was that Bay Chaleur harbored a mysterious radiance, which in scientific terms ought to be explicable but which in popular speech and belief was a phantasmal fire ship.

While examining fire ships as a recurrent folk-narrative type *or* as a frequently observed in unexplained natural phenomenon, so far we have dwelt on these things as if they were peculiar to the northeast coast of America. This impression is as misleading as the most energetic nautical jack o' lantern. If the distribution of the phenomenon and its legendary codicil is not worldwide, the inference is that it does not miss being so by much. Any seagoing community is likely to have its tales of ominous lights, testifying again to that odd uniformity or even predictability that patterns human responses to the anomalous.

The Hooper of Sennen Cove at the foot of Cornwall . . . the Scottish sea fire, water fire or water burn, of which one of the authors was told only in 1992 and in perfect seriousness: we could travel round the world, noting down a tradition of ominously interpreted luminescence over stretches of coastal horizons, lake and loch and estuaries that is virtually universal. But we don't need to travel around the world when there are modern-day explorer-adventurers like John Blashford-Snell to do it on our behalf and write entertainingly about it in books like *Mysteries* (1983) afterward.

A visit to the Black River of Honduras in 1981 introduced Lt. Col. Blashford-Snell to Mr. Green, "a charming old negro who spoke nineteenth-century English" who had this to say of the locality: "Ghostly lights, mister, ghostly lights. . . . When there's a storm you sees a light, just like a lantern on the water off the bar. . . . It kind of floats on the surface across the bar—but there's no one there—it's bad for boats."

An interesting if hardly original statement of folk belief, no doubt, but Blashford-Snell was even more impressed by the semi-sequel that emerged in conversation with ex–U.S. Navy man Joe Garrison later that year when they met on the island of Roatan. Joe had been caught in a bad storm off the Honduran coast and though he came through it his brig was lost soon after. He remembered that at one stage he had seen a single navigation light, belonging to a shrimp boat, he had assumed, some miles astern. The location of this incident had been the bar at the mouth of the Rio Tinto, otherwise known as the Black River.

It would take comparatively little effort to multiply the tally of ghost-light accounts of this type, yet that effort would take us no closer to defining what they are. Ultimately we have to accept that beyond the strong probability that they *are* physical and (as Ganong hypothesized) meteorological-cum-electrical in character, anything else is guesswork. What fascinates us here is the way cultures attempt to explain them. One of the most well-sustained and instructive illustrations of reaction by way of legend-narrative takes us halfway across the world from New England to a famous inland sea of Japan.

A strange and motley crew populates the Japanese spirit world. There are the *kitsune,* "fox spirits": teasing shape-changers that delight in deceiving lone travelers. There are bird-faced, seriocomic *tengu* in the forests and half-human, half-turtle *kappa* in the deep ponds. And of course there are the more conventional ghosts of the departed who cling stubbornly, obsessively, to the things left undone or uncorrected during their earthly existences. Victorian and Edwardian travel writers like Lafcadio Hearn or A. B. Mitsford have made these phantasms accessible to Western readers. But the *shito-dama,* the "fireball spirit," remains a largely unpublicized entity.

In Japan perhaps more than anywhere in the world, spirits of the departed harbor the strongest feelings on justice. Above all, a ghost cannot rest until the wrongs that led to its becoming a ghost have been put right; Nipponese folk tales and mythologized explanations of place names often commemorate some piece of spectacular supernatural revenge that restored this imbalance between living and dead. History, legend, and supernatural revenge—including that wreaked on people not even alive at the time of the original event—figure strongly and concertedly in the tales generated towards the end of the last century by Richard Gordon Smith (1858–1916). During nine years of wide-ranging Japanese travel chiefly spent collecting natural history specimens for the British Museum, Smith had unusual opportunities to talk to fishermen, farmers, priests, and children. He took down their stories. As a result, a number of folk narratives that might never have reached the West were swept up along with the butterflies and reptiles. Many of them dealt with ghosts of the most violent dispositions and none was more puzzling in its malevolence than the fireball-like spirit Smith's informants styled *shito-dama.*

Coincidentally or not, Smith had spent some time on the Gaspé peninsula of French Canada, whose waters, as we just heard, were said to be haunted by a fiery spectre. But it was not until he made one of his several visits to Lake Biwa, the famously attractive stretch of water in the southwest of the main island, that Smith met the Japanese equivalent. To be more precise, he never saw a *shito-dama* for himself, but here and elsewhere he encountered it as a belief, and was patently fascinated.

Biwa-ko was named after a supposed resemblance to the shape of the traditional four-stringed, lute-like instrument of Japan and (equally traditional) it was celebrated as the possessor of "eight Beauties" or panoramic views. The small settlement of Seze (Zeze) was not one of them. In fact, Smith indicates that it amounted to little more than a lakeside cottage occupied by a very old fisherman and his three sons, proud owner-operators under a century-old license from the local *daimyo* (lord) of "an immense fish trap, which runs out into the lake nearly a mile, and is a disgrace to all civilized ideas of conservation." The patriarch was bewildered to find a visitor—a foreigner!—who wanted to hear the simple tales that even his sons didn't care for nowadays, but he obliged with a few of what he called "truths"—true stories, or in our terms, legends—concerning that part of Lake Biwa.

First and foremost was the *shito-dama,* the "Spider Fire of the Spirit of the Dead Akechi." Rooted in local history as all good folk ghosts are, the fireball was a fact as far as the narrator was concerned, "a curious and an unpleasant thing" he had seen at first hand and evidently too much so for his comfort. It appeared on the lake in wet weather, he began, and was none other than the spirit of Akechi, by whom he presumably meant the *daimyo* Akechi Mitsuhide, familiar to generations of Japanese as the "Shogun of Thirteen Days." He owed his folk-hero celebrity to an act of revenge and rebellion. Having waited five years, Akechi had risen up against his liege-lord Nobunaga, whom he held responsible for the death of his mother, and capped the accomplishing of his enemy's death by proclaiming himself Shogun (military dictator—effectually the ruler of Japan). From the time of his rebellion to his total defeat at the hands of Nobunaga's successor Hideyoshi Toyotomi (the dynamic leader who eventually unified the country) and thence to his death in 1582, Akechi enjoyed a paltry thirteen days of triumph: hence his popular if, to our ears, derisive title.

Standard historical sources state that Akechi Mitsuhide died en route to the safety of his castle at Sakamoto, massacred by a peasant mob in the village of Ogurusu. Smith's informant had a more romantic version of that event, investing cold fact with nuances dear to folk narrators and audiences all over the globe, nuances revealing the staple twin elements of Japanese popular lore: betrayal and supernatural vengeance.

According to the fisherman, Akechi had built the now-ruined castle at the foot of the southern spur of Mount Hiyei and when the time came he held it against a siege by Hideyoshi's far larger force. The castle might well have remained untaken had not a fisherman from Magisa told the besiegers the secret of its water supply. Once this lifeline was severed, the garrison had no choice but to capitulate. Akechi and most of his men took the honorable way of forestalling the inevitable disgrace by committing suicide.

As already pointed out, this version of Akechi's bloody end does not square at all with the sober biographical details given in texts like Papinot's *Historical and Geographical Dictionary of Japan.* This should not be surprising if we recall the folklore tenet that oral tradition often fills in the gaps left by the historical record, but just as often ignores those facts that *are* present. More interesting is the way the fisherman's variation lent itself to explaining a menacing local phenomenon. For it was said that ever since the betrayal at Hiyei:

> in rain or rough weather, there has come from the castle a fireball, six inches in diameter or more. It comes to wreak vengeance on fishermen, and causes many wrecks, leading boats out of their course. Sometimes it comes almost into the boat. Once a fisherman struck it with a bamboo pole, breaking it up into many fiery bits, and on that occasion many boats were lost. . . . That is all, sir, that I can tell of it—except that often have I seen it myself, and feared it.

As a meteorological phenomenon—a literal fireball, perhaps, or (to borrow from W. F. Ganong) "a phase . . . of St. Elmo's fire" that coincides with rough weather—the *shito-dama* of Akechi sounds quite believable and in the context of what this chapter has covered already there is no surprise in hearing how this natural phenomenon was interpreted as a *super*natural one. Certain aspects of this process arise from prevailing cultural beliefs against which the story is told. As the narrator underlines in his conclusion, the *shito-dama*'s purpose is revenge on fishermen of Lake Biwa because to this class belonged the man who in distant time offended against a dominant social law: namely, the unchallengeable tenet of absolute loyalty to one's lord. It is true that Akechi himself overturned this law by his act of rebellion and that the *shito-dama*'s application of vengeance seems indiscriminate, falling not merely upon the descendants of the offending fisherman, but on *all* fishermen as a social class. But Akechi was excused by another part of the Japanese social code, which made it a duty for him to exact revenge for his mother's death. The class structure of Japan also stressed that the crimes of an individual might be the responsibility of the immediate group to which he belonged. It is noticeable that the narrator does not contest the fairness of Akechi's descending upon fishermen with no distinctions or exceptions made. The rationale of revenge soars above the fact that it is founded on a literally incorrect historical construction.

The spider fire of the Akechi spirit is another example of popular morality. Murder and all the degrading crimes that go with it will out; punishment is an inexorable consequence. The "Palatine Light" and (in some literary-flavored versions) the Bay Chaleur fire ship are testaments to the "fact" that inhumanity and criminality are, in the words of old Benjamin Corydon, a little more than the Almighty can stand and their manifestations remind us that nothing goes unnoticed by Him. Japanese popular theology is inclined to express itself more physically: the *shito-dama* of Lake Biwa tries to take more direct revenge by sinking fishermen rather than by afflicting their consciences. It's all a matter of cultural degree.

And it seems that at Lake Biwa a certain class of paranormal event had been redefined to meet the needs of a particular situation. Fishermen knew of an odd meteorological effect associated with storms on the lake: an effect characterized as a fireball. They knew also that it was more convenient to classify it as *shito-dama* than as anything else. During his Japanese travels, Smith met the phrase several times without finding it attached to so unique a legend as Akechi's spider fire.

"So much evidence have I got from personal acquaintances as to their existence, and even frequent occurrence," he wrote of *shito-dama,* "that I almost believe in them myself." Indeed, the *shito-dama* seemed integral to the concept of spiritual survival: an astral form that could wander the earth after death. As such, this specifically Japanese entity relates to another universal belief that some part of the human organism may survive the experience of death and be visible in or around the locality of that terminal event. Japanese audiences would have had little difficulty in understanding (and believing in) the pallid lights or "magnetic effluvia" said to have been discernible to nineteenth-century clairvoyants in graveyards, for instance.

Smith's informants divided *shito-dama* into two descriptive categories: those of "roundish oblong tadpole shape" and others "more square-fronted and eyed," as in the cases of those belonging to a deaf man and a fishergirl seen by two or three dozen people at Tsuboune near Naba. Smith's hunter-assistant, Oto of Itami, claimed that he and his son had seen the *shito-dama* of a dead woman that resembled an egg with a tail. At Toshishima a number of elderly men testified that the *shito-dama* of a carpenter had been red, but more typically the witnesses spoke of a smoky-white phosphorescence.

Although *shito-dama* were firmly held to be manifestations of human spirits, they were not to be confused with conventional ghosts of the dead. Generally and regardless of a kind of theatricality or self-dramatization—their love of ethereal garments, the tendency to appear as macabre skeletons—Japanese ghosts are always recognizably human in form or format. The *shito-dama* was nothing more than a moving light, perhaps an abstract of the human spirit. At the same time, the *shito-dama* might be seen alongside and accompanying a more representational phantom. In Smith's ghoulish record of "A Haunted Temple in Inaba Province" the *shito-dama* hovers in jerky fashion and (reminiscent of Pliny's observation of St. Elmo's fire) buzzes audibly as it leads "the luminous skeleton of a man in loose priest's clothes with glaring eyes and a parchment skin!" The narrative makes it clear that both apparitions belong to and are aspects of the same murdered man.

A kind of limited intelligence directs the *shito-dama*'s peregrinations. In common with haunting folk ghosts the world over, its actions seem defined by obsessive thoughts in which revenge or the desire to reveal the whereabouts of its mortal remains are usually paramount.

Again, the *shito-dama* may be concerned to carry out some important act left unfinished by sudden death and these instances tell us a lot about cultural mores at the time the stories evolved. We can understand more of the drama involved when swordsman Rokugo Yakeyi solved the mystery of the *Kubi sagashi no hi,* "the head-seeking fire," if we know that the taking of enemy leaders' heads played an important part in Japanese medieval warfare. The head would be ritualistically paraded before one's own leader as proof the presenter had rendered signal service in removing a hated opponent (or more simply, that he was no longer any threat). It was equally important for retainers on the opposite side to prevent this disgrace to their lord's name and family by getting possession of the head (if not the whole body) before it was stolen. Rokugo, on seeing the *Kubi sagashi no hi* which "moved here and there without noise" as it quartered the ground at a height of five feet, "though sometimes it went lower," also learned that it had been performing in this way for two hundred years. In time and by virtue of his courage, Rokugo discovered the fireball phenomenon was the spirit of a long-deceased yet still faithful samurai carrying out his last earthly duty as he'd been doing when killed and searching for the struck-off head of his general.

Smith's folktales were told to him, and retold by him, principally for their entertainment value. Then as now, folk narrative contained subtextual meanings also; in the instance of the *shito-dama* a phenomenon that may sound to us uncommon but natural has been presented as something spiritual and transmutes into a visual symbol of the soul, the astral body, or some other element superior to bodily death. Stories centered upon it simultaneously have a moral or educative value aimed at the living; they are intended to reinforce deep-rooted ethical teachings about what binds human society: the underlying factors of loyalty and duty. The "head-seeking fire" is an exemplary tale because it shows that these twin virtues survive death. Listeners were doubtless meant to admire and emulate the persisting selflessness of the samurai who sustained the search for his master's head into his post-death existence. Betrayal of trust—a terrible lapse in a hierarchical society like that of Japan—brings evil consequences not merely for the individual transgressor but for generations unborn. Thus in the Akechi fireball tale the fisherman who gave away his lord's secret drew supernatural vengeance on an entire class to which he belonged. We are reminded of the nineteenth-century motif in which the vision of the fiery *Palatine* afflicts descendants of the original wreckers.

At first appraisal, these interpretations may seem irrelevant to cultures outside Japan. But to the contrary, the belief-tale we have given here as *shito-dama* reveals a remarkable conformity of response with those of peoples polarized by geography and (to a lesser extent) by custom.

It may be specious to overvalue cultural echoes between medieval Japan and pre-twentieth-century Britain, but folklorists have always been impressed when two remote cultures have yielded evidence to suggest common modes of interpreting unknown phenomena. So it is at the very least revealing when the attitudes of Smith's Japanese *shito-dama* informants are set beside rural British traditions of wandering luminescences known variously as "corpse lights" or "corpse candles."

Technically though not consistently, corpse lights were believed to be distinct from corpse candles, the latter being described as mobile balls of light that presaged a death in the community; often they were supposed to belong to the spirit of a deceased person who came to warn or welcome the one whose death was imminent. Interestingly, some East Anglian corpse lights were described as red in color, like the *shito-dama* of the Toshishima carpenter. Here again the phenomenon can be summed up as an eerie nocturnal ball of light or flame that tradition asserted was particularly prone to wander when the spirit had been victim of an undiscovered or unpunished crime and could not rest until this issue had been acknowledged. As in the Japanese analogues, opinion on the dangers posed by these itinerant lights differed; some bore no malice towards the living, whereas others were to be avoided at all costs. As late as 1920 rumors of corpse lights sprang up in the wake of a well-publicized and sordid British murder case. Clearly, the victim's spirit was prosecuting its claim for justice, not unlike the way in which the buzzing *shito-dama* of the Inabi temple drew attention to the bones of "a priest who had suffered a violent death and could not rest."

These similar beliefs of uncomplicated (often unlettered) working people have suffered similar attempts at rational deflation from the more scientifically minded. "Wandering fires," be they locally known as will o' the wisp, ignis fatuus, or by some other name, were authoritatively dismissed by Victorian savants as exhalations of marsh gas, perhaps or presumably ignited by some means they rarely identified beyond "spontaneous combustion." Corpse lights (if truly distinct from will o' the wisp) were either fungoid luminescence, spontaneously igniting marsh gas or both; the origins of *shito-dama* could arguably take in those answers as well as the geological and meteorological hypotheses mentioned earlier. But no rationalization process has completely convincing results and none can balance the ease with which folk audiences insisted the phenomenon was a supernatural, paranormal manifestation.

That British and Japanese should both interpret a species of nocturnal light in terms of spirit survival—that Japanese and Americans should regard a meteorological effect as the spirit of supernatural justice/revenge on wrongdoers—matters more than racial distinctions. Folklorists and parapsychologists may dwell on the fact that across the inhabited globe ghosts are popularly endowed with qualities that lay outside narrative form and convention. The uniformity or conformity of narratives suggests that certain ideas, certain values, are integral to every race. The ghost that demands justice is an expression of our own belief in justice—we hate to think it could be otherwise. Man also hates to think that death is the end: a luminous fire in the night stands for the proof of his indestructible soul.

But can a ship have an indestructible soul? Can that soul manifest as a fiery light on the sea? If associated with the savage destruction of human lives, the inanimation—the essential inanimate nature of a ship, that is—becomes irrelevant since the ship becomes a symbol of the sinned-against, suffering mortals who perished with her. Fire-ship stories lacking any "explanatory" phase wherein the phenomenon of the light is attached to some historical tragedy cannot carry that significance, yet it is as if the coidentification of light with fire ship predicates the theory that such a tragedy may have taken place.

In chapter 1 we said that the *Flying Dutchman* represents for some researchers a nautical version-variant of the Wandering Jew. It is logical to suggest (as several nineteenth-century writers did) that St. Elmo's fire is the marine equivalent of the land-based will o' the wisp or corpse light and that the fire ship, related to both genres, derives its motivation from terrestrial, justice-seeking and on occasion disaster-prognosticating ghost stories. If so, and taking the *shito-dama* of Seze as a "nauticalized" version of a more widely spread Japanese type, or as a name conveniently borrowed due to its similarity to the *shito-dama* of nonnautical lore, it seems that we have a conglomerate out of which stories can be molded to suit specific local conditions.

Every example of cultural contouring illustrates a stage in popular dissemination of ideas. If the stories encountered by nineteenth-century collectors show the usage of common legend-types to explain unknown quasi-physical effects only describable as "fireballs" or "lights," they also reveal at various points a less narrative tendency: the invocation of science, often in ways that go beyond the accepted scope of physical sciences, to explain those same effects. Phlogogistous gas and tectonic stress theory are bold attempts to extrapolate from known scientific facts in order to physicalize those mobile, tantalizing blobs of luminescence that in early eras bred ghost and fairy stories.

This being so, fire-ship phantoms retain their old status; they are true sea mysteries still. They hint at electrical and meteorological events that we adapt and adopt according to the imaginative, fictive and scientific propensities of our age and culture. In that respect, the old Seze fisherman was right. Richard Gordon Smith asked him for curious legends; the old man replied that he could tell him a few "truths."

References

The literature on fire ships and other phenomena associated with them in this chapter is a full one. The fugitive nature of much of it, plus natural limitations in the library resources upon which the authors were dependent, has meant that several sources mentioned by earlier writers—and often quoted freely by them—have not been examined by us. Apologizing for these gaps in our research, we include here a number of those items as per other bibliographies; each is marked by an asterisk. While we have attempted to categorize the individual cases separately, many of the articles listed here deal in passing with other accounts subsidiary to the main topic of the title.

General Surveys

*Larry Arnold, "Ahoy, Mate!" *Pursuit* II (Summer 1978): 109, 113–14, and (Fall 1978): 144–50.

Loren Coleman, *Mysterious America* (London: Faber, 1983), pp. 271–73.

Ralph des Childs, "Phantom Ships of the Northeast Coast of North America," *New York Folklore Quarterly* V (Summer 1949): 145–65.

**Fate*, various authors: (Spring 1948): 112, 114–15, 128; (April 1954): 4 (editorial note); (May 1954): 107; (January 1955): 31–33; (July 1958): 6–8 (editorial note); (April 1962): 41–44; (June 1971): 63–67; (September 1973): 22 (editorial note).

Vincent Gaddis, *Invisible Horizons* (New York: Ace Books, 1965), pp. 95–116.

*Charles M. Skinner, *American Myths and Legends* (Philadelphia: Lippincott, 1903) and *Myths and Legends of Our Own Land* (Philadelphia: Lippincott, 1896).

The "Palatine Light"

"Block Island Legends: Folk Lore of the 'Lazy Man's Paradise,'" *New York Times,* October 19, 1884, p. 4.

**Depositions of Officers of the Palatine Ship* Princess Augusta (Providence: General Court of the Society of Colonial Wars in the State of Rhode Island, 1939).

Samuel Adams Drake, *A Book of New England Legends and Folklore* (1884).

*Thomas R. Hazard, *Recollections of Olden Times* (Newport, R.I.: J. P. Sanborn, 1879). See pp. 127–29.

John Kobler, "The Mystery of the Palatine Light," *Saturday Evening Post,* June 11, 1960, pp. 44–45, 55–56, 58.

*Samuel T. Livermore, *A History of Block Island* (Hartford, Conn.: Case, Lockwood & Brainard, 1877), pp. 89–118.

*Edward E. Pettee, *Block Island Illustrated* (Boston: DeLand & Barton, 1884). See pp. 96–106.

John Greenleaf Whittier, "The Palatine," in *The Tent on the Beach* (1867). See any collected edition, e.g., *The Poetical Works of* — (Oxford University Press, 1910), that reproduces Corydon's letter as an afternote.

Also see Arnold and Gaddis as cited above. N.B.: For shorter treatments, see also Richard M. Dorson, *Jonathan Draws the Long Bow* (Cambridge, Mass.: Harvard University Press, 1946), pp. 167–68, with a study of Whittier's treatment of New England folklore on pages 204–214. The same writer's "The Jonny-Cake Papers," *Journal of American Folklore* 58 (1945): 104–112, gives a biographical assessment of Thomas R. Hazard (see above) and commends Albert Matthews's "The Word Palatine in America" (Publications of the Colonial Society of Massachusetts 8, 220 n. 2) for its bibliography on this legend.

Other Fire Ships of Northeastern Shores

*Horace P. Beck, *Folklore of Maine* (Philadelphia: Lippincott, 1957).

Edward Farrer, "Folklore of Lower Canada," *Atlantic Monthly* 49 (1882): 542–50. The article refers briefly to the Cap D'Espoir legend; see also Lambert below.

W. F. Ganong, "The Factual Basis of the Fire (or Phantom) Ship of Bay Chaleur," *Bulletin of the Natural History Society of New Brunswick* 5, part IV (1906): 419–23. Reprinted with some editorial comment in *Journal of the Society for Psychical Research* 12, no. 235 (January 1907): 8–13. For other treatments of the Bay Chaleur case, see also *Fate* (June 1958): 29, and (February 1964): 114–15.

*Sheila Hervey, *Some Canadian Ghosts* (Richmond Hill, Ontario: Pocket Books, 1973), pp. 175–76.

Edward D. Ives, "The Burning Ship of Northumberland Strait," *Midwest Folklore* 8, no. 4 (Winter 1958): 199–203.

R. S. Lambert, *Exploring the Supernatural: The Weird in Canadian Folklore* (London: Arthur Barker, 1955), pp. 51–57.

*L. M. Rich, on the phantom ship of Northumberland Strait, *Fate* (November 1949): 28–31.

*Roland H. Sherwood, *The Phantom Ship of Northumberland Strait* (Windsor, Nova Scotia: Lancelot, 1975). This could be a reworking of Sherwood's version in his *Story Parade* (Sackville, New Brunswick: no date, but pre-1958), pp. 19ff. as cited by Ives above. Ives lists several other tourist-style writeups of the Northumberland Strait fire ship and commends the chapter on phantom craft in Helen Creighton's *Bluenose Ghosts* (Toronto, 1957).

Analogues and Other Background Material

The Black River case: see John Blashford Snell, *Mysteries: Encounters with the Unexplained* (London: Bodley Head, 1983), pp. 65–67.

St. Elmo's fire: see Fletcher Bassett, *Legends and Superstitions of the Sea and Sailors* (1885), pp. 302–330, and George C. Carey, "The Tradition of the St. Elmo's Fire," *American Neptune* 23 (January 1963): 29–39.

Shito-dama: see Richard Gordon Smith, *Ancient Tales and Folklore of Japan* (London: A. & C. Black, 1908).

N.B.: The issue of *Magonia* (November 24, 1986) that carried the original version of Michael Goss's "*Shito-dama*: The Japanese Fireball Spirit" (pp. 2–7) also contains David Clarke's "Spooklights in Tradition and Folklore" (pp. 8–13) and Claude Mauge's "Persinger's Tectonic Strain Theory: Strengths and Weaknesses" (pp. 13–17). Both are relevant to the later-stage material of this chapter.

II

Mysteries Under the Sea

3

Submersibles and Psychism: The *Thresher* Resurfaces

George E. Simpson and Neal R. Burger's *Ghostboat* is what you might call a modern mystery novel. First published by Dell in 1976, it tells of a submarine, the USS *Candlefish*, that disappears inexplicably in the Sea of Japan on December 11, 1944, and resurfaces just as inexplicably on October 5, 1974, fully conditioned and in perfect working order. After thirty years presumed lost she is completely untarnished, but minus her crew. As the pace of the story picks up, a new crew (led by a hero fascinated by the mystery of the Japanese Triangle) prepares to retrace the *Candlefish*'s last journey.

We are not about to give away what happens after *that*. Instead, we want to talk about another mystery submarine—the USS *Thresher*. Unlike her fictional counterpart, the *Thresher* did not resurface thirty years after her seemingly fatal dive toward the sea bottom, at least, not in the normal sense of the word. It is only in the *para*normal sense that this submarine has resurfaced and though we cannot offer a mystery of the Japanese Devil's Triangle, we feel we may be able to perplex you slightly with a real-life submarine ghostboat.

Ghostboat: there is something about a submarine that makes the casual observer intuit that he is not looking at an *ordinary* boat. Perhaps, despite the way technological ingenuity has made us accepting, even blasé toward innovations in travel, there is still something incomprehensible about the idea of a ship that sails underwater. We wonder about it. We wonder about the kind of men who would willingly sail in submarines. And, if we are honest, we make a macabre association of the shark-sleek hull of a submarine and death—not because most submarines are fundamentally warships, but because as we look on a submarine part of our minds starts to wonder what it would be like to be in a *disabled* submarine, doubly entombed under a great depth of water with no hope of escape.

All this is very fanciful. In truth there was nothing very fanciful about the USS *Thresher*, SSN-593. She was commissioned on August 3, 1961, the first of a new class of advanced American attack submarines. Two hundred and seventy-eight feet long and powered by a nuclear reactor, her teardrop-shaped hull and streamlined conning tower radiated an atmosphere of controlled power and deadly menace. Indeed, the motto on her insignia, Vis Tacita, meant "silent strength." *Thresher* had been designed to dive deeper, run quieter, and move faster submerged than any other nuclear submarine ever built. At a cost of somewhere between $49 million and $57 million, she was a hunter-killer capable of seeking out and destroying enemy submarines with the nuclear-tipped underwater-to-underwater "SubRoc" missile, a combinational torpedo and ballistic missile fired via conventional torpedo tubes. *Thresher*'s complement of crew consisted of twelve officers and ninety-six enlisted men who, like their boat, were based in Portsmouth, New Hampshire.

The significance of the new submarine needs to be seen in context of the international arms race whose chief characteristic towards the end of 1961 was a delicate counterbalance of Russian and American nuclear technologies and a marked deterioration in East-West relationships. In July 1962 Nikita Khrushchev announced that to secure its safety the Soviet Union was going to produce nuclear weapons of 100 megatons or more. The tension culminated in October with the Cuban missile crisis, when for seven days the globe lived with the imminent possibility of World War III. Mercifully, the world came through it unscathed, but few Westerners doubted the wisdom of the sharp rise in spending on strategic nuclear forces that had been a feature of that year.

To the uninitiated, the key to domination in the arms race lay on land (intercontinental missiles) or in the skies, where the United States seemed intent on making up lost ground after the USSR and Yuri Gagarin beat them to the making of the first manned orbital satellite flight. For its part the USSR appeared equally concerned with upstaging America's attempts to catch up. In February 1962 John Glenn became the first American in orbit; in May Scott Carpenter became the second. A U.S. senator pronounced shortly afterwards that the United States was forging ahead in the space race, only to have the Russians reply via a *joint* orbit in August. Prestigewise and spacewise the Soviet Union always seemed to have one jump on the United States; on the ground the (apparent) sheer size of their missile arsenal threatened to pulverize the West into a poor second place.

But elsewhere it was a different proposition. Military experts believed that although a future war might be affected by developments on the ground (or in outer space, though the world was still a decade removed from Star Wars technology and even "spy" satellites were blueprints in the war-masters' minds), it might in fact be effectively decided in the sea. The Soviets were believed to have submarines capable of operating under the Arctic: to have, in other words, mobile nuclear-powered nuclear-warheaded missile bases that could secretively bring the war much closer to the United States than any land-mounted missile was able to do. The counter to this was the Polaris submarine fleet and, of course, a new breed of deep-dive American subs that could hunt and kill the Russian marauders before they had a chance to anchor in Chesapeake Bay and provide an undersea variation on Pearl Harbor. *Thresher* was not nuclear-armed, but she was nuclear-powered. She lacked the glamour of a manned orbital satellite, but she had a vitally important role to play in the modern war scenario.

Thresher's keel was laid on May 28, 1958, at the Portsmouth Navy Yard. Early in May 1960, only two months before her launch, the Navy Department and the Department of Defense put the submarine's construction on the "Master Urgency List." This meant that the government wanted *Thresher* to be commissioned and ready to join the active fleet as soon as possible, and that no effort was to be spared in the completion of her construction. The navy yard workers complied with these orders, working swiftly and efficiently to complete the difficult assembly of the new submarine.

On July 9, 1960, *Thresher* was ready for launching. As the first vessel of her class, her launch entailed something completely new for a submarine. Due to the difference in her buoyancy distribution as well as the depth of water at the end of the building ways, SSN-593 slid into the sea bow first. After the monstrous hull had come to a halt, Vice Admiral Harold T. Deutermann addressed the young crewmen into whose charge *Thresher* would be given.

"Your challenge as you enter the realm of the new and the untried is tremendous," said the vice admiral. "Equally great is your opportunity to contribute in very large measure to the new tactics and new capabilities of our Navy today. I know you would not have it otherwise."

A month later, on August 3, USS *Thresher* was commissioned and turned over to her first captain, Commander Dean Axene. The active service life of America's newest attack submarine had begun.

However, *Thresher* had not reached this initial stage of her career without encountering problems. Indeed, deficiencies in her design had already been noted by Vice Admiral Hyman Rickover, deficiencies the admiral felt were serious enough to merit correction during the vessel's construction. Rickover had observed that a silver-brazing technique was being used in the assembly of the submarine's nuclear reactor piping system. Lacking confidence in the strength of this joining method, he ordered the reactor cooling piping to be taken apart and reconnected using welded flanges.

Rickover had good reason to be concerned about the safety of this silver-brazing technique. During the vessel's builder's trials one of these joints failed on a small pipe, allowing sea water to spray back into the submarine's interior. On another occasion a missing gasket caused a one-inch pipe joint to fail during a deep-dive test, and sea water had gushed into the *Thresher* before repairs could be made.

Because of weight considerations, the steel used in construction of *Thresher*'s hull had to be relatively thin but very strong. When the steel underwent the requisite special toughening process, however, it tended to become slightly brittle, thus increasing the possibility of later crack formation. This necessitated taking thousands of x-rays of the submarine's hull plates so that possible defects in the metal might be detected and corrected.

The heavy structural members supporting *Thresher*'s outer skin gave additional strength to the submarine's hull, however. This meant not only that the hull plates did not creak and groan during a deep dive like those of other submarines, but also that the hull would be able to withstand major stresses that might be faced during the vessel's active service career.

Thresher's crew did not anticipate any major problems during their tour of duty aboard the submarine, and the vessel's August 9 shakedown cruise took place without incident. For the next two years Commander Axene put the boat through her paces, testing the vessel's systems as well as her crewmen. Slowly the proficiency of the men grew as they became used to their duties and equipment.

These two years did not pass uneventfully, however, and the term "jinx" might even come to mind in a review of the *Thresher*'s brief career to that time. Of SSN-593's first 625 commissioned days, 406 (about 65 percent) were spent either at her moorings or in drydock undergoing repairs. This was more off-duty time than that required by any other nuclear submarine. Eleven fires broke out on the ship during her active career, six while she was at sea. And these were not the only mishaps sustained by the submarine.

On October 29, 1961, *Thresher* was submerged and moving at eleven knots when her trim system went out of commission, preventing precise alteration of the vessel's buoyancy. Repairs took four and a half hours, the submarine remaining submerged during the whole procedure.

On the night of November 2, 1961, *Thresher* was lying moored at San Juan, Puerto Rico, when her diesel engine, used to provide electricity for the docked submarine, suddenly quit. The ship's batteries did not contain a charge sufficient to run the ventilation or air conditioning systems, and heat from the reactor's steam system quickly began to build up inside the vessel. The temperature soon reached 136 degrees, and most of the crew were ordered to leave the ship, several being overcome by heat beforehand. Four men remained in the engine room and finally succeeded in making repairs, for which they later received Navy commendation medals.

January 2, 1962, saw *Thresher* pulling away from the Portsmouth drydock when water began pouring into her forward compartment escape hatch. The flooding was soon controlled, and a hundred gallons of sea water were then pumped out of the vessel before she proceeded on her way.

On June 1, 1962, the big submarine was maneuvering toward her dock in Port Canaveral, Florida, when a tugboat came near her port side. The tug, moving too fast, was unable to turn in time and rammed the *Thresher* just forward of her conning tower. A three-foot hole was torn in the submarine's port side, extending from one to four feet below the waterline. *Thresher* immediately redocked, and Commander Axene then ordered her starboard ballast tanks flooded. This heeled the vessel heavily to starboard, raising the damaged area of her port side above the waterline so that repairs could be made.

On June 18 *Thresher* was scheduled to take part in a "shock test" off Key West, Florida. The submarine was to submerge to a depth of fifty feet and remain at a prescribed safe distance from a cache of explosives on the sea bottom. The explosives would then be detonated, exposing the submarine to shock waves of a known strength and allowing the Navy to see how well she withstood the stress. Somehow, however, *Thresher* strayed too close to the detonation site, with the result that she sustained a shock 20 percent greater than that absorbed by any other submarine in non-combat conditions. The explosion smashed against the submarine's hull, rocking her violently for several minutes before her crew finally regained control. *Thresher*'s interior was a shambles, with ship's equipment broken and crewmen's belongings scattered everywhere. The vessel was able to surface and proceed back to port under her own power, and Commander Axene probably realized that he and his crew had gotten off lightly.

Thresher continued to undergo shock tests for the next couple of weeks, then headed back to Portsmouth for another session in drydock. She arrived there on July 12, and spent the next nine months undergoing inspections and repairs. She also received a new captain, Lt. Cmdr. John Harvey, who assumed command of *Thresher* on January 18, 1963, while she was still in drydock.

No prototype can be expected to perform perfectly, and the *Thresher*'s catalogue of mishaps does not seem to have had those most intimately connected with her talking of jinxes. That was to come later—with hindsight—when the various malfunctions took on a distinctly ominous overtone.

Giving evidence at a subsequent inquiry on April 13, 1963, retired Navy chief Joseph Shafer affirmed that both of his younger brothers (who were chief petty officers on the *Thresher*) were particularly enthusiastic about the submarine, despite being "not sure" that the overhaul conducted while *Thresher* was drydocked had been done properly. Their attitude was jocular, though; at most they wondered aloud what would go wrong with the ship next time. Cmdr. Howard Larcombe, commanding officer of the diesel-electric submarine *Dogfish* and senior submarine commander at Portsmouth, would tell the court that Lt. Cmdr. Harvey had assured him that both *Thresher* and her crew were ready for trials only a day before setting sail, a vote of confidence corroborated by one of the Navy's leading engineering officers, Cpt. William Heronemus, who as repair and shipbuilding superintendant at Portsmouth had overseen the work on *Thresher* over the past nine months. "I have known no other ship in a higher state of readiness for sea than the *Thresher*," he remarked.

That same day (April 15, 1963) the commander of the Atlantic Fleet Submarine Force, Vice Admiral Grenfell, answered a suspicion which, voiced or not, may have been lingering in many minds: no pressure had been exerted on the shipyard, he said, to accelerate *Thresher*'s return to operational status. Of course, there was no point in denying that there *had* been structural or mechanical problems. The executive officer of *Thresher* from March 1962 to January 1963, William Cowhill, thought *Thresher*'s construction and overhaul at Portsmouth had been excellent, "with one reservation, the silver brazing process on piping"—which may indicate that the replacement joints of the cooling pipes conveying sea water had not been carried out as Admiral Rickover had ordered.

Lt. Raymond McCoole, the ship's electrical officer, missed the *Thresher*'s final voyage due to a lucky accident—not to him personally, but to his wife. He told the inquiry of the trouble that the overhaulers were given by *Thresher*'s main sea water valve (a large valve which admitted water to several of the cooling systems). He testified also to continuing problems with the air systems, the reducers of which had to be replaced frequently. This was a potentially serious defect, as the air systems affected the submarine's ballast tanks and therefore its surfacing capability. There had also been problems with the indicators that showed whether or not *Thresher* was on an even keel, and 20 percent of the valves in the hydraulic system had (like certain periscope mechanisms) been installed backwards. (The statement about the reversed valves, however, was authoritatively clarified by the shipyard's production engineer, Cpt. John D. Guerry, a month later: "Following exhaustive tests none was backwards when the ship sailed," he confirmed for the press on May 7). Finally, the diving plane and rudder mechanisms had been found defective and were replaced no more than twenty-four hours before *Thresher* put to sea.

Taken together, Lt. McCoole's evidence might seem to nonnaval eyes a terrible indictment of inefficiency and/or negligence. Surely no responsible body would have permitted the submarine to leave port in so dubious a condition? But, to repeat, such a conclusion seemed obvious only after events furnished a reason for reviewing the *Thresher*'s history in the hope of apportioning blame or explanation for disaster. There is even some confidence in the idea that, although malfunctions existed, they had been located and corrected. At any rate, naval authorities appear to have been satisfied: the *Thresher* was safe and *more* than safe to begin her sea trials.

This confidence does not appear to have been misplaced. Although a modicum of doubt concerning *Thresher*'s seaworthiness arises from all this—whether she was 99.9 or only 96.3 percent seaworthy—it is unreasonable to suggest that the new submarine left Portsmouth with the reputation of being a disaster looking for a place to happen. *At that time* there were certainly no grounds for supposing her a prematurely doomed vessel. And of prime importance here, more so, we feel, than the debatable issue of how safe the *Thresher* may or may not have been in actuality, is how safe the *crewmen* perceived her to have been. The Shafer brothers' remarks (as relayed by Joseph Shafer at the inquiry) establishes that there was a kind of weary awareness that the sub might "go wrong" yet again, but this was also a humorous, part-cynical response born of the fact *Thresher* had already wearied everyone with her unfortunate record of mishaps. The point is this: evidence of a profound disquiet about the ship's readiness and the suspicion she might venture out in an unsafe condition would assuredly affect our interpretation of any subsequent stories of paranormal warnings (omens, precognitions, etc.) suggesting that she was bound for disaster. On balance, we find that no such deep-seated anxiety existed.

The *Thresher*'s crew worked very hard during her overhaul period to get their boat shipshape and ready for sea again. In spite of her unfortunate safety record during the previous two years, none of *Thresher*'s crewmen expressed any desire to be transferred to another boat. Even so (and perhaps contradicting our assessment that no unusual anxiety existed), as the time approached for her next scheduled sailing, one of *Thresher*'s crewmen *did* experience an overwhelming feeling of uneasiness regarding the upcoming voyage.

The crewman in question was machinist's mate 2nd class George Kiesecker, who was one of *Thresher*'s nuclear reactor operators. A veteran World War II submariner who had taken part in numerous war patrols—according to one quote attributed to his wife, Lily, he had been in submarines since he was seventeen—Kiesecker was certainly not lacking in courage. He was an open, friendly man not given to morbid introspection, which is why his uneasiness about the upcoming voyage was so noticeable to his wife.

"*Thresher*'s a coffin," Kiesecker told his wife a few days before the submarine was scheduled to sail. "I don't want to go on it. I'm scared to death."

In Kiesecker's opinion the work on *Thresher* had been rushed to the point where he did not consider the vessel ready for sea. "There was too much trouble from the beginning," he told his wife. "I know what I'm talking about. I've been working twelve hours a day, seven days a week, helping to get her in shape."

Kiesecker felt so certain about the outcome of *Thresher*'s next voyage that he eventually confided to his wife his ultimate fear for the submarine's safety.

"I have a feeling this will be our last trip, honey," he said. "Before this week is over you'll be a wealthy widow."

Acknowledging the fact that Kiesecker's remarks were based on the belief that *Thresher*'s repairs had been undertaken too swiftly (hurriedly!) for the ship's good—which conflicts totally with the more roseate statements of Grenfell and Cowhill to the forthcoming inquiry—it seems too sensationalistic to argue that the crewman had experienced a veritable premonition. But neither is it wholly impossible: did Kiesecker speak with the odd certainty of disaster that his quoted words imply, or was this another case of a statement of strong probability being tragically corroborated by events? Interestingly, an article in the (London) *Daily Mirror* of April 13 suggests that other wives of *Thresher* crewmen had voiced similar doubts and one of the crewmen, Paul LaFranc, was alleged to have called the ship "a floating coffin." One thing to notice is that the story of Kiesecker's (pseudo)premonition was no late decorative flourish; as we will indicate presently, his widow repeated it within days of the *Thresher*'s fatal cruise out of Portsmouth.

On April 9, 1963, *Thresher* left her berth with her full complement of crew as well as seventeen additional technical observers. She spent the day at sea recalibrating her instruments, diving and resurfacing under test conditions. That evening, having completed her surface trials, the submarine began her journey toward the deep diving area where she expected to rendezvous with her escort ship, *Skylark*.

At 7:45 a.m. the next morning *Thresher* was at 41°44′N, 64°57′W, some 220 miles east of Cape Cod and in position for her deep submergence test. *Skylark* was informed that the attack submarine was beginning her dive, and a few minutes later received the message, "We are now at four hundred feet and checking for leaks."

The outside sea pressure strove mightily to find a weak spot in *Thresher*'s hull, but the submarine reached six hundred feet with all her compartments dry and free from leaks.

"Proceed to test depth," Cmdr. Harvey told his dive officer. At 8:35 a.m. *Thresher* began the really deep part of her dive off the edge of the continental shelf. *Skylark* remained in position over the submerged submarine, monitoring her progress and occasionally exchanging communications with her. *Thresher* continued to descend, eventually approaching a depth of a thousand feet.

At 9:12 a.m., after a few minutes of radio silence, *Skylark* requested *Thresher* to reestablish communication with the surface. The message received by Lt. Watson and Lt. Cmdr. Stanley Hecker on the escort vessel was not the one they expected, however.

"Experiencing minor difficulty," reported a voice from the attack submarine. "Have positive up angle. Attempting to blow. . . ."

Thresher was evidently trying to blow her ballast tanks in an attempt to rise. She seems, however, to have lost her forward propulsion, perhaps due to a leak that shorted out her reactor's electrical power supply. When Cmdr. Harvey ordered his vessel's diving planes turned to the "up" angle, the submarine's forward momentum brought her nose up briefly, but then *Thresher* stalled in the water and began to drop stern first toward the ocean floor 8,400 feet below.

The crewmen on board *Skylark* listened to their radio loudspeaker and heard the rushing sound of compressed air being blown into *Thresher*'s ballast tanks. The submarine was trying desperately to surface.

"Are you in control?" asked *Skylark* at 9:15 a.m., but she received no reply.

Two minutes later, at 9:17 a.m., a garbled message was sent from *Thresher*, a message impossible to understand except for the last two words: ". . . test depth." A moment later the men on *Skylark* heard a sound that several of them recognized from their World War II experience—"a dull, muted sound like that of a ship breaking up," or (in Lt. Watson's phrase) "like a compartment collapsing."

USS *Thresher* had imploded after descending past her test depth. The Navy's newest attack submarine fell to the bottom of the Atlantic in a thousand pieces, taking her entire crew—sixteen officers, ninety-six enlisted men, and eighteen civilians—with her. It wasn't until almost three months later that the deep submersible *Trieste* found the submarine's shattered remains lying in the darkness a mile and a half down.

Meanwhile news of the *Thresher*'s loss had gone round the world. It was reported in the (London) *Times* of April 11, 1963, that the submarine was "overdue and presumed missing," and that four destroyers had proceeded from Newport, Rhode Island, on a "possible search and rescue mission." Two days later the paper confirmed there was "No Hope Now for 129" and, with the passing assurance that the disaster did not pose a threat of radioactive contamination, moved directly to the U.S. Navy's court of inquiry at Groton, Connecticut, part of whose proceedings we have already quoted.

The inquiry—one is tempted to write "inquest"—heard various affirmations to the complete seaworthiness of the *Thresher*; it also heard Lt. McCoole's evidence that perhaps "complete" was not the best word to use, though it is worth emphasizing that the court established that the faults he stipulated had been put right before the submarine left Portsmouth. Watson and Hecker of the *Skylark* also appeared to describe what they knew of *Thresher*'s last moments. The latter was criticized for not having informed Washington earlier.

In their respective ways, the British national newspapers help to gauge the depth of feeling for what was essentially an American tragedy. The queen (like De Gaulle of France) was known to have sent a message of sympathy to President Kennedy; outside these formal expressions of condolence, the peculiar horror appears to have struck a certain core perfectly expressed by the *Daily Mirror*'s headline of April 11: "Atom Sub Is Trapped Under Atlantic." Graphically but aptly described elsewhere as the worst peacetime submarine disaster, the incident may have touched Britons in a peculiar fashion; Britain's first atomic submarine, *Dreadnought* was scheduled to enter service soon. More than that, some readers could recall the drawn-out tension and ultimate dejection of June 1939 when the submarine *Thetis* failed to surface during her acceptance trials in Liverpool Bay.

To complete the analogy with *Thresher*, the *Thetis*—third of the new T class general purpose submarines—had experienced some teething troubles; she went into Liverpool Bay with a history that included steering gear problems, which had propelled her to port when she should have headed starboard, and jammed forward hydroplanes. She submerged with ominous difficulty and did not come up again unaided. Interestingly, if we recall the story of George Kiesecker, a sensitivity to what he felt was an inexplicably depressing atmosphere on board what was otherwise acknowledged to be a "happy ship" persuaded Warrant Engineer Robert Ostler to refuse repeated invitations to sail on *Thetis*'s first sea dive. He resisted even at the risk of compromising his friendship with Roy Glenn, who felt that Ostler's presence was more desirable in view of the fact that every other submarine officer from Cammell-Laird's yard would be going. Hence, unlike Glenn, he missed the dive of June 1, 1939, that ended with *Thetis*'s bows wedged in the mud 160 feet down. Only 4 of her complement of 103 found their way through the hatch of the Davis Submarine Escape Apparatus to safety. *Thetis* was not lost permanently that time. After a July tribunal had established that six sequential factors had contributed to the disaster (the most serious of which was the opening of a rear door while the bow-cap was open to the sea), she was raised, repaired, refitted, and renamed *Thunderbolt*. Under this title she served with notable success in the Mediterranean until depth-charged by an Italian sloop in 1943. Even so, her original denomination *Thetis* was enough to cause grave looks as late as twenty years afterward, when *Thresher* seemed to replicate her tragedy on a more awful scale.

The British press had also detected the stateside rumors that the loss of the *Thresher* was not as unpredictable as the inquiry may have wanted it to sound. "The Jinx Ship?" queried the *Daily Express* headline of April 13 as it related the submarine's previous history of malfunction courtesy of correspondent Robin Stafford in Groton.

The answer to the headline was implied rather than stated. There was the catalogue of accidents. There were the wives quoting previously unpublicized anxieties of their husbands, not the least of whom was Mrs. George Kiesecker. The direct quote that appears a few pages earlier is duplicated, give or take a phrase or so, in the reports published in the *Daily Express* and *Daily Mirror*; no doubt they also found a home in other papers, British and American.

Needless to say, in using this striking material the media did not infer that Kiesecker had been gripped by a paranormal premonition of his coming death. The machinist's words suggested only a deep conviction that repairs to *Thresher* were woefully inadequate and by quoting them so expertly in context of the sub's known, dismal past record for going wrong there was a strong hint of criticism directed at the authorities who had overlooked the evidence. But there was every likelihood that, given a lapse of a few years and a change of focus, those same words would take on a definite "predictive" tone and George Kiesecker would be regarded as one more helpless seer, the kind who sees his fate rolling toward him yet cannot avert it.

This or something like it is what took place when an anonymous author mentioned George Kiesecker's fear for the *Thresher*'s safety in *Fate*'s September 1963 issue. Kiesecker's ostensibly premonitory remarks are quoted accurately enough (presumably from press reports at the time of the accident). But, culpably or not, the boat's history of equipment failures and other problems was omitted, giving the incident a pronounced list toward the Unknown which in our opinion the original context didn't necessarily possess.

We are left with the choice of treating Kiesecker's words (a) as authentically and paranormally predictive, or (b) as an expression of strong anxiety based on an interpretation of what his experience told him—namely, that *Thresher* was not prepared and that disaster was inevitable, regardless of what higher authorities might have thought and said. We, the authors, incline toward the latter view, but we refuse to be dogmatic about it.

Skeptics occasionally protest that newsworthy disasters—wrecks, earthquakes, practically anything that causes loss of life and catches media attention are ready-made for psychic exploration. According to this model, any notable tragedy (or rather, any notable tragedy that generates massive media and hence popular attention) will be followed by a sporadic outbreak of claims from assorted seers, psychics, and other pseudosoothsayers who belatedly announce either that they "saw" the disaster before it happened *or* at the time it happened but before any recognized news agency announced it *or* that they have been blessed with the postdeath confidences of the victims. It's a scenario that is quite easy to lay at the paranormalists' door and unhappily one that is not always inapt.

As far as we can discern, though, the scenario doesn't apply to the *Thresher* episode. While our researches may have been faulty (and probably were) there does not seem to have been a spate of paranormalist material lumped in with the world's worst submarine disaster to date. We submit: *that* absence is interesting in itself.

The *Thresher* was no hush-hush project, but neither was it one accompanied by excessive media ballyhoo; by modern standards the press announcements that accompanied each step of the submarine's career were quite sober, tending to the strictly informative rather than the sensational. The main burst of publicity concerning her was, naturally enough, stimulated by her loss. Even then, the psychic press (which might be expected to seize upon the incident one way or another) did not roar into frenetic life. It's true that *Psychic News,* a British spiritualist weekly noted for a tendency to tie its articles into current events in the nonspirit world, used the *Thresher* disaster in the front-page headline of its April 20, 1963, issue, but it can hardly be accused of milking the possibilities. In fact, it is rather disappointing to find that "Nuclear Submarine in Amazing Trans-Ocean Telepathic Test" does no more than use the *Thresher* as a lead-in to an article about alleged telepathy experiments on a different submarine; it is an early scarifier about the militaristic dimensions into which psi was headed taken from Pauwel and Bergier's *The Dawn of Magic* (of which book more later). The *Thresher*'s role in all this is no more than to provide an introduction. The *Psychic News* journalist, picking on Washington's statement that *Thresher* was a victim of communications failure, boldly attributes the disaster to a Cold War race to find a psychic (telepathic) solution to the problem of communicating with submarines beneath polar waters and then forgets all about the unfortunate vessel itself. In other words, the loss of the *Thresher* was no more than a peg upon which to hang a somewhat dubious article.

We find it significant that there should be so little paranormalist usage of the *Thresher* dating from the time of the actual disaster. The material we *have* found dates not from then, but from a period by which the tragedy had lost its primal sharpness; it was still a tragedy, but a strange glow of nostalgia had surrounded it. Before we attempt further analysis of what this may indicate, we had better give you the stories.

Our first is set *prior* to the disaster (circa 1962) but published only in September 1963 (briefly, and in *Fate* again). It concerns a gentleman named Philip Jenkins of Fresno, California.

Jenkins was an amateur artist who specialized in producing oil paintings of ships belonging to the U.S. Navy. He had just finished a rendering that showed the submerged *Thresher* descending at an angle into the ocean depths.

It was Mr. Jenkins's intention to donate his painting to the *Thresher* herself, hoping that the picture might be hung on board for the enjoyment of the ship's crew. One of Jenkins's friends, however, a man currently in the Navy, told the artist something that made him change his mind about giving the painting to the men of *Thresher*. This friend told Jenkins that the painting depicted the new attack submarine "in an uncontrollable dive position."

Following the disaster, it was wondered if Philip Jenkins might have unconsciously experienced a precognitive glimpse of *Thresher*'s fate while planning his painting of the doomed submarine.

Our personal response isn't favorable to that speculation; we put the entire thing down to coincidence and even that may be flattering. To be fair, the artist did not dress up his story by suggesting that he had experienced any kind of weird premonition about the *Thresher*, nor did he imply that he felt so much as strangely drawn to it as a subject for his latest painting. That apart, we feel that whoever suggested to

Jenkins that his picture was inspired by other-than-normal artists' sources did him no favors.

For a start (and despite what his naval friend suggested) there is nothing overtly significant in Jenkins depicting the *Thresher* in an uncontrollable dive attitude. As far as the inquiry evidence goes, that alignment does not match the boat's last known position at all. The final coherent message suggests that her bow was pointed upward toward the surface, not down at the bottom. Of course, the situation may have altered after this message was sent to *Skylark,* but we cannot be certain that it did. Some might attempt to defend the theory that Jenkins received paranormal insight into the crisis by suggesting his picture was not a literal visualization of the *Thresher*'s last moments, but a kind of dramatization of them; in this model, the psychic element deliberately exaggerates the alignment of the submarine purely to spell out the fact it is sinking (or rather, was destined to sink). The superior power involved was intent on informing the percipient that *Thresher* would go down; it was not particularly concerned with showing exactly *how.* Fine, but it is equally if not more likely that an artist, unlike an experienced submariner, would not have known that no sub could have assumed the angle he chose to show it assuming. In *this* model, Jenkins decided to show *Thresher* in a suitably evocative pose and merely departed from strict technological accuracy: a quite permissible kind of error, especially when we remember that all but a few experienced marine artists might have been tempted to draft a submarine in a bows-down attitude.

So far the reader may feel cheated: we have given *two* stories and, despite transparent efforts to keep the cases open, we have expressed personal distrust of both, at least as far as paranormal interpretations go. Our next offering may appear qualitatively better than George Kiesecker's retroactively ominous words or Jenkins's strangely aligned depiction, since it features an out-and-out ghostly vision.

After the shattered *Thresher* fell to the ocean floor in 1963, it would normally have been expected that new views of the vessel could only be obtained by sending a deep submersible down to photograph her wreckage. This supposition is untrue, however, if we are to believe an article by Raymond Lamont Brown concerning the John S. Schultz family of Boston, Massachusetts.

The summer of 1967 found Mr. and Mrs. Schultz and their three children vacationing aboard their yacht *Yorktown Clipper,* cruising leisurely along the New England coast from Long Island to Connecticut. Early one morning they were a couple of hundred miles east of Cape Cod and sailing through choppy seas toward home when, much to their surprise, a submarine surfaced off their starboard bow.

Mr. Schultz recognized the vessel as an American nuclear submarine, and he was alarmed to see that she had a huge gash along her waterline. He said nothing to upset his family, but he was puzzled about how the submarine was still able to float after having sustained such serious damage to her pressure hull.

Scrutinizing the submarine carefully, Schultz suddenly became aware that his yacht was being observed by two men in U.S. Navy uniform who stood on board the undersea craft. One man was on the submarine's walkway while the other stood on her bows. Both men were peering intently through their telescopes at the *Yorktown Clipper.*

After a few minutes of this mutual examination of each others' craft, the Schultz family was shocked when the huge submarine suddenly rose upwards a couple of feet in the water and then seemed to break in half amidships. The bow and stern sections jackknifed, and the vessel quickly disappeared beneath the surface of the choppy sea. Amazingly, the two Navy crewmen did not move a muscle as their vessel broke up, and they remained standing, stiff and motionless as figureheads, as the two halves of their craft carried them below the surface.

Before she vanished, the entire Schultz family clearly saw the name "*Thresher*" lettered on the submarine's side.

A strikingly dramatic account, to say the least. However, there are some odd discrepancies contained in the above story. Needless to say, the details of the Schultz family's phantom *Thresher* sinking bore no resemblance to the circumstances surrounding the loss of the actual *Thresher*. Another curious detail is that, whereas John Schultz saw the name "*Thresher*" lettered on the side of his phantom submarine, the real *Thresher* bore only the identification number "593" on her bows and on her "sail" (conning tower). The phantom *Thresher* therefore possessed characteristics curiously different from those of her actual namesake.

The most disturbing element of the above story is that, although they were greatly upset by the apparent submarine disaster they had just witnessed, the Schultz family (for some inscrutible reason) decided to keep quiet about what they had seen. Later John Schultz carried out some "discreet research" and learned that there had indeed been an American submarine named *Thresher* which, four years before, had foundered with all hands in the immediate vicinity of his family's odd sighting.

The loss of *Thresher* in 1963 had resulted in banner newspaper headlines the world over. If the Schultz family had somehow managed to remain blissfully unaware of the *Thresher* disaster when it took place in 1963, then—as far as they knew—they had just seen a real submarine disaster take place in 1967. The fact that the submarine bore the name "*Thresher*" on her side should not have seemed odd to the Schultzes, for they were supposedly ignorant of the very existence of the real *Thresher* (and her loss). Why, then, would they not have told anyone of the apparent tragedy they had just witnessed from their yacht? Common sense dictates that the family should have immediately come forward with potentially important information regarding the apparent sinking they had just witnessed. Why would it be necessary for Mr. Schultz to do "discreet research" in order to learn about the real *Thresher*?

Besides the above objections to the purported sighting of a phantom *Thresher*, however, there is another consideration to be dealt with, a consideration much more basic to our understanding of the above account.

Of the macabre detail concerning those two immobile figures who maintained their statuesque poses even as the submarine vanished under the waves, we can make nothing. It is interesting, though, to find the same motif in a *Fate* article about the haunted UB-65 (and by the same writer, no less) which we promise you for a later chapter. Taken with the other problems we have raised, not to mention the writer's failure to say how he came by the story, we are left with a nice little ghost story: one to appreciate in terms of fictive art, but not one that carries any seal of conviction in terms of fact.

A final mystery concerning the loss of USS *Thresher* came to light seven years after the tragedy. It occurred, however, in a totally unexpected place.

Lake Superior is the largest of North America's Great Lakes. Although these huge fresh water basins are connected to the Atlantic Ocean for ocean-going navigation purposes by the artificially constructed St. Lawrence Seaway, Lake Superior is still a long way from the sea.

One day in 1970 Scott Wilson and Allan Mackenzie, two ten-year-old boys from Duluth, Minnesota, were walking along the shore of Lake Superior when they came across something washed up on the beach. Upon closer examination the piece of jetsam proved to be a Navy-issue life ring made in 1950. Although it was broken in half, the two pieces of the ring were held together by a rim rope. Painted upon the white ring were black letters spelling out the name, "SS *Thresher*—Portsmouth."

The two boys kept their find as a curiosity until Dr. Julius Wolff, a University of Duluth expert on shipwreck studies, spoke at their school in May of 1970. The boys then brought their find to the professor for examination.

Wolff was impressed by the life ring, although he could not account for its presence in Lake Superior. Thinking that it may have come from another vessel with the same name as the lost submarine, the professor checked listings of other national and international vessels without finding another *Thresher* listed anywhere.

"Nothing here indicates a hoax," Wolff told the press, adding, "I thought it was another ship until I checked the records."

Left with few other credible explanations, Wolff theorized that *Thresher*'s floating life ring may have become entangled on the rudder of an ocean-going ship, which then dragged it through the St. Lawrence Seaway to Duluth. The Navy was contacted regarding the life ring, but no public statement was ever issued concerning whether or not the artifact came from the ill-fated nuclear submarine.

"This is the strangest thing I've ever run across," concluded Wolff in puzzlement.

In spite of Wolff's statement to the contrary, it seems possible that the broken life ring in his possession may indeed have been a hoax, perpetrator unknown. The evidence for this tentative conclusion is contained in the name printed on the ring—"SS *Thresher*."

"SS" is the standard prefix used by civilian ocean-going vessels. Since *Thresher* had been an American naval warship, it is probable that her life rings—if she carried any at all—would have been marked with the military designation *USS* ("USS" being the American naval prefix).

The life ring found in Lake Superior would appear to have been the work of a not-very-meticulous hoaxer. If only the true nature of George Kiesecker's premonition(?) could be arrived at so easily. . . .

Beyond saying that fake notes in bottles and other memorabilia from famous lost ships are not unknown, and that Wolff may have been victim of a hoax, there's little to add. We are conscious that some readers will be tempted to give up in disgust at the feebleness of these stories. For our part, and taking the line that the important thing about such tales is not whether they are true or false, but that they are told at all, we regard them as not without a certain curiosity value. The timing of these resurfacing stories is not the least intriguing. A few pages earlier we commented on the hypothetical link between media coverage of notable disasters and psychic events allegedly based on them. We invoked the skeptical protest that any major disaster will spawn claims that it was foreknown, foreseen, and generally available through precognition to the gifted few. It is time to readdress that issue.

The *Thresher* accident had numerous features that should have made it magnetically attractive to the psi-mongers. It was a horrifically final, totally unanticipated accident on a relatively huge scale involving a boat that to lay minds must have seemed the latest in modern technology—an emotional factor that undoubtedly explains part of the shock occasioned by the *Titanic* disaster, to take a glaring instance. And the boat in question was a new submarine, a class of vessel whose power over our imaginations we noticed at the commencement of this chapter.

Thresher ought to have generated any number of psychic stories, then. But as far as we can see, it didn't. By way of comparison, the *Thetis* accident of 1939—Britain's equivalent to the *Thresher* affair, as we mentioned earlier—*was* seized upon by the psychic press in a modest but notable way. Whether or not *Psychic News*'s coverage of séances at which victims allegedly "came through" (that is, communicated via) two different mediums be judged exploitational is a matter of taste or personal viewpoint; spiritualists will hardly think that it is. The first report carried in that paper (June 17, 1939) detailed how medium Estelle Roberts had suddenly asked whether any members of her audience at the Aeolian Hall, London, had been "connected with a man in the submarine disaster." According to spiritualist philosophy, spirits of the prematurely deceased are always likely to "drop in" at services and sittings, so perhaps her allusion to the topical disaster was less unusual than it might appear. Needless to say, medium (and spirits) had to guarantee that any relatives, friends, or acquaintances of the deceased mariner would be present in the audience that night, however.

As chance would have it, a man in the audience affirmed that he *had* some connection with a couple of *Thetis* victims. In what follows, we have to remember that the relationships of the man in the audience with *Thetis* crewmen cannot be verified; it remains as much a matter of trust as the medium's statement that there was a spirit present and visible to her.

Roberts described the appearance of the spirit (including "some peculiarities of his teeth") and his age. "Would you know if he is an engineer?" she asked the audience member. Yes, he did, and he was. "He is very agitated and confused," went on the medium, "and keeps saying, 'I must get through. . . . I must get to my wife.' " Then she and the man entered into dialogue that tended to confirm what the other was saying, his personal snippets of information going to corroborate that the spirit was who Roberts claimed him to be. Looked at cynically, it was a mutually supportive process that excluded the possibility that there was no spirit and that the man in the audience knew no one from the *Thetis*.

The most interesting phase of the séance came when the soi-disant spirit told how he had met his end. He'd been in the engine compartment with four others when disaster struck—here the medium mimed a revolving machine part: "He says that something stuck in the engine—and then something snapped. He is showing me a picture of part of the submarine." The spirit said that he had died from fumes from the electrical equipment ("Chlorine gas," supplied someone else in the audience) and he named another victim who had worked "on the electrical side." The medium discreetly gave only the initials of this second casualty, which again received confirmation from the floor. Finally the bodiless visitor announced that the spirits of his shipmates were still attached to the *Thetis*—earthbound, in spiritualist parlance—and part of his purpose in coming through tonight was to ask help in obtaining their release.

At this time, little if anything had been made public about the cause of the disaster. The medium, perhaps significantly, perhaps not, offers few clues about that; she (or the spirit) describes only one local aspect of it, not the overriding reason for the boat's loss. The swiftness with which "fumes from the electrical equipment" entered the picture is less compelling than it is natural in context. Many people would have picked up the fact that chlorine gas released by contact of sea water on batteries was one of the most dreaded phenomena of a submarine accident, if only because early newspaper reports of the disaster had mentioned it. For instance, the *Sunday Pictorial* of June 4, 1939, printed (among even more emotional *Thetis* coverage) Peter Wilson's dramatic tale of a submarine captain trapped in a submerged sub with men coughing as water reached the batteries. (The article appears to have been based on what the writer recalled from the conversation of a man he once met on holiday. Judging from the quantity of direct quotes, Wilson was gifted with a photographic memory. But then, the *Thetis* affair put memoirs of men who'd been trapped in subs and survived at a premium.) The *News of the World* for the same date subheaded its front-page article, "Chlorine Gas Crowned the Final Terrors of Doomed Submarine," basing that statement partly on the technical opinion of a Cammell-Laird official, but moreover on the testimony of Frank Shaw, one of the lucky quartet who negotiated the Davis Submarine Escape Apparatus to the surface.

We may as well concede that nothing of what Estelle Roberts or the unnamed spirit had to say could be checked; the failure to name the communicator (for whatever reason) robs the séance of real evidential value. Better was reported in *Psychic News* the following week (June 24) from a séance held by twelve sitters at the Glasgow Association of Spiritualists. Through the mediumiship of Helen Hughes a far more forthright *Thetis* victim came through, announcing himself as William Orrock, a stoker, and blaming the disaster upon a blocked valve. ("God bless Captain Bolus," he added in praise of his late commanding officer. "He was splendid.") Unknown to the medium, the sitters included Orrock's uncle, who was attending his first séance, and a Mrs. Mary Rae (also a stranger to spiritualism) who had known Orrock in some capacity or other. Both were highly impressed and signed a statement to the effect that they identified the spirit as William Orrock.

A good deal of spiritualist literature seems to deal with the furnishing of what the writers regard as watertight proof of survival. Again and again *Psychic News* flourishes material that it claims will totally defy, defeat, and ridicule anyone who doesn't accept the paper's legend: "You Will Survive Death." It seems odd to us that so much effort should go into proving over and over what the converted readers already accept as a rock-solid truth, but leaving that aside, let's consider how well the Hughes séance does in terms of proving that a *Thetis* victim was indubitably in contact with the living at that Glasgow session.

There *was* a stoker named William Orrock on the *Thetis*. Helen Hughes could have gleaned that much from the papers, of course—full casualty lists had appeared in the papers by this time (e.g., *News of the World* for June 4)—but we have to respect the fact that Orrock's uncle and Rae believed they had grounds for identifying the communicator as the deceased stoker and no one else. Of the purported Orrock's remarks that the submarine was felled by a blocked valve, little positive can be made. The tribunal of July 1939 attributed the cause of the accident to be at least six contributory factors: complete blocking of a test cock in the torpedo tube with bitumastic enamel, the opening of a rear door while bow cap no. 5 was open to the sea, failure to close a watertight door, failure to expel water from two flooded compartments, failure of those outside *Thetis* to render effective aid, and failure of all but four inside her to escape through the DSEA. A blocked valve doesn't figure in this, not as a major factor. But then, William Orrock was a stoker; arguably, he had no technical expertise to guide his analysis and what we get from the spirit here is personal opinion as fallible as any from a living, carnate person.

Rightly or wrongly, we are not concerned here with the truth or falsity of what came through at these séances. We are more interested in the way the *Thetis* tragedy was picked up by the psychic press. By and large, it ignored the *Thresher*. If the skeptical model is to hold up, the incident would have to be found lacking in some essential quality that prevented the seers from foreseeing, the clairvoyants from distant-viewing, and the spirits from communicating. What can this quality have been?

It seems true to say that despite its technologico-military significance (and at a time when developments in submarine warfare were certainly to the fore of public attention—witness Polaris) the *Thresher* was not a high-profile name in media terms. There was *some* prelaunch publicity and some popular awareness of this new hunter-killer along with it. Yet *Thresher* may have failed to generate the kind of excitement or interest outside naval circles that was essential if it was to be the focus of paranormal stories. In more prosaic terms, the full facts of what the submarine was and could do (and the problems it was encountering in its early days) may have restricted the development of such material among the civilian public. The very detail that the victims were military personnel may have lessened the emotional impact of the tragedy likewise; the drowned men were too remote from the mainstream of ordinary life to be accessible (although, as we just heard, the *Thetis*'s crew were also naval men). Again, skeptics are quick to notice how many psychic allegations of disaster extrapolate known (published) details into their fabric, which is quite possible when newspapers print the stories of survivors (as may have occurred in the *Thetis* cases, where the spirits seem to echo some aspects of newspaper-publicized speculation on the cause of the disaster). The *Thresher* incident left *no* survivors.

And however harrowing that disaster may have been at the time, public awareness of it soon faded. It is virtually certain that as early as the year's end it had ceased to dwell in the minds of all save the immediate circle of the crewmen's wives, relatives, friends, and colleagues, who of course had better reason to remember it. The *Thresher* disaster was overtaken in the public mind by larger events, and none larger than the assassination of John F. Kennedy the following November.

And yet it retained a kind of emotional kernel—a once-famous maritime tragedy—which, given time, might provide a basis for odd stories. The fact these came later, when the original impact of the sinking had given place to a blurred memory ("The *Thresher*? Oh yes, that was that sub that sank first time out. Terrible business.") may go to prove that the stories themselves could not flourish closer to the event, but needed time to mellow. Classic ghost stories frequently center upon past tragedy, as if they were folkloric attempts to recall and commemorate the event in question. Often they involve a simple philosophy that the past reminds us of the present through apparitional visions of itself. The forgotten *Thresher* lives on—resurfaces—as a ghost ship.

We cannot outargue the objection that we may have missed other, possibly stronger stories that were related closer to the event or that the time lag in those stories we have found was more apparent than real; that is, Jenkins's account *may* have been contemporaneous with the event, but remained unheard until *Fate* published it. Against this, there is clear evidence that the act of "reinterpretation" that overtook Kiesecker's words to his wife—giving them a premonitory ring—was a late addition, not an inference drawn at the time of the tragedy. The Schultz apparitional adventure off George's Bank dates from 1967, or four years after the loss of *Thresher,* assuming our source (author Raymond Lamont Brown) is correct. The belated discovery of the life ring takes us as far on as 1970 (when the story was first published in the *Detroit Free Press*). It is very noticeable that Raymond Lamont Brown spends some time informing his readers who and what *Thresher* was: a most necessary practice, as only a maritime and/or submarine buff could be expected to know without the telling.

In the final analysis, we are back to the thorny issue of: are these stories true or are they false? Attentive readers will have observed that the present authors prefer to keep our hands in pristine, unlacerated condition; we talk of them as *stories* in the sense that however stolidly they are presented as literal fact, they may be imaginative fiction. As our chapter on the Goodwins Ghost Ship debated, a spurious "true" story should be seen as none the worse for being so; while we have to accept the parapsychologist's rule that unusual stories can only be accepted as facts upon unusually strong evidence, there is another way to proceed: the folklorist's way. To a folklorist, the real significance of a story (or memorate, or account) lies not so much in its absolute truth or falsity, but in its content, style, and underlying meaning. We submit that, taken as legends, folk versions drawing upon historical events, but not necessarily or even likely matching up to the known data of those events, the previous quartet have a definite value. If nothing else, they affirm that the *Thresher* was not lost forever on April 9, 1963. She survived in folkified memory, as a basis for legend.

But then, submarines are peculiarly well adapted to legend-making. Submarines are ships (or "boats," as those who sail in them say) and submariners' legends are only a subtype of the Haunted Ship—the Jinx Ship, the Jinxed Ship. Do you recall how the *Daily Express* headline invited its readers to speculate that the *Thresher* was one? The same motif was evident when the *News of the World*'s Birkenhead correspondent joined the crowds lining the banks of the Mersey for news of the *Thetis* on June 3, 1939, prior to his interviewing Cammell-Laird's managing director, R. S. Johnson. The rumor had got around that *Thetis* was—had always been?—an unlucky ship. The reporter duly challenged Johnson to respond to the allegation.

In point of fact, *Thetis* had not been particularly "unlucky"; much less could she be called "jinxed." Johnson could only remember that she had fouled the dock on her return from inauguration trials and that a hydroplane malfunction had caused her diving tests to be postponed. In the wake of the tragedy, it seemed that some people *wanted* to label *Thetis* an unlucky ship. This is a manifestation of our suspicion that however safe and sophisticated a submarine may appear, it is somehow unnatural: a vessel married to grisly death. Not unlike the *Mary Celeste,* for instance. And yet . . .

A ship of death . . . a derelict manned by a crew of skeletons . . . such ghastly occurrences have occasionally come to pass during man's long and often tragic relationship with his friend/adversary, the Sea. "Who hasn't heard of ships drifting, haphazard, with their crews all dead?" asks Joseph Conrad, recalling in *The Shadow-Line* his days as a young captain whose first command was dogged by fever among the crew and no wind to sail by—circumstances that made the old stories seem less unbelievable to him. Although eighteenth- and nineteenth-century sailing vessels plying the Atlantic might very often vanish without ever being heard from again, a missing vessel might occasionally be sighted long after she was presumed to have gone down with all hands. She would be proceeding under sail and appear to be completely seaworthy, the only odd detail being that there was no visible sign of life on board her. If the ship was boarded, her curious discoverers would learn to their horror that the long-overdue vessel was a floating morgue, her dead passengers and crew lying about the decks or in their cabins with no visible sign of what had caused their deaths. Little wonder that ships like these were regarded with awe by the sailors who happened upon them.

The mere thought of a seaworthy vessel carrying a long-dead crew on a voyage to nowhere is enough to raise the hairs on the back of one's neck and send a thrill of horror prickling down his spine.

Man normally likes to believe that he is the master of his own fate; he feels that by exercising care in his daily life, he can ensure results which, if not ideal, will at least be tolerable to his health and well-being. There is no room in his thinking for the unexpected; if one's plans are thorough enough, he thinks, the unexpected can be met on its own terms and conquered.

This is one reason why, when faced with a derelict ship full of dead men, man's superstitious fear of the unknown is mingled with a haunting desire to find out how the unfortunate mariners were stricken down in such a mysterious fashion.

In the early days of transatlantic travel ships were propelled by sail, were slow (by today's standards), and carried no wireless. Once a vessel sailed out of sight of her home port, she was usually on her own for a long time to come, until she finally arrived at her destination. This meant that a sailing vessel would not be missed by her owners unless she was overdue for an extended period of time, a period during which much could happen.

Although "death ships" might be the subject of superstitious speculation among many sailors, the more down-to-earth mariner realized that such a fate, although horrible, was at least *understandable*: perhaps the sailing vessel had been becalmed for weeks or months until her supply of food and water gave out, resulting in the death of everyone on board. Or perhaps disease had broken out on board the vessel, killing passengers and crew indiscriminately until there was no one left who could navigate the ship. Before the invention of wireless there was no way such a stricken vessel could summon assistance, and so her passengers and crew either lived or died according to the whim of an uncaring Sea. But, regardless of the fate of her passengers, the vessel herself would sail on . . . and on . . .

With the advent of steam-powered, wireless-equipped ships, however, one would expect reports of derelicts manned by skeletons to become almost nonexistent. And so they have, with two notable exceptions.

Our first account originally appeared in a book entitled *Mysteries of the Sea,* written by Robert De La Croix in 1956. Although De La Croix's account is frustratingly vague as far as specific details are concerned, it is still a story that quickly captures the imagination of the reader.

The incident took place in the North Sea in February 1915, and our story opens with German destroyers sighting an unknown submarine off the coast of Hamburg. The sub was half submerged, her conning tower showing above the surface while her hull was awash. The destroyers were certain that the vessel was an Allied submarine lying in wait for German shipping, although they were puzzled by the fact that she did not submerge at their approach. Deciding that caution was the order of the day, the destroyer captains held their fire as their vessels closed on the submarine, and they soon breathed a sigh of relief at their proper judgment of the situation. The submarine proved to be one of the kaiser's warships, a member of his U-boat fleet.

The German submarine seemed to be stationary in the water, with no crewmen visible. The destroyers made several recognition signals to the U-boat, which, oddly, did not reply. Deciding that the submarine must be on some type of secret mission, the German warships withdrew and left the solitary U-boat to go her own way.

A week later a British destroyer was patrolling in roughly the same area when her lookout sighted a submarine about four miles away. The British gunners manned their battle stations and trained their guns on the distant U-boat, awaiting their captain's order to open fire. But the order did not come. The destroyer closed to within two miles of the submarine without shelling her, and the gunners thought their captain's reluctance to open fire would certainly doom their own vessel to destruction by a German torpedo.

But the U-boat showed no sign that she was aware of the British vessel's proximity. The destroyer continued her approach until she was within a few cables' lengths of the German submarine. The British sailors stared at the U-boat as their ship steamed slowly round her, for it was a rare privilege to examine an enemy warship at such close range with impunity. One can imagine the sailors' surprise, however, when their captain eventually gave the order for his destroyer to retire to the northward without sinking the enemy submarine.

Even though the destroyer's seamen were dumbfounded by the action of their captain, the officers on the bridge realized that the captain had been reacting coolly and calmly throughout the entire encounter with the U-boat. He had consulted a table of ships' identity silhouettes, and had even been heard to murmer, "Yes, that's her, all right." This led to speculation among the officers that the U-boat was actually a disguised British submarine whose purpose was to hoodwink real German U-boats and lure them within range of her torpedoes.

A week later another British destroyer sighted the mysterious U-boat, but this time the British gunners opened fire at long range. With shells splashing all around the target and a direct hit only moments away, the destroyer's captain suddenly ordered his astonished crew to cease fire. Like his predecessor, the British commander steamed his vessel inquisitively around the U-boat before turning about and then withdrawing, again leaving the submarine alone in deep water.

Rumors about the mysterious U-boat spread among the British antisubmarine flotilla, but the destroyer captains were the only ones with any inkling as to what was really going on.

"We realize that your crews must be mystified," the captains were told at headquarters, "but you will appreciate that the matter must remain secret until we are sure what results can be expected from the plan. These things soon get about. We are at the mercy of any indiscreet talk. The Germans would at once hear about it through their spies. That submarine mustn't be sunk."

However, as time passed without additional sightings of the U-boat being reported, it began to seem that the Admiralty's intentions, whatever they were, had been thwarted. In spite of diligent searching, nothing further was heard of the submarine, and the Admiralty prepared to write her off as lost.

The Admiralty's fears proved premature. Eight days later a Belgian steamer returning from Africa reported a hair-raising escape from a U-boat off Yarmouth. The Belgian captain reported that his vessel had dodged the U-boat's torpedo before turning tail and finally managing to outrun the submarine. When queried about whether the U-boat had actually fired a torpedo at him, the captain's certainty wavered a bit, but he maintained that he was "pretty sure" the German submarine had attacked his ship.

After the Belgian captain left the Admiralty interrogation room the British officers couldn't help smiling about his "hairbreadth escape" from the U-boat. One of the officers suggested that it was time the truth was told about the mysterious submarine, and that she should now be towed to a British port. Another officer asserted that such was the Admiralty's intention—just as soon as the U-boat could be located again. It was uncanny, but the submarine suddenly seemed to have taken it into her head to vanish completely.

A few days later, however, unknown to the Admiralty, the "ghost submarine" put in a new appearance in front of a German audience. A U-boat returning home from her own wartime patrol encountered her mysterious colleague at sea, saluted her, and asked what inroads she had made on British shipping. When no reply was received, the returning U-boat captain was indignant about the stranger's failure to observe the traditional courtesies characteristic of the German navy.

But now the mysterious submarine was off the coast of England and floating steadily closer to land every day. One morning soon thereafter the U-boat drifted ashore on a beach near Yarmouth, and it was then that her secret was finally disclosed. And what a secret it was: the stranded submarine was found to contain the dead bodies of four British sailors.

The Admiralty's explanation for this remarkable fact was in itself remarkable. The stranded U-boat belonged to a new class of German submarine, the plans for which the British Intelligence Service had been unable to get hold of. In response to this failure, the Admiralty had suggested that four British submarine technicians be disguised as German sailors and infiltrated into the enemy's submarine base. Once there, the four men could steal an example of the new class of submarine and sail it back to England!

And this is just what had happened. One night the British spies entered the German submarine pens and had been allowed to board the new submarine by her caretaker crew. After overpowering the Germans on board, the British sailors found that the submarine had enough fuel on board to see her safely across the North Sea. The U-boat carried no torpedoes, but these would be unnecessary anyway since the German navy would not fire on one of their own submarines; besides, the unit commanders of the British fleet had all been warned to be on the lookout for the stolen submarine, so there would be no risk of being sunk by friendly fire.

All had proceeded according to plan. The British sailors eased the U-boat out of her pen and through the harbor. Daylight found the submarine well out on the North Sea. It took the Germans some time to miss the stolen U-boat, as they thought she had just been moved to another berth for an equipment check. Meanwhile the missing submarine was heading rapidly toward England, her prize crew running her half-submerged for increased speed and decreased visibility.

A day after leaving Germany, however, the stolen U-boat encountered a fierce storm which caused her ballast tanks, already half full, to take on more water. To their dismay, the crew discovered that the submarine's compressed air pumps were not equal to the task of forcing the excess water from the ballast tanks. Running awash through the gale, all the submarine's outside hatches were battened down to keep out the raging sea.

With the outside hatches sealed shut, the air inside the submarine slowly began to fill with carbon dioxide. In an attempt to counter this, the four sailors opened the valves of several oxygen bottles to help freshen the air. This was a mistake which was to prove fatal. Too much oxygen escaped from the tanks, causing the crewmen to fall into a kind of intoxicated state. Having lost touch with their precarious situation, the four men gradually passed into a coma. Oxygen continued to escape from the bottles, the unconscious men's lungs became inflamed, and they lay where they fell until, one by one, they died.

The submarine's engines continued to run normally, although, with no one at her helm, the vessel began to zigzag hither and yon. When her fuel supply finally gave out, the U-boat began to drift wherever the winds and currents wished to take her. Meanwhile, British destroyers reported to the Admiralty that the submarine had been sighted on the surface, so the mission planners felt that success was assured. They were not perturbed by the submarine's overdue arrival date because they realized the difficulties four sailors would face in navigating a submarine from Germany to England. No one in the Admiralty realized that the U-boat was now manned by a crew of dead men.

The submarine's temporary disappearance had no doubt been caused by her ballast tanks slowly filling up with water. After she submerged—according to author De La Croix—the pressure exerted by the oxygen in her hull slowly acted on the ballast tanks until enough water was forced out of them to allow the U-boat to resurface off the coast of Yarmouth. Soon thereafter the submarine grounded, exposing her grisly secret to the world.

The above account is truly intriguing, even though the reader will immediately note that De La Croix is unable to supply any specific details which would serve to document and flesh out his story. We do not know which U-boat was the subject of the British "highjack attempt," nor do we know the date on which the derelict submarine washed ashore in England. All of this makes the event very difficult to authenticate.

In spite of this difficulty, the probable source for De La Croix's story has come to light. The following account (dating from 1929) predates De la Croix's 1956 version, and, although it differs in certain essential details, is so strikingly similar to the later account that it almost certainly served as the the basis for it. (Indeed, De La Croix's submarine story took place in February 1915, while the one we are about to examine began in January 1915 and concluded "six months later"). Let us now look at this second story, which originally appeared in a book by Lowell Thomas entitled *Raiders of the Deep.*

Lowell Thomas, later to gain fame as a journalist and broadcaster, found himself fascinated by the U-boat campaign that had played such an important part in German strategy during World War I. Following the cessation of hostilities, Thomas set about interviewing as many German submariners as he could, and his efforts eventually led him to Adolf Karl Georg Edgar, Baron Spiegel von und zu Peckelsheim. Baron von Spiegel invited Thomas to his Berlin apartment and regaled the young journalist with stories of his wartime service in the kaiser's submarine fleet.

The events that concern us here began on January 13, 1915 (which happened to be a Friday), and Baron von Spiegel emphasized to Thomas that he had good reason to regard the old "Friday the 13th" superstition seriously. On this particular day three U-boats had set out from Wilhelmshaven on combat patrols—U-22 under Commander Hoppe, U-31 under Commander Wachendorff and U-32 under von Spiegel himself.

After nine days von Spiegel's boat had returned to Wilhelmshaven without having seen a single ship, a string of consistent (but ordinary) bad luck. Five days later Hoppe returned in U-22, bringing the tragic news that his boat had mistakenly torpedoed and sunk the U-7 (commanded by Georg Koenig, Hoppe's best friend). Surely such a dreadful mishap could not be described as "ordinary" bad luck.

But the third boat, Wachendorff's U-31, never returned at all. As weeks and months went by and nothing more was heard of her, it was presumed that the missing submarine had struck a mine in the North Sea and gone down with all hands. A logical assumption, perhaps, until one day six months later . . .

Baron von Spiegel's story continued: "A U-boat above water nosed its way slowly along. Nothing seemed amiss. It looked trim and menacing, as if ready to dive and launch a torpedo at any moment. It was drifting before the wind, though, and finally ran ashore on the eastern coast of England. Astonished fishermen sent out an alarm. Naval men came hurrying. The U-boat lay rocking, aground on a sand bar. They boarded the craft, took her in tow to harbour and dock, and discovered an eerie riddle."

The grounded submarine proved to be the U-31, and it was soon learned that she was in perfect working order. The British discoverers were shocked, though, when upon entering the U-boat they discovered her entire crew lying in their hammocks and bunks as if asleep—only they were dead.

The log of the U-31 revealed that its last entry had been dated six months before. Wachendorff's record revealed that his submarine's voyage had been completely uneventful right up to the time when his log entries suddenly and mysteriously broke off.

The U-31 became known as the "phantom submarine."

"It was a nine days wonder," said Baron von Spiegel. "This dead man's boat had seemingly been cruising around for six months over the heavily patroled waters of the North Sea. It sounded like a case of spooks." According to von Spiegel, British investigators could come up with only one explanation for the mysterious death of the U-31's crew, and the veteran U-boat commander felt that this explanation was undoubtedly the correct one.

Baron von Spiegel told Thomas that night may have overtaken the U-31 after she neared the English coast, and Commander Wachendorff probably settled his submarine onto the bottom until daylight. Since they were in no danger from British warships, the officers and men of the U-31 had probably left one of their number on watch and then turned in for the night. However, the stillness of the sleeping U-boat may have lulled the guard into taking an unauthorized nap himself, a lapse that sealed the doom of everyone on board. The batteries powering the submarine's engines may have suddenly developed a leak, causing chlorine gas to seep slowly throughout the U-boat and kill her sleeping crewmen where they lay. The submarine continued to lay on the bottom of the English Channel, but, as the months went by, cylinders of compressed air began leaking their contents into U-31's ballast tanks. Little by little, water was forced out of the ballast tanks until, six months after she had last seen the light of day, U-31 broke free of the sea floor and floated slowly to the surface. Drifting before the wind, the "phantom submarine" soon found herself aground on a sandbar and surrounded by English fishermen. The rest, as they say, is history.

Or is it? Baron von Spiegel was a highly respected veteran of the Deutsche Unterseeboots Flottille, and Thomas had absolutely no reason to doubt the story he had just heard. Since the veteran submariner described the event as having been a "nine days wonder," English newspapers might have been expected to contain thorough coverage of such an event, if only to boost the wartime morale of her civilian population. Indeed, since this is just the kind of story that a maritime historian would love to know more about, a diligent investigator might be expected to search the newspaper archives for additional information on the incident.

Our diligent investigator would be (and, in the present case, *was*) disappointed to find that there is no newspaper record of such a U-boat stranding having taken place in England in 1915, manned by either four dead British sailors or a full complement of dead German submariners. Indeed, there seems to be no record of *any* German submarine coming ashore on the English coast in circumstances similar to those we have discussed above.

So our intrepid investigator might next be expected to consult German naval records pertaining to the last mission and eventual fate of the U-31. The official records are very brief and to the point: "Mined (?) North Sea, January 1915."

In other words, the U-31 was never seen again after she left Wilhelmshaven on her final war patrol. Since no British warship ever claimed to have destroyed her, the only alternative explanation for her loss seems to be that she struck a mine and went down with all hands.

It appears, then, that there is no truth to Baron von Spiegel's dramatic story of the "derelict U-31." But why, we must ask, would he decide to fabricate his dramatic story about the derelict U-boat and relate it to Thomas, who accepted it as true? Alas, we can only speculate on his reasons. Von Spiegel and Wachendorff had been comrades in arms; both had run the risk of losing their lives during the course of their wartime duties. Perhaps it might have been considered permissible for fellow warriors to spin such tales about each other, whereas those same warriors would have regarded the same tale created by a noncombatant as blasphemous. Since Wachendorff was dead (under mysterious circumstances), von Spiegel may have felt that his imaginative tale about the U-31 could do no harm to his late comrade; indeed, perhaps he felt that Wachendorff himself might have enjoyed being the subject of such a gripping story. We can at least be sure that the baron enjoyed telling a good tale; at least one naval historian has said that the veteran submariner dined out on his U-31 story many times during the course of his lifetime. The present authors have little doubt that this is true, for, like the good baron, we regard the fictional U-31 story as being too good *not* to tell.

These stories bear testimony to the imaginative force of the submarine. There is something about the very idea of that kind of vessel that conditions us to believe what we might otherwise dispute. They are, by virtue of their secret mode of operation, ideally suited to the formation of rumors, which folklorists sometimes class as only another underdeveloped or short-lived type of legend, hence the phrase, "rumour-legend." We mentioned in passing Louis Pauwels and Jacques Bergier's *The Dawn of Magic,* a.k.a. *Morning of the Magicians* (1963), though only because the name cropped up in tenuous connection with the *Thresher*. That flamboyant compilation of reports of ancient astronauts, mysterious psychic energies, and other modern apocrypha contains a prime example of a rumor-legend that evolved in response to the Cold War and took as its theme a Jules-Vernishly named sub.

The background to the telepathy experiments allegedly conducted on board USN *Nautilus* from July 25, 1959, onward seems to focus on contemporary research into new submarine-land communications systems. Two years prior to this, a report prepared on behalf of the U.S. government by the Rand Corporation had highlighted the inability of communicating with submarines submerged beneath the North Pole, and it was widely accepted that a fresh approach was needed. Add to this the growing interest in ESP research about extrasensory perception—reportedly among "scientists" and by a small imaginative leap, among *military* scientists: a suggestion by no means ridiculous in itself, as J. B. Rhine's pioneering work in parapsychology at Duke University had done much to legitimize the idea of telepathy and militarists were conceivably obliged to wonder about its possible applications.

According to Bergier (who footnotes an article of his own for *Constellation* 140, December 1959), in July of that year the atomic submarine *Nautilus* took onboard a mysterious passenger, later pseudonymously labelled as "Jones," and sailed out into the Atlantic. Jones, by the way, was a student at Duke University. You may be surprised to learn that somewhere ashore, but in mental contact with this supercargo, evidently, was another pseudonymous person called "Smith."

With *Nautilus* submerged under the Atlantic for sixteen days, alias Smith and Jones went to work. Jones's lifestyle does not sound very exciting. Secluded in his cabin, he saw only the sailor who brought him his food and Cpt. Anderson, to whom twice a day he handed a sheet inscribed with the stars, circles, wavy lines, squares and crosses of a Zener ESP testing symbolism. Each sheet went into a dated-and-sealed envelope marked: "Top Secret. To be destroyed in the event of capture by a submarine."

After *Nautilus* docked at Croyton on August 10, Jones was whisked away under escort to a military airfield and flown to Maryland, where another car was waiting to hurry him to the Westinghouse Special Research Center and Col. William Bowers, director of biological sciences on behalf of the U.S. Air Force. The results of Jones's telepathically received impressions (for such the Zener symbol sheets were) were checked by Bowers against the sheets of the "transmitter," Smith, which had been lodged with him. The outcome was that Jones's impressions had been correct to within less than 30 percent error.

Seven correct out of every ten guesses is an amazingly high success rate in telepathy experiments. We would anticipate that most parapsychologists would be delighted to get them. We also anticipate that, while satisfied that the conditions of the experiment precluded normal communication between sender and receiver, they would demand to know how many trials were run and other details relating to the experiment. And, being in the main ultracautious people, a few would refuse to believe that the experiments took place at all.

But the *Nautilus* story contains a failsafe very common to modern cryptoconspiracy legends: as it was "Top Secret." It is impossible to confirm or refute it and any firm statement that no such experiments were held would be automatically suspect. Quite simply the U.S. government's cryptocrats would issue such a denial as a matter of course. Just as cogently, the cloak of top secrecy means we have no way of proving that the experiments did *not* take place. We are fully in the power of the narrator who, if challenged as to how he penetrated that cloak, will doubtless refer to a leak, a highly placed naval contact or someone similar.

Anyway, this was the source that provided the substance of Anne Dooley's article for *Psychic News,* the article which, as mentioned already, was nominally about the *Thresher* disaster. Having retold Bergier's story of the *Nautilus,* Dooley worked hard to provide further grounds for a reader's belief; she quotes Peter Castriccio, director of the Westinghouse Electrical Corporation's Aeronautics Institute, who admits that he believes in ESP and confirms that American scientists have shown interest in it for "industrial use in long-distance communication systems." She relates that various U.S. laboratories, military or otherwise, are thought to be investigating in this area. A thirty-one-year-old "scientific psychical researcher" named William Lamphrey is prepared to say the *Nautilus* experiments represented a step forward, insofar as they prove that high-powered people and bodies are now taking the psychic world seriously. What Dooley *doesn't* do is provide anything that looks like independent corroboration of what Bergier claims happened.

Perhaps that kind of corroboration is irrelevant. One of this book's authors (M.G.) has met people who are firmly convinced that the *Nautilus* experiment took place—or something like it; what matters more is that the story tapped a burgeoning awareness in the "new" submarines as well as the emergent 1960s' popular interest in parapsychology, one aspect of which dwelt not upon whether ESP existed or didn't, but upon its usage and abusage in world warfare. The *Nautilus* story is therefore an important landmark in an evolving, rumor-based literature of cryptocratical powers waging psi wars that threaten to make nuclear holocaust a tolerable proposition.

The moves toward East-West detente of the late 1980s and early 1990s have not entirely quieted the putative threat. It is interesting that new books on psychotronic weapons have not solved the problem of how to provide independent corroboration of the alarming developments their authors chronicle, but then they do not try too hard to do so. Psi war is a matter of belief or disbelief rather than of proof or disproof. As always, we are reminded that we simply cannot be sure *what* those devious characters are up to. A previously unpublished manuscript that forms a chapter in John White's *Psychic Warfare—Fact or Fiction?* (Aquarian Press, 1988) assures us in lurid first-person terms of what few would have deemed possible back in 1963: the *Thresher* was destroyed by long-distance Soviet psychic transmissions and Nikita Khrushchev was delighted.

We have seen the submarine translated from ultimate aggressor to victim; from doom of ships to doomed ship. In this chapter it has been a ghost boat, a focus of tragic premonitions, a *Mary Celeste* without the canary. We have also seen that submarine stories are . . . well, not as strong evidence for the paranormal as the tellers usually portray them to be, yet as *legends*—stories which express, however distantly, certain items of belief or perhaps attitudes towards submarines (or ships, or the sea)—they have a validity as well as an entertainment value.

Now prepare to meet the finest submarine story (or legend) of them all. Up periscope for the haunted U-boat 65!

References

Thresher

John Bentley, *The* Thresher *Disaster* (Doubleday, 1974). Used for *Thresher*'s career, as well as for story of George Kiesecker's premonition of danger (pp. 7–8).

Raymond Lamont Brown, *Phantoms, Legends, Customs and Superstitions of the Sea* (Patrick Stephens, 1972), pp. 43–45. For the story of the Schultz family's supposed sighting of the "phantom" *Thresher*.

British newspaper coverage, especially *The Times,* April 11–19, 1963; *Daily Express,* April 13 and 17, 1963; *Daily Mirror,* April 11–13, 1963.

Detroit Free Press, July 4, 1970. An account of *Thresher*'s life ring in Lake Superior.

Fate, September 1963, p. 22, a brief account of George Kiesecker's premonition and p. 75, a brief account of Philip Jenkins's painting of *Thresher*.

Robert Gannon, "What Really Happened to the *Thresher*," *Reader's Digest* (May 1964): 111–16. Condensed from *Popular Science Monthly,* February 1964.

Norman Polmar, *Death of the* Thresher (Chilton, 1964). Used for additional testimony regarding deficiencies on board *Thresher* (pp. 90–102).

John White, *Psychic Warfare: Fact or Fiction?* (Aquarian Press, 1989). The *Thresher* destroyed by psychism.

Thetis

British press reports in *News of the World,* June 4, 1939, and *Sunday Pictorial,* June 4, 1939.

Psychic News, no. 369 (June 17, 1939): 1: "*Thetis* Victim's Spirit Message" and no. 370 (June 24, 1939): 1: "Another *Thetis* Victim Returns."

C. E. T. Warren and James Benson, *"The Admiralty regrets. . . .": The Story of Her Majesty's Submarine* Thetis *and* Thunderbolt (London: George Harrap, 1958).

U-31

Robert De La Croix, *Mysteries of the Sea* (John Day, 1956).

Edwyn Gray, *The Killing Time: The German U-boats 1914-1918* (Charles Scribner's Sons, 1972).

———, *Submarine Warriors* (Bantam, 1990).

Lowell Thomas, *Raiders of the Deep* (Doubleday, 1929).

Nautilus Telepathy Tests

Anne Dooley, "Nuclear Submarine in Amazing Trans-Ocean Telepathic Test," *Psychic News* 1611 (April 20, 1963): 1, 6.

Louis Paulwels and Jacques Bergier, *The Dawn of Magic* (1963). Later retitled in Britain *The Morning of the Magicians* (1963, Mayflower paperback, 1971).

4

Hexed, Hoodoo-ed, Haunted: The Enduring Legend of UB-65

> UB-65 was never a "happy" ship, though we were always fortunate in our officers. There was something in the atmosphere on board which made one uneasy. Perhaps, knowing her evil history, we imagined things, but I am convinced myself that she was haunted.

Such was the opinion of a petty officer who served on the German submarine UB-65 from her first commission to her penultimate cruise. There is considerable mystification attached to the end of UB-65; so too is there mystery surrounding practically every event leading up to it.

Take that petty officer to begin with. Precisely who was he, apart from a petty officer soi-disant? Perhaps our introductory sentence should have read: such was the opinion that *allegedly* came from a petty officer who *allegedly* served on UB-65 from her first commission to her penultimate cruise. That might have erred on the side of caution. It would certainly have compromised the beginning of what is, by any reckoning, a wonderful story and a model maritime ghost saga. So we will content ourselves by saying that we would have liked to have given the full name of the petty officer, but cannot, and to have confirmed that we have corroborated the claim that he was ideally situated to vote on whether or not the UB-65 is a tale of hoodoo and haunting rather than a hoax—but we have not been able to.

Hector Charles Bywater was inclined to accept the petty officer at face value, however. In reviewing "the curious case of the 'hoodoo' submarine which is still mentioned with bated breath by veterans of the German U-boat corps" Bywater was moved to declare that it "must . . . go on record as one of the best documented ghost stories of the sea." And who was Hector Charles Bywater? Beyond saying that during the 1920s and early 1930s he was a naval journalist and author widely, even internationally acknowledged as an expert on warships and the strategies relating to them—or that his name must figure largely as we attempt to trace what he calls the "curious history" of UB-65 and its credentials as "one of the best documented ghost stories of the sea"—we will place him on standby. Right away, however, we notice that Bywater's version of events relied heavily on that of another person.

That person, to use Bywater's own phrase, was "the distinguished psychologist Professor Dr. Hecht." It is in Hecht's testimony, a "pamphlet he published after the war" that the unnamed petty officer is extensively quoted. By implication the psychologist's report bears the hallmarks of an officially sanctioned investigation; indeed, one writer (not Bywater) asserts that it was undertaken at a direct request from the German Naval High Command. We are told that Hecht managed to trace and interview some of the latterly reassigned crewmen of UB-65 and that he examined all her extant logs. His conclusion, as paraphrased by Bywater, was that he could discover no rational explanation for what had happened and that "while as a scientist he deprecates the suggestion of supernatural agency, he fails to put forward an alternative theory." Forgetting the "best documented" claim for the present, it can be said that if only a quarter of what we learn from Hecht via Bywater survives scrutiny, the case of UB-65 represents a scarcely equalled maritime ghost story. In that overworked but evocative modern phrase, it is a classic.

The story is a classic in most vernacular senses because it has been retold down successive decades with no diminution of its appeal. Bywater is the person who is to be thanked for that. We hope to prove that the popularization of the haunted UB-65 dates from 1932, when he gave it pride of place among three episodes illustrating "The Queer Side of Things"—that is, three highly unusual incidents in the U-boat offensive—which form the second chapter of his book *Their Secret Purposes.* None of the later versions we have examined adds anything other than minor details to Bywater's original; conversely, all show a mighty debt to it.

For example, Michael and Mollie Hardwick (who cite Bywater as their authority) depart mainly in the heavy use of reconstructed or imagined dialogue; Peter King's 1974 Fate article throws in some supportive historical material on the U-boat war and fills in several fore- or surnames left blank in Bywater: the psychologist is Prof. Max Hecht, an unnamed submarine commodore becomes Michelson, etc. Around the same period Raymond Lamont Brown gave UB-65 two airings in his *Phantoms of the Sea* (1972) and "U-boat 65: Forever Haunted" for *Fate* of June 1977;

we will look at certain additions which seem peculiar to Brown in due course.

So, now that the time has come to retell the story yet again, we do not feel ashamed to confess that what we offer is a fairly solid recapitulation of Bywater. *Our* additions take the form of extraneous historical material meant to place what he wrote in a broader perspective, but also a few extrapolations from the writers just mentioned plus a minimum of comment that is entirely our own responsibility.

UB-65's keel was laid, says Bywater, in summer 1916. As a practical concept submarine boats were only two years old and as far as the German Naval Command's thinking went they had altered beyond all recognition.

The *Unterseebooten* had been conceived originally as a purely defensive force. But when the widely anticipated British naval assault on the German Bight failed to materialize, there seemed an opportunity to utilize the U-boats in a less passive manner. They were detailed to offset what German strategists viewed as an embarrassing and constricting numerical imbalance in warships; they were to attack and whittle down the Grand (British) Fleet's capital ships, which had initiated a dangerous blockade of the North Sea. Even then little was expected of them and at first they appeared to be achieving no more than a little. The opening months of World War I (August to December 1914) saw the U-boats score negligible success. It was undeniable that U-9 and U-21 managed to sink four British cruisers, but they were elderly patrol units, not front-line "Dreadnoughts"; it was impressively true that in November the U-18 had actually penetrated the Grand Fleet's anchorage at Scapa Flow, but only to find that the Grand Fleet wasn't there. In exchange, if "exchange" it could be called, no fewer than five U-boats had been lost.

Although it was not immediately appreciated, however, the U-boats had scored a valuable *psychological* success, one unrelated to the material tonnage they had managed to sink. British naval commanders (and soon after their German counterparts) recognized that the U-boats constituted a definite menace, not least of all in their hitherto underestimated seaworthiness and durability. This was tacitly acknowledged when Earl Jellicoe, the Grand Fleet's commander in chief, began a series of temporary withdrawals from Scapa Flow, hence moving his ships further from the North Sea venues targeted as the most likely theaters of a decisive naval action. The German Naval Command was encouraged to use its submarines more aggressively. One result of this and taken in response to Britain's attempts to strangle German trade by maritime blockade was the declaration of unrestricted U-boat warfare (February 1915) wherein neutral vessels not positively identified as such were sunk without prior warning. As everyone knows and as we repeat in a later chapter, one famous U-boat casualty was the *Lusitania* (May 7, 1915), whose loss brought about an event that Germany had foreseen and tried to avoid: the entry of the United States into the war on the Allied side.

UB-65 came into being at a critical moment. By late 1916 Germany was fully committed to a major submarine offensive; it seemed the fastest way to win the war. Britain reacted by creating an antisubmarine division of its naval staff, introducing measures such as improved mines, depth charges, and other shipboard armaments, patrol vessels and planes and "hunters" (including submarines) that at least made U-boat commanders more cautious. And by the period February to April 1917, with the German population's morale tested by rationing and a harsh winter, Admiral Scheer was prepared to admit that the U-boats represented the last real hope of victory. The order was given for "energetic action." Submariners' leave was curtailed and fourteen-day cruises planned, during which each boat was to fire its full supply of torpedoes. U-boats were to take up station near the English coast where shipping routes converged and remain there even in bad weather. All armed or suspect ships were to be attacked while the submarine was submerged; there were to be no boarding parties and victims were to be sunk with minimum expenditure of time, preferably with just a single torpedo per ship. A total of 105 *Frontboote,* rising to 120 by April, were to implement this policy within a six-month time schedule, that is, before American intervention in the war might make itself felt with uncomfortable clarity.

The strategy seemed to work. April 1917 found the number of merchant vessels sunk by U-boats climbing to a record 413, a sizeable fraction of the February to April total of 977 or 1,945,243 tons. There was evidence that neutrals had begun to shun British ports. Even conceding that ten U-boats had been lost over the same period, the German command worked out that the loss ratio was acceptable. Even Jellicoe felt that if merchant losses continued at that rate, Germany would be triumphant. The only sober note from the German point of view was that on April 6, 1917, the United States had declared war.

The U-boats did not win the war for Germany. The year 1918, when our story is set, marked their decline as a deciding factor. Partly this was due to the circumstance that despite a flat-out construction program of awesome dimensions there were too few U-boats to carry out the destructive strategies on which German success depended; more obviously, the arrival of some two million American troops on the European battle front negated anything that submarines could have hoped to achieve. Convoying alone cast a pall on the U-boats' prospects, with the new "homed" mines biting into their numbers and the floodlit Dover Barrage (introduced in 1918) restricting their access to formerly happy hunting grounds. By late 1917 it was evident that the U-boats were failing: the number of "kills" declined while losses rose fourfold per kill by the period of August to December 1917. The process of defeat was irreversible.

Thus we can say that UB-65's brief career coincided with the climax and collapse of the German submarine offensive. Bywater specifies that she was one of twenty-four "medium" U-boats principally designed to operate from the Flanders coast and he gives her displacement as 510 tons, her surface speed as 13 knots and her complement as three officers with thirty-one enlisted men. From other sources we can add that UB-65 was armed with ten 19.7-inch torpedoes and a 105mm gun, while her commander on four logged tours of duty was named Schelle. The last data, by the way, cannot be reconciled with Bywater's information that UB-65 entered active service on January 1, 1918 (by which time she had already accounted for three of the nine vessels she was destined to sink before her own demise), nor with his informant's statement that she had at least two captains. But, as we averred earlier, it is in the main Bywater's record of events we will pursue.

We will commence by going back to those early days when UB-65 was still an embryonic form on the blocks. How many accidents occur during the construction of a ship, we wonder? How many injuries or even deaths befall workmen as winches slip or supports buckle unexpectedly? The same thought occurred to us when we were compiling our chapter on the *Thresher*; there we found ourselves speculating that if a researcher was to look back into the early history of *any* vessel that latterly came to acquire a "hoodooed" reputation there might be anecdotes of dockyard accidents and/or mishaps during sea trials—things insignificant in themselves, yet enough to convince hindsightedly wise individuals that the ship in question was doomed and dangerous from the very start. The UB-65 arguably conforms with this pattern.

We are told that only a week after work had begun on her a heavy girder fell, killing one laborer outright and mortally injuring another. We are told that not long before she was completed three men were fatally overcome by fumes in the engine room, that on her trial trip a man was lost overboard in a gale, and that during diving tests UB-65 developed a leak in one tank and only managed to surface after a difficult twelve hours, her atmosphere charged with deleterious fumes and half the men on board asphyxiated. If true, these episodes hardly inspired confidence about UB-65's future, perhaps.

But they came, says Bywater, as a minor prelude to what overtook her when she returned from her maiden cruise: during the loading of her torpedoes an unexplained detonation of a warhead killed five people, among them the boat's second officer. This tragic casualty, whom

King's account names as F. Richter, plays a very important part in the story of the Haunted Submarine, since it was his ghost that allegedly haunted it.

Some weeks later, while UB-65 was still in port undergoing extensive repairs, a panic-seized seaman alerted the Oberleutnant that he had just seen the second officer—"the dead officer . . . !"—walk up the gangplank and board the ship. Accusing him of drunkenness was a somewhat perfunctory gesture on the part of the Oberleutnant and the man denied it just as perfunctorily; besides, he added, one Petersen had also witnessed the same thing.

Petersen was soon discovered up on deck, huddled in the lee of the conning tower and pallid with fear. Yes, he had seen the dead officer come on board and walk toward the bows, where he stood with arms folded. Petersen had ducked behind the tower and when he looked out again the figure had vanished.

The two men were sober. A hoax was mooted but ruled out. However the incident might or might not have been explained, it had a bad effect on the morale of the crew, who (in Bywater's words) "were now convinced that the submarine and all on board her were doomed." Petersen's faith in that interpretation was underlined by the fact that two days before UB-65's next cruise he deserted. Evidently the ghostly officer did not.

UB-65 left Heligoland on New Year's Day 1918 (Bywater's dating) and made an uneventful run to Zeebrugge, where she stayed ten days before cruising into the English Channel.

The weather on the evening of January 21 was dirty; a rough sea was breaking over the conning tower as the starboard lookout (whom King names as Erik Molle) surveyed the fifteen miles of water that lay between them and the gaunt peninsula of Portland Bill that juts from the southern English coastline. This, together with the fact that all hatches save that of the tower were battened down, made incomprehensible to him the sight of a figure, "apparently an officer," on the plunging deck. Even as he started to hail the unknown man—to warn him of his danger—the figure turned and gazed up at the bridge, "clearly revealing, even in the twilight that was fast merging into darkness, the features of the second officer, whose mutilated remains lay in the naval cemetery at Wilhelmshaven."

Bywater may have been a fairly conservatively minded journalist for the most part, but like all good writers he had an eye for the telling touch that conforms with the mood and type of a story and communicates directly with his audience. He had by this time written at least one "factious" or "fiction couched as non-fiction" novel—*The Great Pacific War*—and here again he delights in a lurid but well-controlled piece of decorative prose. The incident continues with the lookout staggering back to collide with the captain, who curses him roundly but then sees the apparition for himself. Others who arrive on the bridge seconds afterward are too late: the deck is now deserted.

The air of gloom and doom on board UB-65 deepened, but the cruise was successful; two steamers were sunk and two others hit by gunfire, one of these apparently mortally. Yet, curiously enough, the captain made no attempt to follow up and finish her despite the fact that she appeared to be lowering her lifeboats. Statements of crew members as collected by Hecht suggest this was not a case of unusual clemency or overconfidence in a U-boat commander, but of supreme caution; it may have been that he suspected the stricken vessel was a Q-ship, one of the small, apparently defenseless steamers that actually bore concealed guns with which to handle any submarine decoyed into attacking them. But the inference was that he, too, had come to believe that his boat was ill-fated and in passing up the opportunity he was simply trying to avert the disaster that everyone deemed inevitable.

UB-65 returned unscathed to Bruges. She was lying safe in a bomb-proof shelter during February while an air raid raged all around, but her commanding officer was not as fortunate. Returning from a visit to a casino, he was decapitated by a shell or flying splinter and his body was brought on board the submarine he had commanded. That same night the ghost of the second officer was purportedly seen again.

By this time the German naval authorities had picked up the strange allegations concerning UB-65. She was visited by no less a personage than the submarine commodore, who heard the crew's nervous revelations. Officially, their numerous requests for redraftings were turned down, but unofficially most (though not all) had been reassigned under various pretexts before UB-65's next cruise came round. And, according to Hecht, during her month-long sojourn at Bruges a Lutheran pastor conducted an exorcism on board the haunted submarine. This only served to unsettle the new crewmen and to aggravate the unease of such as remained of the original complement.

Nevertheless, UB-65 entered a relatively happy phase of her existence. The next two cruises were successful in terms of ships sunk; from May 1918 she had a new captain in Lt. Commander Schelle, who let it be known he would have no tolerance for talk of ghosts and the like. But the hoodoo-haunting, if there was one, had not been driven out by the pastor's prayers or by the new captain's skepticism.

Bywater allows the rest of the story to be told by the anonymous petty officer whose verdict on UB-65—"never a 'happy' ship . . . I am convinced that she was haunted"—introduced our chapter. This extended opinion, which takes up three pages in *Their Secret Purposes* and which appears in considerably doctored form in Brown's 1972 version, adds a vivid tone to a tale already colorful and on the strength of it alone we might feel that Bywater was quite justified in calling it "one of the best documented ghost stories of the sea." Even if we accept its documentary value—for any first person account is calculated to enhance a ghost story's credibility in a way that a third-person recitation of details cannot—we ought to bear in mind that the litany of weird events was merely *one* person's version of what happened. His interpretations and emphases may have distorted the facts of the case; there is no guarantee that other crew members would have agreed with them.

Yet we can anticipate from Bywater that UB-65 was regarded as a submarine with an evil history and a propensity to become worse. It may be that such a reputation was sufficient by itself to generate other "phenomena," or, as the petty officer said, to make her crew "imagine things." Later on we will examine the possible relevance of the great stress under which all German submarines labored at this stage of the war: the declining tonnage of kills against the rising casualties among U-boats, the evidence of mental or spiritual deterioration among the men who sailed them and the evolution of a kind of "U-boat psychosis." In the light of these ideas, a "hoodoo submarine" may not only have represented an extension of the psychosis, but may have acted as a focus or outlet for it.

The unnamed petty officer claimed to have seen the apparitional officer several times. "He was not one of us," he affirmed. "I only caught a glimpse of him, but a shipmate who was nearer swore that he recognized our former second officer, who had been killed long before by a torpedo explosion." The petty officer saw the figure on deck at sea; he saw it walking below decks, always going into the forward torpedo room but never emerging from it. "Several of the bluejackets saw the ghost quite often, but others were unable to see it, even when it was pointed out to them standing only a few feet away." Seekers after a purely psychological explanation of UB-65 will find that last remark highly significant. Lt. Cmdr. Schelle evidently was among the nonpercipients, but the petty officer doubted his sincerity. Although he refused to admit the existence of anything supernatural, Schelle seemed agitated when others on the foredeck claimed to see it; he called them nervous fools, but was overheard to say that his ship was "haunted by devils."

May 1918. Now part of II Flotilla, UB-65 cruised the English Channel and Spanish coast on what the petty officer called "the worst trip of all." It was only a few days old when the torpedo gunner Eberhard went berserk, screaming that the ghost was after him. He was tied up until a dose of morphia appeared to have calmed him enough to allow him on deck. Eberhard promptly jumped into the sea and never came up. Off Ushant the U-boat hit bad weather; the chief engineer fractured his right leg in a fall. Next they chased a tramp steamer and lost it. They also lost Richard Meyer as a big sea broke over the gun he was trying to load. Then a very close brush with disaster: diving hurriedly to escape an enemy patrol, UB-65 put her bows down too sharply and had to make a hurried return to the surface. Only some fortuitous mist prevented the patrol from seeing her a paltry half-kilometer away.

The men were like sleepwalkers, said the petty officer; they started at sudden noises and performed their duties mechanically. "We all knew these successive misfortunes were not mere accidents," he went on. The unspoken question was, "Who is to go next?" During the cruise the ghost was reported to have been seen three times.

Even the achievement of slipping unscathed through the Dover Strait, known among German submariners by now as a U-boat graveyard, brought little elation. The crew mentally rehearsed the names of the boats that had been lost recently: UB-33 (April 11—mined in the Dover barrage), their "chummy ship" UB-55 (April 22—same cause and location), UC-79 (March—cause unknown, though the petty officer may have blamed the Dover defenses yet again). It was pessimistically thought that they had run the gauntlet successfully only to succumb on the return passage. As if to confirm that the war wasn't over, UB-65 was detected and subjected to depth charging for more than an hour, while coxswain Lohmann fell and fractured three ribs, sustaining internal injuries from which he died a week later. And even when the ship defied all despondent predictions by returning safe to Zeebrugge and thence Bruges, the witness concludes, "so far from being relieved at our escape, most of us felt that it was merely prolonging the agony."

Luckily for him—and we can easily understand why he felt it was lucky—the petty officer went down with rheumatism and consequently he missed UB-65's next cruise. The day before she sailed he was visited by a messmate named Wernicke, who came to bid him farewell in a sense more permanent than the word normally conveys. Both men believed Wernicke would not come back from the trip; he went as far as asking the petty officer to take care of some personal effects and to send them to his wife when "the news comes in."

UB-65 left Heligoland on July 2, 1918. The "news" that Wernicke had euphemized came in on July 31, when the submarine was officially posted as missing, presumed lost.

Lost she certainly, irrefutably was, but under what circumstances? "It is true that a mystery envelops the end of UB-65," Bywater writes, and no student of the 1914–18 U-boat war is likely to disagree with him. Typically enough, while it has no room for ghosts or hoodoos, R. M. Grant's monograph, *U-Boat Intelligence* (1968), unflinchingly refers to the incident as "one of the most baffling mysteries" of the conflict. And to that book we now turn for a full explication of the last days of the Haunted Submarine.

II Flotilla records indicate that on July 4, 1918, UB-65 was in the North Sea (51°7′N, 9°42′W) where the British submarine G-6 fired three torpedoes at her and missed with each. It next appears that UB-65 was sighted six days later by the American submarine AL-2 under Lt. Forster, which at 6:30 p.m. was patrolling off Fastnet. She was not identified immediately; what Forster saw on the surface some three miles off resembled to his thinking a buoy. We can dismiss Raymond Lamont Brown's allegation (1972) that then or shortly afterwards the lieutenant made out the lettering "UB-65" on her hull, since Grant makes no mention of this event. In fact, it is evident that at no time did Forster discern the enemy craft's hull plainly or unambiguously. This makes it easier to discard Brown's second offering: that the same witness's periscope revealed the figure of a man on UB-65's bows, his arms folded in majestic calm even as the doomed submarine went down forever.

AL-2 spent the next five minutes maneuvering closer to the half-submerged object; some writers aver that she was lining up a torpedo shot at it. Before any such thing could take place the American sub was shaken by a violent explosion. Some eighty yards away a geyser of water flew up and as it fell back Forster saw six feet of enemy periscope about a hundred feet to the rear of the turbulence. Putting AL-2 into a crash dive, he attempted to ram the suspected U-boat and heard the noise of high-speed propellors churning close by, followed a few minutes later by the sound of two submarines communicating by the C-tube: one near at hand and running fast, the other moving slowly. Within the next twenty minutes the faster submarine was silent, but the second continued to signal. On his return to Bantry Bay Forster learned that the two U-boats had been signaling for an hour before AL-2 came on the scene and that one of them had done so (presumably while sinking) at midnight on July 10.

Grant pronounces it "practically certain" that UB-65 sank at this time. He is less definite about other aspects of Forster's testimony. Conceding that UB-65 was one of the submarines, what was the other? Grant deduces that the only ones likely to have been in the area in question were the U-60 (whose log, however, mentions only routine matters) or, less likely, the UB-108, which had left Flanders for the western English Channel approaches on July 2. This is very unlikely, since despite

King's assertion that UB-108 was present, she is believed to have been sunk as early as July 4. The lieutenant of AL-2 was positively convinced that *two* U-boats were involved and his testimony is hard to shake; nonetheless, Grant concludes that despite all appearances to the contrary there was only one—the hoodoo-afflicted UB-65.

Deciding that UB-65 was blown up on July 10, 1918, is one thing; explaining how it came about is another. Either she was destroyed by another submarine or, bizarre as it may sound, she destroyed herself. The former scenario necessarily revives the "second U-boat" mystery. As the kill was never claimed by any Allied submarine, it follows that the hypothetical culprit belonged to Germany—in other words, that UB-65 fell prey to one of her own side. Such "cannibalism" was recognized as an unpleasant hazard of the undersea war and at least one U-boat (U-7) is known to have become a victim of it when in January 1915 she failed to respond to U-22's recognition signals. But then again the German naval command would almost certainly have admitted the embarrassing fact eventually, if fact it was; instead, they appeared to have been as befogged for an answer about the loss of UB-65 as their Allied counterparts. On balance, it seems more credible that UB-65 destroyed herself in some unpredicted fashion.

Assigning a feasible cause to that event presents a moderately circumscribed choice of proposals, all centering upon some form of torpedo malfunction. Bywater approved of Hecht's idea that the submarine's torpedo tube, unbeknown to anyone on board, had become torn or distorted so that when UB-65 attempted a shot, presumably at AL-2, the torpedo fouled an obstruction, detonating not only itself but others in that tube. Gray's proposition, which seems to fit the observation of Forster quite well, was that the magnetic pistol in a torpedo snout had gone off prematurely, exploding the charge closer to the submarine than intended and before she could make an evasive run to the surface. As we just heard, she got no closer to that goal than six feet of periscope.

Either or neither theory may be right; of more interest to us here is the obvious manner in which UB-65's enigmatic end appears to conform with her hexed and haunted past record. It takes little literary skill or effort to make that event sound like the culmination of a curse, like an inevitable, supernaturally governed finale for a ship doomed before she had cleared the dockyards.

Placing the loss of UB-65 into the greater context of the chronicles of the U-boat war does not spoil its mystery, let alone solve it. On the other hand, it might make that incident seem somewhat less remarkable and decidedly "unsupernatural." Briefly, then, across the full duration of that war (August 1914 to November 1918) Germany lost a total of

178 U-boats; compare this, if you like, with 1,305 merchant vessels destroyed by them or the mines they laid. The causes by which 37 of the U-boats were lost remain conjectural or totally unknown. For the January-to-December 1918 period during which UB-65 disappeared a total of 69 U-boats went missing and of these 14 (or 18.8 percent) were listed as "unknowns." A closer look at this record shows that the German authorities were inclined to attribute two of those casualties to putative mines of the Northern Barrage (U-92, U-102) and one apiece to those of the Dover Barrage (UC-50) and Zeebrugge (UB-57), but the others—UBs 12, 17, 63, 66, 70 and 113, UCs 77 and 79, and U-93—were beyond their powers of guesstimation.

UB-65 was not even put down as a "pure unknown"; it was registered as an accidental loss, one of 19 that occurred throughout the war. This could mean that, strictly speaking and as mysteries go, UB-65 is less of a breath-snatching conundrum than many other German submarines that went out and didn't come back. But, of course, *they* were not endowed with the reputation of being jinxed; none of them carried a Jonah-like apparition of a former officer. The ambiguous end of UB-65 (which, as we just conceded, *was* a genuine piece of ambiguity, though perhaps not more so than could be found in a baker's dozen of other cases from the last year of the war) came as a gift to writers intent upon ending a good ghostly tale on a shuddersome upbeat. None of them chose to turn it down.

But, greater or lesser in character, the mystery of UB-65 remains. Even ignoring the end of the story—tagging it ambiguous without being paranormal, that is—can we make anything of what leads up to it? Was she plagued by an unaccountable, uncoincidental run of bad luck? Was she haunted by the spirit of a former officer? Or, if these questions be too difficult to answer, how might the belief in both or either phenomenon have arisen?

The solution to that may be deeply rooted in the mental and spiritual conditions that prevailed among Germany's navy and her dock towns toward the end of the war. Edwyn Gray writes in *The Killing Time* that by 1917—year of the mutinies at Wilhelmshaven and Kiel—the U-boat men were experiencing the strain induced by losses, near-misses and the need for unrelenting vigilance. He quotes Baron von Spiegel as recalling that the submariners

> were likely to break down with nerve strain of some kind or other and were constantly being sent away to recuperate. The ordeal of life aboard the U-boats, with the constant stress of peril and terror, was too much for human flesh to bear for long stretches. Some men went mad. Others, after periods of rest and medication, came around and

were, or perhaps were not, fit for undersea service again. All felt the grinding pressure.

Von Spiegel, let it be said, may not be the perfect witness; it was he who created the legend of the U-boat crewed by corpses with which we tried to entertain you in chapter 3. Yet it seems overly skeptical to reject his testimony on this subject, especially when other contemporary writers seem to confirm it. Bywater mentions "obvious signs of disintegration among German crews" during the penultimate stages of the war, "and still more among the dockyard staff."

We can believe in a depressing atmosphere characterized by high levels of anxiety, a dearth of reliable information (arguably worse among the dockyard workers and their families than among the personnel actually on board the submarines) and, as always, a proliferation of rumor and wild, strange tales to take the place of that information. Further, we might posit that under these conditions people were more than normally prone to accept ideas that in ordinary times they would have rejected. Add to this the traditional element of sailors' superstition. All this is not to say that the uncertainties and vulnerability to suggestion made people see ghosts, but they may have been all the readier to believe that others had seen them.

However hard it may be to estimate the dimensions of this abnormal mental climate, we can believe that it existed, and that Allied propagandists exploited it. A former British intelligence officer confessed as much when he recounted how, on perceiving the state of unease over U-boat losses that possessed German dockyard towns and the resultant problems experienced in getting new recruits for the submarine service, Northcliffe's Ministry of Propaganda managed to have full details of each U-boat lost or captured published in Hamburg. The result, he claims, was "an almost total stoppage of recruiting for submarines and something approaching mutiny among the existing crews."

So far, then, we have been considering the UB-65 story a virulent expression of a "doom" or "curse" that was supposed to dog the U-boat fleet, a rumor-legend that made concrete all the terrors apprehended by the mariners themselves, by their families, by those who lived and worked near them. We have been tempted to regard it as a focus, perhaps one of such power that it actively caused men to imagine things, to misinterpret mundane instances of bad luck as a pattern of supernaturally managed evil, to see things: as a kind of "U-boat psychosis" in which the factuality of the things being reported became subordinate to their emotional value. But now we have to reorient ourselves and ask: could the UB-65 story have been a strikingly successful piece of propaganda?

As a propaganda tactic aimed at undermining the morale of the dockyarders and submariners, the UB-65 story would rate as a more outlandish exercise than the release of official figures on U-boat losses just mentioned. Its outlandishness is one of the chief arguments against labelling it as a possible propaganda extravaganza, however.

World War I saw the first fully coordinated attempt to employ propaganda as a military weapon; more than that, it was perhaps the first war in which the civilian population of the enemy was deliberately targeted. That the British, operating through a number of official departments culminating in the establishment of a Ministry of Information in March 1918, were both extremely active and successful in this field will not be denied; that some Germans should latterly attribute their nation's defeat almost solely to the pernicious undermining effects of Allied propaganda must, however, be taken in the nationalistic context that argued that Germany had not been defeated in a true military sense. The ultimate strategy of the propagandists was to work upon the opponent's perceptible weaknesses, particularly those signs of unease and uncertainty that manifested as he tired, for as Sidney Rogerson observed from his experiences as a WWI intelligence man, "propaganda against the enemy is only deadly when he is tiring and beginning to doubt the rightness of his cause or the invincibility of his arms." Theoretically, any story that contributed to the doubt and anxiety of the opponent was a legitimate tool.

But the main *practical* tool of propaganda is factuality. As surprising as it might appear to outsiders, propaganda always tries to be factual; to be effective it must be based on a measure of demonstrable truth, not upon imaginative fabrication or obvious invention. The infamous "Kadaver Works" rumor singled out by Rogerson as an example of poor propaganda failed because it was too easily discredited; indeed, it was the kind of story that threatened to boomerang and embarrass its promoters.

The Kadaver Conversion Works story of 1917 encouraged people to believe that the Germans maintained factories—*secret* factories, of course—where human corpses were converted into fats for explosives (or, in another version, soap). It seems to have originated in Belgium and, to be strictly accurate, was taken up by the British Ministry of Information with no great enthusiasm, not least of all because they felt it rested upon very flimsy evidence. In fairness again, there were several stories of far more dubious character that significant numbers of people were prepared to believe: Arthur Machen's Bowmen of Mons come to mind at once, with the troops so speedily whisked from Russia that the snow on their boots barely had time to melt. That these magnificent yarns passed muster even for a moment tends to reinforce what we said earlier about war conditions reducing the credulity barrier. Finally, we have to admit that the Kadaver Works tale was not recognized for what it was until it had been disseminated in pamphlet form through Portugal, Spain, Sweden, and Holland (not to mention Britain and the English-speaking world) and that it was not officially repudiated until 1925.

Does the creation of "A Corpse-Conversion Factory" (London, 1917) make it seem less improbable that the secret agents of propaganda would not hold back on a haunted U-boat? Perhaps so, but the reservations expressed by Ministry of Information leaders as much as the story's overall failure suggest that rumors that tested the target population's sense of the credible were not popular. Fundamentally, British propaganda's output was designed to arouse outrage against German militarists and it presented material based upon verifiable and topical fact towards that aim. (Naturally, the interpretation and/or relation of the facts in question were given a specifically British slant, in which contradictory German versions of the same events were ridiculed or suppressed. Propaganda may pose as objective reportage, but seldom presents the opposition's viewpoint accurately.) "Prussian" atrocities against the Belgians, or Turkish atrocities against the Armenians and the execution of Edith Cavell, all based to some degree upon actual events that could be proven to have been so: these were the typical themes of British propaganda during World War I. The Kadaver Works story seems to have been a momentary aberration.

Few if any British propagandists would have had time for a haunted U-boat. As a story, it lacked any "atrocity" element; it did not present a favorable view of Britain by juxtaposition of any view of Germany. It lacked bloated Prussian militarists; the crew of UB-65 sound like quite unexceptional mortals. The story patently lacked all the things it needed to persuade audiences in neutral countries—perhaps the main target of much Allied propaganda—that the Germans were the bad guys in this war. As a weapon for attacking audiences in Germany, civilians as well as service people, it lacked a good deal more. It lacked credibility.

UB-65 was much too improbable. It was too easily laughed out of court. It was more fanciful than the corpse-processing factory by far. A related argument against it as a potential propaganda story is that, given the unwritten law that the more improbable your propaganda seems, the less likely it is to be taken seriously, even the cleverest rumor's effectiveness is likely to be uncertain. It is faintly possible that *some* Germans would have swallowed a hoodoo-haunted submarine, perhaps—but what would that have achieved? Even if the story exploited a pre-existing *German* rumor with a similar narrative line, would it have bred alarm and despondency? Would it have curtailed the dwindling stream of new submarine recruits as decisively as the publication of U-boat losses is said to have done? The uncertainty of the German response—bug-eyed fright, tremors of doubt, or roars of laughter—would have made the UB-65 a doubtful propaganda weapon.

But the mention of propaganda arouses the suspicion of espionage; the two go together naturally. That the Allies maintained a highly active spy network in Germany both before and (of course) during World War I, that dockyards and submarine-related sites were of major interest to it, and that the mood of dockyard towns was as subject to espionage agents' reports as actual ship construction developments or naval movements, is not to be doubted.

Our leading authority for this statement is, yet again, Hector C. Bywater, whose credentials for writing on WWI espionage will become blindingly apparent in a few pages' time. The topic was of great interest to him, providing the theme and material for at least two of his later works: *Strange Intelligence* (1931) and *Their Secret Purposes* (1932). In fact, *Their Secret Purposes* is choc-a-bloc with accounts of ingenious, often daring undercover work and examples of wartime information-gathering ploys in which, by the author's reckoning, the British excelled. It also has a tendency to make constant reference to U-boats. "In the latter part of the war," Bywater states early on, "there was nothing our Intelligence Division did not know about the ways and wiles of the U-boats."

So theoretically they would have been aware of any weird rumors that a particular U-boat labored under a supernatural curse. They would have known when despondency and anxiety made it the right time to circulate a rumor that a certain U-boat labored under a supernatural curse. And if what Bywater wrote of Allied agents' ingenuity was correct, they may have done even more than that.

Espionage, or rather sabotage, is a theory cautiously approached by the Hardwicks in their retelling of the UB-65 story. They speculate that the first appearance of the ghost, which you may recall took place soon after the death of the second officer by an exploding torpedo, and which was supposedly attested to by Petersen and another man, may have been a "faked appearance" aimed at creating an atmosphere of expectancy and hysteria—in which it certainly succeeded. The writers concede that it is hard to imagine how an Allied agent might have contrived the episode and also that the subsequent accidents like the decapitation of the commander or the washing overboard of the gun-loader could only be regarded as coincidence. "But the whole thing has a very strong smell of sabotage. Another possibility is that the 'ghost' and various disasters were the work of some Till Eulenspiegel with a grudge, or a taste for

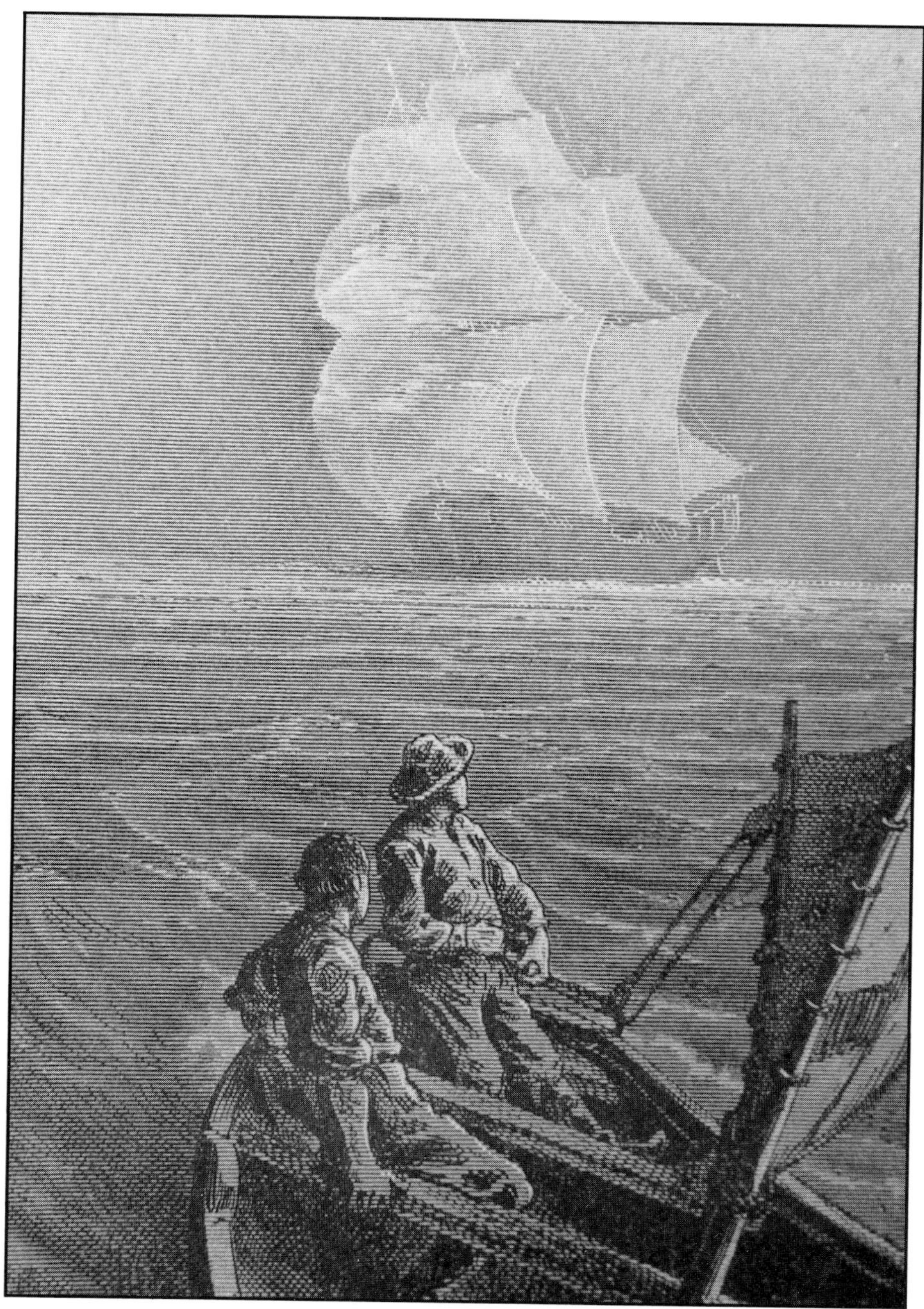

For centuries the Phantom Ship, conventionally depicted as a pale antique vessel, served as a recurring symbol of maritime mystery. (From Fletcher S. Bassett, *Legends and Superstitions of the Sea and Sailors,* 1885)

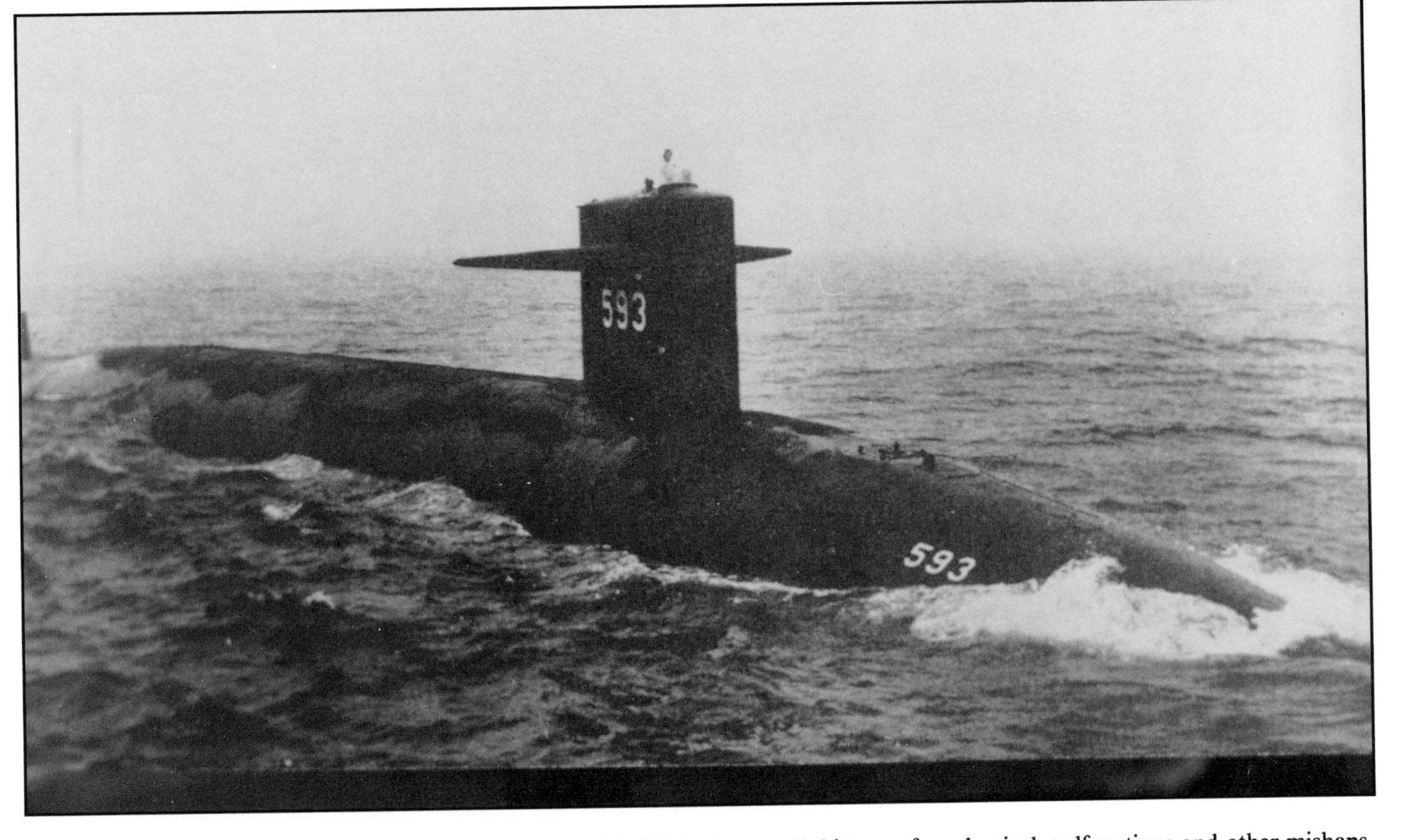

The American nuclear submarine USS *Thresher,* SSN–593. Might the vessel's history of mechanical malfunctions and other mishaps have influenced those of her crewmen who experienced "feelings of foreboding" prior to her loss? (U.S. Navy)

A deck scene aboard U–35 in 1917. This photo suggests the view experienced by horrified crewmen of UB–65, who reportedly saw their boat's deceased second officer standing, with arms folded, on the U-boat's bow. (U.S. Navy)

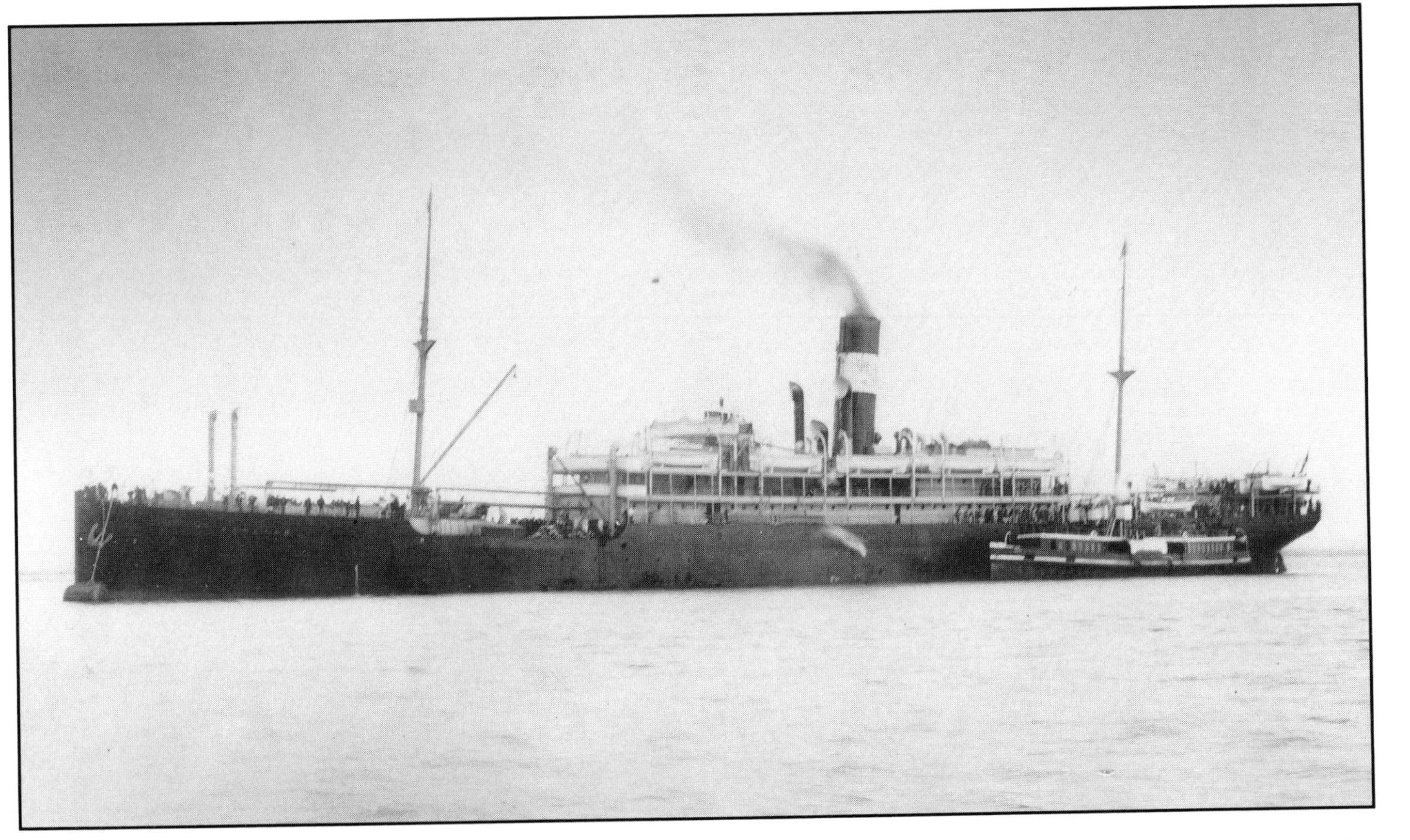

One of the very few known photographs of the Blue Anchor Line's *Waratah,* which vanished mysteriously in 1909. (The Peninsular & Oriental Steam Navigation Co.)

Edward Dorking experienced a "vision" of his loved ones while he himself was freezing to death in the icy waters over the *Titanic*'s grave. This illustration chillingly depicts the hopelessness of most of those people who went into the water with Dorking. (Logan Marshall, *The Sinking of the* Titanic *and Great Sea Disasters,* 1912)

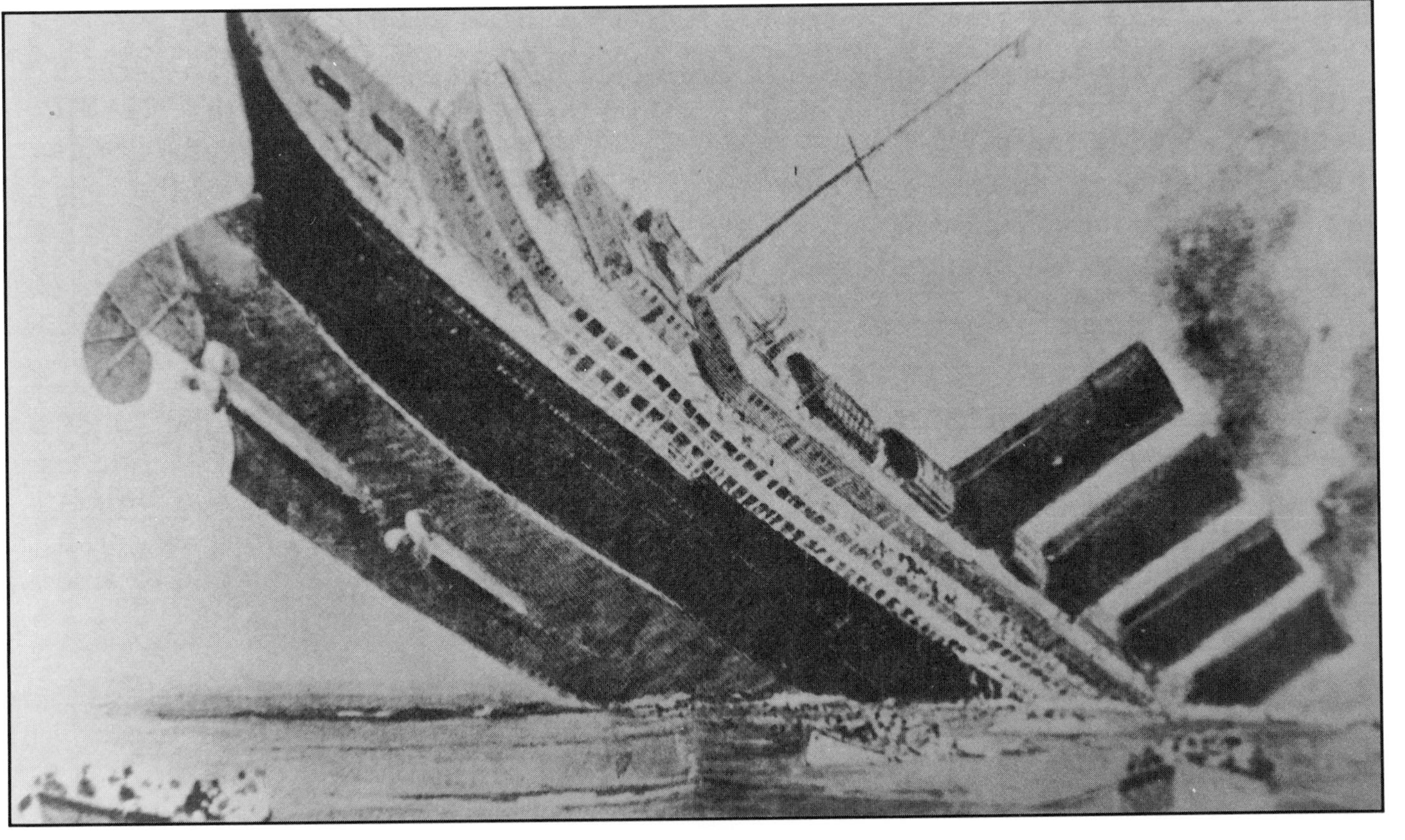

The sinking of the *Lusitania.* Does the horror of a major sea disaster send ripples through the fabric of time that can be "picked up" by people with precognition ability? (Author's collection)

The *Carmania* was one of several ships involved in attempts to aid the fire-stricken *Volturno*. This view, showing smoke billowing from the *Volturno*'s forequarters, was one of the first that rescuers had of the disaster. (Arthur Spurgeon, *The Burning of the* Volturno, 1913)

This dramatic painting by Henry Reuterdahl depicts dazed crewmen abandoning the *Aboukir* as she begins to capsize. The stricken *Hogue* (in background) lists heavily to starboard as the sea pours into her vitals. (Francis March, *History of the Great War,* 1919)

killing. If the last accident of all was a planned one, the saboteur must have blown himself up with his victims."

The concept of the haunting of UB-65 as an espionage maneuver has the makings of a great film script, but that makes it no more or less improbable. Acknowledging all the grievous difficulties facing an agent who wanted to infiltrate an enemy submarine and plant a ghost story when and where he could more easily have planted a bomb, we have to say that it is not a ludicrous suggestion. Yet it seems to us a very indirect mode of procedure. In these circumstances a bomb has a marked advantage over a faked-up ghost. If you aim to destroy a submarine and the morale of a submarine fleet along with it, a bomb is pretty decisive; either it goes off or it doesn't. The results of spreading a ghost rumor are less calculable; it *may* foment terror and thereby vitiate the enemy's efficiency, but it may do absolutely nothing. No, give us the old infernal device every time.

And why target UB-65? She was not an exceptionally brilliant star of the submarine fleet and the only grounds for singling her out could have been that she already possessed a conveniently bad reputation as a hoodoo boat *or* that the circumstance of the torpedo explosion rendered her not only ripe to feature in a disaster-horror rumor but physically laid up (in dock) so that a fabricated ghost could get on board her. Our former objection that the theory requires a rather hit-and-miss approach to espionage/sabotage work still applies.

In the long run, it may be unnecessary to credit alien agents for what the imagination of German nationals was capable of producing unaided. If UB-65 had accrued a record of mishaps before she came into service—culminating, let us say, with the accidental death of her second officer—it may have been that the timeless process through which people begin to talk of jinxes as if by instinct came into play; we gave you a taste of this in our chapter on the *Thresher* and *Thetis*. Consider now the impact of the second officer's death on the crew; it would not be unremarkable that a few men should start thinking of ghosts and it would only require a couple of them to think they had seen one for the ship to become haunted—haunted, that is, by the belief that it was haunted.

Bywater's text reads more emphatically than this. He dwells on the detail that the apparition was clearly recognized by men well qualified to recognize him through past association. We might wonder whether a climate of hysterical expectancy may have clouded the witnesses' judgment, prior events leading them to accept (a) the likelihood that some paranormal force dwelt in or upon UB-65, (b) that the tragically killed officer would be "bound" to the submarine, and (c) that when they saw (*imagined* they saw) a strange figure on board it could *only* be the spirit of that officer. No espionage agent could hope to achieve effects like that. There was no need for any "agent" beyond the minds of the men who, like the second officer though in a different sense, were bound to UB-65.

All this is a series of explanations based on the assumption that there is something that needs to be explained. That would be to treat it as a priori fact. Suppose it was fiction. Might the haunting of UB-65 be no more than a story?

As we said earlier, submarines possess the power, the charisma, to attract legends unto themselves. In chapter 3 we told you how Baron von Spiegel passed off the *Schudderoman* of the U-boat crewed with corpses on the unsuspecting Lowell Thomas and dined out on the story for many an evening. It may not hurt to throw in here the hoodoo of U-30, which began her career quite modestly in early 1915 by sinking a couple of cargo ships and then in the same year sank herself in Emden harbor with all but three of her crew trapped on board. All rescue attempts failed and after three days the faint tappings on the hull by the unlucky men were heard no more. Three months later U-30 was salvaged, the dead were buried and the submarine was refitted for sea.

In October 1916 U-30, her diesel engines broken down, was crawling homeward off the Danish coast under escort from Schwieger and the U-20: the man and the submarine collectively reviled or lauded for the sinking of the *Lusitania.* Dense fog led to both U-boats ending up on a mudbank; ironically, it was U-30 that managed to free herself while U-20 remained stuck fast. Schwieger sent out distress messages. They were received by Admiral Scheer—who, rendered desperate at the thought of the Allies capturing a luminary of the U-boat fleet, personally led four capital battleships to the rescue—but also by the British submarine J-1, which arrived in time to inflict serious damage on two of the rescuers. Scheer was severely reprimanded by none other than the kaiser for risking two of his beloved battleships in exchange for a submarine. As hoodoos go, U-30 seems to have been contagious. Schwieger might have thought so; he was subsequently reallocated to U-88, which was sunk by mines off Terschelling on September 5, 1917.

This is another story that Bywater tells and with some relish. Some aspects of it are genuine history; other parts are imaginative revisions. (For example, we have seen it published that U-88 fell victim to a Q-ship, contrary to what official records have to say.) A legend is at heart a folk version of historical fact; submarines and U-boats especially seem to act as foci for these part-real, part-fabricated accounts. At the start of our research for this chapter, we guessed that the real story of the

UB-65 might have been subject to "legendizing"; as we had it from Bywater and the writers who evidently followed his version, the text seemed too dramatic to be true. What we said of the gap between fictional ghost stories and parapsychologically verified accounts of apparitions in chapter 1 applies here. That the UB-65 story should resemble a fiction writer's output did not mean it was not factual, but we wanted to see some good historical data corroborating that even a part of the things described actually took place. Despite the abundance of names and other details in Bywater, we were not optimistic. Names can be injected to give a tale an air of credibility; some, like "the distinguished psychologist Professor Hecht," impressed us as possible "authority figures" whose purpose is to enhance that quasireliability of the fabrication still more. We suspected, but certainly had not decided beyond the point where our minds could be changed by contrary data, that the UB-65 story as most writers told it was a legend.

Here is a summary of the impressions we formed as our research developed. We felt it likely that a rumor of a haunted and hexed U-boat had circulated in German dock towns around the end of World War I and that it might have been a loud echo of some "U-boat psychosis" afflicting the submariners. We toyed with the idea that the rumor was a creation of Allied propaganda and/or of British intelligence agents, perhaps as a result of reports concerning an already-established rumor having filtered back to Allied naval intelligence. The tactic, either in utilizing this extant rumor or in manufacturing a new one from nothing, would have been to alarm and unsettle German submariners and anyone connected with U-boats in any way whatsoever. But the practicalities of the thing worried us—we could not see why UB-65 should be so targeted. Furthermore, the likelihood of British intelligence committing itself to a plan of such uncertain effect seemed poor and in any case we found no evidence of propaganda-espionage having played a part in the story. We shelved the idea.

Was there independent evidence of supernatural disturbances in official records—in the UB-65 logbooks or her "war day-book" (war diary), for instance? Perhaps a U-boat captain would not enter such data in places reserved for terse observations of courses set and followed, ships seen, ships attacked, evasive actions taken and so forth, but if the disturbances were as violent as we had been led to believe—surely so much as to constitute a dangerous breach of discipline that affected smooth performance of duty!—we felt that he was bound to have done so. That, too, would have to be checked.

Another not-too-inspired guess led us to think that Bywater had been involved to some degree in naval intelligence. At this point we had not given up the hypothetical espionage-propaganda scenario completely; we half-thought that Bywater may have been the person who came up with the idea of using a haunted submarine to torpedo the German U-boat command. But to the best of our knowledge Bywater had not written about UB-65 until 1932, fourteen years after the end of the war. What purpose would he have had in maintaining the deception at this late stage?—unless, of course, Bywater was a cryptoconspiratorial sort of man who enjoyed leaving his public believing what he knew to be a flagrant fabrication, or perhaps an author whose new book needed the spice of a true and authenticated ghost mystery. It soon became clear, however, that Bywater enjoyed exposing the "secret war" with all its dramas; that he was especially fond of revealing cases where British Intelligence signally outwitted the enemy. Had UB-65 been any kind of intelligence trick, Bywater wouldn't have missed the chance to tell the story at some convenient point in *Their Secret Purposes.*

Anyway, we kept coming back to this Hector Charles Bywater, seemingly the prime source for the story of the Haunted Submarine. Who was he? Was he reliable as a writer and naval historian? The entry in *Who Was Who 1929–40* was enough to confirm our suspicions that Bywater *was* a World War I intelligence man. But he was considerably more than that, as we found out after reading William Honan's gripping biography, *Bywater: The Man Who Invented the Pacific War* (1990).

Honan's choice of subtitle relates his belief that Bywater, a now-neglected writer whose theoretical contributions to naval strategy seem to have escaped the notice of historians, may have influenced Japanese policy leading up to World War II. That is, during the 1920s he published a number of popular studies, of which *Sea Power in the Pacific* (1920) and the fictional *The Great Pacific War* (1925) were most influential, which predicted a drastic maritime collision between Japan and the United States. It should be said that Bywater believed such a conflict would only be inevitable if the nautico-political trends analyzed in his works were not reversed; that he believed his books might help to prevent it through their stark exposition of what it would mean to both countries; and finally that not all historians will agree with Honan's assessment of Bywater's importance. The fact remains that Bywater seems to have predicted with awful accuracy a series of events that lay fifteen to twenty years in the future.

The struggle to win naval control of the Pacific would be initiated by a Japanese preemptive strike against the U.S. Navy before war had been formally declared. The place where Bywater conceived this would occur was Hawaii, at Pearl Harbor. In concert, they would attack America's crucial Pacific staging posts of Guam and the Philippines.

(Bywater went as far as mapping out the landing points on Luzon and Mindanao that they would go for and his reckonings were not far out.) The United States would hit back in a series of "island hops" that would carry the conflict to Japan's back door—again Bywater mapped out the route they would take—and would score a major sea victory against the enemy fleet en route. Eventually, Japan would be defeated. Ignoring the details that Bywater had Pearl Harbor's fate decided by conventional battleships rather than aircraft carriers and wrote "Yap Island" when he should have written "Midway," there isn't much to quarrel with in his prophecies. Honan also believes that the books containing them were carefully digested by Japanese naval strategists and that one who particularly benefitted from them was Yamamoto, the man who planned and executed the attack on Pearl Harbor. National pride, however, forced the Japanese to reject the way Bywater had ended the story.

Interesting as it is, this material doesn't bring us much closer to Bywater's role in the UB-65 mystery. Yet the early chapters of the Honan biography ought to help here. Its opening sentence portrays Bywater as "a convivial, pub-crawling English journalist, author, spy and raconteur who knew more about the navies of the world in the 1920s and 30s than a roomful of admirals"; he was in addition a man who "could hold a packed pub room in rapt attention when he told anecdotes," but also was compulsively secretive, as befitted a former undercover operative and information gatherer. So here we have him: Bywater had a nautical journalist's background, he had experience of and contacts within British intelligence, he enjoyed good stories, and knew how to tell them.

Gifted with a precocious grasp of naval tactics and their geopolitical implications—his birthday, after all, October 21 as most Britons know, was the day Nelson fought the battle of Trafalgar—Hector Bywater was a professional naval correspondent by the time he was nineteen. By that time he had also lived in Britain, the United States, Canada, West Africa, and Germany, returning to the last-named in 1907. It goes without saying that he spoke the language fluently and idiomatically—a great advantage for someone who collected data on the escalating efforts to build Germany's navy to a state of war-readiness. This was what Bywater was doing, at times under close scrutiny of the espionage-conscious German police. Indeed, says Horan, he became "one of the best spies the Royal Navy ever had."

Bywater was formally recruited into the foreign section of the British Secret Service not long after, collecting some highly detailed material under cover of writing for the Dresden *Daily Record.* At least one exciting adventure attributed to an anonymous agent in *Strange Intelligence* wherein he describes hazardous visits to a German submarine yard north of Danzig and observation of their trials, was apparently written from personal experience; the anonymous agent was Hector C. Bywater. Although he left the service in 1910 and returned to full-time journalism, the connection with espionage was not severed and by the outbreak of World War I he was back in Germany and undercover except for periods at the Naval Intelligence desk translating German publications. And despite having formed a low opinion of the espionage agent's life before the war ended, Bywater was still carrying out sporadic operations for intelligence during the 1920s.

We have established that Bywater had intimate access to confidential sources of information on German naval matters. He habitually read German papers and journals for material useful to the career of a naval correspondent, a vocation in which he excelled internationally during the interwar years. He had informants in Germany to alert him to anything he may otherwise have missed. Sandwiched in all this, we note evidence that Bywater was particularly interested in espionage stories relating to U-boats, a theme recurrent throughout *Their Secret Purposes,* which makes it the more improbable that if the UB-65 story had been a product of intelligence he would not have written it up as such.

And now, how reliable is Bywater's writing? The style in which *Their Secret Purposes* is presented suggests that the author aimed to entertain; as we observed earlier, Bywater does not despise the occasional florid touch. At the same time, the book is unpretentiously factual—authorities are cited, quoted and footnoted and statistics are fluently interwoven into the text—so that we can regard it as a kind of popularist history with a clear bias in many chapters toward anecdote, which is most evident in the portions dealing with untold espionage dramas. It is nowhere apparent that when he wrote the secret chronicles of UB-65 Hector Bywater was trying to make fiction pass in disguise as fact.

At the risk of sounding grossly repetitive: we have found no evidence to suggest that the "haunted UB-65" story was known, in Britain, at least, before Hector Bywater wrote of it, which he did only as late as 1932. If Bywater put it into print before the publication of *Their Secret Purposes,* we have been unable to establish where and when. If the story exists in any version independent of Bywater (or of Hecht, which amounts to the same thing) we have been unable to trace any such version. But of course UB-65 herself was more than a story—she was a fact of history. Are there then no official documents, *German* official documents, contemporary with the events upon which Bywater wrote so fluently?

There are. The *Kriegstagbuch* (or "war diary") of UB-65 exists for the period August 18, 1917, to July 2, 1918; that is, from her entry into active service up until the last cruise from which she never returned, the data on which event are covered by a handful of manuscript notes preserved likewise. These original documents were located for us in the Bundesarchiv Militärarchiv in Freiburg, Germany, by Roland Hauser, and we subsequently learned that a copy of the same, microfilmed by American Naval Intelligence after the war and before return of the originals to Germany, was located at the Directorate of Naval Staff Duties (Foreign Documents Section) of the Ministry of Defence in London. In toto, these give a reasonably complete picture of UB-65's wartime career: her day-to-day movements, her encounters with and actions against hostile vessels, end-of-cruise summaries of kills and misses, positional charts, and even details on weather conditions and ballistics.

We have inspected these records as far as our imperfect German allowed, with closest attention to the "critical" dates suggested by Bywater. Additionally, we have consulted relevant portions in Arno Spindler's *Der Krieg zur See,* an official multivolume history that draws patently and heavily upon the manuscript sources we just mentioned. It seems fair to guess that Bywater, whose reservations about the truth of the "haunted UB-65" story are hinted at broadly in the introduction to *Their Secret Purposes,* could not have seen her *Kriegstagbuch.* Putting the matter less obliquely, anybody who had done so could not have placed much reliance in Hecht's version of that submarine's adventures; and that person would scarcely have dared to repeat it as factual history.

It may not matter too much that whereas Bywater's source allotted no less than three commanders to UB-65—the first being allegedly killed during a bombing-raid on Bruges, the second a determined skeptic and the third Lt. Schelle—*our* sources permit her one commander and one only. This was the same Kapitanleutnant Schelle who served on *all* her cruises from the first to the last. At the same time, we might overlook the fact that by the time Bywater's version had her entering active service the real UB-65 had already completed two war cruises. Discrepancies like these do not generate confidence, but they could be passed over, were it not for the fact that Bywater consistently misplaces UB-65 in locations where her log insists she was not and has her doing things her log insists she never did.

We have to confess that Bywater is not overgenerous with precise dates, but we can use what he wrote to reconstruct UB-65's movements as follows. He says that she came into active service on January 1, 1918, by which time the second officer was not only dead but had already begun to inflict his ghostly semblance on the crew, starting with Petersen and at least one other man. The apparition was allegedly seen on January 21, when the submarine was fifteen miles off Portland Bill; this was the cruise on which she sank two steamers, hit two others, and was unnerved by a putative Q-ship. On her return to Bruges, the commanding officer was decapitated by a shell splinter during an air raid. The Lutheran pastor's exorcism ceremony was held during her month-long sojourn in dock.

The next two cruises, we are told, were under a new skipper and were relatively accident- and ghost-free. Schelle took over in May, which was the month UB-65 embarked on "the worst trip of all" through the English Channel and down the Spanish coast. This was the occasion on which the crazed Eberhard leaped into the sea; the chief engineer hurt his leg off Ushant; Meyer was swept away as they chased a tramp steamer and Lohmann fractured three ribs, dying a week after the return to port. The last cruise began on July 2, 1918; as we have heard, it is thought to have terminated horribly for UB-65 on the tenth of the same month.

And now here is what the *Kriegstagbuch* has to say of the life and times of UB-65. We must start by going back a few months prior to the January 1918 debut offered by Bywater. The maiden voyage of UB-65 (October 10 to November 4, 1917) took the new submarine from Bremerhaven to the Shetlands and Hebrides and back. In military terms, it was a "blank cruise"—no ships were sunk—and one that passed almost without accident save for the one that overtook stoker Franzel, who mutilated two fingers of his right hand in the diesel he was servicing. This episode and the successful amputation of the fingers above the middle joints was duly noted in Schelle's "war diary." We do not mention these details because they tend to confirm allegations that UB-65 was jinxed by accidents; indeed, the accident was relatively trivial. The impression that Schelle's entry *does* reinforce is that any accident to a crew member would have been logged, an important point we will address presently.

More serious matters occupied the diary of the submarine's second cruise (December 6 to 29, 1917). Passing through the "U-boat graveyard" of the English Channel, she took up station in the Bristol Channel before moving into the southernmost reaches of the Irish Sea. Here, in St. George's Channel, she scored some notable successes. Two enemy ships were sunk between December 12 and 15—one of them supposedly an armed British steamer that Spindler subsequently identified as the *Arquebus*—and on December 28 a Dutch vessel named *Minerva* was halted but allowed to proceed. UB-65 came home having experienced little worse than an encounter with an airship (December 15) and some depth charging.

What of the hauntings—what of the dead officer? You may recall that he is supposed to have manifested himself in moderately spectacular fashion off Portland Bill on January 21, 1918. If he did, UB-65 was not there to see him. She saw in the new year in port and did not leave until February 2, when she undertook a short cruise from Heligoland and back to Wilhelmshaven on the tenth of the same month, leaving on the nineteenth for her former hunting grounds across the North Sea past Orkney and the West Hebrides and down into the Irish Sea. This time she claimed two steamers totalling about 5,500 tons before returning along the same route to Bremerhaven. It is evident that Schelle felt that the Irish Sea was a profitable quarter.

His next visit, the cruise of April 22 to May 19, 1918, must have confirmed that view. This was the period coinciding with what the anonymous officer-informant of Prof. Dr. Hecht called "the worst trip of all." Judging from the official records, that verdict was singularly misplaced. Bywater raises hopes that the log would situate UB-65 in the English Channel and off Spain; she was nowhere near either. The same writer raises ghoulish hopes of a catalog of disasters: Eberhard driven mad by the phantom and jumping into the sea plus a small hospital of injuries lurking in his wake. Not according to that disappointingly prosaic war diary, however.

UB-65 ran a course that was much as before: from Heligoland past Orkney and west Hebrides down into the Irish Sea. Far from being the worst trip of all, it was her finest hour. She sank four vessels prior to returning to Wilhelmshaven and a note reproduced in Spindler makes it apparent that Schelle intended to return to so rich a locality with its brisk steamer traffic. In fact, he appears to have been engaged in exploiting these opportunities on July 10, 1918, just eight days after leaving Heligoland, at which point a series of laconic fragments in the record signify the end of UB-65.

Thirty-seven men disappeared along with her. Their names are reproduced alphabetically in one of Spindler's appendices; perhaps it is not remarkable that Wernicke, the pessimistic or forewarned friend who takes a last and poignant farewell of Hecht's valued informant in the "primary" version of the story, does not appear among them. It is not remarkable because practically nothing of the story that has come down to us from Bywater can be corroborated in the official archival material, the ghostly happenings that are the kernel of that story least of all.

For a moment we entertained the dubious notion that a U-boat captain would deliberately suppress any such paranormal evidence when writing his official log; it would, after all, be read by his superiors and episodes of a spectral type would not reflect well on his running of the submarine, perhaps. But, as we just implied, the moment and the dubious notion soon passed. It is true that not every incident on board would find its way into the diary, yet events of the magnitude suggested in

Bywater would surely not have escaped entirely, the more so as they blatantly affected the smooth operation of the submarine. As we saw a moment ago, the accident that led to the removal of Franzel's fingers was recorded officially; it is hard to imagine that an incident like Eberhard's insanity would be omitted and the idea that Schelle diplomatically forgot about so serious a disruption to the boat is not credible.

Bywater, it is true, never states that the successive phases of the haunting were logged, but his source—Hecht—is supposed to have written his report after scrutinizing the official documents relating to UB-65. Time and again we come back to the crucial importance of "the distinguished psychologist Prof. Dr. Hecht" and "the pamphlet he published after the war": were it not for Bywater's citation of both, we would have to suspect that he had received the story from some vague oral source that featured a very garbled, fanciful version of the facts. We have already indicated that Bywater had plenty of opportunities to pick up the material he used subsequently in his books during an espionage career that took him to Germany as an undercover agent. There again, his wartime desk work also included translation of German documents and after the conclusion of hostilities various correspondents kept him informed on journalistically useful events in that country. These, not to mention Bywater's regular scrutiny of German newspapers and books concerning naval matters, *could* have alerted him to this remarkable story.

There were also the after-work drinking sessions with the "Fleet Street Press Gang," a group of naval journalists and correspondents who met to swap stories and gossip at pubs like the Old Bell or the White Swan. The haunting of UB-65 has the "feel" of the sort of story told over a few drinks—a typical ambiance for the recitation of weird tales, perhaps, and a pursuit in which Bywater's skill as a pub raconteur led him to excel, according to Honan's biography. The problem is that if Bywater came by the story in these ways he would probably have acknowledged as much in a footnote to his book, if not in the main text. It is a procedure he follows throughout *Their Secret Purposes.* The only source he acknowledges for UB-65 is Prof. Dr. Hecht and his postwar pamphlet.

Bywater appears to have been highly conscious that the credibility of the haunting of UB-65 rests upon Hecht and his pamphlet. He introduces and cites the psychologist's name quite early in his account, as if all too aware that he requires maximum and authoritative support for the outrageous story he is about to relate. This, of course, is a common strategy among ghost-story narrators; the opening statement that the tale is based upon a private document is as standard a feature in the printed tale as the assertion that the speaker knew a friend of the original narrator is among oral equivalents. The focus upon the reliability of that informant—here he is patently trustworthy because he is a "distinguished psychologist"—is an equally popular narrative device. In one of the last paragraphs of his introduction, Bywater writes: "To forestall possible criticism of the chapter on the haunted German submarine, I may state that the data which reached me on this subject were carefully scrutinized and, as far as possible, checked before being used. As to the why and wherefore of the phenomenon described, readers must draw their own conclusions."

How carefully scrutinized? Where checked or with whom? If we are to take this assertion as more than a standard narrative device—if we want to do more than sit back and enjoy the haunting of UB-65 as more than a story—it becomes essential to revise those questions or to ask a fresh one: who was Hecht, apart from being (on Bywater's say-so) a distinguished psychologist?

We may as well admit that we haven't been able to find out. Fairly extensive inquiries amongst libraries and psychological associations in Britain and Germany turned up no record of either Hecht or his pamphlet. It seems particularly odd that, for an allegedly distinguished psychologist, the object of our search appears to have been unusually reticent about committing himself to print; that is, we would have expected a distinguished psychologist's name to have appeared (if not frequently) in the pre– or post–World War I literature of the subject. With this in mind we scanned two obvious bibliographical sources: the *Psychological Review* (1917–36) and *Psychological Abstracts* (1927–32). This search unearthed three Hechts, two of whom were of no apparent relevance to our inquiry. The third, S. Hecht, however, seemed to merit the epithet "distinguished"; he was a highly prolific writer of scientific papers and it was a poor year that failed to carry a reference to at least one such contribution.

Unfortunately, S. Hecht's speciality was not parapsychology nor abnormal mental phenomena. He wrote chiefly on the psychology of perception with a special interest in such arcane but unparanormal topics as the kinetics of dark adaption, visual acuity in insects, photosensitivity and the photochemistry of animals' sensitivity to light. We found no evidence that he ever strayed into, say, studies of hysteria or hallucinatory states. Unless the war had created an acute shortage of psychologists, it is hard to conceive the German naval command delegating the investigation of a haunted submarine to a man who was more at home with the visual prowess of honey bees.

We began by trying to locate a distinguished psychologist named Hecht, but soon would have settled for being able to prove Hecht was any kind of psychologist whatsoever. In the end, we found ourselves disposed to doubt he had ever existed.

At any rate, Hecht doesn't sound like a distinguished psychologist to us. He sounds far more like an "authority figure": one of those spurious but credibility-reinforcing characters invoked in legend-like tales to allay the audience's skepticism. Intentionally or not, Bywater drops Hecht's name to that effect. So do the writers who follow Bywater. Hecht is "the well-known German psychologist" whose report appeared in "an official survey of his findings . . . (details of which were never published)," according to Brown's 1972 version. He becomes "a renowned psychologist" acting at the request of the German naval high command in King's 1974 variation (which, however, merely paraphrases Bywater). King is unique in bestowing on Hecht the forename "Max," incidentally; the only Max Hecht we have been able to trace wrote not on ghosts but upon the equally mysterious fossil bird-reptile Archaeopteryx. For our part, we cannot believe that he was either "well-known" or "renowned" as a psychologist, but we may as well move on to other things.

If Hecht is a shadowy figure, his pamphlet takes on the hues of blackest night. We could find no library that had heard of it, let alone one that possessed a copy. Of the writers who follow Bywater only one—Raymond Lamont Brown—goes into more detail concerning it. In 1972 he stated that the contents of Hecht's investigation "were never published"; in 1977 he decided that the unpublished report is or was lodged in the Staatsbibliothek der Stiftung Preussicher Kulturbesitz, Marburg, while the logs consulted by Hecht can or could be found at the Institut fur Zeitgeschichte, Munich. To clarify the situation further: a "full report" went to Admiral von Capelle, the secretary of the Imperial German Navy, who felt it represented an attempt to discredit the German navy, and a copy passed to the naval Intelligence. Hecht's report is "an analysis" added to the intelligence dossier and it is this that Brown describes as "never published." We just speculated that Bywater had access to secret or semisecret German documents, of which Hecht's report/analysis may have been one, but Brown's description hardly conforms with Bywater's reference to "a pamphlet published after the War."

Our German informant Roland Hauser looked into these citations for us and found nothing of the kind. The UB-65's logs are not held in Munich, but in the Bundesarchiv Militararchiv, Freiburg. The Staatsbibliothek at Marburg held no record of Hecht's name in their catalog (and, need we repeat, no copy of his pamphlet). They checked their magazine file lest he had contributed it to a periodical and also their manuscript collection in case, as Brown asserts, the document was unpublished and existed in purely holographic form. The result: *nichts.*

Bywater gives neither the full nor partial title of the pamphlet. He does not give date of publication. We are left wondering whether he actually saw a copy of it, or took its existence as genuine on someone else's assurance. Careful rereading of what he sets down in his introduction highlights phrases like, "the data which reached me," which doesn't entirely rule out the idea that he had only *heard* of the pamphlet and the gist of its contents, but may *not* have seen it. But what in that case constituted the careful scrutiny and the "as far as possible" checks of which he speaks? And surely his account contains too much detail, some of it as direct quotes from the former UB-65 officer, to be the product of memory. The only other possibility is that Bywater did not need to tax his memory—did not need to consult anyone's pamphlet, either!—because he made up the entire story.

That much is certainly possible. Yet we retain a feeling that Bywater must have seen a printed . . . something, which he describes (perhaps loosely) as a pamphlet—but, as we've remarked before, he gives no details of it. Still more to the point, we cannot trace it. Whatever it was, Hecht's piece of work sounds a rather fugitive kind of publication and it is remarkable that it should appear so given the importance Bywater places upon it.

Back to the ever-mysterious Hecht. Interestingly enough, we ran into a case of outstandingly strange phenomena testified to (and greatly substantiated) by a putative psychologist just a few years ago; in that instance the "phenomena" resolved themselves into a wonderful hoax and the "psychologist" was actually a playful journalist. As we recall, he justified styling himself a psychologist by virtue of the fact his story was an ad hoc experiment in human suggestibility—that is, credulity. Could it be that a fictioneer created the haunting of UB-65 and that Bywater didn't detect the sleight of hand?

It so happened that the name "Hecht" rang a few bells with us straight off, though not in any psychology sense. We take no credit for that; the Hecht we had in mind was *Ben* Hecht, one of the most prominent U.S. playwrights of the 1920s and 1930s. Born in 1894 in New York, Hecht served as a journalist on the Chicago *Daily News* and *Journal* before scoring significant successes as a novelist and dramatist. Later he turned to writing Hollywood screenplays that included *Wuthering Heights* (1939) and the Hitchcock classic *Spellbound* (1945). The youthful experiences in Chicago journalism, as related in his autobiography *Child of Century,* included a variety of stunts that would have made the fabrication of a haunted U-boat saga seem tame; he also served as the *Journal*'s foreign correspondent in Germany at the end of the war.

Did Ben Hecht's early work include a masquerade as a distinguished professor of psychology? Was "Prof. Dr. Hecht" a pseudonym or narrative persona of Ben Hecht? On the face of it, the suggestion does not seem outrageous. Making up the most bizarre news stories was a workaday feature of Hecht's career on the *Journal.* As he himself puts it, "Tales of prodigals returned, hobos come into fortunes, families driven mad by ghosts, vendettas that ended in love feasts, and all of them full of exotic plot turns involving parrots, chickens, goldfish, serpents, epigrams and second-act curtains. I made them all up."

And submarine crews driven mad by ghosts, with or without assistance from parrots? Hecht produced scoops to order: a Chicago earthquake (which needed two hours spent in digging the fissure for the accompanying photo), a Romanian princess discovered as a waitress in a Greek restaurant, and so on. Yes, a haunted U-boat would hardly have tested a creative imagination like Hecht's. The only but insurmountable difficulty is that Hecht never claimed credit for the UB-65 fantasy, not as far as we have been able to establish. Another resides in Hecht's claim that by the time he had graduated to more serious journalism—about the time he went to Germany, perhaps?—Hecht had foresworn invented news and stuck to more conventional approaches to reporting that did not necessitate making up news to fill gaps in the papers. We throw in Hecht's name as one that suggested itself to us when we were casting about for a solution to the identity of Bywater's distinguished psychologist. However much it would have delighted us to prove that he was the author of the seminal pamphlet—or perhaps was named as such in something written by someone who knew of Hecht and his track record in perpetuating ersatz true-life sensations—we have been signally unable to do so.

Despite our prestated doubts about the lack of evidence proving that Hecht and his pamphlet existed, we take the optimistic view that Bywater's chapter was based upon *something* he had seen and read. But why should he believe the story?

Bywater does not appear to have been a credulous man, although it is true that he swallowed the tale of the U-boat crewed by corpses—the tale upon which von Spiegel later claimed to have dined out to his heart and stomach's content—as one of the strange but true dramas of the war. Where nautical history was concerned his bent was largely factual. Yet there is in his writing an element of romance, a controlled fantasy that enabled him to visualize fictive scenarios inside factually governed parameters, as he did with striking success in his *Great Pacific War*. He was also a five-star raconteur, a man who loved a good story and who knew how to tell one. His later books, including *Their Secret Purposes,* have a confessedly anecdotal character and hints of literary artifice. There is no reason to doubt that he had access to the "secret" Whitehall room in which, he claimed, lay folders dealing with "complete records of every incident that occurred at sea during the Great War"

(*Their Secret Purposes*, p. 257) and that he heard numerous yarns of "mysterious incidents . . . upon which light has been shed by post-war disclosures." UB-65 may have been one of these and, for a writer, an example too good to ignore. The doubt remains whether Bywater checked the story as thoroughly as he wishes his reader to believe.

So our final impressions are as follows. Official documents make it extremely difficult to believe that UB-65 was haunted or even troubled by bad luck beyond what was experienced and accepted on board many a WWI submarine. Nevertheless, the story has evolved that it was or had been and the responsibility for that rumor-like legend in all its dramatic detail cannot be traced back with any certainty before Hector C. Bywater.

And Bywater, we feel, believed the story—believed it because he liked the story and wanted to retell it in one of his books. We do not feel that he checked it in any detail. Bywater's ultimate authority for it was someone named Hecht, though we are less certain that he actually read the pamphlet he cites to such great effect and we are virtually certain that Hecht (if he existed at all) was not the distinguished psychologist Bywater took him to be. We cannot prove there was any Hecht pamphlet, yet we can accept that a story (verbal or printed) came into Bywater's possession; it may have been in circulation for some time before it reached him.

Our grounds for guessing so reside in a comment made by Robert Casey in his *Battle Below* (1945). The haunted UB-65 appears there in a chapter on "Things Which Never Happened" and the story was, he asserts, current towards the closing stages of World War I. Casey adds that although he is not sure he can believe the yarn, he never met a submariner who *didn't*.

Our admittedly incomplete survey of newspapers for 1918 has so far failed to confirm expectations raised by this statement, which is a pity. It would be more than useful to find the story in circulation by the end of the war and therefore more than a decade prior to the occurrence of the thing in Bywater's book. Not least of all, it would render Hecht's role redundant, since we could be sure that the story predated his rumoured pamphlet ("published after the war"); beyond that, it would prove the story was *not* fabricated or refabricated by some post–WWI fictioneer.

But when exactly did the submariners mentioned by Casey hear the story? Were they *WWII* submariners who got it (indirectly, one presumes) from Bywater? If so, the detail would prove only that by World War II the haunting of UB-65 had passed into naval lore and more specifically into the imagination of the men in the submarine service.

Reverting to our previous speculations, there is little to prevent readers from agreeing that the Haunted Submarine *may* have been known earlier than Bywater's book—or to allow them to hypothesize that some kind of "hoodoo-haunted" rumour concerning UB-65 may perhaps have been current around the end of World War I, most likely in the early postwar years and amongst submariners for whom it would contain particular horrors. That rumor may well have focussed initially on the ambiguous demise of the submarine with a species of hindsighted backtracking creating for the boat an ominous and supernatural history. It wouldn't be surprising if this process utilized other, earlier rumors (though we found no evidence of them). But in type and quality the imagined and ghostly history of UB-65 is no different from the other "unlucky sub" stories we gave in our last chapter: what we have here is a further testament to the way in which the submarine can act as a focus for our darker fantasies simply by being a submarine.

But UB-65 lives on in legend—lives on *as* a legend. And legends sometimes develop new plots. We leave you with a little episode that may indicate that UB-65 is not quiescent just yet. It comes from Raymond Lamont Brown's 1977 *Fate* version and we find it a little odd that he didn't find room for it in the version he gave in book-chapter form some five years earlier.

July 10, 1968: Sven Morgens-Larsen of Baltimore, his American wife June, and two children were sailing their yacht *Grey Seal* along Cape Clear off the Irish coast and as far as Fastnet rock, which they reached sometime after lunch. At 6:30 p.m. they heard a muffled explosion; a few hundred feet away the sea frothed and churned as the conning tower of a submarine broke the surface. On a point close to its prow stood a motionless figure. He disappeared—the submarine melted into vapour—but not before Sven thought he could make out the markings on her side . . . including the numerals "65."

You may have guessed what happened when the Morgens-Larsen family notified the Irish Coast Guard. They had no knowledge of a submarine in the area. Nor was there any trace of wreckage nor oil slick. But once home in Baltimore, Sven set out to research the incident. In the Johns Hopkins University Library he read about the American submarine (A)L-2's encounter with a U-boat that apparently self-destructed, and although it is in no account of that episode that *we* have seen, Brown notes that Foster of the L-2 had also seen a motionless man on the enemy craft's bows.

As it appears that Foster never *saw* the submarine he was thinking of attacking (which is hardly strange when we recall it was submerged!), we can't see how he could have seen the mysterious man on the bows. The incident isn't unparalleled, however; if you turn back to chapter 3, you will find that when the Schultz family saw the ghostly *Thresher* in summer 1967, she also had a stiff and motionless figure—no, a pair of them!—who stood unresisting on her bows as she sank. Brown wrote *that* story as well. As to the story's envoi, in which Sven Morgens-Larsen visits Munich and the naval archives of the Institut fur Zeitgeschichte and learns the full and peculiar story of the haunted UB-65. . . .

But no, there's been enough critical comment from us. Brown entitles his magazine article: "U-Boat 65: Forever Haunted," and although we'd hesitate in applying the phrase literally, we would agree with it. Like all great legends, UB-65 *is* forever haunted, because it haunts us forever.

References

Our primary source for the haunting of UB-65 was Hector C. Bywater's *Their Secret Purposes* (London: Constable, 1932), pp. 18–34. Most of this was excerpted for *Fifty Strangest Stories of the Sea* (London: Odhams, no date). A similarly titled book containing this story is John Canning's *Fifty Strange Mysteries of the Sea* (1979). Michael and Mollie Hardwick follow Bywater's account very closely (but with much added dialogue) in their *The World's Greatest Sea Mysteries* (1967), pp. 82–89. Three shorter but important treatments to which we have referred frequently in our chapter are Raymond Lamont Brown's *Phantoms of the Sea* (Patrick Stephens, 1972), pp. 25–31, where the submarine is mislabelled U-65; the same writer's article, "U-Boat 65: Forever Haunted" in *Fate* (June 1977): 70–75; and Peter King's "The Haunted Submarine" in *Fate* (August 1974): 47–53. Robert Casey's *Battle Below* (Bobbs Merrill, 1945) mentioned that the tale of the haunted U-boat was (apparently) current in the latter days of World War I.

On the history of the U-boat war of 1914–1918 we consulted the following books:

R. M. Grant, *U-boat Intelligence 1914–1918* (1968), especially pp. 171–73.

Edwin A. Gray, *The Killing Time* (1972).

Arno Spindler, *Der Krieg zur See 1914–1918* (Berlin and Frankfurt, 1941), principally vols. 4 and 5.

V. E. Tarrant, *The U-Boat Offensive 1914–1945* (Arms & Armour, 1989). Key manuscript sources are as noted in the text of this chapter.

Also useful was a longhand manuscript in the Royal Navy Submarine Archives at Gosport, Hampshire, *The U-boats: activities and losses of*

German U-boats 1914–18. Its account of UB-65 (vol. 1, pp 188–91) seems to follow Bywater.

Additional works consulted for this chapter included William H. Honan's *Bywater. The Man Who Invented the Pacific War* (Macdonald, 1990); M. L. Sanders and Philip M. Taylor, *British Propaganda during the First World War, 1914–1918* (Macmillan, 1962); and Sidney Rogerson, *Propaganda in the Next War* (Geoffrey Bles, 1938).

III

Lost Liners

5

Waratah: "The Man with a Sword"

At about 8 p.m. on July 26, 1909, the *Waratah* sailed out of Durban harbor and into maritime legend. The mystery surrounding the disappearance of the 16,800-ton Blue Anchor Line steamer is really three mysteries in one—or possibly four, if we care to ask what unique quality the event possessed to qualify it as a maritime legend. Let us start there.

Statistically and logistically, the loss of the *Waratah* may not appear overremarkable if we regard her as the opening to a four-act nautical tragedy. The *Waratah* may well have struck Edwardians as a terrible business, but—coldly rational as it may seem to put it this way—she was soon upstaged by the greater dramas of the *Titanic* (1912), the *Empress of Ireland* (1914), and the *Lusitania* (1915). Inasmuch as she did not carry wireless, her abrupt vanishing may seem the opposite of incomprehensible. And measured on the scale of lives, the *Waratah* and her human cargo of just over two hundred pales beside the *Titanic* and her fifteen hundred lost souls. But then, as we hope to show in a later chapter, in comparison to the *Titanic* all sea disasters look pallid.

It is unjust to compare *Waratah* with *Titanic, Empress of Ireland,* and *Lusitania,* to imply that her tragedy was lesser than theirs because it was numerically subordinate. It would be fairer to see it, as contemporaries did, as the worst passenger ship loss to date; only history seems to upstage or diminish its significance. But then again there is the crucial element of uncertainty about "why" and "wherefore" that distinguishes the event. We know what happened to *Titanic, Empress,* and *Lusitania*; in the case of the *Waratah* we are reduced to making guesses, educated or not so educated. *Those* three ships left survivors; the *Waratah* did not. And as John Harris remarks in his highly readable *Without Trace*

(1981, 1988) one survivor is enough to prevent a sea tragedy from becoming a sea mystery.

Abruptness and uncertainty. The *Waratah* was a new ship on only her second voyage. She had all the paper qualifications of seaworthiness that the Board of Trade (BOT) and a Lloyds 100-A1 certificate could guarantee. More practically, she had sixteen lifeboats capable of holding 787 people plus a spare boat that could take another 29, three rafts with a 105 total capacity, two dozen 16-ounce rockets, ditto socket distress signals, 14 lifebuoys with lights that ignited on contact with the water and 930 lifebelts. Inevitably—for in the appalling and unexpected event of her loss how could it have been otherwise?—allegations came from sailors who had worked on her: from Alfred Philip Pinel, to name one, who said the boats were made of "green wood," or from the boatswain who in the hearing of Samuel Lyons and Steward Fred Carl Lusatkin, called them "the awfullest boats he had ever seen in his life." That wasn't the sort of verdict to inspire confidence, but his follow-up had been even gloomier: "By heaven, I would not like to be in this ship in a storm. She will go to the bottom."

But perhaps the boatswain was one of those saturnine individuals who are only happy when they are being miserable and happier still when they can pass on their despondent imaginings to someone else. Some of the *Waratah* men, as we'll hear shortly, appear to have been of that ilk. So the boatswain may not have been the ideal witness for the prosecution. Nicholas Sharp, who'd left *Waratah* at Sydney, was even less so. Sharp was the agent for some colorfully forthright criticisms, of which those relating to the state of the lifeboats—faults and patches masked by heavy paint and putty malgre the BOT certificate!—formed only a part. Sharp was to tell the court of inquiry that he'd resorted to "cracking on he was sick" to be paid off. "He left her because he was frightened of her," ran the report. Even though "he had done no good since. . . . He would not have gone back in the *Waratah* for a thousand pounds."

All very emphatic stuff. But as it happened, Nick Sharp wasn't in need of money; it transpired that he had boasted to Able Seaman George Doughty Short that he was currently "doing all right out of the *Waratah*, answering questions for a weekly newspaper." Very likely he made sure his copy was as dramatic as required. Incidentally, it is to Short whom we owe the information that the lifeboats were fine—that the davits worked (contrary to what others claimed)—and that the boats *had* been tested in the water. It is fairly obvious that, inspections or not, the *Waratah* had gone on her maiden voyage with a set of lifeboats that left something to be desired, safety-wise; but Lund could point to records of costs for making them sound after an emigration official had passed unfavorable remarks about them. The Board of Trade felt no doubt about the boats' adequacies for the second and as it transpired last voyage of the *Waratah*.

These critics aside, we would be justified in saying that the *Waratah* was as well-equipped with safety devices as most ships in the early 1900s could hope to be. We are also justified in saying that none of them made a jot of difference to what befell her. The *Waratah* steamed out on the Durban-Capetown leg of her journey, much as we described; she was "spoken" to by another ship some hours afterwards and may have been sighted by a couple of others, as we will detail later. And thereafter . . .

Thereafter she disappeared from human ken. There were reports of wreckage, of lifebuoys, of bodies; these we will mention in due course. There were, need it be said, speculations and theories that were poor substitutes for definite facts; there were searches which failed to produce definite facts, either. What *can* be said (echoing the *Times* of February 1, 1911) is that she "had absolutely vanished, not in mid-ocean, but whilst on a short voyage of 700 miles round the coast, almost entirely in sight of land in a frequented track." That alone called for comment. The problem: though it was patently obvious before long that the *Waratah* had sunk, nothing and no one could prove how or why; not even the official Board of Trade inquiry conducted from December 1910 to February 1911.

No confirmation, no solution. As always, rumor stepped in to fill the gap left by the paucity of genuine facts. The *Waratah*, it now appeared, was a drawing-board disaster that had come to actual disaster; she should never have been allowed out of the shipyard, let alone out of port. These and other, wilder suggestions bred of hearsay and hindsight generated an outrage that the court of inquiry was in part convened to assuage. Even so, there is a good chance that the loss of the *Waratah* might have been forgotten in time (with or without the greater disasters of the *Titanic* et al.) but for the interest shown in it by J. G. Lockhart.

By now readers will have gathered that we are more than slightly interested in the sources for classic sea legends—how they come to be seen as such and/or who first presents them in that light. They will also have noted our great debt to J. G. Lockhart and especially to his *Mysteries of the Sea* (1924), in which the *Waratah* forms the concluding chapter.

In suggesting that Lockhart popularized the *Waratah* mystery, we certainly do not intend to imply he created, nor in any way sensationalized or exaggerated it. This writer's first and possibly major contribution was to recognize that the *Waratah* case was indeed a mystery of the sea—

one which by 1924 had been partially forgotten—and, with skilful use of personal informants as well as careful study of other source material, he brought the story to life in all its puzzling detail. He did so in a manner that has made every other writer who handles it indebted to him. Naturally, the present authors cannot and do not wish to divorce ourselves from that ruling. However, although what follows will draw on Lockhart's versions of the case, we have tried to do more than present a resume of chapters in *Mysteries of the Sea* and its sequel, *Strange Tales of the Seven Seas* (1929). This applies most strongly to our analysis of the two "sub-mysteries" that append to the mighty question: *What happened to the Waratah?*

So to the story then. We began with the *Waratah* clearing Durban, which, paradoxically or not, is close to the end of the narrative as far as certain facts go. Now we need to go back a little, beginning with the ship as the central issue of a contract between her owners, the Blue Anchor Line, and her builders, Barclay, Curle and Co. of the Clyde.

The *Waratah* was built to the Blue Anchor's specifications: a twin-screw vessel of the spar-deck class measuring 465 feet in length and a little over 59 feet in breadth. Her displacement was 16,800 tons, but her gross and registered tonnages were, of course, considerably lower: 9,339 and 6,003 respectively. These figures do not represent any true discrepancy, though John Harris observes that it was not uncommon for shipping lines to cite the highest of the three tonnages in their advertising material, thereby hoping to impress potential customers with the size and (implied) opulence of their new vessel. When delivered on October 23, 1908, she became the line's sixth ship and, as F. W. Lund was to say when representing the owners at the BOT inquiry, an improved version of their proudest possession to date, the *Geelong*. To sail her: Cpt. Josiah E. Ilbery, who had served the Blue Anchor Line for forty-two years. *Waratah* passed builder's and owner's inspections, but more importantly those of the Board of Trade, Lloyds, and (since she was planned to take part in the lucrative trade of carrying newcomers to and from the British colonies) an inspection held necessary by the emigration authorities.

More specifically, she was signed for the London-Australia run, stopping off approximately midway at the Cape of Good Hope—which, if you remember the legend we dealt with in chapter 1, was once considered *Flying Dutchman* territory. But no omens of ill-luck and, come to that, no ill luck seemed to attend when the ship undertook her maiden voyage over that course, which she commenced on November 6, 1908, arriving back in England the following March. We might conclude that none of the 67 cabin and 689 steerage passengers, not to mention the 154 crew, found anything to complain of about the *Waratah*'s performance, except that subsequent and officially investigated reports indicated that it might have been otherwise.

It would have been usual for Captain Ilbery to tender an official report of that first voyage, but it appears that he did not (or, as some think, was not requested to do so). Instead there was F. W. Lund's assurance to the BOT inquiry that Ilbery had been very satisfied with her—that he had professed her "an easy ship in a heavy sea," though "in a light condition he did not think she was as stable as the *Geelong*." Aware of rumors that the commodore had been rather more explicit than this, Lund hastened to tell the court that Ilbery had *not* affirmed that the *Waratah* was less stable than the *Geelong* at sea, and in any case Lund disagreed with him. It was likewise untrue that Ilbery had threatened to leave if the boat-deck wasn't removed; he'd had ample opportunity to make any kind of suggestion toward improvement. It *was* true that the captain had drawn the attention of the line to *Waratah*'s inability to shift in dock without ballast—that much *was* a matter of record. But it turned out that that detail had been a part of a ploy to gain advantage in the owner's dispute with the builders over demurrage (a legal term for compensation arising from undue delay in handing over a vessel, amounting in this case to $50 per diem). Practically speaking, as Lund worked hard to prove on this occasion, Ilbery had said nothing to suggest the *Waratah* was in any way unseaworthy. Whether that silence was an accurate assessment of affairs was, it transpired, open to dispute.

Captain Ilbery's apparent failure to place his thoughts about the *Waratah* on written record came as an unwelcome surprise to the inquiry. For want of them or it, the court entertained a number of secondhand testimonies, of which Lund's was just one. There seemed no agreement on the subject. Worthington Church said the captain had responded to his observation that *Waratah* was top heavy, rolled and quivered at the end of each roll, by saying he was not altogether satisfied with her and that he felt more at home on the *Geelong,* though he hastened to add that Church's fears were groundless. This didn't conform precisely with Lund's version of how Ilbery felt about the vessel. Marine Supt. Captain R. F. Bidwell had heard complaints from neither Chief Officer Owen nor from her master; in fact, he'd heard Ilbery call the rumors mere "idle talk." Ilbery had supposedly complimented the *Waratah* in John Charles Neill's hearing, but according to Adelaide pilot John McDiarmid he might have said something about her being a bit "tender." Several Australian officials who had worked with the *Waratah* denied hearing any adverse comments about her from Ilbery. The report that he had told the captain of the Peninsular and Occidental's *Mongolia* that this would be his last voyage in the *Waratah* "unless she was very materially altered when she got home" seemed to corroborate a statement passed on by Able Seaman Edward Dischler that the captain had avowed a second voyage on her would be his last—"that either his reputation or the vessel would be lost." The problem was that the *Mongolia*'s master denied having met Ilbery and that Ilbery undertook that supposedly fatal second journey regardless.

As late as 1955, and as an unexpected result of having done a BBC broadcast on the *Waratah*, Alan Villiers was told by friends of Ilbery that the captain had been notably less cheerful than usual after the maiden voyage and *had* said he was unhappy with his new ship. Elsewhere we may find room for other testimony to this effect; for now we might conclude that, even allowing for the possibility of exaggerating how deep his "unhappiness" lay or what it amounted to, it seems a fair bet that Captain Ilbery had reservations about the *Waratah* (especially after having sailed the *Geelong*), although he never formally expressed them in ink.

Regardless of whatever Captain Ilbery may have said or did not say, the *Waratah* left London on her second voyage on April 27, 1909, arrived at Adelaide on June 8 and after travelling on to Sydney (on June 17) and Melbourne (June 28) returned there ready to commence the home run via Durban and the Cape, for which she started out on July 7. At Durban on July 25, she unloaded 240 tons of cargo of coal, bringing her cargo weight on departure to somewhere around 10,000 tons. (These figures, theoretically relating to the question of her stability, were routinely analyzed at the court of inquiry.) Then she and her 92 passengers and 211 crew set out on July 26 for the easy-sounding trip down the coast of South Africa to Capetown.

It would have been literarily satisfying to have been able to conclude that last paragraph with the terse statement, "and nobody ever saw them again." Unluckily for us, it would be untrue. The *Waratah* certainly was seen again, and only eight or ten hours later; the vagueness here arises from our different sources putting the hour at either 4 a.m. next morning or 6 a.m. But there is no doubt that the ship with which *Waratah* exchanged messages by signal lamp across a distance of about two miles that early morning was the *Clan MacIntyre,* a steamer that had left Durban some time before the larger, faster vessel cleared. The dialogue was limited to:

Clan MacIntyre: "What ship?"
Waratah: "*Waratah,* for London."
Clan MacIntyre: "*Clan MacIntyre,* for London. What weather did you have from Australia?"
Waratah: "Strong southwesterly to southerly winds, across."

Clan MacIntyre: "Thanks, goodbye. Pleasant passage."
Waratah: "Thanks, same to you. Goodbye."

As he watched *Waratah* go, *Clan MacIntyre* Apprentice S. P. Lamont thought she was "sailing like a yacht" with a strong starboard list and her propellers showing out of the water. It came as a surprise to him when Chief Officer G. P. Phillips told the inquiry he had noticed no such thing. Within a few hours, the *Waratah* was gone over the horizon.

Where and how far? The master of the *Clan MacIntyre* estimated that by 9:30 a.m. she ought to have been abeam the Bashee River and some twelve miles outside it. Following the southwest-northeast slope of the South African coast on a map, this would situate the ship about midway between Durban and East London. The name "Bashee River" and the proposition that the *Waratah* might have got that far takes on relevance later in the story.

So too does Phillips's evidence that by this time the wind had freshened and by evening of the July 27 was at gale force from the southwest—a prelude to squalls of hurricane strength next day. It was, he testified, the worst storm he had experienced in thirteen years' sailing off Africa. *Clan MacIntyre* was slightly sheltered by the coastline; the *Waratah*, forging further ahead, would have been less protected. If she suffered from any structural flaws, this weather might have found them out.

Even now, we cannot indulge ourselves and write: "and no one saw her again." As the *Waratah* graduated from being overdue in Capetown to missing and feared lost, several ships came forward to claim they *might* have seen her.

Here we stay with those claims that, even if unfounded, were based on honest belief. The story of how a Capt. Brendon "of a steamer said to be called the '*Talis*' " testified to having seen the *Waratah* between 5 and 6 p.m. on July 27 can be eliminated as not belonging in this category. Lund had started this particular hare in all good faith; he testified that a man who identified himself as Brendon had called on him with the information that when twenty-five to thirty miles from East London on her London-Valparaiso run (*sic*) the *Talis* had seen the *Waratah* cross her stern, going "splendidly and easily." It was not Lund's fault that the BOT could find neither name of master nor ship in the marine registers, nor that when they called at the address Brendan had given nobody seemed to have heard of him. The *Talis* affair has all the marks of a hoax and, as it turned out, where *Waratah* was concerned, hoaxes were too common.

Albert John Brice, captain of the *Harlow*, was available to give evidence. Heading northeast along the coast on the July 27—that is, in the opposite direction to the way the *Waratah* ought to have been heading—they sighted what looked like the smoke of a steamer at around 5:30 p.m., leading Brice to exclaim: "Damned if I don't think she's on fire." Later two masthead lights and a red side light were visible astern and a couple of hours afterward, when the *Harlow* was off Cape Hermes, these lights seemed to be ten to twelve miles away. Brice was returning from the chart house to the bridge when two bright flashes, one a thousand feet high, the other three hundred feet high, came from somewhere behind them. An explosion? queried Brice; bush fires, replied Chief Engineer Robert Parkin Ovens.

All this seemed suggestive when Brice learned of the *Waratah*'s disappearance after the *Harlow* had reached Manila. But it could be put down to a natural inclination to reinterpret the evidence in view of that new knowledge. The inquiry listened carefully to Brice's testimony, then deemed it irrelevant. It is easy to see why. Had there been an explosion—in the coal bunkers, for example, as Brice suggested—the *Harlow* must surely have heard it. And in that eventuality distress flares would have been sent up. All they saw was a volume of smoke with a glare seemingly enclosed by it—explicable, as Ovens said, in terms of the bush fires prevalent at this season. The lights might have belonged to some vessel other than the *Waratah* or to the Cape Hermes signal station (which reported no flames as described by Brice). Perhaps more cogently, the lights would have implied that the *Waratah* was sailing in the wrong direction—back to Durban instead of away from it, as per her true and last-known course.

The claim of the Union Castle's *Guelph* to a "last sighting" of the *Waratah* ran into similar objections. The incident took place around 9:30 or 9:51 p.m. (our sources diverge again) on the night of July 27 when the *Guelph* was some eight miles abeam of Hood Point near East London. Here she swapped signals with a cargo-passenger ship, but evidently not too successfully, as Third Officer Blanchard could only decipher the last three letters of her name: *Tah.* Discussing the episode when they reached Natal, he could only conclude that he had been in contact with the missing *Waratah.* The supposition seemed reasonable, even inevitable, except that the BOT inquiry felt unhappy about the positioning of the mystery ship. Taken at face value, it meant that the thirteen-knot *Waratah* had covered a meagre seventy miles after "speaking" the *Clan MacIntyre* earlier that day. It seemed highly unlikely unless she had suffered some engine trouble—but if so, why had the *Clan MacIntyre,* which was bound on the same course, not overtaken her?

There seemed to be two possibilities. The less likely alternative (whose credibility diminished with each passing month) was that the *Waratah*, crippled and helpless due to engine, steerage, or other problems, had drifted far from the normal shipping lanes; she was (on Lund's reckoning) well-provisioned for five to six weeks and there might be survivors if only prompt action was taken. The second, gloomier but stronger possibility was that she had foundered; if so, it was only logical to expect traces (wreckage, jetsam) to record that fact.

The first of the searches began in the autumn of 1909; the last and less hopeful were still continuing when the Board of Trade was trying to set up its inquiry in 1910. Messrs. Lund hired the salvage steamer *T. E. Fuller,* which sailed from Cape Town on July 31 with extra assistance leaving Durban the next day in the shape of the *Harry Escombe*; both returned a week later, defeated by bad weather. From August 4 to 22 three British warships, the *Pandora, Forte,* and *Hermes,* were detailed to investigate a trapezoid area whose angles (Cape Town, Port Natal, lat. 35° 10'S long. 38° E and lat. 40° 15'S long. 25° E) took in the coast from Port Natal to Algoa Bay. Meanwhile the Australian government sent the *Severn,* which covered 2,700 miles in a month-long hunt.

The extent of the probable search areas, let alone the possible ones, was daunting in the extreme, but those in charge of planning the expeditions responded with some ingenuity. Recalling how in 1899 the disabled *Waikako* had drifted out of the waters whence the *Waratah* had vanished, only to be discovered fourteen weeks later at the obscure island of St. Paul a little over halfway between the Cape and West Australia, the Blue Anchor Line chartered the *Sabine* to sail over the same course. She left on September 11, 1909, and spent eighty-eight days at sea, during which time she covered 14,000 miles within a 3,000-square-mile area and saw many traces of wrecked ships, but none of the *Waratah.* In 1910, public subscriptions in Britain and Australia raised the £5,000 needed to send the 4,072-ton steamer *Wakefield* on a similarly adventuresome route to the extreme southeast of the Cape: from Prince Edward Island and the Crozets as far as the Kerguelen group on the fringes of the Antarctic. These searches deserved to succeed, but didn't.

All ships eastbound from South African ports between August 2 and September 10 had been put on the alert for signs of the missing vessel. The idea that the *Waratah* could not go down without leaving some telltale sign of her going—some kind of wreckage—was almost as old as the first rumor-suspicions that the ship had been sunk. It took some highly dramatic forms, not least among which was the belief that the steamship *Tottenham* had sailed past a number of bodies somewhere between the mouth of the Bashee and East London on August 11. This story, which the BOT inquiry took seriously enough to have the *Tottenham*'s captain appear in person at the hearing, constitutes the second element of the *Waratah* mystery and we are inclined to reserve it for a more detailed analysis; all we need say here is that after hearing the evidence, the court pardonably ignored it. Other flotsam and jetsam stories included more blatant hoaxes. At one stage, BOT investigators were excited by an announcement in Brisbane newspapers of a message found in a bottle washed ashore that read: "At sea, latitude 40S—Steamship *Waratah* broken down August 23, drifting South." The signatory, J. G. Jones, asked the finder to write to Mrs. J. G. Jones of 58 George Street, Sydney. As it happened, a Jones appeared on the *Waratah*'s lists, but there was no trace of her at the stated address (and, come to that, it was known there was no Sydney passenger named Jones at all). It had seemed at first to be an outside chance; it proved to be yet another message-in-a-bottle hoax, one of five *Waratah* bottle hoaxes to be washed onto Australian beaches.

In or around March 1910, about three weeks after a hatchway was alleged to have been found, supposed wreckage washed ashore at Mossel Bay, South Africa, including a cushion marked "W." Suggestively truncated identifying names, like the incomplete message received by the *Guelph,* are a feature of latter stages of the story; the problem is (as we comment elsewhere about the "*Thresher*" life ring in Lake Superior) nothing is quite so easy to fake as a memento from a lost ship that has caused a lot of excitement. Most relics, however, seem to have been honest or over-optimistic errors of identification. The deck chair washed up at Coffee Gove on South Africa's east coast in December 1910 and originally reported in *African World* as being marked *Waratah* showed on closer inspection to bear the unconnected name "Moir" and the letters "N. R." A lifebuoy that the *Times* heard of from Waiuitu the following year was similarly ambiguous; in their haste to remove the barnacles from its name the children who found it reduced the last two letters to mere traces. The remaining five, though, sound interesting: "Warat." Another hoax? If these were rumors and fantasies that took a concrete form, the purely verbal variety were even more common. Up until now, the image of the *Waratah* as a fine, modern passenger carrier had gone unquestioned—or rather, any criticisms of her performance at sea had gone unpublicized. Now the reverse applied. The distinction between rumor and actual belief is often a fine one; to whichever category they belonged, the verbal and occasionally printed criticisms tended to blur that distinction still further.

Thus: the *Waratah* had always been an unsafe ship. She was said (as the *Times* summarized from the first day of the inquiry's cautiously worded introductory remarks) to have "behaved in an extraordinary manner at sea," (though the speaker correctly pointed out that not everyone who'd sailed on her said so). She had shown herself to be top-heavy—rolled even in the calmest weather—listed at the slightest puff of wind. Senior Engineer Fraser Chapman had left her due to his fears about her top-heaviness; it was in the papers. (Or, more likely, *one* paper—*John Bull*, the egregious weekly whose interest in the *Waratah* will become apparent later in this chapter. Chapman subsequently let the inquiry know the story was totally untrue. To the contrary, he thought *Waratah* a steady ship and he had left her only because his wife was in bad health. Actually, his wife had sent a correction to the paper responsible for promoting the misconception, but they hadn't published it.) Others were supposed to have "deserted" too. There was the tale of Ilbery wanting to quit which, as we heard, Lund negated, and other variations on the same theme.

More and worse: the *Waratah* was said to have gone aground on Kangaroo Island after she left Sydney; the BOT was able locate a passenger named Samuel Trott who testified to this incident (strangely missing from the ship's log) and promised to examine the depth charts to see if it was feasible. (Although there was some "vague corroboration" for the story, the court eventually discounted it.) At Adelaide (also allegedly) the ship had nearly turned turtle. On her maiden voyage her decks had broken loose. And so on. Best of all, overheated imaginations turned a cargo of coal and frozen meat into an unspecified and perhaps inestimable treasure hoard.

Moving closer to home, Dame Rumor declared that the *Waratah*'s design was the subject of disagreements between owners and builders, and, more invidiously, that she was heavily insured. In fact, as Lund pointed out, the ship wasn't insured for her full £150,000 value, but for only £135,000—not that the detail would convince anyone who was not disposed to be convinced. Lastly, perhaps in response to the claim that the *Waratah* had made Durban a day ahead of schedule, Cpt. Ilbery was said to have been under "secret orders" to drive her flat out in what hindsight declared was a dangerously irresponsible manner. (The same accusation was voiced after the *Titanic* disaster, although with slightly better reason.)

Quite obviously a Board of Trade inquiry was called for. All rumors aside, the significance of the *Waratah*'s loss was overwhelming.

At the risk of sheer reiteration, the first and greatest mystery concerning the loss of the *Waratah* is what happened to make it happen. A large new ship "constructed by builders of great eminence," equipped with seaworthiness certificates from five authorities, a much-experienced commander and all the safety gear of the period, had sailed into oblivion. Not unnaturally, people wanted to know how and why; they had begun to concoct their own theories or to listen to the ungracious theories of others. The Board of Trade confronted these facts squarely. Despite all the problems of bringing a small crew of seafaring witnesses together in one place at one time, the inquiry eventually opened at Coxton Hall, Westminster (London) on December 15, 1910.

December proved to be a remarkable climax of the journalistic year. It was a news-packed month; the *Waratah* inquiry found itself facing heavy competition for space in the papers with other disasters—gales and heavy flooding across Britain, three policemen shot dead and two others injured in trying to foil a raid on a Houndsditch (London) jeweller's, not to mention a crucial election the same week, and, perhaps ironically, the record-breaking feats of the latest in passenger-liner luxury, the *Mauretania.* We have neither the space nor inclination to reproduce all the evidence from the protracted hearing which, after a recess over the Christmas period, finally wound up the proceedings in February of the next year. Significantly, most of the proceedings focused on the *Waratah*'s performance at sea, upon her stability or, as it became plain early on, upon her reputed lack of it.

The first day's hearing had draughtsman Thomas Miller and other Barclay & Curle employees answering questions about the *Waratah*'s performance in ballast; during the second, director Noel Peck said there had been no complaints about the ship on her first voyage, but confessed to some "as to her ability to shift in dock without ballast"—also that there was some evidence that she was not as stable as the *Geelong*. Former Third Mate H. M. Bennett testified that the *Waratah* had behaved well on that maiden run despite a 4° to 5° list in strong wind and a slow (but normal) roll. He forcefully denied having told Mrs. Gibbs, who had lost a son on the *Waratah*, that he intended to leave the ship because she was going to be altered (meaning, inferentially, that there was something so terribly wrong with her as to require urgent rethinking of her design or that the repair, as he understood it, would make her even worse?). He had only left the *Waratah* when promoted to another ship. When Mr. and Mrs. Gibbs called out from the audience that he *had* vowed to leave her for the reasons he now contradicted, Bennett persisted in his denials. The court took his word.

As Admiral Davis had stated that day, the stability of the *Waratah* was a crucial question. C. G. Sawyer, the last witness of the session, had plenty to aver on the subject, but him we intend to hold over for a few more pages. Now (day three) came a parade of witnesses, all of whom tended to oppose the confident opinions of the builders' men. Frederick Little, a general servant on the *Waratah* until Durban (July 1909), said he'd noticed that the ship rolled heavily and recovered slowly, and that he had heard stewards saying she was top-heavy. Worthington Church agreed. The *Waratah* had a penchant for a prolonged roll ending with a quiver and many female passengers had been affected by it. He himself had arranged to swap to a new cabin because of the rolling. Leslie Augustus Wade recalled seeing an unscheduled entertainment on the maiden voyage, one that featured Cpt. Ilbery chasing a piano across the dining saloon. Chief Officer Owen made the mistake of asking A. W. Sedgwick if he thought the ship top-heavy and got the tart reply: "I don't think it, I know it. I am not a landlubber."

Mr. Herbert, former *Waratah* steward, spoke of the ship listing constantly either to port or starboard on the maiden voyage and of crockery being smashed when she rolled or pitched. Also, you could put your finger in between the deck plates and the beams they were supposed to be bolted to; then there was "a terrific creaking noise" as she rolled, especially in rough weather. Although he'd been assured that all new vessels creaked, Herbert made sure he left *Waratah* when they reached London "because he did not like the ship." Nor did E. Pask, also present on that first voyage. He thought the *Waratah* top-heavy, having observed her long, slow roll and delayed recovery as well as her tendency to list with the slightest change of wind. Pask also left the ship when they docked in London.

Notwithstanding their maritime experience, none of these men could be called an expert on a ship's seaworthiness. W. H. Bragg (arguably and at least in theory) could; he had not only sailed on the *Waratah* all the way from Adelaide to London, but was the Cavendish Professor of Physics at Leeds University. When a physical scientist testified with reference to the ship's "metacentre" the inquiry was inclined to harken. The listing had been pronounced enough for him to discuss it with the chief engineer and to ask Ilbery for a look at the *Waratah*'s stability curves (which he could not provide; they were not on board). Thanks to Bragg, it became apparent that the listing had been a breakfast-table topic of conversation among the passengers. Albert Vandam, who'd done the Cape Town-Sydney journey out, affirmed that the same phenomenon had been something of a joke. "How are you up there?" passengers would call to their counterparts on the other side of the ship. "How are you down there?" those counterparts responded gaily. No, Vandam wasn't worried, not even when the ship rolled so badly that crockery was broken. The marine inventor E. Crossley could not agree that sailing on the *Waratah* was jolly fun, however. The ship's chief officer had told him otherwise. According to Crossley, he had been "very dissatisfied" and said she "did not behave as she should do," got on one side, didn't right herself, "she fell more than rolled and got hit back again." The majority of her officers, added Vandam, wanted to leave the *Waratah* or complain about her, or both.

More evidence of the ship's top-heaviness followed next day, but there is a repetitive tone to it that encourages us to pass on to other matters. It is very noticeable that the owners (now known as Messrs. Lund, having sold their entire Blue Anchor fleet to Peninsular and Occidental some time after the *Waratah* disaster) took every available opportunity to contradict assertions that the ship was unstable. There were also intimations that they were prepared to go to unconventional lengths to do so. Several of the employees who testified in a manner favorable to them revealed under questioning a kind of vagueness that the court found unhelpful. When Cpt. R. F. Bidwell, Lund's marine superintendent, testified concerning certain rumor-like allegations the inquiry wished to probe, it was with an odd unconcern that moved Admiral Davis to remark that there seemed to have been quite a few matters about which he had not troubled his head—implying that a man in Bidwell's position ought to have done so.

Again: Messrs. Lund could not provide exact data on how the *Waratah* was loaded when she left Durban—only reconstructions of that detail—and, as we said before, there was no captain's report of the ship's performance on the first voyage. It seems likely that the court half-suspected the company of suppressing documents that might incriminate them. Bidwell confirmed that some such might have been destroyed the previous February, when Lund sold out to P&O, but he felt they had nothing to do with the *Waratah*; one wishes he could have been more certain. The dearth of written records, plus a desire to investigate every possible avenue of information, accounts for the way in which the Inquiry admitted evidence that can only be called hearsay—one person's account of what another absent person had told him and so on. In many respects, that concession to circumstance was forced upon them.

To the lay reader it may seem almost certain, or beyond all reasonable doubt, that the *Waratah* in fact *was* an unstable ship: that she listed, rolled heavily, and took her time about recovering herself. Failing that, we could temporize by saying that the *Waratah* was normally stable, but under certain conditions had the propensity to be the opposite and that her fault was fatally exposed by the first heavy storm she encountered. True enough, the smaller *Clan MacIntyre* met the same southwesterly gale and subsequent hurricane without worse effect than being forced back in her tracks, but besides the fact that a smaller vessel may often weather out conditions that destroy a larger one, *Clan MacIntyre* was, as it were, already storm-tested. "She is a good stable ship," confirmed Chief Officer Phillips. "I have been in many a storm in her." The *Waratah* had never been tested by serious seas and winds.

Such might be the conclusion drawn from the mass of testimony heard by the court, where many a statement about the "extraordinary behavior" of the *Waratah* leaps out of the page to catch the eye. But it goes against the inquiry's final opinion and also ignores testimony from witnesses that, though less dramatic, frankly disavows the suggestion of instability. Whom do we believe? Were those who emphasized the listing, rolling, plunging, and hanging merely nervous passengers lacking the kind of marine experience to know what was usual and unusual in a ship's behavior? Had the seventeen months (or more in some cases) that had elapsed between the disappearance of the *Waratah* and their appearance on the stand at Caxton Hall—and the atmosphere of rumor that surrounded conversations about the loss of the ship over the same period—encouraged them to reevaluate their past experiences on board her and possibly, knowing now that the ship *had* been lost, exaggerate the past "dangers"? Were the crewmen who testified in these same terms also affected by the process? And was steward B. J. Shore right to say the crew's dissatisfaction with the *Waratah* had been limited chiefly to the older men, who dramatized the peril of the situation to enhance their own prestige: a kind of assertion of their special sea-salted status as men of no ordinary landlubber mold? The court found it significant that former pilots had noticed no signs of rolling, listing, or intractability. Does a pilot's word count for more than that of someone who has been on a ship in open ocean? We won't presume to say.

Of course, several of the witnesses were far from being inexperienced ocean travelers and at least one—Bragg—seemed well-qualified enough technically to avoid charges of landlubberly naiveté. But even there doubt existed: passenger David Tweedie had sat near Bragg at mealtimes but couldn't recall hearing him complain. No, indeed—to Tweedie's judgment, the *Waratah* "seemed to go through the water like a duck." Like his assertion that in sixteen ocean voyages he'd never known a better passage or a better ship than *Waratah,* these sentiments might have carried more conviction had he not turned out to be "an old friend" of her owners.

Nonetheless, there is no escaping the fact that for nearly every negative statement about the ship and her brief career at sea, there was a positive or placatory one to offset it. Able Seaman Edward Dischler called the *Waratah* "the unsteadiest ship I ever voyaged in" and, like the onboard surgeon, Dr. Harold Skarrett Thomas, who'd complained of being upset in his bath by her listing and jerking, left her when they reached port. (Thomas once had to grip a bunk rail to prevent being thrown out of bed.) John F. Ryan, the fourth engineer on the maiden voyage, said, "She neither pitched nor rolled anything out of the ordinary," and Morley Johnson said that the vessel behaved quite equal to any he'd been on—

the roll was not unusual. Nobody seemed to care that William Saunders had been scared by the rolling. After all, he'd only been on the *Waratah* as a stowaway. Even the fact that it was costing ratepayers the four shillings a day the BOT allowed as his expenses seemed to go against him.

From Vandam's testimony it is clear that some passengers regarded the ship's gymnastics as a joke. Theirs was the sort of humor that feeds on mild nervousness and insecurity, or perhaps upon the kind of assumed pessimism that leads us to pretend that anything we engage in is bound to be a disaster. Thus a seaman might agree that his ship was doomed simply to enter into the spirit of the thing, and, perhaps, by superstitious magical logic, to fend off the possibility that it *was* doomed. George S. Richardson, the chief mechanical engineer of Geeling Harbour Trust, claimed that when he'd told the passengers cited as witnesses in Sawyer's testimony that, "One of these days she will drop her nose down too far and not come up again," he'd only meant it in a jocular way. Even Able Seaman Dischler (no great admirer of the ship, as we just saw) admitted that talk of disaster was a sailor's conventional gambit. On joining the *Waratah* he had been warned she would not make Las Palmas, but hadn't been intimidated—"he had often had similar advice as to other vessels." There was also talk among the men about not signing on for another voyage; Captain Ilbery had supposedly made that remark about a second voyage meaning the loss of either his reputation or the ship. But most *had* signed on for that second voyage, Ilbery at the head of them.

It was a paradox: so many men had (allegedly) expressed grave doubts about *Waratah*, yet had followed her to the grave. Second Officer Henry, for example, who met the inquiry of John Latimer, a shipping clerk to the *Waratah*'s agents, with words to the effect of: "I don't like her at all. Between ourselves, I think she has a deck too many. . . . I'm different to a seaman, and an officer cannot throw up his job when he likes, but I intend to get out of her as soon as I get a chance." If the chance came, he did not take it; Henry numbered among the lost. Disgruntled cook Samuel Trott left the ship, it is true, but his dislike of her did not extend to preventing his son from going as pantry boy on the second voyage. It seems that quite a few unenamored people overcame their quotable fears and suspicions in the same way.

Not Dischler, however. He had tried to leave at Melbourne, only to be told by the captain that he wouldn't get his pay; leave he certainly did at Sydney, after telling Ilbery that he was going whether he was paid or not. His desperate determination suggests a man for whom an old nautical joke was a joke no longer. It is possible to disregard what Able Seaman Nicholas Sharp claimed Owen had told him when he was thinking of signing on for the *Waratah*—"If you can get anything else, take it, because this ship will be a coffin for somebody"—since, as we saw a few pages into this chapter, Sharp was not the most credible of witnesses and may have had financial motives for blackening *Waratah*'s reputation. But some doubt remains, and Sharp, too, got off at Sydney.

Was Owen joking when he said that to Sharp?—if he said it at all, for Alan Melville claimed to have heard the chief officer call *Waratah* a splendid ship and say that he had never been on a better one in a seaway. Or did Owen laugh when a passenger called Duncan Mason (holder of a first engineer's certificate and a man with thirty-three years' nautical experience behind him) said: "Owen, if I were you, I would get out of this ship. She will be making a big hole in the water one of these days"? Perhaps not if the reply attributed to him is correct: "I am afraid she will."

The reaction of Sir William White to this piece of testimony symbolizes the owners' response to any such damaging allegations about the *Waratah*. Testifying on the stability and related questions, the former director of naval construction at the Admiralty was effectively appearing on behalf of Messrs. Lund and his analysis of Owen's putative remark was to refuse to believe the chief officer ever made it.

"It seems you are skeptical about all witnesses," said Mr. Dickenson from the chair, in what came as close to a caution as anything during the inquiry. "There is evidence, on oath, and there is another witness confirming it." Sir William drew a breath and said he couldn't account for the chief officer having made such a statement.

None of this is conclusive, however. Was the *Waratah* unstable or was she not? Writing in his *Some Ship Disasters and Their Causes* (1968) K. C. Barnaby developed an idea contained in several inquiry-witnesses' statements: the *Waratah*, though normally stable, was inclined to be a "tender" ship. This nautical expression indicates she responded skittishly to changes of conditions, including those influenced by how her cargo was stowed. Barnaby felt that there may have been insufficient time in the ship's brief career to learn how a cargo might best be disposed and that the Durban arrangements did not cope with the severe weather she ran into within hours of leaving port. In essence, the *Waratah became* unstable under those trying conditions and capsized, going to the bottom rapidly and upside down—too rapidly for rockets or boats to be launched and in an inverted position that trapped everything and everyone on her. Hence no wreckage, no bodies.

Since—curiously and some would say suspiciously—there was no authenticated original plan of how the cargo was stowed at Durban, this must remain conjectural. Lund attempted to reconstruct its distribution, using (he said) what he had learned from stevedores, from a plan drawn up by the captain and chief officer and from weights shown in the manifests; new figures prepared by request of the court gave the cargo's weight as being between 6,253 and 6,425 tons, which, when coal, crew, stores, passengers, and sundries were on board, meant she sailed with a combined weight of about 9,961 tons. But the best of estimates is just that.

The two experts who (in our opinion) seemed less impartial, objective theoriticians than witnesses for the defense were volubly dismissive of the instability hypothesis. Sir William White, as we heard, descended on evidence conflicting with that view with a lofty skepticism that appeared to irritate the court; naval architect Robert Steele saw no indications of top-heaviness and testified on the arcana of stability data with great aplomb. "Some sort of accident must have happened," he concluded. Whether that took the form of rudder damage, engine stoppage, or something else—hatches left unbattened or else knocked off by heavy seas, for example—he was not prepared to say. But the *Waratah* had possessed ample stability, so in his opinion it had nothing to do with that.

Of course, it was very much in Messrs. Lund's interest to establish that instability or any other construction flaw had played no part in the *Waratah* tragedy. Rightly or wrongly, owners are always liable to be blamed whenever a ship goes down, at least in part, and their counsel, Leslie Scott, labored hard to dispel the impression that the generalization might apply here. His address to the court on its thirteenth and fourteenth (and final) days of hearing evidence took an urbane way of dealing with all those allegations about *Waratah*'s seaworthiness: quite simply, they were made by persons not competent to judge these things.

"On the question of stability, the evidence of no observer on ship or shore could be accepted as comparable to that of men who had knowledge of questions of stability," he stated with slightly ovoid logic, "the evidence adverse to the ship given, mostly in depositions, by persons not qualified to give such an opinion. . . ." And then, with a flagrant belittling of these opponents: ". . . such as stewards, pantry cooks, a stowaway, and men who were working their passage out."

How Prof. Bragg may have felt about being lumped with stewards and pantry-cooks—not to mention stowaways, of whom there was actually only the one called to testify—has gone unrecorded. Our opinion on whether having to work your passage on a ship makes you a less worthwhile witness than a personal friend of its owner (like David Tweedie) had better go unrecorded as well. But Scott hadn't quite finished. Next he singled out E. Crossley, who had passed on the nettling remarks about Owen definitely not being happy with the *Waratah*'s performance. "Mr. Crossley was described as a marine inventor," said Scott, uncaring of the fact that the man was occupying a seat not too far away from him, "and I am almost inclined to describe his evidence as a marine invention." A neat turn of phrase, but Crossley objected audibly to it, as did the court. Scott was reminded that he was referring to "a man of experience" who'd "been four times around the world." The counsel merely repeated that he found Crossley's reports of officer dissatisfaction incredible. In his summing up next day, he asked the inquiry "to say in the clearest possible terms" that the *Waratah* had not been lost due to want of stability "and that the owners sent to sea a ship well constructed, well found and with ample stability."

In *round* terms, this was indeed what the inquiry said. What it did *not* say "in the clearest possible terms" was what beyond all doubt had caused the loss of the *Waratah*.

At some point close to where the *Clan MacIntyre* met her—lat. 31°36′S, long. 29°58′E—the *Waratah* had been "lost in a gale of exceptional violence, the first great storm she had encountered, and the vessel capsized." But *why* had she capsized? The report stressed that the inquiry regarded her as stable with her cargo correctly stowed, that she had sufficient safety and emergency gear, that no fault could be found in her construction; there was no evidence that hatches had been left unbattened or that any other safety measure had been omitted. It expressed incomprehension over Ilbery's total silence, maintained even in letters containing myriad trivial details of his daily life, concerning so exciting and dominating a prospect as his new ship, the more so as the inquiry would have expected him to make some reference to her stability and behavior at sea as a matter of course: "The court is unable to understand how silence could have been preserved on such an important and interesting subject." From the wording of this sentence it seems likely that the Blue Anchor Line was suspected of having suppressed or withheld certain information prejudicial to its reputation, interests, or future prospects. And notwithstanding Lund's explanation of the demurrage dispute ploy and his simultaneous qualification of the captain's remarks about the *Waratah* not being as stable as the *Geelong*, the owners were also criticized for what the court read into that episode. The stability of passenger ships must be reviewed, ended the findings of the inquiry.

But these were virtual asides. They did not answer the crucial question of why the *Waratah* was capsized (if she was) or how she came to vanish (if by some other cause). To look closer into that we need to move beyond the BOT inquiry's findings, and we cannot do better than to turn to J. G. Lockhart.

Lockhart reduced the possibilities to five. The first of these, namely, that the *Waratah* had been disabled and drifted off course to some remote

Southern Ocean corner, we have already looked at; though the fact that several expeditions covering increasingly large areas did not find traces of her is not absolutely conclusive, it is very suggestive. And again, if disabled, why was she not overtaken by the slower-moving *Clan MacIntyre*? If, as some predicted, her steering system had been affected, why did she not engage the handsteering gear, the work, as Barclay & Curle's superintendent engineer James Shanks testified, of only four or five minutes?

We have also considered the view that the cargo taken on board was badly stowed (or, if we posit that the *Waratah* was a "tender ship," that its disposition counted against her in the storm). At the same time we mentioned that the theory must be treated as conjectural. Not unrelated to this is the proposition that the 614 tons of coal in the spar deck had disturbed the vessel's center of gravity. It was known that on two occasions coaling had to be suspended because the ship was showing increasing signs of "tenderness." The coal storage in general had been examined closely by the court. Lund calculated that the *Waratah* had left port with a little under 2,377 tons on board; P. A. Marshall calculated that her dead weight overall was 9,204 tons, taking into account the coal supplies on the upper and lower 'tween decks. Whatever the figures, the spar-deck bunker does not seem likely to have upset the ship. As Messrs. Lund's superintendent engineer, James Shanks, testified, a spar-deck coal load of 600 tons was not unusual on vessels at this time and the *Waratah* might have sailed out with only 250 tons in her spar-deck bunker.

Conventional safety precautions may have been neglected, but again we have pointed out the unlikelihood of this possibility, especially under a commander as experienced as Ilbery. Finally, Lockhart sifts over the stability issue, noting the divergences of opinion between expert and non-expert. There is no need to go over that again.

Summarizing and drawing his own conclusions, Lockhart takes the view that the *Waratah* went down in the bitter storm of July 29 (and too suddenly for launching of boats or even distress rockets) because, though ordinarily stable and capable of withstanding the conditions of ordinary seas, she ran into conditions with which her design and construction were unable to cope. Failure of her steering gear, a cargo shift or unbattened hatches may have contributed; it is easy and safe to say we will never know for certain. Returning to the subject in *Strange Tales of the Seven Seas* five years later, he had little to add beyond pointing out that there were survivors enough from the *Vestris, Trevessa,* and *Shahzada* to prove that sometimes (happily seldom!) a healthy ship will founder for no apparent cause.

John Harris's *Without a Trace* struck us as the best post-Lockhart description of the *Waratah* mystery; it contains a perfect and meticulous summary of the court of inquiry proceedings, for example, if you cannot get hold of the official report, and it has a good deal to say on the matter of theories concerning disappearance. We can start by noticing his evidence that the waters in which that event took place have a reputation for sudden and fierce gales. Percy Evans, chief officer of the *Raboul,* apparently told Lockhart in 1936 how he'd been caught on a sound, stable 11,000-ton steamer by one such; gigantic waves smashed hatches and the front of the bridge, making it seem less incredible that the *Waratah* might have come to grief this way. Evans believed the ocean bed fell steeply at the point where a huge wave took the ship, explaining the lack of wreckage. Or there is the "blow hole" theory wherein the *Waratah* was sucked into a gulf in the ocean and drawn by powerful inshore counter-currents into some submarine cavern.

The notion of a powerful, vacuum-like effect lurking off the South African coast—a strange, deadly combination of gale, current, and ocean bed contours capable of drawing a ship down and perhaps of keeping it forever—may seem uncomfortably close to the romantic occultist excesses of the "Bermuda Triangle." Or, less perniciously, to one of the three "vile vortices" located between 30° and 40°S of the southern hemisphere, as described by Ivan Sanderson in his *Invisible Residents* (1970): places distinguished by abnormal surface currents where hot and cold water meet to create atmospheric and meteorological disturbances and all associated with unusually high numbers of vanished ships and planes. Such concepts could be unnecessary luxuries. According to Cpt. W. S. Byles of the *Edinburgh Castle* and another Harris source, we may need look no further than the swell that can develop in heavy seas off that part of the Cape. A change in wave patterns—the ship caught before she had time to recover and ploughing into the next wave at 30°, taking sea on board: that ship might, in a graphic phrase, drop into a hole in the ocean—not a literal hole, but a metaphorical one. Or perhaps it would take no more than a freakishly large wave, the kind that might trouble a modern steamer let alone an Edwardian one, which could smash wooden hatches and flood the forward holds: once again, the apt image would be of a ship pulled down.

* * *

Our second installment in the *Waratah* mystery may, after the first, seem anticlimactic, but it is worth recording, containing as it does a hint of an unsolved enigma and (even more blatantly) evidence of a cover-up.

Three ships claimed some sort of contact with the *Waratah* after she left the *Clan MacIntyre* behind. The third of these was the *Tottenham* and in her case the contact allegedly took the ghoulish form of sailing through bodies that probability suggested might have come from the lost ship.

At 12:05 p.m. on August 11, 1909, the Antwerp-bound *Tottenham* was somewhere between the mouth of the Bashee River and East London, which lay twenty to twenty-five miles to the north-northwest of the *Waratah*. The initial alarm seems to have come from Third Officer E. F. Humphrey, who said he had seen two objects twenty yards away on the port side: objects that "appeared to be human bodies face downwards." Apprentice M. W. Curtis was more specific: to him, the four-foot-long thing apparently wrapped in red was a little girl wearing a red dressing gown. For a second he "saw something like a head, but no limbs."

On hearing Humphrey's report—for it seems he either did not hear Curtis's version or disregarded it—Cpt. Charles Edward Cox ordered the ship to alter course, but they failed to get a more positive sighting of whatever was in the water; there were (according to Humphrey again) two more bodies, one with a gull perched on its head, and a white floating shape that could have been a sheet or tablecloth. Cox appears to have gone about with no great expectation of finding corpses and some sources state that he was already convinced that all they'd see were sunfish or dogfish. Sure enough, he would later claim that they "found nothing but a big sunfish" and "several pieces of matter which [he] took to be dead fish," or, in the light of other evidence, blubber; after all, these were whaling waters and whaling is a messy operation.

The *Tottenham*'s second mate, John Noble Day, was to tell the inquiry that he and Cpt. Cox had hurried to the bridge "and saw all round the ship pieces of fish floating . . . one piece larger than others with an albatross on it." There were some discrepancies between his testimony and Cox's, however; Day, who some sources claim had also spoken of what he saw as a little girl of ten or twelve, dressed in red hood and cape, bare-kneed, which sounds remarkably particular, asserted that the captain had examined the larger piece of flesh through the glass and pronounced it the trunk of a body!

The *Tottenham* sailed through bits of fish until 1:30 p.m., when engineers came on deck saying they had seen a small girl's body close to the ship. Chief Engineer John C. Hammond had been at dinner when the second engineer asked: "What is that in the water?" Up on deck, Hammond evidently heard Cox's remarks about sunfish, flesh and/or blubber; though some writers report that he confirmed Humphrey's verdict, the *Times* quoted him as saying that the "little girl" had proved to be a four-to-five-foot-long roll of paper with a dark red wrapper round its middle "such as was used for printing." Another skeptical view came from the masthead, where Chief Officer David E. Evans had been on watch for half an hour—some of it spent concentrating on a brown object that he eventually identified as a big skate—and on two pieces of what he simultaneously deglamorized as flesh-like blubber.

The evidence of the remaining witnesses is soon dealt with. Second Engineer T. Stewart (whom we just heard of drawing the attention of his senior to something in the water) thought he had seen the body of a little girl ten years old, the trunk of another body just below the surface, then a mattress and a sheet. Engineer Artificer A. J. Tucker also thought he may have seen a little girl in a red mantle. And lastly there was the enigmatic koan-like brevity of the Chinese fireman: "Plenty bodies sea side."

But were there? The *Tottenham*'s evidence is scarcely unchallengeable, especially when the certainty of Cox and Evans is opposed to it. As just mentioned, there would be nothing remarkable about blubber (or "fish") in the waters off this part of South Africa and presumably Cox was sufficiently experienced to know this; he could also anticipate that "bodies" would most likely turn out to be sunfish. The obvious conclusion is that the *Tottenham* had sailed into a field of ichthyological debris left by whalers, fishermen, or both.

It may seem odd that others among the crew, chiefly those who thought they'd seen a body or more than one, did not recognize this possibility. Alternatively, acknowledging as they must have done the difficulty of making exact identification of strange objects partly submerged as they float by in the waves, it seems peculiar they should fix so specifically on a little girl in red. Why did they not entertain the idea that the object was more likely a fish, blubber, or something less dramatic than a human corpse?

But then, they all knew that the *Waratah* was missing. At Durban there had been orders, *strict* orders, said Day, for them to look out for her or for signs of her. It is quite obvious that they were obeying those directions. This was, moreover, the time of the first organized searches; on board *Tottenham* there may well have been an expectation, expressed or tacit, that they might come upon traces of the lost ship and that in all probability those traces would be bodies. We can imagine a mood of expectancy throughout the ship that some officers may have been unable to resist.

A strange object is seen in the water, not so strange in reality, perhaps, if you have seen the debris left by fishermen or whalers, but certainly exciting to a mind primed to be on the lookout for things more dramatic than sunfish, skate, or blubber. There is no need to accuse the *Tottenham*'s crew of leaping to false conclusions. But once the rumor-like quasi identification of the object as being *like* a little girl in red was voiced (and regardless of whoever made it first) it acted like a powerful suggestion. It gave intelligible form to a previously unintelligible focus; even when aware that the object might *not* be a body of a little girl, it was hard to avoid repeating the description. Possibility became belief. The talk of the little girl in red filtered through the ship and it is not impossible that it conditioned how the anomalous object was identified or at any rate how it was described.

The theory seems quite acceptable, but it is not a good reason for dismissing the incident forthwith. Interestingly, apprentice Curtis appears to have stuck to his original opinion—that the object was a human child—even after hearing Cpt. Cox's firm statement that the red-streaked thing they had seen was a sunfish (or more than one). Many things might have been solved if Cox had taken the logical step of lowering a boat to investigate more closely. He thought of it; for various reasons, he did not do it.

On the same day and also off the Bashee estuary, but not precisely in the same place as the *Tottenham,* the British steamer *Insizwa* allegedly sighted four bodies in the water. What we know of this is partially colored by journalist J. H. Blenkin's account in the *Rand Daily Mail* of December 1, 1928, which provided insider information on an episode nearly twenty years old.

The *Insizwa* had reported its sighting of the "four supposed bodies trending south-west, and a large number of birds same direction" via the Cape Agulhas lighthouse on August 13, 1909. With a newsman's enterprise, Blenkin arranged to be first to get on board the ship not long after she arrived at Table Bay, where he interviewed Cpt. Moore in his cabin.

Officially, the incident was closed; a government tug had been sent out from East London and was said to have found only blubber and offal. But Moore had a different story to tell: "I have not the slightest doubt they were bodies of human beings. Two were clad in white and two in dark cloth . . . floating in close proximity to the ship and I was able to see two of them out of the cabin window. The others were observed on inspection from a higher point." He had not lowered a boat; there were ladies on board and he had not wished to alarm or distress them . . . the *Insizwa*'s cargo had shifted, she had a dangerous list, and it would be dangerous to bring her to a halt in the heavy seas. Even without having taken that measure, the captain sounded full of conviction about what he'd seen in the water.

The curious thing is that when he saw his testimony in writing—which he did after Blenkin reported the contents of the interview to

Sir David Graaf, the colonial secretary—Cpt. Moore seems to have undergone a change of heart and a change of mind. He grew reserved, cautious, vague. It was comparatively easy and perhaps advisable for the court of inquiry to disregard what he said.

Blenkin attached a serious suspicion to Cpt. Moore's unexpected change. Lockhart (*Strange Tales*) quotes him as believing that, "On board the *Insizwa* was someone in authority in the company that owned the vessel, who immediately realized that if Cpt. Moore persisted in his statement both he (the captain) and the steamer would be held up, and the service of the line disorganized by the compulsory attendance of himself and some of the crew at the Cape inquiry which had been forecasted."

Considered in tandem with the *Tottenham* evidence, this anecdote may suggest that the crews of two different ships were identically deluded by floating blubber or fish detritus; or conversely that the two ships separately encountered floating corpses, possibly though not certainly victims from the *Waratah*'s last voyage. And taken in combination, the *Tottenham* and *Insizwa* cases may point to some kind of deliberate suppression of vital evidence: a cover-up.

Cryptoconspiracies always make good reading and allegations based on that sort of motif are fairly easy to construct. J. H. Blenkin may have been a frustrated sort of journalist; Cpt. Moore may have availed himself of the universally followed privilege of reassessing at leisure what he had said in haste (and, as per proverb, repenting at leisure). His lapse into vagueness might have been a result of natural self-doubt. But we cannot rule out Blenkin's suggestion that the captain's vacillation was induced by pressure from unknown person(s) in authority over him. No captain, no ship owner, is fond of delay; it breeds passenger complaints and costs money. An Edwardian captain, regardless of his service record, was a paid servant of the line owner and often at the mercy of his employers. Some anecdotes relating to Ilbery of the *Waratah* imply strongly that he felt he had not received the full recognition that his four decades in the Blue Anchor Line merited and there is an inference that to some extent he was not in a position to influence the owners' decisions. But Ilbery was in a stronger position than most masters. In an era where company loyalty was an unwritten qualification for captaining a ship, Moore may have felt it tactful to strike his colors when someone pointed out the inconvenience of the statements attributed to him by Blenkin.

Was Cpt. Cox under pressure (overt or understood without being told) to suppress the facts of what the *Tottenham* saw? Or was he the sole source of the pressure?

For pressure seems to have been exerted. Once again, the witnesses' versions do not dovetail, but such is the impression of the authors of this book after dividing up the statements in favor of and against it. Third Officer Humphrey recalled how, on the evening the ship docked at Simon's Bay, Cape of Good Hope, he had heard Cox telling Evans that if asked about the incident, they—he and Evans? the ship's crew as a whole?—should say they had seen nothing unusual. It seems reasonable to conclude that the captain feared it likely that someone would ask. And sure enough, they were interrogated by an officer from the *Forte,* one of the H.M. vessels involved in the search for the *Waratah.* The chief officer duly replied that . . . they had seen nothing unusual.

For his part, Humphrey remained convinced that he had seen bodies, not blubber or sunfish. He was equally certain that the captain "did not want to know." The most destructive remark he imputed to Cox was that he'd excused himself by saying that "his owners would have a very poor opinion of him if he bothered about picking up these bodies and conveying them to the nearest port when there were ships out there paid to search." This was rather more explicit than what Day claimed the captain had told them—to wit, that "it would be best to say nothing of what had been seen as it would cause controversy and delay." It almost certainly would have.

The apprentice, it seems, remained a security risk. Young Curtis had not heard Cox caution anyone to keep quiet about the affair, but in due course he was challenged to repeat his version of events in front of the ship's agent and he insisted on saying once again that he'd thought he had seen the body of a small girl in red. This apparently took place at Melbourne (presumably on the *Tottenham*'s next outward-bound run) and Cox warned him against mentioning the story "as it might cause friction in the town." This was true as well; Australians had been lost with the *Waratah* and feeling ran high in the ports with which she was associated. There would have been severe inquiries as to why Cox had not stopped to pick up the bodies or at least to have confirmed that there *were* no bodies. Someone might well have asked why he did not lower a boat.

John Day, the second mate, was to tell the court of inquiry the seas were too heavy for the launching of a boat; the same explanation was one of two or three interrelated reasons given by Cpt. Moore for not stopping the *Insizwa.* But Humphrey said that the *Tottenham* was in smooth waters and in his opinion a boat could have been launched. From his own comments as reported in the *Times,* it appears that Cox had ruled out the idea even before he put the *Tottenham* round because he already believed the "bodies" were some kind of fish. It is tempting to think the incident may have created a division among the crew members or that it exploited existing ones; the tenor of Humphrey's evidence reveals a barely disguised animosity towards his captain and this he may have shared with others on the ship. At any rate, it is interesting to see that Cox received support from only two of the *Tottenham*'s crew who gave evidence at the inquiry, and that both were seniors on board the ship. Chief Engineer Hammond maintained that the captain had expended considerable effort to investigate the bodies in the water; Chief Officer Evans said that allegations of Cox ordering a discreet silence about what they had seen were false. There seemed no compromise between the opposing views experienced by the *Tottenham* witnesses.

It seems nearly certain that Cox did talk about the advisability of hushing up what they had seen. He may not have passed orders to that effect, but by virtue of his position the statements assigned to him by three different witnesses came across as directives rather than pieces of advice. He may also have conceded that perhaps the floating objects *could* have been bodies and, in admitting that, simultaneously conceded that he ought to have investigated more closely. But this may not have been the case at all. Cox may have been motivated purely by the belief that any doubt on the subject of what they had seen would cause delay and that he would be held in disfavor by his employers. Humphrey claimed the captain had predicted this would be the outcome "if he bothered about picking up these bodies and conveying them to the nearest port." But it might have been the same if he'd spent time looking for bodies that turned out to be lumps of blubber; the delay would have been less, but there would still have been delay. This, and not the fear that he *would* discover actual bodies (and hence be saddled with all the responsibility that went with them) was probably the real reason he refused to lower a boat.

If Blenkin was right about Moore's strange onset of vagueness—if the captain of the *Insizwa* truly came under pressure from some higher authority to change his account, the motive being to avoid all the disruption to the ship's schedule that an inquiry would entail—we can believe that Cox anticipated the same kind of prejudicial response from the owners. And yet the *Tottenham* was allegedly under strict orders to look out for traces of the *Waratah*. Admitting that these orders (or should we read "instructions"?) may have come from someone other than the ship's owners, it seems incredible that Cox should suppress evidence of the very sort he had been encouraged to look for and report. Cox may have assumed his employers would cast a jaundiced eye upon his becoming too assiduously involved in the search when "there were ships out there paid to search," and he may have been right about that; nor would we seriously expect to find any record of them expressing such a callous view. But we cannot confirm that he was acting on such unspoken orders rather than upon his own estimation of how they would react. The owners may have been a good deal more lenient, more humane, than Cox supposed; they might have regarded his situation as unavoidable. For all we know, the company might have been delighted at the publicity-value of one of their ships being the first to locate indisputable traces of the vessel for which so many were searching. They might as easily have held that it was his duty to investigate those objects in the sea, regardless of whether they were bodies or not.

And it may strike some readers that Cox was belatedly conscious of this. He may have known that a few people, or a great many, would believe he had acted in a summary fashion: that he had deliberately taken the easiest way out of risking delay to the *Tottenham* by overruling all opinions contrary to his own. He may (and we, the authors, tend to believe he did) truly think the objects nonhuman. But there would be criticism that he had not been vigorous enough in checking. That Cox appears to have been concerned about this is indicated by his remarks on the need to avoid "controversy and delay." Although he never went to the extent of issuing an "official version" or of telling his fellow sailors that they had to "get their story straight," he definitely urged a uniformity of negative reporting. Was this, as he implied to Curtis, to spare people's feelings, or had he a more personal motive?

Over the past four pages we must have used the word "may" a dozen times. For a writer, this is unpleasant; it gives what he is saying a tentative feel of which readers cannot approve. In the *Waratah* case, though, it is the only realistic style to adopt. We *don't know* what happened to the ship and virtually every event associated with her is fringed by conflicting evidence or, more frequently, by conflicting opinion. As we enter now into a still more shadowy realm of rumors, allegations, and unlikely stories (not to mention lies proven or suspected) we need to appreciate that probability may have to do duty for certainty.

Our third and final *Waratah* mystery may not be intelligible unless it is presented in the context of a certain climate that prevailed when the loss of the ship seemed an inescapable conclusion: a mental mechanism that underwent sporadic revivals long after the event ceased to be topical and became history instead. We have noticed the gap between what informed people thought concerning the *Waratah*'s stability and what less informed ones were liable to think or conjecture. Once the spotlight moves away from all the stability curves, stowage plans, latitudes and longitudes, and other hard data of workaday nautical life, this "belief gap" grows wider and less cautious. The stories that follow exploit the fact that people wanted sure information and in its absence would accept, partially or wholly, some very peculiar replacements, no matter how many years or decades elapsed between the vanishing of the ship and their oft-unexpected appearance.

There were variations on the hoaxer's perennial favorite, the message in a bottle, some averring that the *Waratah*'s passengers were still alive. The reflection that comes to mind when you are watching a particularly boring conjuror suggests itself in these cases: it's not a question of *how* they do it, but of *why* they do it. The audacity of the hoaxers did not stop at tricks with bottles, however; over the years there were a few ambitious spirits who came as if from nowhere claiming to have survived the destruction of the ship. Perhaps they were inspired by rumors that there had or may have been survivors, or by nebulous quasiidentifications of amnesiac individuals as *Waratah* survivors. Such a man, says Lockhart, had allegedly been found wandering the veldt close to Port Elizabeth: he bore no identification and only the vaguest account of himself except that he had come ashore from the *Waratah*. To borrow something that Charles Fort wrote of a similar amnesia case, there may have been doubt about where he came from but there was no doubt where he was going after telling a story like that: the mysterious survivor was dispatched to Grahamstown Asylum.

Two other claimants appear to have been in full possession of their faculties. The proud boast of the Irishman named Staunton that he had survived the wreck of the *Waratah* lasted about as long as it took someone to think of checking the lists of crew and passengers (whereupon his name proved not to figure among them). John Noble—no relation to the second mate of the *Tottenham*, we hope!—enlivened the year 1922 with a highly creative lie about having transferred from the *Telemachus* to the *Waratah* some time after the latter left Durban, after which he survived the capsizing, reached the shore, and got to Cape Town. Finding no one to believe his story, Noble took ship on the *Telemachus* once more and never mentioned his adventure again until (for whatever reason) he went public with it some dozen years afterward. The fact that a ship called *Telemachus* was found to exist was more than slightly outweighed by the fact that back in 1909 she wasn't within a thousand miles of the *Waratah*.

If you couldn't be the last person on the *Waratah*, you might be the last to have set eyes on her. A number of people claimed the honor of having seen her go down—from some vantage point on the shore, obviously—or had it claimed on their behalf. Lockhart tells of a letter from H. D. Barry to the *Daily Mail* (1928) that was based on what he had heard while visiting the Transkei area between East London and St. Johns in 1913. Among the inhabitants of Willowvale it was "common knowledge," he wrote, that a white man had witnessed the end of the *Waratah* and Barry had travelled out to his camp on the Qoka River to talk to him. The rediscovered witness said he had seen the steamer come close inshore on that wild, storm-tossed night, but she had vanished before he could fetch night glasses to study her. The man also claimed to own a piece of wood with the letters "War" carved on it.

Unfortunately, but perhaps predictably, the story was vigorously spiked by Harry Hulse, ex–Cape Mounted Rifles, who had been one of those who had searched for wreckage of the *Waratah* at the time. He could not agree that there was any element of "common knowledge" about what Barry had written; he had not heard of a ship close to shore then and he had not heard of it since. Not unreasonably, he wanted to know why the Qoka River man had not come forward when the search was in progress—when his information was most needed.

Perhaps the witness had some personal motive for keeping quiet, as (according to Frank Price in 1954) had Jan Pretorius. Price said he had met the elderly Boer around forty years before and was sworn by him not to repeat the story while Pretorius lived—the story being that he had seen *Waratah* wallowing in porcine state close to shore, heeling over, disappearing. Pretorius didn't publicize the episode because that would have meant publicizing himself when he had been where he should not have been doing what he shouldn't—illegally prospecting for diamonds. From what little we know of the prohibitions surrounding the South African diamond trade, this motivation towards secrecy seems reasonable; but would Pretorius really have lived in fear of reprisals forty years after the event? Was he still liable for prosecution, or was he still active in the illicit pursuit of diamonds?

If the *Waratah* sank close to the shore—if!—then somebody might have seen her doing so. The immediate objection to that is: if she went down so near the shore, and if the sharks snapped up any bodies (as some suggested), surely the wreck itself would have been spotted sooner or later. According to a final collection of regrettably unconfirmed stories, it was—later.

In the winter of 1942 South African Air Force pilot Lt. D. J. Roos noticed a submerged wreck during a mail run over the area where *Waratah* had vanished. No wreck had been reported from here and Roos sketched a map that ought to have led anyone to corroborate his sighting. One Durban newspaper tried, but the chartered plane was balked by engine trouble and bad weather. Roos died in a car accident some time afterward and his map was lost until 1973, when it was located in a family album.

But it is not thought that he had rediscovered the *Waratah*. The wreck Roos saw lying on its side upon a rocky shelf off Mazeppa Bay could have been one of many victims of the U-boats; the Dutch passenger liner *Columbia,* torpedoed by U-156 in 1942 while serving as a submarine depot ship, has been suggested as a likely candidate.

Another airman contributed to the discussion in March 1973. Former Royal Air Force Wing Commander C.V. Beadon calculated that the *Waratah* could be found at 29°46′E, 32°36′8″S in 21 to 24 meters of water, which was where novelist Geoffrey Jenkins had placed her two years previously. So much for theory; more intriguingly, a South African Airways pilot was said to have seen her (or something like her) not once but several times at the spot indicated by Beadon. Do we put this down to an instance of someone seeing what he has been led to expect he will see? Or do we believe that Pat McGahey, the mayor of Grahamstown and the origin of this story about the pilot, did exactly what he claimed—checked the report, visited the spot and found the wreck in about 30 fathoms north of the Fish River? Whether he did or did not, the *Waratah* remains officially undiscovered.

The survivors who weren't, the last sightings, the rediscoveries, are all variations on the theme of confirmation. Each in its way answered a question for which official channels held no solution; for want of certain fact, imagined or rumored semblances came into currency. The same dearth invited information from inspirational sources. At the same juncture, the shocking unexpectedness of the event encouraged stories that expressed a belief that no tragedy is ever unexpected; that nothing occurs without warning. One symptom of this were the hindsighted declarations of those who "knew" the *Waratah* was doomed; the symptoms (her instability, her unseaworthiness) they said, were all signs crying out to be read and acted upon. Allegations that the tragedy had been foreseen—paranormally, precognitively—served the same function. And other psychic revelations, notably from those who received by allegedly supernormal channels information about what had happened to the ship and why, served the former: they purported to fill a gap in the understanding.

Paranormal claims of both types seem to have associated themselves with the loss of the *Waratah* from the moment it entered the public consciousness. There is nothing derogatory in stating that. For anyone believing that he or she was possessed of abilities beyond the normal, or that he or she knew someone else who apparently possessed such abilities, it became logical to attempt to glean information from those faculties, the more so as information didn't seem to be forthcoming from more orthodox ones.

We are tempted to believe that there were many more attempts of this kind than ever reached the printed page and even more certain that many more accounts reached the printed page than we have seen. Anybody who wants to follow up that hint could do worse than scan the Durban and Cape Town papers for the period about August 1909 onwards. South Africa had a number of small but flourishing spiritualist circles at this time (as correspondence and lecture-tour reports in publications like *Light* and *Two Worlds* indicates) and the Cape seems to have been a regular port of call for British mediums; it is very likely that proselytizing individuals would have passed on *Waratah* communications and clairvoyant episodes to the press as a matter of course. For ourselves, we are content to offer a sample from what may be an undisclosed library and hope that the sample makes its point.

Passing hurriedly over John Harris's mention of a King William's Town (South Africa) woman named Morris who was supposed to have seen the *Waratah* striking a rock during a storm and going down funnel first, we come to the tale of an unnamed fifteen-year-old schoolgirl who told her friends of a warning dream in which she saw the ship sink with loss of all on board, herself included, presumably. When the *Waratah* prepared to leave Durban the girl had to be pulled up the gangplank by her parents. These are good stories, but they lack all necessary detail for sound analysis.

For different reasons, two mediumistic accounts published in the spiritualist paper *Two Worlds* as late as 1937 seem beyond the scope of any kind of analysis; either they speak for themselves or they don't. The first of these (from Louis S. Vernon-Worsley in the edition of June 25, 1937) is not even a personal experience. It merely relates with some minor variation the strange case of a passenger with which we will deal more thoroughly in a moment. The other (C. W. Hutchins, July 16, 1937) was a report of what trance medium Miss A. Nuthal of Brixton, London, had revealed during a home circle or private seance at the writer's house. An entity identifying himself as the *Waratah*'s captain had come through at or about the time of the ship's disappearance, describing a failure of the steering gear; this, as you may remember, was a theory taken up by quite a few people, so in itself it was less than fantastic. The same hardly applied to the rest of his narrative. The *Waratah* had drifted into the "Saragossa Sea" (sic), her crew had mutinied, the captain had been killed. Hutchins concluded with a remark that it would be interesting if any of this could be confirmed. Well, yes . . .

Another phenomenon with which we deal more thoroughly in our chapters on the *Thresher* and the *Titanic* is the "vague feeling" that with hindsight becomes a manifestation of psychic power. A person may at any time experience an odd suspicion that something may happen; the sensation may seem in defiance of what that person's logic declares probable or it may be little more than an admission of some outside probability that the unlikely event could happen. If the event then occurs, however, there is a good chance that the experient will come to believe the vague sensation or impression was a veritable psychic assurance that the event was going to transpire. Simultaneously, other people—writers hard-pressed to fill a book on true-life accounts of the supernatural, for instance—may seize upon the experient's vague impression and represent it as a veritable example of clairvoyance/precognition/etc. in action.

The case of Robert Dives, a member of the Institute of Mechanical Engineers at Newcastle-upon-Tyne and a minor figure at the *Waratah* inquiry, may seem to afford a typical illustration of this process—only he himself did not see matters in that light. Dives testified that he'd gone to see the *Waratah* in Durban harbor on July 26 because of "a sort of premonition that if he did not go and see the vessel then he would never have the chance again." He went away with a poor opinion of the ship's high bridge—too high for her stability, as it seemed to him—and was laughed at when he broached his opinion to others.

At first glance this doesn't sound too impressive and not much like a psychic "message." To suggest otherwise might risk placing a false stress on Dives's choice of phrase; "a sort of premonition" could be no more than one of those formless feelings we just spoke of and perhaps an expression of a probability: he had no way of being certain that he'd ever be in a position to inspect the *Waratah* again. Later we will be discussing what Maj. Butt of the *Titanic* could have meant when he spoke of wanting to see Westminster Abbey because "if I miss the Abbey now I shall never see it again." Butt wasn't a young man; he probably had no idea when he would be in England again (if ever) and it must have seemed to him that he'd not get the opportunity to visit this attraction if he passed up this one. On the face of it, Dives's comment about the *Waratah* amounts to the same thing.

Fortunately for us, someone at the inquiry thought it worthwhile to inquire how Dives was using the word "presentiment." Was he, then, a believer in clairvoyance? "I am a believer in divine inspiration," qualified the witness. "I think I was led to notice this peculiar bridge and to consider it a source of danger." Not that we can be sure it *was* a source of danger, nor that it caused or contributed to the loss of the *Waratah*: all we can say here is that Dives appears to have thought he received some kind of paranormal insight into the fate of the ship. Skeptics, knowing how we tend to reevaluate these momentary sensations when events transpire as to make them seem both extraordinary and uncannily accurate, may feel unimpressed by his conviction.

Quite a few of the inquiry witnesses' statements take on this quasi-predictive tone thanks to hindsighted knowledge of what happened to the *Waratah*. Duncan Mason's remark to Owen that she'd make a big hole in the sea one day demonstrates this. Here and elsewhere we have to distinguish between a personal belief or opinion (couched in the most vivid language!) that is justified by later events and an oracular, psychically received statement of fact before the event proved it to be a fact.

Most psychic anecdotes concerning the loss of the *Waratah* were, strictly speaking, peripheral to it. By contrast, Claude Sawyer's was on the way to being an integral part of the mystery. It was not a digression, but was presented at the court of inquiry as a thing of unusual importance. In the introductory phase on the first day of the hearing it was promised that,

> A gentleman named Claude G. Sawyer, who was a passenger and who had joined the ship at Sydney, was now in London. He had intended going in her to Cape Town, but he left the ship at Durban because he had apparently satisfied himself that she was dangerously top-heavy, and there could be no doubt that it was in his mind when he left the ship, because he telegraphed to his wife "Booked Cape Town. Thought *Waratah* topheavy. Landed Durban." His decision was biased to some extent by two dreams which he says he had. It was proposed to call him and he would tell the Court what the dreams were.

Sure enough, Claude Sawyer's evidence dominated the second day of the inquiry and consequently the news media's reportage of that session. Two-thirds of the *Times*'s coverage was taken up by it, other papers reflecting its uncommon interest to much the same degree. It should be said that few showed signs of giving undue prominence to the supernatural elements of the story; all dwelt attentively upon the more prosaic observations that preceded it. But a glance at the headlines confirms that for most editors the real newsworthiness of Sawyer's testimony lay precisely there and nowhere else. "A Warning Sword," said *Reynolds's Newspaper*; "Vision of the Sword," replied the *Daily Express*. "The Man With the Sword," was the *Daily News*'s slightly more precise offering. "Warned By Dream," the *Daily Mirror* preferred. "Saved by Dreams," chorused the *Daily News* in its follow-up piece. *Lloyd's Weekly News* took a deep breath and came out with something that almost managed to subsume everyone else's headliner: "Dream Man's Drawn Sword Vision That Warned *Waratah* Passenger."

The reverberating key words alone told a good deal of where the story's focus lay: "dream(s)"—three usages; "sword"—three; "warned" or "warning"—three. It is no misrepresentation to write that if Sawyer's testimony dominated the day's events, his account of the ominous dreams that had "to some extent" influenced his decision to quit the *Waratah* dominated the rest of that testimony.

He began, however, with an impressionistic catalogue of all he had noticed wrong—all he'd heard described by fellow passengers as wrong—with the ship. Traveling home to England from New Zealand, Sawyer found at Sydney that the only ship available to him was the *Waratah*; he booked as far as Cape Town with a reservation to continue to London and was given berth 122, a cabin on the port side of the promenade deck. Why he didn't book through to London right away is not stated. It may be worth mentioning that our hero was experienced in ocean travel; this trip was actually his thirteenth voyage by sea. Number thirteen—unlucky for some, as they say, but not absolutely for Claude G. Sawyer.

The *Waratah*'s limitations soon came to his notice; indeed, he made it sound as if even a blind man would have been aware of them. He recalled that she left Melbourne with a "big list to port" and that afterwards, as though by way of compensation, also listed to starboard (and hung there for a distressingly long time) whenever she met a patch of disturbed water. Fine weather in the Bight made no difference and passengers complained of the rolling, though perhaps they would have done better to reserve their criticisms until the ship left Adelaide when the roughening of the weather caused the ship to roll in earnest, "in a very disagreeable way," so that *Waratah* took her time about recovering her balance and gave a decided jerk on reassuming the horizontal. Several passengers had more cause for complaint than most; Sawyer testified that they had taken a few falls.

Not long after this Sawyer noticed that when the *Waratah* performed one of her rolls, his bathwater took an angle of 45 degrees. He discussed the rolling with the ship's officers (who were noncommittal) but also with two fellow travelers, one of whom was a Mr. Ebsworth—then a solicitor, but formerly a sailor for seven to nine years. All three studied the way their vessel pitched heavily forward; on going into the trough of a first wave she would keep her nose down into the second and instead of rising to meet it "simply ploughed through." As he clutched at a railing to preserve his balance, Ebsworth remarked that he'd never seen a ship remain in that position for so long.

By now Sawyer was thinking seriously. He knew this was only the second voyage of the *Waratah*; he seems to have been negatively impressed by the damage sustained by his shipmates. Among the victims was Mrs. Caywood, who had hurt her arms and hip in a fall, spent two incapacitated days in the saloon and eventually reached her destination at Johannesburg in an invalid chair. He had also seen Dr. Fullford and Miss Lascelles flattened by one of the *Waratah*'s idiosyncratic jerks as they crossed the deck—in fine weather with a smooth sea. With Durban still ten days distant, Sawyer decided he would not be going on to London—he would not be going on to Cape Town, even. He informed Cpt. Ilbery that Durban was as far as he was sailing on the *Waratah*. He didn't tell him why, but when he announced his decision to other passengers (Mr. Muller, Mrs. and Miss Hay) he was less reticent.

And then on the night of July 21, with Durban only four days away, came dreams. When Sawyer testified that dreaming was "unusual for him," he obviously meant that usually he didn't remember his dreams, but these dreams were not the kind a person would forget. "He saw a man with a long sword in his left hand, holding a rag or cloth in his right hand saturated with blood." Sawyer added here that immediately the thought occurred to him that "I will know it again": we could take "know" in the sense of "to recognize" (if he saw it again), but Sawyer seems to have meant he would *experience* the same dream again, which is what he said happened. In all he dreamed the dream three times that early morning and "the last time he looked so carefully that he could almost draw the design of the sword."

Such was the outline of Sawyer's three-times dream as reported by the *Times*'s correspondent (with a few minor borrowings from other newspaper accounts by way of clarification). And, presumably, as he himself described it to Ebsworth. We aren't told precisely when, but that may not matter. Ebsworth, according to Sawyer, "said it was a warning," at which time Sawyer became "anxious to get off the ship." There's little surprising in that, we might well imagine.

On docking at Durban on the July 25, Sawyer discovered he had neuritis. At least, this was what the *Times* understood him to have said. By implication, he blamed this condition on all he had endured aboard the *Waratah*. The obvious and skeptical response would be to insist that his experiences on that ship, including the weird dreams—perhaps most especially the weird dreams—were the *product* of neuritis, rather than the experiences acting as the cause of it. The point matters somewhat, since our medical dictionary makes it clear that neuritis is not merely a flashy term for "nervousness," an important distinction, because at least one writer has described Sawyer as "a nervous man," which tends to detract from the evidential value of his warning dreams. Quite simply, if Sawyer suffered from "nerves" he would appear a far less credible witness. That much appears to have been in Counsel Scott's mind when, examining Sawyer on behalf of the *Waratah*'s former owners, he made a point of asking Sawyer if he suffered from "nerves" or "nervousness."

This was when Sawyer mentioned that he had discovered he had neuritis—though he specified (and the *Daily Graphic* duly reported) that he had only been told so when he reached London, not Durban, as per the *Times.* Again the point may be too fine to matter much, yet it deserves a few more moments of our concentration.

Technically and properly applied, neuritis is a name given to the inflammation of a nerve or nerves. It can be localized in one part of the body or generally distributed as "multiple neuritis." Symptoms can include vague pains, tingling sensations in the limbs, muscular weakness, loss of voice and feeling, as well as other, more marked effects. Our medical dictionary does not suggest that a person could contract neuritis simply as a result of worry or stress, the kinds engendered by a voyage on an ostensibly dangerous ship, for example, or that its symptoms run to odd dreams and hallucinations (of sword-bearing men, for instance). It *does* say, however, that multiple neuritis takes two to three weeks to develop, making it unlikely yet not impossible that Sawyer succumbed to or contracted the ailment while on the *Waratah.*

Sawyer claimed that he was told he had neuritis when he finally reached London; he doesn't say by whom, though we might anticipate that person to have been a doctor. Nor does his response to Scott's question really help us to decide what part neuritis might have played in his experiences. Are we to assume the onset of this illness predated his passage on the *Waratah*? That the onset of its more notable symptoms coincided with the time he spent on her (and culminated in his alarming dream)? Or conversely, that when Sawyer claimed to have neuritis he did so without medical sanction, the diagnostician *not* being a trained doctor after all? It may be that he was led to attach a fashionable or convenient term (spuriously) to what was actually a kind of overall nervous debility, rather like a headache sufferer will say he has migraine and a cold in popular parlance is always "flu." And it may be that neuritis/ nervous debility does not relate to Sawyer's dream experience at all.

After his arrival at Durban, Sawyer's course of action was not that of some chronic invalid. On July 26 he called at the offices of the Union Castle Mail Steamship Company to arrange a passage home on another vessel and, coincidentally, while he was there he met Charles F. H. Hadfield, the clerk who had booked him to Cape Town some months before. Sawyer told him of his recent adventures, confiding that he regarded the *Waratah* as top-heavy; by strong inference, the experiences he talked of included the ominous dream, but we will examine that part of his conversation later. The couple must have met again on a separate occasion, too, after the *Waratah* was long gone, since Hadfield allegedly called Sawyer a lucky man, saying that he must be gifted with second sight because the ship was overdue at Cape Town and that a steamer had been sent to look for her.

It cost or lost Sawyer more than £8 and the difference in fare to London to transfer ships. He was in place to watch the *Waratah* leave that evening. On board her were Ebsworth, and the Hays women, who'd not responded to his advice to do as he had done. *Waratah*, he noted, was listing slightly to starboard as she sailed out into the Unknown.

Sawyer also telegraphed his wife, informing her he had broken his journey because he "thought *Waratah* top-heavy"; he produced a draft and the cable for the inquiry's interest. That was not until August 4, though, which means he did not notify her at the earliest opportunity, but at a time when it seemed obvious to many the *Waratah* had foundered. Quite conceivably, the cable was to allay any alarm she may have had about his safety. In fact, Mrs. Sawyer probably hadn't heard of the *Waratah*'s disappearance yet, but her husband was not to know that. Next day (August 5) he took the *Kildonan Castle* to Cape Town, whence he returned courtesy of the *Galician* to England.

In between these activities, Sawyer had one last nocturnal visitation. No man with a sword this time: in the dream that came to him on the night of July 28, he was not on the ship but looking down on it from a distance. He saw the *Waratah* amid big waves, one of which broke on her bows and pressed her down; the ship rolled onto her starboard side and vanished. As a purely imaginative scenario it was no more fantastic than most of the theorized ends that had been, or would be, put forward. As a genuine psychic impression, it was more than that; for as a certain Nepesh wrote in *Light,* "If Mr. Sawyer's vision be true in detail, it is probably the only precise information we shall ever have as to how the *Waratah* went down."

The inquiry offered Sawyer hearty congratulations on being with them to give his evidence. Though its summing up observed the fruitlessness of passing opinion on what clairvoyants had to say of the *Waratah*, the fact remains that Sawyer had been taken seriously enough to warrant an invitation to give testimony in person; that testimony had been listened to, dreams and all. It does not follow that Claude Sawyer displayed any particular courage in repeating his story under such formal conditions and in front of a critically aligned audience; contrary to common belief, witnesses of the paranormal are not uniformly intimidated into keeping silent about what has happened to them and in our experience many are more than willing to publicize their adventures. Despite that, Sawyer deserved some credit for putting his dream warnings on the BOT record and his posthumous reward has been that no one who writes on the *Waratah* in any real detail would want to omit the part about "the man with a long sword in his left hand, holding a rag or cloth in his right hand saturated with blood."

But not every writer who mentions that incident chooses to do so in precisely those terms. Over the years some decidedly odd versions of Sawyer's dream have appeared, perhaps no more than slenderly related to the story as it was just told.

As we mentioned, our account (and the direct quotes given in it) derives from the *Times*'s report of day 2 of the inquiry—December 17, 1910—with a few extra details from other papers. Sawyer had been waiting the better part of a year and a half to present his evidence and all the laws of common sense dictate that he must have recited the story of his dream on any number of occasions before then—perhaps, we conjectured at one stage, to a journalist or two. Retellings nearly always breed variations and perhaps embellishments. It seemed to us when we began to dig into the episode that some earlier version of the story—earlier than what we took as the "official" version in the *Times,* that is—could exist and that certain odd fluctuations in it as told in later sources might have arisen from it.

So it turned out, insofar as a published, pre-*Times* version of the story existed, evidence that Sawyer had told the story to the press before he appeared at the inquiry. But, surprisingly enough, it contained very few variations of detail and none of them significant.

"The Mystery of the *Waratah*" appeared in *John Bull* for January 22, 1910—eleven months before the BOT inquiry. It was in many ways an unlikely venue for a story of this kind and the placement came about in an indirect fashion; evidently Sawyer told of his dream to his friend the Honorable Southwell Fitzgerald, who wrote of it in earnest, cogent terms to *John Bull*'s editor, the excitable Horatio Bottomley, member of Parliament for Hackney South. Being equally impressed, Bottomley invited Sawyer to call at the weekly journal's offices, which he did, confirming all the details Fitzgerald had set down. Bottomley (even more impressed now—possibly scenting a sensation) printed it.

As *Light* commented when summarizing the article, Fitzgerald's concluding assurance that the informant was no believer in the world of dreams, spirits, and visions was equally true of *John Bull.* Those entities smacked of the chicanery and crankishness which it was the magazine's self-perceived, self-appointed role to mangle and mutilate in its strident, hectoring columns. Under the bluff patriot symbol of John Bull, the proud and tough archetypal Briton—not to mention the politicized guidance of Bottomley, for whose ideas it was little more than a mouthpiece—the paper attacked cant, deception, governmental dereliction and, oddly enough, "killjoys" with solid enthusiasm. The paper could be atrociously self-congratulatory, too, as when it lauded itself as "a wonderful—in many respects, the most wonderful—institution in the journalistic world" at the start of its January 1, 1910, number. By form, *John Bull* should have flayed Sawyer's dream and made its hide into a football. Instead, it gave both dream and dreamer its seal of approval.

"We are very skeptical as to dreams," warned the authorial voice at the start of the article. "We have heard of many wonderful dreams presaging events, but we have always heard of them *after* the event." That Fitzgerald was able to convince *John Bull* of the dreamer's integrity—that Sawyer was able to convince *John Bull* that he had told the story to others prior to the confirmatory event, though as the magazine remarked they were no longer around to corroborate that detail—made all the difference. The dream of Claude Sawyer was published, not as an interview per se, but in the words of Southwell Fitzgerald.

It was much as we heard before: a thorough report of the *Waratah*'s failings as noted by this observer and then the supernatural portion. Sawyer had a vivid dream, three times over, and on each occasion he saw it after he was sufficiently awake to sit up in bed. The dream or apparition was "that of a man standing at the head of his cabin, with his left foot forward, with a long straight sword in his left hand, holding up a rag saturated with blood in his right hand," large drops of blood falling on the floor. "The sword was between Mr. Sawyer and the rag, as if to keep him off." Fitzgerald wanted especial note taken of the "fact . . . that Mr. Sawyer actually sat up in bed and saw it each time." And, of course, he had told others about it, including Hadfield. *John Bull* concluded, not very originally, that here was one of those cases of truth being stranger than fiction.

The article was a moderate success. *John Bull* was able to run a short series of "Mystery of the *Waratah*" pieces on the strength of it, each one presenting views from what was alleged to be a large reader response. Strangely, perhaps, the correspondents seemed to respond most forcefully to the first part of Sawyer's account. They agreed the *Waratah* was top-heavy or unstable; there were trenchant notes from a naval architect and reports of how the *Durham Castle* had sailed a few hours ahead of her into seas like walls, causing one of her officers to comment that *Waratah* would never survive it and would go down like a stone. Copeland K. Etheridge, who had known Ilbery, voiced the belief that her steering gear or rudder was disabled and the hope she might yet be found drifting somewhere. But only one of these selected correspondents tackled the subject of Sawyer's dream and he, a "merchant service officer," had little complimentary to say about it.

Ignoring the additional data provided by this article by Southwell

Fitzgerald, we can compare Sawyer's story in *John Bull* with the "authorized" or notarized version recorded in the *Times* almost a year later. There are no major variations of detail between them; they are remarkably consistent. By the conclusion of our research we had studied ten different newspaper reports of Sawyer's dream, all but one taken from his testimony at the inquiry in December 1910. The same consistency emerges. Of course, there may have been other accounts prior to that date that we have not seen, and if so there may have been divergences from the way the story was told in our ten sources. Allowing for that possibility, we feel fairly confident that the striking embellishments to the plot as outlined so far were not the responsibility of Sawyer, but of writers who handled the story of his dream long after its debut appearances in print.

Turning to those later versions, we find J. G. Lockhart a reliable reporter and, as already acknowledged, a source for many if not all who came to retell the *Waratah* story in his wake. He introduces only a couple of details not mentioned in *John Bull* or the *Times.* These arrive early on, where he has Sawyer describe his dreams in the following way (the italics have been added): "I saw *a man dressed in a very peculiar dress which I had never seen before* with a long sword in his *right* hand which he seemed to be holding between us. In his other hand he had a rag covered with blood."

The man of this version appears to have swapped the sword from his left hand to his right, not that the alteration suggests very much. In point of fact (and contrary to the *Times,* which specifies that the left hand was the sword hand) some other press reports of the inquiry place the weapon in the dream figure's right; *Lloyd's Weekly News,* for example, which also uses the phrase "dressed in a very peculiar dress." Lockhart must have worked from one of these alternative sources. Assuming that *John Bull* and the *Times* were correct—assuming Sawyer said the man had the sword in his left hand, not in his right—the discrepancy could be explained as mere inference; most of us are right-handed and a journalist mishearing or failing to note accurately what the witness actually said may have taken for granted that apparitions lead with their right hand as well. That reporters at the inquiry nodded occasionally is shown by the way the *Daily Chronicle* alone made the dream figure's *thumb* saturated with blood instead of the rag or cloth he carried.

The other change is more interesting. The *Times,* and *John Bull* before it, didn't pick out the witness's making any assessment of how the man was attired; now it seems that it was "very peculiar" in its choice of clothing and wore a garb that Sawyer "had never seen before." It would be helpful to know what was so peculiar about the figure's dress—in what ways so original that it defied tighter description.

Another kind of journalistic inference takes over in later versions like Lauber's (*Famous Mysteries of the Sea,* 1962). The man is still a southpaw, but the detail about the sword—and also, perhaps, an attempt to clarify in what ways his dress was strange—have transformed him into a *knight in bloodstained armor,* a more dramatic creation by far than the one in our original. We can partly understand how all this came about; a "man with a long sword" certainly suggests a "knight" from popular iconography; the bloodstained armor is a more flagrant translation of the original blood-saturated cloth. But would Sawyer describe a knight in bloody armor as "a man in a very peculiar dress which I had never seen before"? Everyone, surely, has seen pictures of knights in armor; why didn't Sawyer *say* the man was a knight if that was what he resembled? Perhaps Sawyer wanted to indicate he had never seen any *living* person dressed that way (in armor) or that he had never seen armor like it before. The variation is hard to reconcile with his original, *Times*-quoted statement or that in *John Bull.*

Still, these details do not alter the fact that these accounts remain fairly consistent. In other versions, however, writers appear to have gone beyond inferences of the "sword = knight = knight in armor" variety and some major pieces of dramatization appear.

In the Hardwicks' *The World's Greatest Sea Mysteries* (1969) Sawyer's dream depicts him leaning on the rail of the passenger deck, gazing out across the ocean; there rises from the waves a knight in bloody armor who holds as before a bloodstained cloth and a sword (which he brandishes). But in this version the mouth of the apparition opens and shuts as if speaking and Sawyer, by a species of lip-reading, makes out the words: "The *Waratah*! The *Waratah*!" before the figure sinks beneath the waves. He interprets the knight as a form of murdered man. Finally, Sawyer is supposed to have told fellow passengers of this to their amusement, but to the disapproval of Cpt. Ilbery, who has an officer caution Sawyer privately about spreading alarm on the ship. This version is certainly more energetic than the previous ones we've looked at. The ominous significance of the dream is augmented (perhaps redundantly) by the detail of having the knight name the ship, thereby underlining the fact that his message surely relates to the vessel Sawyer is already worried about; there are also elements of irony (the other passengers laugh at Sawyer, but he will have the last laugh, of course) and of cryptoconspiracy (Cpt. Ilbery orders a hush-up operation). The treatment here suggests a wish to entertain by making more of a story than the earliest versions contained.

Bill Beatty (*A Treasury of Australian Folk Tales and Traditions,* 1960) subscribes to the same view. The scene at the Union Castle office where Sawyer tries to explain to the manager (Hadfield or his substitute) why he wants to change ships is a moderately racy affair; our hero's dilemma is that he's forced to admit that he is prepared to lose a couple of weeks all because of a dream. The manager, who in fictive narrative terms is the token skeptic, suspects that Sawyer is mad, but the customer denies the imputation, asserting that he's "not the psychic type . . . I'm a very ordinary bloke . . . just a commercial traveller." (Actually, Sawyer described himself at the inquiry as a company director, but let that pass.) The dream itself is presented as a first-person account featuring "a figure of death. A corpse-like creature in a strange dress like that of a matador" with sword and bloody cloth. If, as we said earlier, the act of identifying Sawyer's swordsman as a knight was a piece of fair inference, we have to concede that the original description might fit a matador just as well. But Beatty's character is no bit player; he acts, he talks, and there's no need for Sawyer to lip-read. The figure draws aside the bed curtains in the best tradition of the ghost in a gothic novel and on the third occasion it declares: "Leave her! This is the last warning to leave the ship!" Now, that's more like what we expect from spectral knights in phantasmal armor.

Bill Beatty is writing a popular-style book of folk tales and, although folklorists may not thank us for saying so, you can get away with quite a lot in books of that kind. To Sawyer's dream he welds an account that we have not found elsewhere in the *Waratah* mystery, reintroducing Chief Officer Phillips of the *Clan MacIntyre,* who allegedly told this story to an English newspaper. When you read it, you may guess why he didn't trouble the court of inquiry with the same information.

After the *Waratah* swept by his ship in a hurricane-force gale, said Phillips (oddly forgetting that the gale didn't occur until many hours after that brief encounter), he sighted from the bridge an old-fashioned sailing vessel that, astonishingly, was sailing into the teeth of the wind.

"I'm not a superstitious man," Phillips said,

> but I know my seafaring lore. The rig of the strange craft immediately brought to mind the legend of the *Flying Dutchman*—the phantom ship of Venderdecker [sic] who played dice with the devil, lost, and, as a penalty, was doomed to sail for eternity in a ship that steered herself and never reached port. The phantom ship held me spellbound. It disappeared in the direction taken by the *Waratah*, and I had a feeling that it was a sign of disaster for the liner. When I told the other ships' officers of the vision they just laughed and joked about it. But when we arrived in London and heard that the *Waratah* was missing they regarded the episode in a very different light.

It's a pleasure to renew acquaintanceship with our old friend from chapter 1. Bearing in mind exactly where the *Waratah* was lost and the reputation of the Cape as Vanderdecken's old sailing grounds, the story would seem oddly incomplete without him. As far as authenticated sea mysteries go, however, Claude Sawyer's dream seems a much better proposition. We have not been able to track down the newspaper to whom Phillips communicated this extra nugget of information and we suspect that others before him had raised the apparition of the notorious Dutchman; but let us treat the story we just heard as a not-totally unexpected supercargo and go back to Sawyer.

The preceding versions of Sawyer's dream have been adduced as typical specimens; there is no doubt that prolonged search would turn up dozens of others. But without additional help our sample indicates a process of gradual aggrandizement, an editional or authorial program in which a somewhat meager outline is filled in, fleshed out, dramatized. Recent additions to the canon (e.g., Palmer, 1980) add no new plot details or developments. This possibly indicates that the story has become a fossil; no fresh variations on it are possible.

And as far as we can tell, there have been no variations whatsoever of Sawyer's later dream, the one in which he saw the *Waratah* overwhelmed by a large wave, roll on her starboard side, and vanish. All writers tell it more or less the same way, which is the way Sawyer told it. Perhaps by its nature it created no misunderstanding and permitted no improvisation. As we argue presently, it was also a rather different type of experience; for now, with due caution, we proceed to analysis of the first (triplicated) dream.

The first observation relates to the timing of the dream. This occurred, Sawyer said, on July 21, when the *Waratah* was three or four days away from Durban, which means it postdated his decision to leave the ship—taken, as he also informed the court, about *ten* days before she reached Durban. There is no sense that Sawyer decided to quit the vessel solely because of the warning dreams. The inquiry's introductory address paraphrased Sawyer as saying that his decision was "biased to some extent" by the dreams, not that they formulated his resolve to get off the *Waratah*. Sawyer was pressed to clarify this point, perhaps because it affected his status as a witness—frankly, a person who would leave a ship simply because he'd had a weird dream (even one that seemingly came true) was a lot less impressive than one who would leave due to his impressions of her mechanical faults.

Would Sawyer have left the *Waratah* even if he hadn't had that dream? asked Laing, the BOT counsel. Sawyer considered the question. "It reminded me I had made up my mind to get off," he said, though he admitted that he was less keen on doing so than he had originally been, now that he had "got settled down." On balance, he felt he would have left the ship even without the encouragement of the man with the sword and bloody cloth.

So the dream acted as reinforcement of a course of action already decided upon. Can we go further and suggest that it arose as an indirect expression of the nervousness Sawyer had already manifested concerning the ship and perhaps add that his "predisposing nervousness" was a direct result of a series of conditions with which he was not familiar? Earlier we quipped about unlucky thirteen, this being Sawyer's thirteenth ocean voyage, by his reckoning. If he was a superstitious man, this numerical bad-luck tradition may have affected him; we do not know that he was superstitious or that he expected thirteen to be unlucky for him. Patent in his testimony is the fact that he seemed all too aware that this ship behaved (or misbehaved) like none he had known before. A good few other people—some, like him, experienced ocean travelers—made similar disquietening observations about the listing, plunging, rolling. But we have no record of anyone else having a warning dream as a result of this unease.

The old adage about things going in threes comes to mind when trying to analyze Sawyer's dream. In other words, he had the same one three times. Recurring dreams are not unknown to psychologists, but they may be even better known to folklorists, the latter being educated in the way popular narratives often feature trio sequences: three characters sequentially performing the same actions (and probably reciting, rote-like, the same identical speeches)—reference Goldilocks and the Three Bears, Sir Patrick Spens's ship going "a league, a league and barely three," and so on. "Trio-isms" of plot serve to reinforce narrative structures and may heighten suspense merely by prolonging the story, but they also draw upon the audience's awareness that the third element in the series will bring a sort of climax: we could guess that after the sword-and-rag bearing apparition's *third* appearance in the *third* dream, Sawyer would receive no more visitations—no more warnings.

That dreams came true sometimes, that they occurred in threes occasionally, was an article of faith for previous generations. Literature students may recall how Chanticleer, the engaging cockerel hero of Chaucer's "Nun's Priest's Tale," works hard to convince his wife that dreams ought to be taken seriously as warnings by regaling her with the old legend of a murder revealed by a tripartite dream (and by a host of other examples to be found in Cicero, Valerius Maximus, and other "olde bookes"). He and his creator might have had little trouble in crediting Sawyer's dreams despite the fact that they had a certain monotonous repetitiveness; the ghostly visitor did not reveal the full story in three continuing episodes, but merely repeated the same story over and over. And, critically regarded, where *was* the story? Sawyer's dream, unlike the one cited by Chanticleer, revealed nothing; it merely suggested something. If we are to accept the account as more than a modern folktale with an undeveloped trio motif, we should look more closely at the content of the dream, which sounds more symbolic in nature than explicit or definitive.

The nature or choice of the symbol here was, of course, personal to the dreamer. It is easy to see the "man with a long sword . . . holding a rag or cloth . . . saturated with blood" as a vivid dramatization of the anxieties Sawyer experienced as a result of the *Waratah*'s unseaworthy behavior. None of the published sources have Sawyer stating that he made this connection, and in fact one earlier version (*Times,* December 17) gives no indication that he placed *any* particular interpretation upon his dream; he only says that it happened as described. Nonetheless, it seems safe to aver that the vision served that expressive function—and that it carried a warning.

That warning was directed against violent death, the inevitable outcome of Sawyer's remaining on the ship. The Hardwick version has him interpret the figure as that of a murdered man; that, too, is acceptable because the oddly dressed individual might have signified Sawyer himself ("murdered" by the *Waratah*) or the sum of humanity doomed to premature death when she sank. The bloody cloth would simply stand for blood shed (lives lost) by that misadventure.

Should we accept the post-Sawyer identification of the figure as a knight (which we claimed earlier was an inference) the interpretation becomes more interesting still. Despite the sword, this knight is not an aggressive character; in Lockhart he holds the sword between himself and Sawyer in what may be called a fending-off or protective manner. ("The sword was between Mr. Sawyer and the rag, as if to keep him off"—Fitzgerald in *John Bull*). So the "knight" could be regarded as performing the knight's traditional function: protector of the weak and perhaps also symbolizing justice militant. Close to Sawyer's own time, Algernon Blackwood invoked the idea of an apparitional knight as personal defender in one of his supernatural stories, which ends with the hero escorted through a crowd by this guardian, visible only to his eyes, who fends them off with his sword. Then there is Beatty's suggestion that the man was a matador; this has certain visual attractions, the bloody rag perhaps identifiable as a muleta and the image overall working as another metaphor of violent death. But if the figure was meant as a contribution to the warning function of the dream, why was the symbolism not more explicit—less capable of misinterpretation? Other writers seem to have wished the same thing, hence versions in which the "message" of the dream man is made more obvious by having him speak.

The second of Sawyer's dreams, wherein Sawyer witnessed the sinking of the *Waratah* as if from a distance, was more direct, less ambiguous, presenting what purports to be a cinematic view of the event instead of wrapping it up in symbolism. There is no need to presume it was literally that; the final lolling-over roll of the ship may have been a dramatic construct based on Sawyer's alarmed observations of her behavior up to this point and consequent imaginings of what would occur if she ever met a really big wave. As mentioned before, his dream—literal record or imaginative scenario—may have been quite correct; so too could Nepesh's verdict that Sawyer's vision might contain unique information on how the *Waratah* was lost. But we are left with the question: why are *some* warning or precognitive dreams so often expressed in symbols while others, including the clairvoyant kind, pose as direct representations of events? We ask that same question again in our *Titanic* chapter.

Now to the character of the witness, which is another way of talking about his reliability. Since it was not Sawyer but his friend Fitzgerald who contacted *John Bull* about the dream sequence, it seems unfair to suspect him of seeking publicity or notoriety; if, as seems likely, he talked about it to others, he can also be excused on the grounds that it was not the sort of experience a person can undergo and then forget about. The authors feel that if such a dream occurred to either of *them,* they would find extreme difficulty in keeping it to themselves.

But what kind of man was Claude Sawyer—what do we really know about him? To the stray biographical items that have emerged so far—married, an experienced ocean voyager—could be added the identifying notes to which he attested at the start of his inquiry appearance; job; company director; address: 23 Phoenix Lodge Mansions, Brook Green, Hammersmith, London. The press doesn't appear to have been over-interested in him as a person and only one of our ten sources offers any description. That rare pen portrait appeared in the *Daily Express,* where the witness is said to be tall, broad-shouldered, and possessed of iron-grey hair and moustache plus "the air of a poet rather than a businessman"; leaning on the rail of the box, Sawyer describes his dream vision slowly, "as if he could still see it." While that makes Sawyer a little more interesting, perhaps, it scarcely fills in the blanks; Southwell Fitzgerald's piece in *John Bull* is slightly more helpful. His friend had lived for three years in Natal, had spent the same duration in India and eighteen months in German South Africa. He came from an old Berkshire family of Haywood near Toplow and was "a man of absolute integrity," not one given to forming hasty conclusions. More to the point, Fitzgerald affirms that Sawyer was not "nervous" nor a spiritualist, nor as a rule a believer in dreams, which matches Sawyer's own self-assessment at the inquiry. Apparently there are no grounds for thinking him a credulous or committed occultist who intended to promote the truths of the Spirit-World through the newspapers and/or a public appearance at a formal Court of Inquiry.

A more pertinent question might ask: was Sawyer a reliable-sounding witness in matters unrelated to his dream? Is what he had to say of the *Waratah*'s performance prior to convincing? In most respects it is; many witnesses independent of Sawyer testified to the same or similar effects as those that disturbed him—the pitching, listing, rolling, the unsteadiness—and some even more outspokenly. Yet Sawyer's evidence on these issues frequently evoked hearsay; he repeated secondhand opinions, which, as events had dictated, could not be corroborated. It seems odd that the passengers who, according to him, voted the *Waratah* a frightfully unseaworthy vessel, nonetheless elected to stay on her to Cape Town. Sawyer failed to persuade the Hays to leave her at Durban, likewise Ebsworth; moreover, the last-named had heard the details of the ominous dream (again, according to Sawyer) and had said it must be a warning. Perhaps Ebsworth felt it wasn't a warning that applied to him. Or perhaps Sawyer exaggerated the depth of concern felt by his fellow voyagers, particularly that of Ebsworth. Two documents provided by Ebsworth's widow—a letter of July 19 and a diary covering the period July 8 to 24—indicated to the court that Ebsworth, a former second mate, was not at all unhappy with the *Waratah*, which he called "a fine sea-boat."

None of this invalidates the proposition that Sawyer's testimony was an honest reflection of personal observation and private opinion. The final discussion point reverts to his dream. Is there any evidence that Sawyer had one, let alone three?

We cannot confirm the contents of someone else's dreams. When a person says, "I had this really weird dream the other night," we are helpless to prove whether or not what follows is a fair and accurate reconstruction or indeed whether the informant dreamed anything at all. In the present case the legitimacy of Sawyer's claim rests upon whether he told anyone else about his dream *before* events took place to bear out the interpretation placed on it. This was the crux of the matter, and the thing that persuaded *John Bull* that Sawyer's dream merited an airing in its pages: he had told other people about the dream before it came true—or before the disappearance of the *Waratah* made the omen-like dream seem justified. He had told Ebsworth (who had interpreted it as a warning) and Miss Hay (who had said, "How horrid").

There was a logical factor militating against asking either to corroborate it, though, as *John Bull* acknowledged: "They are at the bottom of the sea." In the same article it is stated that Sawyer also wrote to his wife giving a full account of his dream, but there is no indication of when he did so (after sending the August 4 cable and en route for England?) nor of which dream he wrote (the man with the sword? the capsizing of the *Waratah*?) and in any case no one seems to have asked her to confirm or deny that claim. The only person remaining who could corroborate that Sawyer had mentioned his dream prior to the loss of the ship was the passenger clerk Charles F. H. Hadfield.

In *John Bull* again, Sawyer/Fitzgerald asserts that Hadfield was told of the dream and all *Waratah* chroniclers accept that he was. The first problem: which dream was he supposed to have heard about? Sawyer and Hadfield met at the Union Castle offices on July 26 at about 9 a.m.—that much is certain, and likewise that Sawyer told him he was leaving the *Waratah* because he felt she wasn't safe. As we just said, there is a strong inference that the unnerving experiences described by Sawyer on that occasion must have included the man-with-a-sword dream. But this is rendered meaningless by the remark attributed to Hadfield in several newspaper reports, where he is said to have told Sawyer he was a lucky man and second-sighted because the *Waratah* had been posted overdue at Cape Town and that a ship had been sent to search for her. At about 9 a.m. on July 26 the *Waratah* was not overdue anywhere. She was still in Durban harbor.

The only explanation is that Sawyer met Hadfield on some second occasion: after the aforementioned search ship had gone out (July 31/August 1) and, obviously, before he sailed for Cape Town on the *Kildonan* (August 5). The dream of which he told Hadfield did not concern the swordsman, but the *Waratah* capsizing (which he said took place on the night of July 28). But look! Bearing in mind that the dreams were equally inexplicable and equally substantiated by the fact the *Waratah* was lost, it ought not to matter which dream Sawyer told to Hadfield. All that has been said of the dream being corroborated if there is proof that the witness gave prior notice of it to a second party applies just as well to the capsize vision. You could even say that anybody who wants proof of clairvoyance might cite that dream as readily as the other one. As long as Hadfield could corroborate hearing it from Sawyer when Sawyer said he told it to him.

But here comes the next problem. It may have been that way, but that isn't quite what Hadfield says in his testimony to the inquiry. When they met at around nine o'clock on July 26, Sawyer told him the *Waratah* "was not in his opinion seaworthy, and that he had decided on the voyage to get off her at the first port of call, which happened to be Durban. He said . . . that she was top-heavy." To repeat ourselves: Sawyer may also have spoken about his dream, but in this version Hadfield does not confirm that he did so. Nor does Hadfield mention having met Sawyer a few days afterward and hearing of his dream then.

We cannot confirm someone else's dream. We cannot rule out the possibility that there was no dream—that Sawyer invented the dream he told the court. If he did so, it hardly matters whether he waited a few days or a few months; any claim made after loss of the *Waratah* became publicly known (as a fact or as a strong likelihood) would be automatically invalidated. Since we have found no independent evidence that Sawyer told any producable witness about his dream before the disappearance of the ship was established (again, as fact or strong likelihood) we cannot, according to the strictest criteria of parapsychology, rule out the possibility that he fabricated it in all particulars. Yet, for what the personal opinion of the present authors may be worth, we are inclined to believe otherwise. We think that Claude Sawyer may have had a peculiar dream not dissimilar to the one he described to the BOT's court of inquiry. He may have told people about it, too, and before the loss of the *Waratah* appeared a stark fact rather than a pessimistic conjecture. But we also believe that Sawyer's dream is not the irreproachably inexplicable story it has been made out to be.

Let us, for the sake of argument, suppose that we are wrong, that our interpretation of dates is faulty, that either or both of Sawyer's dreams can be accepted without reservation as genuine. The essential character of the two dreams has already been delineated: while the second dream of July 28 was a direct representation of a distant event arguably taking place at the time (clairvoyant), the first dream, of July 21, represented a still-distant circumstance (precognitive), allowing the dreamer a chance to act and alter his personal future. There is a possibility thrown out by Fitzgerald's article that it was not purely and simply a dream; his phraseology vacillates between "dream" and "apparition," emphasizing the "fact . . . that Mr. Sawyer actually sat up in bed and saw it each time."

So the experient was not asleep and dreaming, but awake and engaged in a sort of "waking dream," as Fitzgerald interprets the episode. However, the distinction may not apply. This could have been one of those not uncommon lucid dreams wherein the act of being awake is part of the dream setting. Or if, as some versions have it, Sawyer states that he could still see the figure when he woke and sat up, the situation becomes one of a person caught in some transitional state where the imagery of a dream continues momentarily into waking: a hypnopompic hallucination, perhaps.

Could the dreams be accepted without deeming them relevant to what became of the *Waratah*? Sawyer was obviously worried over certain aspects of the ship's behavior and, as we have said, the man with a sword appears to have been a dramatic conclusion drawn from what he inferred about its failings. But that conclusion—the *Waratah* would go down sooner or later—was not a certainty. The *John Bull* correspondent who signed himself as a "merchant service officer" scoffed at the suggestion that Sawyer had predicted or foreseen any fixed event: "How many nervous passengers dream the ship is in danger and survive," he demanded rhetorically, "but of course one only hears of these things when by a coincidence it comes true." That is a fairly common and a commonsense argument, yet it seems rather timid to use it as an escape route here. If we accept the authenticity of Sawyer's dreams, there remains the salient fact: the dream was borne out by the circumstance that the *Waratah was lost.*

While we are indulging in realms of speculation or prediction, we would like to offer one of our own. We hereby predict that the lost *Waratah* will be found one day. Dr. Ballard's outstanding feat of locating the *Titanic* with a collation of historical data (some of it subsequently proven flawed) and submersible robot camera technology has opened a new era of submarine exploration. On paper at least the problems that oppose the rediscovery of the *Waratah* are no more daunting than those confronted and overcome by the searchers after the *Titanic*; they may even be, for the next generation of undersea submersibles, lesser problems. The *Waratah* could be resurrected, not physically, but metaphorically. As they used to say at the start of each "Million Dollar Man" episode: "We have the technology."

But how to probe a story like Claude Sawyer's—how to make sense of it! We do not have the technology for that.

References

The Waratah*: Technical data, history, and inquiry into her loss.*

Our main source on these aspects of the story was the *Times* (London), particularly those issues covering the Board of Trade inquiry. See especially the reports of December 16 to 21, 1910 (all on p. 3 of the individual editions), January 10 to February 2, 1911 (pp. 3 or 4), plus February 23, 1911. The court's findings were summarized in the financial, commercial, and shipping supplementary section of the latter. Other select items on searches for the *Waratah*, reports of jetsam etc. appeared in the same paper: January 11 (p. 19), February 7 (p. 12), March 3 (p. 14), June 25 (p. 15) in 1910, and December 28 and 29, 1911 (both on p. 4).

The Board of Trade Court of Inquiry's report no. 7419 on *Waratah* (S.S.) was published on March 17, 1911. It contains somewhat less material than the *Times* gleaned during its coverage of the "live event," but as it stands as an official version of transactions we have incorporated several details from it into our chapter. Other major sources included J. G. Lockhart: *Mysteries of the Sea* (1924) and *Strange Tales of the Seven Seas* (1929) while John Harris's *Without Trace: The Last Voyages of Eight Ships* (Guild, 1988) updates the story considerably.

Some secondary sources:

Michael and Mollie Hardwick, *Famous Mysteries of the Sea* (1969).
Patricia Lauber, *Famous Mysteries of the Sea* (Thos. Nelson, 1962).
R. DeWitt Miller, *Impossible—Yet It Happened!* (New York: Ace, 1947).
Vincent Gaddis, *Invisible Horizons* (New York: Ace, 1965).

On the more minor psychic-and-related episodes:

See Harris for the briefly mentioned vision of Mrs. Morris. Chris Palmer was our sole source for the story of the fifteen-year-old who had a warning dream; see *Titbits,* week ending March 29, 1980, p. 38, for his "Mystery of the Nightmares that Foretold Tragedy." This article was almost certainly taken from some other text that we have not seen. Robert Dives's "presentiment" was reported by the *Times* of December 21, 1910, as part of its inquiry coverage; cf. *Reynold's Newspaper,* December 25, 1910. Of the home seance revelations reported by C. W. Hutchins, see *Two Worlds,* July 16, 1937, p. 464.

Sawyer's Dream

All major and secondary sources listed above give versions of this incident; see also Bill Beatty, *A Treasury of Australian Folk Tales and Traditions* (Edmund Ward, 1960), and R. L. Hadfield, *The Phantom Ship* (Geoffrey Bles, 1937).

We chose as our primary informant the *Times*'s reports of December 16 and 17, 1910, not forgetting Hadfield's evidence as published in the January 18, 1911, edition (p. 4). The versions there were compared with *John Bull*'s "The Mystery of the *Waratah,*" 8, no. 190 (January 22, 1910): 102–103. This article was summarized in *Light* 30, no. 1516 (January 29, 1910): 49, with a discussion from Nepesh following (February 12,

1910, p. 78). Cashing in on the popularity of the piece, *John Bull* then published a series of "The Mystery of the *Waratah.* What Others Say" items consisting of readers' responses: January 29, 1910, p. 136; February 5, 1910, p. 167; February 19, 1910, p. 236—"Some Notes By a Naval Architect"; February 26, 1910, p. 271—including the "merchant service officer's" ruminations; and March 19, 1910, p. 398.

Finally, we studied the treatment of Sawyer's dream in a sample of other papers, as follows: *Lloyd's Weekly News,* December 18, 1910, p. 6: "Dream Man's Drawn Sword Vision That Warned *Waratah* Passenger"; *Reynold's Newspaper,* same date, p. 8: "A Warning Sword"; *Daily Graphic,* December 16, pp. 7, and December 17, 1910, p. 10: "*Waratah* Mystery. Passenger's Dreams During and After the Fatal Voyage"; *Daily News,* December 16, 1910, p. 9: "Saved By Dreams." *Daily Chronicle,* December 17, 1910, p. 3: "Saved By Dream"; *Daily Mail,* December 16 and 17, 1910, both p. 5: "Mystery of the *Waratah*"/"*Waratah*'s Fate"; *Daily Mirror,* December 16 and 17, 1910, both p. 4: "*Waratah*'s Last Signal"/"Warned By Dream"; *Daily Express,* 16 December 1910, p. 1 ("The Liner That Vanished"), and December 17, p. 5: "Vision of the Sword."

6

RMS *Titanic*: The Unsinkable

She has lain in dark silence for over three quarters of a century now, lost in her memories, a prisoner of the icy blackness that surrounds her. But she is not alone, for she did not die alone. Her death throes claimed the lives of two thirds of her passengers and crew—fifteen hundred people—whose presence was felt by the explorers who finally discovered her resting place. Torn in half, she now lies on the sea bed, her innards scattered around her in the desolation.

But once she was a queen, the largest and most beautiful ship in the world. A few fortunate people can still remember viewing her magnificence with their own eyes. Fewer still are those who sailed on her and were lucky enough to survive. But everyone, even today, recognizes her name.

She was the *Titanic*.

The month of April 1912 was a high point in the annals of the White Star Line, one of Britain's leading steamship lines. RMS *Titanic*, the newest addition to their stable of thoroughbreds, was about to enter service as a carrier of passengers and mail. She was the largest moving object ever created by the hand of man—882 feet long, 92 feet wide, 46,000 tons. A double bottom had been built into her hull, with transverse watertight bulkheads spaced along her length dividing her into sixteen watertight compartments. This, it was felt, would be more than enough to insure the ship's safety in event of a mishap. Any water which somehow managed to get through the double bottom and enter the hull would be contained in one of these compartments, allowing the rest of the ship to continue normal operations.

But there would be no mishap. There *could* be no mishap. The mere sight of the *Titanic* was enough to inspire total confidence. Her four great funnels towered into the sky, a symbol of the final mastery of man over nature. A serious accident to the ship was unthinkable. Indeed, her master, Cpt. Edward J. Smith, has been quoted as saying, "Modern shipbuilding has gone beyond that." The British Board of Trade seems to have complacently agreed with him; their lifeboat regulations, long out of date, required that any ship of 10,000 tons or more must carry only sixteen wooden lifeboats. The *Titanic*, at 46,000 tons, was carrying the required sixteen boats, with an additional four Englehardt "collapsible" boats thrown in for good measure: total lifesaving capacity: 1,178 people. The *Titanic* was certified to carry a maximum of 3,000 people, but nobody seems to have given much thought to this enormous deficiency in life-saving equipment. Word of mouth had it that the great vessel was unsinkable, so what was the use of cluttering up the deck with more lifeboats? A single look at the sumptuous public rooms on the great vessel made one almost forget that he was even *on* a ship. What could possibly go wrong?

And yet, there *were* people who, for some unexplained reason, became absolutely certain that something was going to happen to the *Titanic* on her maiden voyage. Although a few of these people had no direct connection with the ship, others were among those who had booked their passage on the great liner. Of the latter, several people took their presentiments so seriously that they actually cancelled their passage, preferring to take *any* other ship rather than sail on the *Titanic*. Others, in spite of grave misgivings, retained their bookings for the maiden voyage of the great vessel.

Many of them paid for that decision with their lives when the *Titanic* foundered after striking an iceberg in the mid-Atlantic.

The sinking of the *Titanic* was the end of a legend, a legend that married technology to opulence, materialism to romance, illusion to fantasy. But it was also the birth of a new legend, or rather, an entire album of legends that took as their theme an idea that the loss of the great ship was, if not foreordained by some power bent on punishing humanity's overweening confidence and hubris, then at least rendered foreknowable to a randomly chosen few.

At first sight the evidence suggests that the randomly chosen few amounted to dozens and perhaps hundreds; interested readers can confirm that by looking into coauthor George Behe's previous book. We're talking, needless to add, of more *Titanic* premonitions, predictions, presentiments, precognitions: a bundle of human documents suggestive of the fact that awareness of the disaster preceded the event (or in some cases preceded public announcement of it). In setting forth a mere sample of the stories told and retold on this theme, we have been concerned with choosing a representative mixture; the moderately well-known and the obscure, the highly dramatic and the near-banal. Taken *en bloc,* they are representative of the new legend of the *Titanic.* Scrutinized analytically, even skeptically (as we plan to do, albeit briefly, toward the end of this chapter), they are not all equally convincing, not all equally evidential.

Repeat, rephrase: not all the premonitory accounts relating to this epoch-making tragedy can be taken just as they appear at first sight: that is, as authenticated or suggestively cogent instances of the paranormal. Although many examples of apparent premonitions of the *Titanic* disaster have been recorded, it would be unwise to categorize all such incidents as having had a psychic origin. Some odd-seeming occurrences were merely the result of ironic coincidences being viewed later with 20/20 hindsight.

One such case is that of an Englishman named Frank J. Goldsmith, who worked for Aveling & Porter, a firm that manufactured steam vehicles. Goldsmith had always had a desire to emigrate to America, and had finally saved enough money to fulfil his dream. Due to his fear of seasickness, however, he postponed his family's departure until he could book their passage on a large ship that would ensure a smooth passage. He chose the *Titanic.*

Goldsmith worked near two friends in the Aveling plant, one of whom was a certain A. Chantler. One day Goldsmith told his chums that he would soon be taking his family to America to make a new start.

"What about you chaps giving me something to remember you by?" he asked the two men jokingly.

Chantler took Goldsmith's question at face value and gave him a pair of outside calipers to use in his new job in America. The other man gave Goldsmith a pair of inside calipers to complement Chantler's gift.

"What's the good of your having them?" teased Mr. Chantler, gesturing at Goldsmith's new tools. "You'll get half way across the Atlantic, and down will go the boat—and down will go our calipers!"

"There is no fear of that," replied Goldsmith. "This is a brand new boat, practically unsinkable."

This sounds all very casual; a kind of familiar exchange wherein Goldsmith merely picks up Chantler's pseudomorbid remark and negates it. ("The ship's bound to sink." / "Oh, no, it won't.") We commented on this kind of "false pessimism" when assessing the climate of unease that allegedly existed among the crew of the *Waratah,* where we suggested that a species of "preventive magic" may lead us to voice gloomy remarks that latterly—but only latterly—appear precognitive. Here again a person can be heard "predicting" that a ship will sink when all rational evidence said it would not, as if by stating the unbelievable the speaker would ensure that it wouldn't happen.

Reading more into this seems as inappropriate as complaining that Chantler's "prediction" was hopelessly off the mark because the ship did very much better than only getting *halfway* to America before the accident occurred. How many other such chaffingly pessimistic statements of doom must have been uttered during this period and forgotten, unless, as for the "seer" in this episode, events gave cause for them to be remembered? Let us accept that there is such a thing as coincidence that can and does impart an ironical coloration to comments made in passing. And let us not forget the equally understandable feelings that overwhelm us when they do so. It is clear that Chantler had only been jesting with his friend, and that he had not experienced any actual premonition of danger regarding the *Titanic*. One can imagine how he must have felt later, though, when he learned that Goldsmith had perished on the *Titanic* after putting his wife and little son into a lifeboat. Indeed, Chantler regretted his little jest with Goldsmith for the rest of his life.

A few *Titanic*-related cases are on record that are not quite so clearly the result of coincidence. Three such cases involve Sophia Laitinen, a thirty-eight-year-old Finnish woman who booked her passage to America on *Titanic* and who later perished in the disaster.

Several weeks before she left home Laitinen borrowed some money that she intended to hold in reserve in case she couldn't immediately find a job in America. She entrusted this money to a friend for safekeeping, asking him to send it to her only if she asked for it. Laitinen's final instruction to her friend regarding the money was, "If I should go to the bottom of the ocean on my way, then pay it back."

Although this last comment seems prophetic at first glance, it was probably just Laitinen's witty way of ensuring that the lender of the money would be repaid even though she herself might encounter some unexpected difficulty. Laitinen seems to have been a thorough woman who was very careful about planning for her own future. Her remark (like Chantler's to Goldsmith) only takes on a vaguely precognitive flavor by virtue of the fact that "go to the bottom of the ocean" she did; without that pseudocoroborative element the remark might even be judged ephemeral to the point of forgettable. But Laitinen's story doesn't end there.

Before the date for her departure from Finland, Laitinen had an odd dream that she later recounted to a friend. In her dream she found herself standing next to a well, dipper in hand, along with some companions. The dipper slipped from her grasp and dropped into the well; Laitinen leaned over in an attempt to catch it, lost her balance, and plunged into the icy water at the bottom of the well.

"Is the water always so cold here?" she called up to one of her friends.

"Yes," he answered, "and it is running."

Laitinen's friends later recalled her description of this dream and wondered if she might have experienced a premonition. Not surprisingly, they couldn't help but compare the young woman's plunge into the cold well water with her later immersion in the icy seas that were to take her life. Although this comparison is interesting, it must be admitted that the overall content of Laitinen's dream was not strikingly similar to the experience she was to go through on board the *Titanic*. It is entirely possible that Laitinen's dream had a normal origin, any hint of "paranormality" coming from the witnesses' attribution of its relevance to her icy death in the cold, running waters of the North Atlantic. On the other hand, she appears to have been sufficiently impressed (disturbed?) by the dream to have related it to her friends. A skeptic could say that we all have bizarre dreams, often far more bizarre than this one; that many of us insist upon sharing them with friends; and that when coincidence dictates that some features of those dreams are approximated by postdating events we all leap to unwarranted supernaturalistic conclusions. There's little to gainsay that, but for a person disposed to think more kindly of psi, there remains the possibility that dream-based precognition does not involve literal perception of coming events, but a more figurative or metaphorical process to which we'll return at the end of this chapter.

In any case, much more impressive was a second dream experienced by Miss Laitinen before she left Finland to board the *Titanic* in Southampton. The "message" contained in this second dream was specific, leaving absolutely no room for misinterpretation.

Laitinen worked as a hostess and housekeeper in the home of a Helsinki merchant. After an old woman in the merchant's household died suddenly, Laitinen had a dream centered on herself and the other members of the household. She dreamed that a second (older) person in the merchant's home would die soon, followed by a third (younger) person. Another older family member's death did indeed occur following Laitinen's dream, but it turned out to be Laitinen herself who became the third, younger member of the household to lose her life.

Some readers may recall Thomas Hardy's famous *Titanic* poem, "The Convergence of the Twain," with its doom-laden line: "The Immanent Will that stirs and urges everything," not to mention "paths coincident" and the "Spinner of the Years." Frankly, it does not seem too imaginative (nor literary) to prefigure in accounts of this type a dreadful irony of the sort Hardy might have appreciated. The visionary dreams true, but cannot see that the warning is meant for herself. Laitinen seems to have been unaware that her own death would fulfill the conditions of her dream. Other people, however, were experiencing definite feelings of personal unease in connection with their upcoming voyage to America. One such person was Anna Ward.

Ward was the maid of Charlotte Cardeza, a Philadelphia society figure who spent much of her time travelling around the world. Ward had made a number of worldwide voyages with Cardeza and had just spent the winter touring Europe with her, but she was doing it against her better judgement. Before leaving Philadelphia Ward had confided to her mother that she did not want to make another voyage across the ocean. Ward's father later elaborated on his daughter's feelings about the voyage:

"She feared that something was going to happen, although she could not tell what made her fear another voyage. We laughed at her and told her that her fear was groundless, and she was persuaded to accompany Mrs. Cardeza. She said that this would be her last trip, and it came pretty near being so."

Ward was one of the fortunate few to find a place in one of the *Titanic*'s lifeboats. She survived the tragedy. Other people were luckier than Ward, however, and avoided the disaster altogether by heeding their forebodings of approaching danger and declining to board the *Titanic* on sailing day.

Tom Sims was a merchant seaman who had applied to join the crew of the prestigious new liner *Titanic*, and he was very proud when the White Star Line accepted his application and assigned him to the ship. Tom's mother, however, was not at all pleased with his impending transfer to the *Titanic*.

Elizabeth Sims was half-Welsh, and her family knew that she often had "fey premonitions" about future events. At this time Sims was worried about the safety of her son. She was absolutely convinced that the *Titanic* would be a tragic ship, and she insisted that Tom remain on his present vessel instead of transferring to the huge new liner. So certain was Sims that the *Titanic* would meet with disaster that she even visited the London offices of the White Star Line and insisted that her son's name be withdrawn from the *Titanic*'s crew roster. Tom Sims apparently acquiesced to his mother's insistent plea, for he was not part of the *Titanic*'s crew when the great vessel sailed on her maiden voyage.

Applying the strictest critical standards, we might reserve judgement on Mrs. Sims's history of fey premonitions (about which it would be interesting to know a lot more!) and attribute her anxiety to a more rational process. The *Titanic* was new—untried, we might say; its presailing publicity, with great emphasis on its unsinkability, struck some folk as daring Fate, God, or both. Reinforced by belief in her own precognitive powers, Mrs. Sims may have reacted to this generalized sense of unease with the results we have seen; once again the paranormal interpretation is justified merely by the fact of the accident.

Any number of *Titanic* premonitions might be reduced to this formula: actions attributable at the time to some nebulous (but not precognitively precise) sense of disquiet over the new and much vaunted ship subsequently "confirmed" as paranormally prescient by the (accidental) fact of the sinking. It is a near-perfect example of Catch 22: a prediction of a certain event taking place can only be confirmed if that event actually happens. And if it *does* happen, it might well have happened anyway even minus anyone's prediction that it would. And then there is the vagueness of it all. Why did Mrs. Sims feel that the *Titanic* was a tragic ship? In what ways did she foresee (or suspect) that it would be "tragic"? We are not told. If Mrs. Sims was reinforced in her thinking by a previous record of fulfilled predictions, as seems likely, do we disregard this personal factor as nonevidential or accept it as further corroboration that her "feeling" about the *Titanic* was authentically precognitive? Surely much depends on the proven accuracy of her prior premonitory experiences: was she always right, right half the time, right on some occasions but not upon others? We are not told.

Without denigrating (much less explaining) the incident, it seems fair to notice the part played by Mrs. Sims's commitment to a belief in the paranormal. Arguably, such a belief might account for the preservation and retelling of the story—by Mrs. Sims herself, by her son, by both of them; perhaps we receive a faint impression that while the episode was told in corroboration of the claim that Mrs. Sims foresaw the loss of the *Titanic* (in some way, on some ill-defined level) the reference to her previous premonitions was intended to raise credence in the fact *this* one was reliable. In other words, we are asked to believe her *Titanic* prediction because she had a record of (accurate?) family-oriented premonitions in the past; we can accept the implied accuracy of those prior premonitions on the grounds of her accuracy in the present case. We can shelve until later any questions as to how a commitment or predisposition towards belief in the paranormal may affect the telling of a story, but (*caveat emptor!*) those questions invade several of the cases to which we turn now.

A premonition not unlike Mrs. Sims's was suddenly experienced by the friend of a woman whose husband was also a crewman on the *Titanic*. The names of the people involved in this case were not made public in the original report. For the sake of convenience, pseudonyms will be used here (except for the name of the unknown *Titanic* crewman and his wife, where use of a pseudonym might hinder their possible identification at a later date).

On March 26, 1912, Angus McCormack and a friend called upon Edward Henderson for the purpose of having an informal discussion on spiritualism. Mr. Henderson was out at the time, but Mrs. Henderson asked the two gentlemen in to wait for him. The three chatted together pleasantly.

Suddenly McCormack's attention was arrested by a small photograph hanging on a nearby wall. The picture was at such an angle that he could not discern its subject matter, but a subtle, subdued light seemed to surround the picture, playing around it in an odd manner. Impressions about the photograph began to form in McCormack's mind.

"Is that a photograph of a lady?" McCormack asked his hostess, to which she replied in the affirmative.

"Is she about twenty years old?"

"No," replied Mrs. Henderson, "but the photograph was taken a few years ago, and she would have been about that age then. You know her, it is Mrs. K——."

"You have seen her today?" asked McCormack, and again he was answered in the affirmative.

"She is in some anxiety or trouble?" he continued.

"No, not specially," responded Mrs. Henderson. "But her husband is starting on a new voyage, and it may be that. She is always naturally anxious at such times."

So far it might appear that McCormack was a victim not only of some peculiar psychological aberration induced (perhaps) by the chance refraction of light on a picture, but of Mrs. K——'s own anxieties at her husband's imminent voyage. From what follows—as from what preceded—it seems probable that he knew a little of the lady in question, but not enough to make the ensuing scenes intelligible.

"He has got a better job, hasn't he?" continued McCormack, "with a step up and more money to it?"

"Yes," answered Mrs. Henderson. "He is going on this new liner the *Titanic*, and it is a step up for him."

Although he had never met Mr. K—— or heard any details about his career, McCormack suddenly became depressed and agitated when the *Titanic*'s name was mentioned. His impressions continued.

"I don't like that ship," McCormack stated flatly. "There's something wrong about it, I can't make out what, but there's something the matter with it. It doesn't seem very serious and seems to happen before it gets out of port, but I don't know. I don't think it's serious. Mr. K—— will get back all right; I don't think you need worry. I don't like that ship. There's a hole right through the skin of it. I don't think it's serious, but there's a hole right through its skin."

The conversation of the three people moved on to other topics, and the above exchange was almost forgotten until two weeks later, when the *Titanic* went down.

During the first few days after the sinking, published lists of survivors were so incomplete and contradictory that no one could be certain who had survived the disaster. It was during this period of uncertainty that Mrs. Henderson's husband called upon Angus McCormack and remarked upon the singular impressions McCormack had experienced regarding the *Titanic*. Mr. Henderson was a spiritualist and had been attempting to contact the "other side" to find out if Mr. K—— had survived the sinking or if he had perished with the majority of the *Titanic*'s human cargo. Mr. Henderson had received no definite answer, however, and he feared that K—— was among the lost.

Unsatisfied with this verdict, however, McCormack stated that he could not believe K—— was dead, and that he was almost certain that he would be found among the saved. A few days later McCormack's intuition was justified when K——'s name appeared on the list of survivors.

Suppose that McCormack knew a lot more of Mr. and Mrs. K—— than this summarized account allows us to assume. Suppose, particularly, that he knew that Mr. K—— was on the *Titanic* before Mrs. Henderson informed him of the fact; his remark about K——'s having "got a better job . . . with a step up and more money to it" rather implies that he may have heard of the man's promotion (and to which vessel), even if he had forgotten about it. If so, McCormack may have been voicing yet more of the general malaise concerning the unsinkable and awesomely huge new ship, a disposition augmented by those understandable fears attributed to Mrs. K—— who was "always naturally anxious at such times," fears of which he may have been aware also. But what can we make of the predictive phase that followed this prelude?

At first glance, Angus McCormack's original impressions about the *Titanic* seem to be very wide of the mark. After all, he said that something would happen to the *Titanic* before she got out of port, but that it would not be serious. What could be further from the truth?

In reality, McCormack's impression was 100 percent accurate! Although not widely known, an incident occurred to the *Titanic* at Southampton that fills the bill exactly.

After *Titanic* had left the White Star dock and begun steaming slowly through the harbor toward the open sea, she passed near two steamers moored side by side at another dock. The outermost ship, the *New York,* was closest to the *Titanic* as the great liner moved slowly past. The huge amount of water being displaced by the *Titanic* drew the smaller vessel away from the quay, snapped her hawsers, and pulled her out into the channel. The *New York* drifted helplessly toward the *Titanic*, pulled relentlessly along by suction from the great liner. The stern of the smaller vessel swung toward that of the *Titanic*, just barely missed it, and then drifted along the entire length of the *Titanic*'s port side separated from her by a matter of feet. Only quick work by several tugs prevented a collision right there in the harbor.

Reviewed again in this light, Angus McCormack's impression of a "not very serious" accident to the *Titanic* while in port is right on the money. True, he mentioned that the *Titanic* would suffer an injury that would pierce her hull. Is it possible that McCormack was "picking up" and confusing two separate impressions about the *Titanic*—one impression concerning the accident in port and another impression concerning the fatal collision with the iceberg? Whatever the case, his final impression concerning the safety of K—— was also proven correct.

Another premonition was experienced by a friend of someone who intended to sail on the *Titanic*. Unlike the above two examples, however, this story did not have a happy ending.

William T. Stead, the well-known crusading editor of the *Review of Reviews,* was planning to sail to the United States in April 1912, having been invited there by the U.S. president himself. Stead was not as excited about his presidential invitation, however, as he was about the huge new passenger liner he would be traveling on.

One day Stead and an up-and-coming young journalist named Shaw Desmond were walking together along the Strand in the heart of London. Desmond was attempting to discuss an article he was writing for Stead's *Review of Reviews,* but the older man kept steering the conversation back to his own upcoming trip. Stead announced that he would soon be sailing on the *Titanic*, a new ship reputed to be unsinkable, and he waxed eloquent on the vessel's size, speed, and other outstanding qualities. Shaw Desmond had never heard of the *Titanic* before listening to Stead's monologue on the subject.

The two men continued along the Strand together until, at one point, Desmond drew slightly apart from Stead. It was then that an odd feeling suddenly gripped the young journalist, a feeling that he later described as follows:

"There came to me for the first time in my life, but not the last, the conviction of impending death. In this case, that the man at my side would die within a very short time. It was overpowering and I felt rather helpless, nor did I for a moment associate it with the liner of which he had been speaking."

Desmond decided not to mention his sudden forboding of Stead's fate, and the two men eventually went their separate ways. It is doubtful whether Stead would have responded to the warning anyway. If the material relating to psychic adventures surrounding the loss of the *Titanic* says nothing else, it confirms that he was on the receiving end of enough premonitory cautions from seers professional and amateur to fill a modest library; one more prediction of impending doom could hardly have shaken his sang-froid. Most of these clairvoyants seem to have been negligent in the recording of their premonitions about Stead until long after the event—a regrettable lapse that greatly reduces their evidential value. When Desmond arrived home, however, he was astute enough to jot down a brief notation regarding his premonition about Stead, and he dated it "for future reference."

It was only a few days later that news of the *Titanic* tragedy reached England. Although there were early rumors that Stead had survived the liner's sinking, Desmond felt certain that the rumors were false and that his own premonition about Stead's fate would prove accurate.

"He is not saved," Desmond told his wife. "He is drowned."

Desmond's forboding of his friend's approaching death proved to be accurate. William T. Stead met his death on the *Titanic.*

Other persons' warnings aside, it is a moot point whether Stead himself experienced some kind of premonition about his coming demise on the *Titanic.* A number of his ostensibly casual remarks (recalled to mind after the event, admittedly, and usually out of context) have inclined a few people to believe so, yet on balance he does not seem to have experienced any "feeling" specific enough to deserve the term "premonition."

The reverse applies in our next case, where the percipient can be seen to labor under a distinct feeling of approaching danger, albeit not enough to cancel his passage. As a result, his life was forfeited.

Maj. Archibald Butt, military aide to U.S. President William Howard Taft, was also a close friend of Theodore Roosevelt. When the Republican Party could not decide whether Taft or Roosevelt should be their presidential nominee for the 1912 election, Butt was distressed by his divided loyalties. Both nominees were his close friends, and he felt enormous pressure at being caught in the middle of their conflict.

Aware that Butt needed to get away from these problems for some much-needed rest, his friend Frank Millet, a noted artist, asked him to accompany him to Rome in March. Although Butt accepted the invitation, he immediately felt guilty about "deserting" the president during a critical time.

In late February Butt wrote a letter to his sister-in-law in which he informed her of his travel plans.

"Don't forget that all my papers are in the storage warehouse," Butt told her, "and if the old ship goes down you will find my affairs in shipshape condition." Aware that this statement might alarm the good woman, he added a good-natured disclaimer. "As I always write you in this way whenever I go anywhere, you will not be bothered by my presentiments now."

"*As I always write to you in this way whenever I go anywhere*": the statement alone seems to rule out any overemphasis by the writer, and as readers we have to bear that in mind. Nonetheless, it seems clear that Butt *was* having strong forebodings of some approaching personal danger. Although his friends attributed his uneasiness to the stress he was under, Butt himself told them that he had "never had such a peculiar and constant feeling of impending trouble."

This feeling may have had something to do with what Butt did next. In spite of having agreed to accompany Millet to Rome, Butt awoke on February 26 determined to remain in America. He sent wires cancelling all his sailing arrangements, then told President Taft what he had done. The president would not hear of Butt's change of plans, insisting that his aide go abroad as originally planned.

Resigned to making the trip to Rome, Butt drew up his will and asked several of the president's Secret Service people to witness it for him. Butt told these men that he had "an unaccountable feeling that he would encounter some terrible danger before he returned."

A day or two before he left Washington, Butt walked through the White House grounds with a friend, and the two men discussed the major's upcoming trip. Butt told his friend that he "had the strangest feeling he had ever had in his life that he was to be at the center of some awful calamity." Butt said he had had this feeling for several weeks and could not shake it off.

Butt sailed for Naples with Frank Millet on March 2, 1912. After delivering messages from President Taft for the pope and the king of Italy, Butt relaxed and tried to build up his strength. Both he and Millet made reservations to return to America when the *Titanic* sailed in April.

Although Butt's presentiments of danger may have continued throughout his vacation, he seems to have felt that, by booking his passage home on the *Titanic*, he would avoid the last possible source of danger his trip might present. He told Baron Carlo Allotti that his vacation had been very pleasant, but that he wanted to get back to America in a hurry.

"I'll get to Washington in time," said the major, "because I am fortunate enough to have a reservation on the new *Titanic*. When I step aboard the *Titanic*, I shall feel absolutely safe. You know she is unsinkable."

By the time that Butt and Millet arrived in London, however, Butt's presentiments seem to have returned and intensified. A close friend said later that, although usually of a lively and genial temperament, Butt was strangely depressed for several days before the *Titanic* sailed, so much so that his friends were concerned about him.

"I must go along to see Westminster Abbey," Butt told them on April 9, "because if I miss the abbey now I shall never see it again."

A typical-enough statement from a man unused to foreign traveling, we might feel; a man voicing every tourist's fear that unless he sees such-and-such a sight *this* time, the opportunity might never come again. But how are we to account for Butt's severe depression prior to sailing? Normally a cheerful man, Butt *should* have been looking forward to returning home and resuming his interrupted work on behalf of President Taft. It is difficult to fathom why Butt's depression would suddenly become so acute as to elicit comment from his friends.

On April 10, 1912, Butt and Millet arrived in Southampton and sailed at noon on the *Titanic*. Five nights later they perished when the vessel foundered.

On April 10, as the *Titanic* had been about to leave Southampton on her maiden voyage, a British woman named Estelle Barnes arrived on the Southsea Beach in Portsmouth. Barnes's fiancé was sailing to America on the *Titanic*; the two sweethearts planning to be married upon his return. The young man had asked Barnes to come to the Portsmouth beach and watch as his ship sailed down from Southampton and out onto the North Atlantic.

As she gazed out to sea Barnes saw the *Titanic* sail into sight from behind a tall rock in the distance. The great liner steamed slowly and majestically past the wide, red sand beach, and the young woman stood there alone, lost in thought about her future husband's journey to America.

"There goes the *Titanic*," said a voice from close by. Startled, Barnes glanced to her left and saw a woman in a golden brown dress with a matching hat and parasol. The woman was looking directly at her.

Estelle Barnes had been alone on the beach only a moment before, and she wondered where her new companion had sprung from so suddenly. Being preoccupied with thoughts of her departing fiancé, however, her attention quickly returned to the steamer in the distance. A few moments later, however, the voice again called out to her. Looking to her right this time, Barnes saw the woman with the parasol standing about twenty feet away and still watching her.

This time the woman told Barnes to call the police and the White Star Line and tell them to order the *Titanic* to return to port. The woman explained that, unless the *Titanic* turned back now, tragedy would overtake the ship in just a few days' time.

Barnes glanced out to sea at the departing *Titanic* before looking back to where the woman with the parasol had been standing only a moment before. There was no one there. Barnes was once again completely alone on the beach.

Barnes returned to the Apartment Hotel in Portsmouth and told her fellow guests about the warning she had just received from the lady in the golden brown dress. Some of Barnes's listeners believed in her story; others thought the whole idea was crazy. Barnes was afraid to approach the police or the shipping line and ask them to abort the *Titanic*'s maiden voyage, fearing that these officials might consider her a lunatic and make trouble for her. In that she was probably correct.

The *Titanic* continued on her way, carrying Estelle Barnes's fiancé and twenty-two hundred other people toward their rendezvous with destiny. Barnes never saw her sweetheart again.

Even by *Titanic* standards, this is a highly dramatic account. There is a possibility that it is too dramatic to be strictly or literally credible and Barnes's standing as a spiritualist may be forced into the reckoning: of all the cases dealt with in this chapter, hers is by far the most theatrical and, to be honest, the least acceptable in terms of conventional thinking. But this isn't to say that it stands completely alone. Not far removed from it in dramatic impact is the curious dream of one M. Abrahams.

On the night of April 13, 1912, four nights after the *Titanic* had sailed from Southampton, M. Abrahams retired to the bedroom of his comfortable English home. Although aware that his nephew had left home on April 9 to begin a journey somewhere, tonight Abrahams did not give the matter a second thought. It had been a long day, and he soon fell asleep. Abrahams was not destined to sleep very soundly this night, however, for he began to dream.

In his dream Abrahams found himself standing beside his son at the dress circle of a theater. Something suddenly attracted his attention, and Abrahams looked up at the left side of the theater gallery. Much to his surprise he saw the side of a ship where the theater's wall should have been. To his alarm Abrahams could also see his nephew by the ship's side. The young man's face was haggard and very white as he raised his arms imploringly toward his uncle. Abrahams noticed that he could see his nephew only from the waist up.

This dream left a very strong impression on Abrahams after he awoke on the morning of April 14. He could only recall four other times in his life when vivid dreams like this had made such a deep impression on him. All four of these dreams had come true shortly after he experienced them, so Abrahams was naturally concerned about what the dream might mean.

He did not have to wait long before its meaning became apparent.

Although Abrahams had not known it, his nephew had travelled to Southampton on April 10 and booked his passage to America on the *Titanic*. The young man was destined never to reach the New World, however. He was one of those fifteen hundred people who went down with the ship the night after Abrahams experienced his curious dream.

Another odd occurrence took place in Groton, Massachusetts, on the night of April 14, 1912. Mrs. H. M. Chase had spent the early evening hours with her daughter, the two women laughing and enjoying each other's company. By 10 p.m., however, Chase retired to her study, her mind occupied with the domestic duties she faced during the coming week.

As she stood alone in her study, Chase's orderly planning of the next day's breakfast menu was interrupted by an unexpected manifestation. A face suddenly appeared—disembodied and floating at arm's length in front of her. It seemed to be composed of a chalky white light, and the image undulated slightly as Chase stared at it in surprise. Portions of the image were slightly darker than the lighter areas, but the features of a bearded man could be plainly distinguished in the hovering vision.

Looking at the image very closely, Chase saw that there were deep lines between the eyes that gave the face an expression of puzzled surprise. The forehead was high while the beard and hair were quite full, the whole giving the impression of great power of mind and physical endurance. Chase felt that the face was that of someone who had died with great suffering, and she noticed that both the hair and beard of the apparition were "stringy," as if wet and windblown.

The next morning Chase said nothing to anyone about her experience of the night before. By the evening of April 15 newspapers were reporting the *Titanic*'s collision with an iceberg, but there was still no hint that the vessel had foundered. Chase, however, was somehow certain that different news would soon arrive regarding the liner's fate.

On the morning of April 16 a friend phoned with the news that fifteen hundred people had perished with the *Titanic*. After receiving this message, Chase decided to tell her daughter about the face she had seen two nights before.

"I wish I could know any individual among the *Titanic* passengers who was elderly and had a face like the one I saw," said Chase.

Later that afternoon Chase's daughter bought a copy of the *Boston American*. On page 4 was a photograph of W. T. Stead, the British journalist who had perished on the *Titanic*. Although the face in the photograph seemed younger, Chase immediately recognized it as the same visage she had seen in her own study on the night of April 14.

Perfectionists may lament that Chase did not confide in her daughter sooner—say, before learning of the loss of the *Titanic*—but the fact remains that she appears to have instinctively made the connection between the face of her vision and the fate of the ship as relayed by her friend's phone call; indeed, she seems certain that the bearded features belonged to one of the *Titanic* passengers. Why, then, should she "see" W. T. Stead? There is no implication that she had any relationship with him, intimate or otherwise, although it seems probable that she would have heard of the celebrated journalist and, quite conceivably, his imminent arrival in the United States for a well-publicized peace conference at Carnegie Hall. And not the least interesting feature of this account is the *timing*.

Although the above experience might seem at first glance to be an encounter with the "ghost" of W. T. Stead, Chase's vision actually took place well before the *Titanic* went down. In fact, Chase actually saw Stead's disembodied face just ten minutes after the *Titanic* had struck the iceberg, or two and a half hours before the vessel sank. Stead was still alive and well at the time.

Was Chase's experience an imaginary one, or did she really undergo a paranormal experience that was somehow connected with the approaching disaster to the *Titanic*? And again: why should she single out W. T. Stead (or he her), when to all appearances no close tie existed between them? Excusing Stead any part in the process, we could hypothesize that what Chase experienced was not a sense of *personal* loss, but an awareness of something more universal; the loss of the *Titanic* was symbolized for her in the forthcoming death of one of its more celebrated passengers. If she was conscious of Stead's fame as a crusading humanitarian—and unluckily we can't be sure of that—the loss of fifteen hundred lives and the end of a luxurious dream vessel may have been encapsulated in that strange, transient visage that grew from thin air in her study. Even had she not known of W. T. Stead, nor of his presence on the *Titanic,* the speculation wouldn't necessarily collapse. Something—some communicating power—wished to make Chase conscious of the disaster; it visualized the event in a symbolic fashion, using Stead as a kind of metaphor that stood for the disaster. Why Chase and not somebody else? Not for the first time in this chapter, we cannot say; the laws or lack of laws that enable a person to tap into that hypothetical communicating power aren't easily apprehended, except perhaps by confirmed spiritualists, who will have little trouble in identifying said power as W. T. Stead himself.

Spiritualist or skeptic, it will be patent from this chapter that visions such as those encountered by McCormack and Chase (and perhaps Barnes, too) are merely enhanced waking versions of what others encountered during sleep contemporaneously with the disaster (or nearly so).

One *Titanic* passenger, however, experienced a dream during the liner's maiden voyage that may have been instrumental in saving his life. Bert John was a Lebanese immigrant who had booked his passage to America in the steerage section of the *Titanic*. Even though the third class accommodations could not compare with the richness of the rooms in first class, John was pleased with his surroundings. His cabin was located deep in the *Titanic*'s bow, as were the rooms of his cousin and all the other single men on board.

The first few days of the voyage passed pleasantly enough for John. The weather was good, and there was always something novel to see or do in the massive new ship.

On the night of April 13 John went to bed expecting to sleep as soundly as he had the previous night. It was not to be, however, for he experienced a very vivid dream. John dreamed that something had happened to this huge new ship that was carrying him to America. He could see that the ship was sinking. Then he found himself placed in a casket and carried from the lower decks of the ship all the way up to the top deck, where the lifeboats were. John struggled to release himself from the coffin, finally succeeded, and then leaped desperately from the ship's deck into a lifeboat.

At this point John awakened from his dream drenched in a cold sweat. He wondered if the dream held any special significance—it was so vivid! He spent all the next day, Sunday, April 14, wondering what the dream might have meant. John could see, though, that nobody around him appeared to have any worries about the ship's safety, and his mind was put somewhat at ease. That night he went to bed at his usual time.

John awakened to a rumbling noise at 11:40 p.m., and he realized that the ship was trembling. Sitting up in his bed John listened intently. The ship's engines continued to turn, however, and he soon decided to go back to sleep. Very shortly, though, someone was shaking him awake.

"The ship's broke! Get up!" shouted his cousin. John hurriedly put on his clothes and accompanied his cousin up to the boat deck. There they watched women and children being ushered into lifeboats that were being prepared for lowering. John tried to enter several different lifeboats, but each time was ordered away by the officers who were supervising the loading. The young immigrant was becoming frightened, as he could see that he would never be allowed to enter a boat as long as women and children remained on board. He became desperate.

Looking over the side of the ship, Bert John saw a lifeboat that had been lowered a little way down the ship's side. Realizing that it was now or never, John jumped over the railing and dropped down into the lowering lifeboat, landing on a woman seated there. A man in the boat attempted to throw John overboard, but the young immigrant got down in the bottom of the boat and held onto the woman's leg. The woman spoke up in his defense, and the man finally left him alone. It was in this manner that John survived the sinking of the *Titanic*.

It is interesting to note the symbolic quality of the dream that John experienced twenty-four hours before the collision. He had dreamed that the ship was sinking, that he found himself fighting to get out of a coffin, that he succeeded, and that he finally jumped into a lifeboat. John's struggle to escape the coffin might be interpreted as his effort to escape death on the sinking ship in his dream. He was able to escape "death" in his dream by leaping out of the coffin and into a lifeboat. This parallels the way John actually *did* escape his *real* death on the *Titanic*—by leaping from the doomed ship into a lifeboat. One wonders if Bert John, right before making his desperate leap for life, might have recalled his dream and realized that it had shown him the only possible way he could survive the sinking of the *Titanic*.

Still on the subject of dreams, another gentleman, this one safe in his bed in England, was having a restless night during the wee hours of April 15. Alfred Adler woke up suddenly from a dream that was still sharp and vivid in his memory. In his mind's eye he could clearly envision the scene of a huge ship going down in mid-ocean. Adler's dream had not depicted the cause of this calamity, but the vividness of the scene was very striking.

When Adler eventually heard about the loss of the *Titanic* he realized that his vivid dream experience had occurred at the same time as the real-life tragedy. Adler was no believer in paranormal phenomena, however, and he eventually convinced himself that his dream had had a commonplace origin. Having just sent the only copy of his new book manuscript to America by ship, Adler decided that his unusual dream merely reflected his anxiety for the manuscript's safety while seaborne. And perhaps he was right.

Let us borrow Adler's cool, collected reaction to his ostensibly preternatural dream. A measured, analytical approach to the paranormal is more easily advocated than practiced; the subject is notorious for lapses from self-imposed standards of objectivity, with special pleading on one side balanced only by instances of rabid skepticism on the other. That apart, there is a tendency to assume that because there are so many accounts of precognition or clairvoyance associated with the *Titanic*, the law of averages must apply: in other words, that *some* of them *must* be regarded as authentic or (conversely, due to their prevailing anecdotal character) that these apparent exceptions only prove the rule that there are *no* genuine, authenticated accounts of paranormal prevision of this, the twentieth century's greatest peacetime maritime disaster.

How do we, the authors, feel about this? The answer, hopefully, will have emerged already from our previous chapters. Our general approach is one of skepticism in the original meaning of that word. We feel obliged to examine the evidence, to note its limitations. We do not feel obliged to come down heavily on one side or the other, and where we speculate it is usually with the intent to ponder how a thing *might* be explained . . . or explained away. While this kind of tactic will satisfy neither of the committed parties (the arch-believers, the convinced skeptics) we're happy with it—and with the overall plan employed in this chapter, wherein the feel and quality of the *Titanic*'s vast store of paranormal episodes is represented in a meager dozen examples. Yes, there are other and possibly better stories—ones that "prove" the authenticity of the paranormal and others that "*dis*prove" it. But imagine: if our twelve accounts were the only ones to stand as evidence, what could we learn from them? What dare we advance on the strength of them?

To open this review, we need to look most critically—and perhaps least sympathetically—at the six cases of verbal apposition, episodes in which the paranormality rests solely upon remarks taking on a somber and precognitive significance in the light of events that followed (namely, the sinking of the *Titanic*). Coincidence is an austere way of reacting to these cases wherein a speaker's words seem in retrospect to have come literally true despite the obvious impossibility of his or her being able to realize that he/she spoke more truly than he/she knew at the time, doubly so when we remember that we do not know what "coincidence" really amounts to and that for most of us it is no more than a term of convenience. To reject all these six cases as "coincidence" proves very little if the noun actually stands for some force that in itself is a paranormal mechanism.

That said, and conceding that a person's words can *come* true in the most ironical way *without* invoking the theory of precognition, we could start by ignoring Chantler's ill-made throwaway line about the uselessness of giving friend Goldsmith the farewell calipers: "You'll get halfway across the Atlantic and down will go the boat." This, despite the neat parallel with the fact the *Titanic* in fact *did* go down (though not halfway across the Atlantic) sounds nothing else than a pure verbal coincidence, a lucky hit or, if you prefer, an *un*lucky one. Conceivably, the same would be true for Sophia Laitinen's comment about repaying her loan. "If I should go to the bottom of the ocean . . ."—were it not for the sequel of her two "warning" dreams.

Elsewhere, we deal with premonitions that a reductionist would scoff at as little more concrete than "strong feelings." Annie Ward's fear, groundless as it must have seemed to her parents, could have been a subconscious reaction to all the sea traveling undergone in Mrs. Cardeza's employ; perhaps she had come to feel that each successive voyage brought her closer to the possibility of shipwreck, just as a pessimistic motor-racer may come to dread getting into his car purely because each race brings him statistically closer to an occupational hazard he has so far avoided: crash, pile-up. Granted, her account doesn't read that way; her father's testimony that she displayed particular irrational fear of *this* voyage deserves to be taken seriously. Yet the possibility remains, and could be extended to cover the deliverance of Tom Sims, whose case is elevated from the mundane chiefly by the family legend of Mother's fey premonitions, which, however, we have to take on trust.

What impresses most in these two incidents is the allegation of the sheer strength of the percipient's belief they precognicized disaster (which, in the Sims case, greatly influenced the behavior of two people: we are led to believe that Mrs. Sims did everything in her power to get her son to change ships and that he eventually acquiesced, if only to allay her fears, we might suppose. Unfortunately, there is no way of distinguishing between a genuine premonition and a "strong feeling," even when the latter seems borne out by subsequent events. Add here Shaw Desmond's "conviction of impending death," and the still more ambiguous responses of Maj. Butt. If any reader feels these convictions were more valid than the hypothesis of coincidence allows, the authors would not argue. If any parapsychologist should object that they are suggestive rather than evidential, the same.

The problem is that the *Titanic* set sail amid circumstances well calculated to rouse vague feelings of alarm. Wyn Craig Wade handles this aspect superbly at the end of his *The* Titanic*: End of a Dream* (Weidenfeld & Nicolson/First Futura, 1980). The dream he writes of there was a technological one born in the Gilded Age; if the unsinkable *Titanic* represented complacent materialism, luxury, and arrogance, she also stood for vulnerability and hubris punished by the gods after the old manner of Greek tragedy.

We do not know whether any of the people featured in these pages felt this way; we can only expect that the very hyperbole of the *Titanic*—its aura of indestructable grandeur, its sheer celestial scope—inspired feelings of unease. We are taught that pride comes before a fall. Is it so incredible to suggest that, in the face of all the vaunting and crowing, some people experienced a primitive suspicion of divine retribution? Or that a few whose anxieties were abetted by more personal worries might acknowledge the possibility as a "strong feeling" or premonition? A mature man like Butt might eventually quell such irrational fears, taking confidence in the "unsinkability" tag; others, whether on board the *Titanic* or off, may have found solace in the ordinary fact that we can't worry too much over what we cannot control.

In the final analysis, a "strong feeling" *or* a premonition is an expression of *one possible outcome* of an unresolvable situation. Event A (the sailing of the unsinkable *Titanic*) throws out corollaries B through Z; and let us say that the possibilities from P through Z range across varying degrees of disaster, arrayed in order of decreasing likelihood. In fixing on the total loss of the ship (which would lie toward the end of the alphabetical scale, though not at the *very* end—there were *some* survivors), our strong feeling/premonition might be a visualization of the more pessimistic of numerous possible outcomes; perhaps even a magical, prerational mode of trying to avert the worst through an act of admitting that it *is* possible. On these highly hypothetical terms, the seers were right by virtue of being proven right. They had predicted or guessed the one outside possible outcome from a whole range of other candidates. Whether they had supernatural aid in defying the long, long mathematical odds of being correct is—well, as always, a matter of private opinion.

But of course, the other material—the dreams, the visions—appears more conclusive. Are we guilty of bias in regarding them as more evidential? The plain fact of their superior narrative interest cannot be avoided, though we will attempt to prevent this quality from unsettling our judgment.

We have, then, a total of four "warning" dreams (Laitinen's two counting as one, and Abrahams, and John, and Adler) and three of what we might style "spirit visions" (McCormack, Barnes, Chase). In many ways the division between "dream" and "vision" is artificial (as we saw in the case of Sawyer's *Waratah* experience) and we use it here simply for amenability. Taken within the overall grouping of *Titanic* premonitions, they are patently more dramatic, explicit, and memorable, if only because they seem more likely to compel readers' attention than our foregoing "strong feelings" material.

One clue to the artificiality of separating dream from vision per se appears immediately: of the five dreams documented here, only two resemble the ambiguous, disorderly parade of images we connect with the word. To the contrary, the dreams experienced by Abrahams, John, and Adler (though more or less difficult to interpret at the time!) seem oddly specific—curiously well organized. The converse applies to those of Laitinen. The dream of falling into a well of cold water, sans the guiding fact of the *Titanic* to give us benefit of hindsight, appear incapable of decipherment. As we commented when reviewing that episode, the elements of this dream seem heavily symbolic: the well and cold running water (grave; sea of death?) appear apt metaphors, but perhaps only when we have before us the fact of how Laitinen met her end. Similarly, the precognitive element of her second dream (concerning further deaths in the family that ironically proved to encode her own death!) are far from blatant until we have that same information.

Judging from common nocturnal experience—the usual nature and caliber of how dream-narratives are presented—and the commonly accepted paradigm that the unconscious expresses itself in symbols rather than through direct, unequivocal statement, we might guess that any precognitive dreams relating to the *Titanic* took this unhelpfully allusive format. But this does not appear to have been the case. As we saw several pages ago, Bert John's dream may have contained an element of symbolism: the casket or coffin sounds, given his subsequent situation, a fairly obvious symbol at that. But despite this, the whole experience seems oddly direct, while that of Adler, the scribe worried over the fate of his precious manuscript, seems more specific still: the fact he dreamed of a ship sinking in mid-ocean impresses more than the detail that he did not immediately recognize it as the *Titanic*. Ah, but there is the confusion that Adler's interest lay in that manuscript and, moreover, that he himself attributed to that anxiety the substance of a dream that seems nonetheless clairvoyant in its aptness to what was going on some fifteen hundred miles away. All we can remark here is that whatever drew Adler's sleeping mind to the event, the coincidence of the dream with it is noteworthy.

We return to the half-theory postulated before: in *all* these cases, the dreamers may have focussed upon one fearful possibility of peculiar relevance to themselves that they selected from a cast of hundreds or thousands. I *may* drown . . . I *may* be getting into my coffin when I get onto that ship . . . for all *I* know, the ship *may* go down and take my manuscript with it. Perhaps M. Abrahams's personal fear dwelt on the possibility of losing his nephew. As we know, that is precisely what happened and as per the terrible theater-balcony dream. We have no means of knowing whether the pale, haggard face and upthrown arms were a supernaturally transmitted or received image of the nephew's last moments, nor whether some especially close link existed between him and his uncle to make the idea feasible. The episode carries a certain credibility; what little we know of psi suggests that an emotional bond between percipient and subject is likely to increase the likelihood of an "impression," though perhaps it will not take the form of a literal or absolutely accurate representation of how the "sender" fares at the time. A review of relationships between the people mentioned in this chapter includes two cases of friendship (Goldsmith/Chantler; Stead/Desmond) and one tenuous connection wherein the seer (McCormack) knew the victim's wife (Mrs. K——, perhaps only slightly) but apparently did not know the victim at all. Chase does not appear to have had any intimate connection with Stead. Finally, blood ties affect the cases of Sims and Abrahams (the percipients being mother and uncle respectively) while Barnes was engaged to a victim.

It needn't be said that none of the preceding validates the evidence for dream precognition in our *Titanic* sample. A further and possibly more damaging issue that needs to be raised concerns the question of how these stories came to be told, or who recorded them, and (by invidious implication) why. That barbed question enters greatly into our analysis of the yet-more-dramatic spirit-vision precognitions.

Facing the issue squarely: in matters paranormal, some sources are traditionally afforded higher respect than others. Cases documented by the British or American Societies for Psychical Research or comparable bodies composed of accredited parapsychologists tend to carry more weight since, though far from being beyond criticism, these organizations are blessed with reputations of strict scientific objectivity, if not healthily constructed skepticism. By contrast, an account in a national newspaper or commercially oriented magazine may (rightly or wrongly) be open to charges of bias; the argument is that such publications exaggerate, color or otherwise "adapt"—or falsify—their material to suit the perceived tastes of a particular, often uncritical, unobjective and nonscientific readership. Finally, and not far removed from this category, certain specialist publications may be accused of utilizing unreliable material not for direct financial gain but to promote a defined view or belief system favored by the editors and/or the readers.

Here are our three spirit-vision cases together with the sources from which we took them: (1) McCormack's impression of Mrs. K——'s photo: *Occult Review,* May 1912. (2) Estelle Barnes and the vanishing woman in golden brown: letter from Barnes quoted in Frank J. W. Goldsmith manuscript in the Titanic Historical Society archives. (3) Chase and Stead's visage: *Journal of the American Society for Psychical Research,* 1919.

People need outlets for their unusual experiences. They relate them to others, verbally and through the medium of print. We would like to suggest this process is not created from a desire to self-publicize, but from a natural dèsire to share, and frequently, where the unusual encompasses the putatively supernatural, to canvass explanations. The possibility that narrators of ghostly yarns also crave a species of admiration cannot be ruled out, of course, but it remains minimal. Any storyteller, be he Joseph Conrad, Bret Harte or the man behind the counter in McDonald's who told you how he met the apparition of his deceased grandfather, is an entertainer, but his motives for button-holing us with his story may not be financial (to sell books) or to win our approval of him as storyteller and all-round good fellow. His right to take up our time rests in the narrative itself. To invoke Thomas Hardy yet again: "A story must be striking to be worth the telling." But in parapsychological terms, a story must not only justify itself by being striking; if it proclaims itself a *true* story, it must evince evidence to back up that peculiar claim.

Obviously the narrators of these visionary episodes felt them striking enough to warrant telling outside a purely local, personal circle, of family and friends, that is. Others—the editors of the journals involved—obviously agreed that their stories merited retelling to larger audiences (and printed them on that understanding, though given the character of the magazines, presumably not for payment). Can it be argued that they did so in the hope of promoting a particular set of beliefs or (which amounts to the same thing) of meeting the interests and beliefs of a specific audience? And did the writers approach the editors in the knowledge that what they had to offer would be accepted on those terms?

The tentative answer is "Yes" and . . . "No." Chase forwarded her account to the American Society for Psychical Research on the clear understanding that what she had to say would interest that learned body, but in publishing it the ASPR did not put its cachet of approval on the incident; rather, as an organization committed to the scientific investigation of allegedly psychic accounts, it threw the matter open to wider scrutiny. The ASPR was recording (and would continue to record) all and any reliable-sounding first-person experience of premonitions centered on the *Titanic*; the Chase account is just one of many. But by its very nature there was little in the narrative to be investigated further. A credible-enough-seeming witness reported an event whose corroboration rested upon the details that a) she actually mentioned her vision of the floating face of W. T. Stead *before* she identified it from the *Boston American* photograph, and b) that the face of that photo truly matched the one of her vision. We are told that both events took place; realistically, sympathetically, we have no reason to reject the statement. Conversely, we cannot be sure that Chase "saw" W. T. Stead's visage at all, nor that what she saw (if anything) was authentically identical with the photo. Could the vision have been "fed" by a subconscious recall of Stead who, as predicated earlier in this chapter, may have symbolized the *Titanic* for her? But Chase, like a few thousand others, had no reason to be worrying over the *Titanic* at that time; as far as everyone was concerned, the ship was quite safe. And if we try to discredit Chase's story on grounds of retroactive cognizance—allowing that she saw *a* bearded face, but insisting she was led to put a name on it by seeing the famously hirsute features of Stead in the paper—we have done little more than complicate the issue. Why should Chase see a bearded apparition at all? As long as the factor of this witness having seen something of the sort is unchallenged, the account remains suggestive. If we accept the coincidence of the fact that she experienced it at or about the time of the *Titanic*'s accident (and that the ship contained at least one person to fit the facial identity of the apparition), it might be better than that.

A dramatic experience Chases's certainly was, but far inferior in histrionic impact than that of Estelle Barnes. Her encounter on Southsea Beach with the mysterious woman in golden brown who, having uttered a prophecy of disaster (and somewhat impractical advice as to how Barnes could avert it), vanished as abruptly as she had come has, as we said before, a decidedly theatrical flavor. But then, apparitional encounters not infrequently do. Again, little is explained by the "all in the mind" hypothesis; stating or suggesting that the woman in golden brown wasn't there in objective reality, but only as a hallucination in the percipient's interior vision of it, scarcely removes the oddity, nor yet its suggestiveness in tandem with the tragedy that followed.

The provenance of Barnes's evidence is quite interesting. It appears in the Goldsmith manuscript (source also of the Chantler story summarized in this chapter) lodged with the Titanic Historical Society; this manuscript was forwarded to the THS for publication in booklet form by Victoria Goldsmith, his daughter-in-law. The account was actually sent to her husband (who survived the *Titanic*) by the alleged percipient, Barnes, in a letter dated June 9, 1973. It qualifies, therefore, as a private memorandum not necessarily intended for publication, although it seems likely that the writer would have had no objection to seeing it used in that manner.

The letter is that of a committed spiritualist. The Rev. Estelle Barnes, as she signs herself, does not question one iota of the events she describes; there is a deep, religious tone to it that thwarts all attempt to examine the alleged experience. As far as she is concerned, the thing happened; it was an example of God working in wondrous ways and critical analysis would presumably be a kind of heresy. Barnes ends her letter with the claim that her warnings have saved no less than four U.S. presidents; "Colonel Lindbergh's baby son would have been saved, had New York and New Jersey police took my advice," Barnes concludes.

So Barnes was a spiritualist. In our book, that makes her neither liar nor fantasist, but it might explain the sheer drama of the episode, always conceding that it doesn't do so completely. Some spiritualistic accounts suggest that a believer is less prone to criticize a subjective experience than other folk, overemphasizing its "evidential" aspects, perhaps, and tending toward a literary format wherein spirits act with a freedom not common in other parapsychological documents. Spiritualism in its early-twentieth-century phase was a crusading movement, and its literature promoted a dramatic image. You *will* survive! The departed *can* be seen and spoken with. What looked suspect to a severe rationalist was quite orthodox to a proponent of the truths of spiritualism.

Barnes's account has the "feel" of a narrative told in prosaic, unquestioning style by one who believed what she was saying. To call it "lie" or "fantasy," or hallucination is beyond the point; Barnes accepted it. If we regard it as too incredible, we have no need to do so. Most spiritualists maturely accept the gulf or credibility gap that lies between themselves and nonbelievers. It is simply that in retelling this story Barnes was attesting to the truths of spiritualism as she perceived them, as she had encountered them. We cannot say that she embroidered all or part of her experience, nor that she fabricated it. The reliability of this account derives largely from how we react to spiritualism and, of course, to spiritualists.

The same thing applies to many of the incidents contained in this chapter, beginning with the McCormack episode. We cannot be certain that McCormack was a spiritualist; against this, he was patently interested in spiritualism, as evidenced by the fact his vision took place at the house of a spiritualist, Edward Henderson, to which he'd gone for the purpose of discussing this subject informally. The free manner in which McCormack launched into an expression of his fears bears a certain resemblance to the style of a medium "thinking out loud"—recording impressions, commenting upon them ("I don't think you need worry") and generally acting a role he had played before. In the context of the Henderson circle, such a performance would not have been deemed remarkable. Could we go further and speculate that the setting—the predisposition towards acceptance of the paranormal—created favorable conditions in which a paranormal event took place?

McCormack's vision was presented less than one month after the tragedy for the delectation of readers of the *Occult Review,* a commercial magazine with a small, well-defined audience. (The nearest analogue to the *Occult Review* nowadays would be *Fate,* whose blend of personal accounts and discursive, essay-like material and newsy items it predated by some thirty years.) There was no guarantee but a strong likelihood that the readers would have found nothing to dismiss in it. Speaking for ourselves, we find McCormack's story quite credible (and for the reasons mentioned earlier); the fact that he was or may have been a spiritualist is neither here nor there and the fact it appeared in a magazine devoted to publicizing the supernatural no bar—perhaps the writer felt that *Occult Review* was more likely to find space for it than any other publication. At the same time, we notice that Abrahams sent his dream vision to *Light,* then a weekly spiritualist newspaper whose news items would not always satisfy the most astringent evidential demands of scientific psychical research.

So it is not permissible to reject our dozen cases merely because some of them suggest a "taint" of spiritualism. Laitinen, to the best of our knowledge, was not a spiritualist; being the experience of a confirmed skeptic did not prevent Adler's dream from appearing in the ASPR *Journal.* As for journalist/novelist Shaw Desmond: it so happens that he was a spiritualist and, according to Nandor Fodor's entry on him in *An Encyclopedia of Psychic Science,* a most proselytizing one: president of the Survival League, believer in his own personal survival as an inevitable fact, lecturer on spiritualism over three continents and in sum "an eloquent propagandist of Spiritualism." We could ignore the detail that, according to accepted canons of parapsychology, Desmond recorded his experience right after it took place because we aren't informed that he showed it to anyone who might confirm that important allegation. We could even claim that his story, told years after in a popular autobiographical book, was part of an attempt to aggrandize the writer, spiritualism, or both. Yet when we look at the story itself, we see *not* a suitably exciting premonitory dream or waking vision, but a strong conviction amounting to a certainty.

If Desmond had wanted to fabricate a wondrous tale that worked on the susceptible reader's conviction, he could have done much better. So too with the other witnesses discussed in these pages: they could all have done better. Even the spirit visions, dramatic as they are, could have been more obvious. If we learn anything from them, it is that the mechanism that provokes paranormal precognition does not function in an obvious fashion.

We are safe in assuming, however, that any paranormal experience relating to the *Titanic* will have this personal, ambiguous quality. We close now with a nice little story of one more *Titanic* passenger who underwent a curious experience even as the great liner was making her final plunge to the seabed two and a half miles below. It may be that no particular time is more suitable for a psychic event than another, but even so . . .

Nineteen-year-old Edward Dorking had decided to leave his mother's home in Liss, England, and live with his aunt and uncle in the United States while seeking his fortune there. Originally intending to sail in mid-April 1912, Dorking was excited to learn that the *Titanic*'s maiden voyage would take place a few days earlier than his own scheduled departure.

The young man decided to change his reservations so that he could sail on the huge new liner when she left Southampton on April 10. Even so, Dorking came close to missing the *Titanic* due to his train's late arrival in the port city on sailing day. The young man considered himself lucky as he walked up the gangplank and boarded the great vessel shortly before her departure.

Dorking was traveling as a steerage passenger, and he met two other young steerage men on the ship who were also on their way to the United States. He chummed around with these two fellows during the early days of the voyage.

Dorking was asleep in his steerage compartment when the *Titanic* struck an iceberg on the night of April 14. By the time he and his friends were allowed up onto the boat deck the ship's lifeboats were already being lowered away with the women and children. The young man attempted to take a seat in several different lifeboats, but he was ordered away from each boat at the point of a revolver. Realizing that they would be unable to enter a lifeboat, Dorking and his two friends made their way to the ship's stern, which was now rising out of the sea as the bow submerged. Pausing a moment to say a silent prayer, Edward Dorking and his companions stepped over the railing and dropped down the side of the ship into the sea.

Fighting their way back to the surface and almost paralyzed by the numbing cold of the icy water, Dorking and his friends struggled to get away from the ship's side. Looking back periodically, Dorking could see the *Titanic*'s brightly lit stern rising majestically into the sky. When the ship's lights finally failed he could still see the great stern towering vertically into the darkness above him.

Suddenly Dorking found himself surrounded by hundreds of fellow human beings who had jumped from the ship as she poised herself for her death plunge. It was then that the screaming began. Gasping men and women clutched blindly at Dorking as he struggled to get clear of the dying liner. Kicking and fighting them off out of sheer self-preservation, the young man managed to get through the crowd alive and continued swimming away through the freezing water into the blackness beyond.

Dorking had no idea where he was heading, and the terrible cold was quickly taking its toll of his strength. The freezing water nearly had its way, and Dorking's head was just beginning to submerge when the *Titanic* herself went down. The passing of the great ship proved to be instrumental to Dorking's deliverance, for the wave that rolled outwards from her gravesite picked up the young man and washed him close to an overturned lifeboat that was floating nearby. Seeing the half-submerged boat ahead, Dorking drew on the last of his strength and swam desperately toward his only refuge from death. His stiffening limbs were rapidly freezing up, while exhaustion clutched at his very soul. He struggled weakly toward the boat, his arms and legs moving automatically, instinctively.

Suddenly a black cloud seemed to enshroud Dorking, obscuring everything around him. But then the young man found that he *could* see something after all, a sight that was completely unexpected. As he later told a fascinated audience, "I thought I saw my people at home before me."

Dorking's vision did not last long, however, for his hand suddenly touched the side of the upturned lifeboat. Someone on the boat grabbed hold of him, causing his vision to vanish as quickly as it had come. Dorking and thirty other men spent the rest of the night standing on top of their slowly sinking refuge from death. At dawn they were taken on board another lifeboat before finally being picked up by the rescue ship *Carpathia*.

Of course, Dorking's vision might have simply been a hallucination experienced by an exhausted man who was rapidly freezing to death. It sounds like one; it probably *was* one. But one wonders if Dorking might possibly have been undergoing what is presently termed an "out-of-body experience." Could the dying young man have actually been "seeing" his family at their home in Liss?

It would be interesting to know if Dorking's brief vision of his family corresponded with their actual activities during the time he was strugging for his life in the mid-Atlantic. But if Dorking ever tried to confirm the details of his vision of his family, he never took the time to record the results of his inquiries.

A pity. But at least the coauthors of this chapter have the satisfaction of knowing that Edward Dorking's story had a happy ending.

References

Abrahams account: *Light,* May 4, 1912, p. 215.

Adler account: *Journal of the American Society for Psychical Research,* 61 (January 1967): 77–80. (The account originally appeared in Phyllis Bottome, *Alfred Adler: Apostle of Freedom* (Faber and Faber, 1939).

Barnes "ghost" account: Manuscript by Frank J. W. Goldsmith in the archives of the Titanic Historical Society.

Butt account: *Southern Daily Echo* (Southampton), April 22, 1912; George Behe, Titanic: *Psychic Forewarnings of a Tragedy* (Patrick Stephens, 1988), pp. 120–22.

Chase account: *Journal of the American Society for Psychical Research* 13 (1919): 31–36.

Desmond account: Shaw Desmond, *My Adventures in the Occult* (London: Rider and Company, circa 1946), pp. 41–42.

Dorking account: *Los Angeles Express,* November 6, 1912.

Goldsmith account: Manuscript by Frank J. W. Goldsmith in the archives of the Titanic Historical Society.

John account: *Port Huron Times Herald* (Michigan), April 29, 1912; April 17, 1932; April (?), 1962.

Laitinen account: *Uusi Suometar,* April 23, 1912 (a Finnish newspaper); "The Commutator," vol. 13, no. 2, 1989, *The Finnish Immigrants of the Titanic* by Kalman Tanito.

"McCormack" account: *Occult Review* (May 1912): 7–8.

Sims account: *Courier* (a British newspaper from near Southampton?), date uncertain: September or October(?) 1985. The clipping came from the boxed *Titanic* file in the Southampton Public Library.

Ward account: *New York Times,* April 17, 1912; George Behe, *Titanic: Psychic Forewarnings of a Tragedy* (Patrick Stephens, 1988), p. 94.

7

RMS *Lusitania*: The Unthinkable

The people of Queenstown, Ireland, stood hatless all morning long as a procession of carts slowly wended its way through the town and toward the cemetery two miles away. A British army band played Chopin's "Funeral March" as the carts carried their burdens on into the sunlit afternoon. Ninety-two rough wooden coffins lay on these carts, each one carrying the mortal remains of a person who, only three days before, had been on board an ocean liner bound for the coast of England. Even now, in the sea just a few miles from this somber procession of carts, floated the remains of more than a thousand other human beings, fellow passengers of these ninety-two people now awaiting burial in Irish soil.

Only ten days earlier, on May 1, 1915, these same passengers had been preparing to leave New York on board the largest ship still plying the steamer track between America and England. World War I had been raging for the past nine months, and the *Lusitania* was now the only four-funneled British liner that had not been requisitioned by the Admiralty for use as a troop carrier. Although Germany had recently declared the waters around England to be a "war zone" and had expressed her intention of sinking any British vessels found therein, little anxiety was expressed by the people preparing to board the *Lusitania* on May 1.

To be sure, a minor sensation had occurred just that morning when a newspaper advertisement (placed by the German embassy) appeared right next to the *Lusitania*'s sailing schedule. The German advertisement was a notice to travelers warning that British ships ran the risk of being torpedoed in the "war zone" around England, and that anyone sailing on a British vessel did so at his own risk.

When reporters got wind of this German warning, they flocked down to the pier of the Cunard Line to interview passengers intending to sail on the *Lusitania*. Sir Hugh Lane gave the reporters short shrift, however, telling them that the German warning was "too absurd for discussion."

Charles Frohman, who was also about to sail, was asked, "Aren't you afraid of the U-boats, C. F.?"

"No," came Frohman's quick reply. "I'm only afraid of the I.O.U.s."

The New York reporters continued making their rounds of the pier, trying to obtain printable quotes from the more noteworthy of the *Lusitania*'s passengers. Some of the reporters began to mention mysterious telegrams supposedly sent to a few of the *Lusitania*'s passengers, telegrams warning that the great vessel would be destroyed before she reached England. These messages only served to fuel the rumors being bandied about the pier, and photographers cracked jokes about the sailing, saying that they intended to entitle their photographs "The Last Voyage of the *Lusitania*."

Although these goings-on may have affected the nerves of some of the ship's passengers, most of them did not believe that a German submarine would dare attack a passenger liner the size of the *Lusitania*. In addition, everyone knew that the *Lusitania* boasted a speed of twenty-five knots while a German U-boat was capable of only twelve. Even if a U-boat did attempt to intercept the fastest liner afloat, nobody felt that the attacking submarine would be able to catch the big Cunarder.

Curiously, it did not seem to occur to the *Lusitania*'s passengers that the speed of their great liner was far less than that of that a German torpedo, which could travel at a speed of forty knots. They were also unaware that, due to an economy move, six of the *Lusitania*'s twenty-five boilers would remain shut down during the voyage to England, reducing the liner's top speed to only twenty-one knots.

Tragically, the jokes of the newsmen on the Cunard pier did not remain jokes for long. The *Lusitania* left New York on May 1 and headed for England with 1,959 passengers and crewmen on board. On May 7, off the coast of Ireland, a torpedo from the U-20 slammed into the side of the big Cunarder. Twenty minutes later the *Lusitania* rolled onto her side and went down, carrying 1,195 of her passengers and crew to the bottom with her.

As has been mentioned, rumors that Germany intended to destroy the *Lusitania* were circulated on the pier before the great liner sailed from New York, and it is almost certain that the ship's crewmen were aware of the rumored danger to their ship. Seamen are a notoriously superstitious lot anyway, so the rumors may go a long way toward explaining the crew's reaction when Dowie, a black cat kept by the *Lusitania*'s stokers as a mascot, jumped ship in New York on the night of April 30. After being deserted by their mascot, some of the crewmen recalled how they had recently been forced to rescue the cat after it had twice leaped overboard. Dowie had seemed determined to leave the *Lusitania* even though he had lived there quite comfortably for four years. Seamen set great store by "omens," and some of the *Lusitania*'s crewmen felt sure that desertion by their cat meant that the liner would be sunk by the Germans. A number of firemen were said to have heeded their mascot's "warning" and deserted ship that same night, preferring to remain in New York and return to England later on a "safer" vessel.

If we are honest, most of us have a soft spot for "lucky pet"-type stories. When the lucky pet is also a psychic pet, the appeal grows stronger. Does it help or hurt to say that a similar story attended the loss of the *Empress of Ireland* on May 28, 1914—an event that neatly forms the middle strut in a trio of nautical tragedies that has the *Titanic* at one end and the *Lusitania* on the other. According to James Croall, the *Empress*'s yellowish tabby cat chose the penultimate moment to announce her retirement from two years of active duty by fleeing down the gangplank and taking refuge in the shelter of a freight shed. The cat had the sense of precognition to stay there until the *Empress*'s plank was taken up and only came forth to join spectators as the liner slipped out toward open water, uttering, it was said, a valedictory mew to match the ship's sirens.

A precognitive cat may strain the imagination; safer, perhaps, to class this as one of those "traveling legends" retroactively attached to the tragic loss of any great ship. (We suspect, but cannot prove, that a survey of marine disasters might reveal other examples of cats reduced in this fashion to eight lives instead of the proverbial nine.) But then, precognition in anything, human or animal, is bound to strain the imagination and we are reluctant to scoff at the *Lusitania* lucky cat episode, or at the crewmen who allegedly acted on the warning at the time.

These deserting stokers' superstitions may well have been fueled by the rumors of possible danger awaiting the *Lusitania*. Other types of warnings, however, were vouchsafed to several people who were to sail on the *Lusitania,* warnings that seem completely independent of those circulated on the pier or published by the German embassy. Indeed, many of these warnings do not seem to have had a "normal" origin at all. Perhaps a *para*normal origin is the only one that can adequately explain the curious events we are about to examine.

In discussing the question of whether or not a certain number of people might have been "precognitively aware" of the *Lusitania* disaster before it occurred on May 7, 1915, it might be interesting to examine material obtained by several mediums at a series of prewar 1914 sittings. In 1923 an investigator named J. G. Piddington undertook just such a project for the Society for Psychical Research, and his report was published in their *Proceedings* for that year.

Piddington was interested in finding out whether any communications obtained by mediums in the weeks prior to the the outbreak of war might have contained evidence of paranormal foreknowledge of that sad event. He examined transcripts of messages obtained during independent sittings with several mediums: Mrs. Verrall, Mrs. Salter, Mrs. Willett, Mrs. Holland, and Mrs. King (the Hon. Mrs. Alfred Lyttelton, a longtime SPR member). The scripts were obtained by means of automatic writing, table-tilting, planchette, and clairaudience.

Although produced independently, each medium's messages had been intended to form an interlocking series of scripts (or "cross-correspondences"). Examined together, they would reveal a complete message, much like putting together the pieces of a puzzle. The analysis of such scripts depends on recognition of certain themes and phrases, especially when repeated. Evidence of such in the work of several independent automatists can suggest a uniformity of topic, hence perhaps a common "communicator" whose message can only be determined by reading the disjointed messages of the individual scripts as a whole.

The above scripts, rich in biblical and literary allusions, are among the most complex and hard-to-assess documents in psychical research. But why, one wonders, should the "communicator" try to express prediction of the coming war (if such it was) so cryptically—by snatches of nursery rhyme or other (often obscure) literary allusions? Piddington felt the "communicator" was simply unable to be explicit, but moreover wished to conceal the meaning of his message from the automatists and (for a time) from the analysts. The "communicator" may have been forced to use indirect or symbolic modes due to limitations of the medium at the time, adapting to the consciousness of the writer.

In any case, our present purpose is to determine whether the scripts suggest any paranormal awareness of the upcoming disaster that befell the *Lusitania*. Although they are rather ambiguous on this point, their content is nonetheless intriguing.

On February 20, 1914, King produced a script that mentions the name "Lusitania" in two separate places. The script opens with lines that string together quotes or allusions to the Gospels of John and Matthew and a hymn. It then continues: "Lusitania, foam and fire—mest [sic] the funnel in broken arcs—" Then, typically, it moves on to speak of rest, peace, vision, and so forth.

Piddington believed that the context of the name "Lusitania" along with "foam and fire" clearly indicates the ship of that name. Mention of "the funnel" might also be a reference to the *Lusitania*, which had four funnels.

On May 14, 1914, King wrote, "Open your hearts to the unknown—fear is the arch-enemy [reminiscent of Robert Browning's "Prospice"]. Lusitania. . . ."

Piddington felt that the double appearance of the name "Lusitania" in these scripts, which seemed to contain predictions of the coming war, was "very odd," although he was unable to decide whether or not it might have been due to chance coincidence.

On the one hand, the repetition of the ship's name in scripts relating to the war and the sinking—an outstanding event in that war—seems more than accidental. On the second occasion the reference to "fear is the arch-enemy" might seem appropriate to the ship's fate.

On the other hand, the foreseeing of the *Lusitania* being lost might be thought very improbable a year before it occurred. More specifically, the scripts do not mention destruction by an enemy—"foam and fire" sounds more apposite to a fire at sea. It is even possible that the phrase does not refer prophetically to a forthcoming disaster, but echoes retrocognitively a past one: the loss of the 3,600-ton British steamer *Volturno,* which burst into flames en route for Halifax, Nova Scotia, and New York from Rotterdam on October 10, 1913, some four months prior to the king sitting. (Incidentally, this dramatic event resulted in at least two allegedly psychic incidents. A "home circle" of amateur psychics from Haywards Heath, Sussex, believed they had picked up telepathic impressions of the blazing *Volturno* before news of the accident reached England, as we detail in a separate part of this book. A stronger if still anecdotal case involved the ship's junior wireless operator, Christopher J. Pennington, who reportedly made a written request for a reassignment following a recurrent dream of himself at the Morse key of a ship on fire.) So we are left with an uncomfortable choice. Either King's communicator's "foam and fire" was a not-so-dim memory of the much-publicized *Volturno* and the rescue attempt that had so excited newspaper readers back in October 1913, or that reference was an oblique warning that the *Lusitania* was to go the same way as the *Volturno,* albeit not quite literally. After all, a torpedo *is* a kind of fire and it *does* create a kind of foam.

Mrs. King also said that "fear is the arch-enemy"; this could refer to the emotions experienced by passengers and crewmen facing the prospect of a fiery death at sea. Clearly, though, the overall content of King's communications could easily be a general reference to the type of end facing the *Lusitania*, a violent end rather than a quiet death in her old age at the hands of a shipbreaker.

Piddington finally reviewed the evidence that the references above could be seen as genuine prevision of events not predictable by ordinary processes of thought. He regarded them as inferior in this respect to some other statements—they might merely be "fortuitous," though he could not entirely dismiss them as chance coincidences. In the end, he suspended judgment.

If genuine, the "Lusitania" reference supposes a feat much harder and more precise than, say, predicting the war itself, which many guessed was inevitable. Suppose the "communicators" had foreseen it and conveyed as much in two references: why, as in other instances, had they not emphasized it by frequent repetition? Maybe they saw the sinking as only a possibility: something that might *not* happen, and hence they restricted themselves to just a couple of remarks (easily overlooked if the event fell through). By contrast, war looked a certainty. Or perhaps they knew of German plans to hit the British mercantile marine and chose the *Lusitania* as a symbol of it. Again, Piddington advises suspension of judgment.

As the date for the *Lusitania*'s final voyage grew nearer, the number of possibly paranormal "warnings" of her approaching demise seemed to increase both in number and in strength. A possible case of precognition regarding the *Lusitania* disaster was reported in connection with John H. McFadden, a wealthy Philadelphia cotton broker who had booked passage for himself and his family on the May 1 voyage of the great liner. Two months before the date arrived, however, he cancelled his booking and transferred to a ship sailing in early March. It was said that McFadden had experienced a premonition that the *Lusitania* would be the victim of an accident during her May 1 voyage.

A similar experience was reported by Edward Bowen of Boston, although Bowen waited longer than McFadden to change his travel plans. With luggage already packed and a room reserved for himself and his wife on the overnight train to New York, Bowen suddenly phoned his travel agent.

"Will you please contact Cunard," he instructed the agent. "We're not sailing tomorrow on the *Lusitania*."

Bowen was later asked why he had so suddenly changed his plans to sail on the great liner.

"A feeling grew upon me," he replied, "that something was going to happen to the *Lusitania*. I talked it over with Mrs. Bowen and we decided to cancel our passage—although I had an important business engagement in London."

A more specific warning of possible danger to the *Lusitania* was experienced by Prof. I. B. Stoughton Holbourn of Oxford University, who had been lecturing in the United States for almost a year before beginning preparations to return home to his wife in Scotland. While in America Holbourn had lived at the home of his friend T. A. Shaw, a New York publisher, and it was to Shaw that the professor described his odd experiences. On at least three separate occasions, the professor told Shaw, he had dreamed that the steamship *Lusitania* had been torpedoed and gone down. In spite of the obvious impression these vivid dreams had made upon him, however, Holbourn went ahead and booked his passage to England on the *Lusitania*. (As we shall see presently, Holbourn was not the only member of his family to undergo a curious experience connected with his voyage home.)

A very graphic premonition about the *Lusitania* disaster was experienced by Blanche Marshall on about April 10, 1915. Marshall, her husband, Jack, and little daughter Joan were staying in New York City at the time, but Mr. Marshall had booked their passage back to England on the *Lusitania*'s May 1 voyage. The family's tickets and luggage stickers lay on the sitting-room mantelpiece against the time they would be needed.

Mrs. Marshall was sitting quietly in the sitting room when her attention became fixed on the steamship tickets. A sudden certainty filled her whole being. "The *Lusitania* is going to sink on that voyage," Blanche Marshall told her husband. "Jack, change the reservations!"

Noticing that little Joan was in the room, and not wishing her to overhear this alarming conversation, Mrs. Marshall told her daughter to run along to bed. The little girl could hear her father beginning to argue with his wife even as the door closed behind her.

Later that evening Joan heard her parents come upstairs, and she crept out of her room to listen to their conversation behind a closed door. Her father had already contacted the Cunard Line by telephone and switched his family's reservations to an earlier sailing. Joan would remember this conversation for a long time.

"Well, it's the best I can do," Mr. Marshall told his wife. "I spoke to nearly everyone in the Cunard office, but the only alternative accommodation they could offer was for a sailing the day after tomorrow . . . on the same ship."

"Oh, that's all right," replied Mrs. Marshall calmly. "The *Lusitania* is not going to sink until the voyage we were going on. I suppose she will be torpedoed, as it is too warm for icebergs. Poor things, I feel so sorry for them! However, there is nothing we can do about it in wartime, so I had better go and tell Kate to start packing."

Marshall was not at all upset by the knowledge that her family would still be travelling on the *Lusitania*, even when she learned that their present cabins were very small and inferior. She seemed to know exactly which of the *Lusitania*'s voyages would be the fatal one, and was quite content to sail on the vessel as long as that one voyage could be avoided.

Although Marshall seemed to intuitively "know" that the *Lusitania*'s May 1st voyage would end in tragedy, a warning experienced by Alta Piper came in the form of a verbal warning, although the identity of the "speaker" remains unknown. Significantly, perhaps, she was a daughter of Boston's famous spirit medium, Leonora Piper.

The arrival of the spring of 1915 heralded the approaching marriage of the eldest daughter of Sir Oliver Lodge, and Alta Piper was asked to be the principal bridesmaid at the wedding. Piper looked forward to sailing to England for the wedding of her friend, but an unexpected illness forced her to delay her trip until the last possible moment. Piper neveretheless began to make preparations for her departure, her excitement being shared at first by her mother, Leonora. As the wedding date approached, however, Mrs. Piper's enthusiasm for her daughter's trip began to fade, even to the extent of urging Alta to forget about attending the wedding. Unwilling to miss the event, the young woman continued with her plans to sail to England.

During the final week of April 1915, however, it looked as if the final decision would be taken out of her hands. The U.S. State Department returned Alta Piper's application for a passport, stating that "pleasure" was insufficient reason for an American citizen to be traveling abroad during these troubled times. Piper resubmitted her application along with a letter explaining her reasons for traveling abroad, urging the authorities to give priority to her request since she was planning to sail on the *Lusitania* on May 1. Piper received a telegram stating that if she would send the State Department the address of her New York hotel, her passport would be sent there to await her arrival. The young woman complied.

Piper was ready to leave Boston on the afternoon of April 30, intending to spend the night in the New York hotel before boarding the *Lusitania* the next morning. As Alta's cab pulled away from the Piper resedence, Leonora watched her departing daughter in great distress, and she remarked to her remaining daughter, "If that child sails on that boat we shall never again see her alive."

But Alta's friends saw her off at the railway station, loading her up with gifts of magazines and flowers, and the young woman was in high spirits when she arrived in New York. Another friend met her there, and they spent a very pleasant evening together before Piper was deposited in front of her hotel at around midnight.

"Goodnight," said the lift boy pleasantly as Piper stepped out of the elevator near her room. "Tomorrow will be a good day for the sailing."

Agreeing with the boy's statement, Piper entered her room in a tired but happy mood, closing the door behind her. Suddenly and unexpectedly, however, her mood changed. Piper unaccountably experienced a vivid awareness of some sort of "impending evil," and the young woman shuddered involuntarily.

"Stupid," she thought to herself. "I must be overtired." Piper prepared for bed, but found herself too restless and uneasy to go to sleep. She paced the floor trying to shake the feeling of dread that had taken hold of her, but without success. The feeling intensified until Piper thought she was losing control of her senses, at which point she suddenly heard a faint whisper. It was indistinct at first, but grew steadily louder Miss Piper could clearly hear the voice's message: "If you get into your berth, you will never get out."

Piper was now far too alarmed to think about sleeping, and she remained awake the entire night. Much to her distress the mysterious voice repeated its warning several times during the night, and Piper realized that the "berth" the voice was referring to was her own berth on the *Lusitania*'s upcoming voyage.

At 6 a.m. Piper's telephone rang; it was the desk clerk obeying her instructions of the night before to awaken her in the morning. The seeming "spell" of the endless night was broken with that phone call, and Piper began to calm down as the dawn crept through her bedroom window.

Piper dressed and went down to an early breakfast, for the *Lusitania*'s passengers had all been requested to board the vessel between eight and nine o'clock that morning. She then went back up to her room to make sure that her luggage was ready to be taken down by the porter. No sooner had she reentered her room, however, than an icy chill suddenly shot down her spine, and the mysterious voice of the night before again delivered a warning message, this time slightly different than the first one, however.

"There is still time," the voice said, "but if you get into your berth, you will never get out."

At that moment the porter knocked on her door. Compelled by a force she could not resist, Piper told the man that she had changed her mind and would not be sailing. She then hurried out of the hotel and over to the Cunard office, where she attempted to cancel her passage on the *Lusitania*. While doing so she suddenly realized that her passport had not been delivered to her hotel as promised, and she used that as her excuse for cancelling her travel plans.

The Cunard agent, however, assured Piper that this unforeseen difficulty would pose no problem, as Piper and her family were known to the captain and her passport could be forwarded to her after she arrived in England.

Determined that there was nothing on earth that could make her board the *Lusitania*, Piper observed that it was after nine o'clock, pointing out that she could not possibly return to her hotel for her luggage and return before the ship sailed. The Cunard agents, not to be denied, insisted that this could indeed be managed successfully, and Piper left them with the understanding that she would attempt to do so.

Once outside, however, Piper decided to assert her independence. She took her time returning to her hotel, arriving there just after eleven o'clock—too late, she thought, to sail on the *Lusitania.* However, an agitated desk clerk handed her an envelope containing her passport and said that a Cunard official was waiting on the telephone to speak with her. Picking up the phone, Piper was told that the *Lusitania*'s sailing had been postponed till noon and that a Cunard official was awaiting her arrival on the pier to see her safely aboard the vessel. Piper was assured that her "missing" passport would be forwarded to her in England.

Without telling the official that she had received her passport, Piper muttered some vague reply into the telephone and then fled panic-stricken up to her room. Terrified that she might somehow be forced to sail on the *Lusitania,* Piper flung open her trunks and threw their carefully packed contents all over the room. Since she could not leave until her trunks were packed again, the frightened young woman felt certain that this precaution would ensure that she would be unable to reach the *Lusitania* before noon. For the next three-quarters of an hour Piper continually packed and unpacked her trunks until, at twelve o'clock, the distant, deep-throated voice of the *Lusitania*'s whistles told her that her ordeal was finally over—the big Cunarder had cast off from the docks and begun her final voyage to England. Calmly and quietly, Piper repacked her trunks and was soon headed for Grand Central Station. From there she cabled Sir Oliver Lodge's daughter in England and told her of her change in plans, then boarded the one o'clock train back to Boston.

During her rail journey Piper tried to make some sense out of her nerve-wracking experience of the previous twelve hours, but was unable to rationalize her unusual behavior. Deep in thought, she happened to glance at the newspaper being read by a nearby passenger, and a headline leaped out at her: "*Lusitania* Passengers Warned Not to Sail."

Piper's mother was the only person who seemed glad that she had canceled her travel plans; everyone else thought that her behavior had been decidedly odd. On May 7 the Pipers were having tea and discussing Alta's odd experience in New York when the telephone rang. Alta's sister got up to answer it. When she returned, her face had gone white.

"Mr. Hill has just telephoned that the *Lusitania* was sunk off Ireland at noon today, with the loss of nearly everyone on board!"

Another example of paranormal foreknowledge of the coming disaster took place a few days after Piper's odd experience, this one occurring on the night of May 6, 1915. Marion Holbourn was in Scotland awaiting the return of her husband, Prof. I. B. Stoughton Holbourn, from America. As we related earlier, Holbourn had been on a lecture tour in the United States and had booked his passage home on the *Lusitania* in spite of his dreams that the vessel would be torpedoed.

On the night in question, Mrs. Holbourn went to bed at around 11 p.m. Just as she began dropping off, however, she had a very strange experience. She suddenly "found herself" on a sinking ship, the vessel being down at the bow and listing heavily. Crewmen were doing their best to lower the lifeboats, and a great crowd of frightened people milled around the boat deck or looked for their friends.

Holbourn was struck by the strangeness of the experience she was undergoing. Her "vision" was so realistic that it seemed as if the event was actually taking place around her. "How strange," she thought, "that I am seeing all this while I am wide awake."

Again caught up in her vision, Holbourn seemed to reach the upper deck of the sinking vessel. She saw a young man in uniform and asked if he knew the whereabouts of her husband.

"Oh, he is all right," the crewman replied. "I think he got away in one of the boats; anyway, he is safe."

Greatly relieved, Holbourn continued to watch the tragedy unfold around her, but was then overcome by a feeling of guilt.

"It is very selfish of me," she thought, "to see all this distress and yet to be unmoved just because my own husband is safe."

When she awoke on the morning of May 7, Holbourn told members of her household about her experience of the previous evening. Everyone regarded it humorously, agreeing that the Germans would not dare to attack a passenger ship.

That evening a neighbor called to Holbourn from the garden gate and told her that the *Lusitania* had been torpedoed and sunk. The poor woman came close to fainting, but tried to fortify herself with the memory of her vision.

The first thing the next morning Holbourn obtained a newspaper and read of the enormous number of lives that had been claimed by the disaster. Soon thereafter, however, she received a telegram telling of Prof. Holbourn's safety. She eventually met her husband at Birmingham, there learning that he was accompanying a rescued child to her grandparents' home in Fakenham.

The little girl's name was Avis Dolphin, and she had been traveling in the care of two ladies, Miss Ellis and Miss Smith. They had all been in the dining room near Prof. Holbourn when a torpedo had struck the *Lusitania*, this being followed immediately by the crashing of crockery as the ship listed heavily.

"No danger! Keep your seats!" shouted the stewards, but Prof. Holbourn knew better. He hurried Avis to his own cabin and strapped a lifebelt on the girl, then grabbed one for himself and rushed back up to the boat deck. Here they encountered Ellis and Smith, the latter of whom did not have a lifebelt. Holbourn offered his own to the woman, who refused it because the professor had a wife and children. It was agreed that he would keep the lifebelt if he could put Smith and the others into a lifeboat.

Seeing one lifeboat smashed against the ship's side and another launched empty, Holbourn herded his charges to the starboard side. Putting them into a lifeboat, the professor gave Avis Dolphin a message for his own wife and children, then ran forward and jumped into the sea as it washed over the boat deck. As he did so, Holbourn watched in horror as the lifeboat containing his friends plunged down the side of the ship and smashed into the sea.

Hopelessly, Holbourn fought his way through the tangle of ropes and wreckage, finally getting away from the ship's side. A few moments later the *Lusitania* went down.

When Holbourn was rescued and taken to Queenstown later that day, he asked if there was any news of the little girl. At around 3 a.m. the next morning he learned that she was alive, and she was brought to him when daylight came. It was then that Holbourn learned that Ellis and Smith had perished in the disaster.

After Mrs. Holbourn met her husband in Birmingham, they both accompanied Avis to the home of her grandparents in Fakenham. Upon their arrival, Mrs. Holbourn asked the elderly Mr. Dolphin when it was that he had learned of the *Lusitania* disaster. She was surprised by Dolphin's reply that he had known about it on May 6.

"But it did not happen till May 7!" exclaimed Mrs. Holbourn.

"Yes," replied the old gentleman, "but I knew it on the previous day."

"Do you mean you 'saw' it?" asked Mrs. Holbourn, remembering her own vision of the disaster.

"Yes," replied Dolphin. "I saw a small boat capsize and a little girl came to the surface and I said to my wife: 'Depend upon it that's our Avis!' "

Mrs. Holbourn asked Dolphin what time he had experienced his vision and was told it had been about 11 p.m. This was almost exactly the same time that Mrs. Holbourn had experienced her own vision of the tragedy. When she related her own experience, Dolphin was not at all surprised to hear that she, too, had 'seen' the sinking of the *Lusitania* before it happened.

One case of apparent paranormal awareness of the *Lusitania* disaster happened to Nell St. John Montague, a well-known London society figure who was also reputed to be gifted with psychic ability. One of Montague's favorite methods of inducing these paranormal experiences was to gaze steadily into a crystal, where scenes of distant happenings would soon become visible to her.

On May 7, 1915, Montague was alone in her Irish home when she had a sudden urge to look into her crystal. She did so, and a vivid picture soon became visible to her.

"I saw what appeared to be a wide expanse of sea," Montague said later. "Next moment I was filled with horror, for on the surface of the sea I saw struggling human forms. . . . Then the vision was lost in the mist, out of which arms appeared beckoning."

Later that same day Montague heard that the passenger liner *Lusitania* had been torpedoed. Could her brief vision in the crystal have been a glimpse of what was taking place off the coast of Ireland that same day? That is the implication of Montague's story.

A couple of *Lusitania*-related cases are on record which took place after the great liner went down. One of these concerns a possible communication with the surviving personality of one of the victims.

Sir Hugh Lane, a well-known authority on pictures and art, had gone to America on business in the latter part of April 1915. He had not, however, told his friends exactly when he would be returning to England or upon which ship he might be sailing when he did return.

On the evening of May 7 Lennox Robinson, a noted Irish playwright, had planned to attend a small séance at the Dublin home of Hester Dowden, a medium. At about 5 p.m., while on their way to the medium's home, Robinson and Dowden saw newspaper posters on the street that said, "Lusitania Reported Sinking!" They did not buy a paper, however. Except for this vague report, the two friends knew nothing else about the ship or the passengers she was carrying.

After arriving home, Dowden and the playwright were joined by the Rev. Savell Hicks, who was to record the messages that might be spelled out by the Ouija board during the sitting. Just before the session commenced, however, a feeling of profound depression settled over Dowden. The feeling was so overwhelming that she went up to her room and stayed there alone for awhile. Eventually the medium managed to regain her composure and at 8:30 p.m. came downstairs to begin the evening's sitting. Dowden and Robinson sat down at the table, were blindfolded by Hicks, and then placed their fingers on the planchette resting on the Ouija board. Hicks then seated himself with pencil and tablet to take notes on what happened during the sitting.

After a few moments the planchette began to move under the fingers of the two sitters. Pointing at first to one letter, then another, the planchette slowly spelled out the words, "Pray for the soul of Hugh Lane," which Hicks recorded without comment. The message continued to come while the two blindfolded sitters chatted amiably, still unaware of what words were being spelled out beneath their fingers.

After a couple of minutes Hicks addressed Dowden and Robinson.

"Would you like to know who is speaking?" he asked. "It is Sir Hugh Lane. He says he has been drowned, and was on board the *Lusitania.*"

The shocked sitters ceased their light conversation, and Dowden asked the Ouija board, "Who is speaking?" The reply came immediately. "I am Hugh Lane; all is dark."

At that moment a news extra was being shouted in the street below, and Robinson hurried down to buy a newspaper. A quick examination of the *Lusitania*'s published passenger list confirmed that Sir Hugh Lane had been on board the liner when she was torpedoed.

Greatly disturbed, Dowden and Robinson resumed their places at the Ouija board. Lane then gave the sitters a description of what had occurred on the torpedoed liner, telling of panic and the attempt to lower the lifeboats. He said that he had finally stepped into a crowded lifeboat but had fallen overboard, and that he had known nothing further until he "saw a light" at the sitting.

Lane went on to describe his last meeting with Dowden, and he also gave her messages to be delivered to mutual friends in Dublin.

"I did not suffer," said Lane at the close of the sitting. "I was drowned and felt nothing."

Several days passed before confirmation arrived that Lane had perished when the *Lusitania* went down.

The next account we shall examine also took place a few hours after the *Lusitania* went down, and concerns another of her passengers. Indeed, this account may well be the most striking of all those connected with the disaster.

Charles Frohman was a prominent New York theatrical manager who was often called "the Napoleon of the drama." He had built the magnificent Empire Theater, and his office at the rear of the building's fifth floor was his base of operations.

Frohman obtained most of his plays in Europe, and he did not allow World War I to interfere with his routine. He continued to make regular trips to England, booking his passage on the *Lusitania* for another such journey.

Like several other *Lusitania* passengers, Frohman received a number of mysterious messages warning him not to sail on the great vessel. These messages did not deter him, however, for the United States was not yet in the war and there were plays in England that he wanted to see. Frohman's entire staff, including one "Big John" Ryland, went to the pier to see Frohman off when the *Lusitania* sailed on May 1.

Now, it was Ryland's nightly duty to inspect the offices over the theater after they had been cleared for the day. He usually did this during the first act of whatever play was being presented on stage.

On the night of May 7, Ryland was making his rounds of the offices over the theater, checking doors and making sure that everything was all right. All seemed normal until he approached Frohman's private office at the rear of the fifth floor. As Ryland opened the door to the darkened office he received the surprise of his life.

There at the big desk, illuminated only by the desk lamp, sat Charles Frohman. His desk was covered with books of press clippings, set designs, pictures of stars, and other memorabilia of a life connected with the stage. Frohman looked up as Ryland opened the door.

"I thought you were almost in Europe by this time, sir," stammered Ryland.

"No, John," replied Frohman with a smile, shaking his head. "I had to come back. I had to look at all this again before I left."

"Did you forget something?" asked Ryland. "Can I help?"

"No," replied Frohman, again shaking his head. "You can't help me, John. Just leave me alone here for a few minutes. Thanks—and goodbye."

Ryland closed the door to the office and immediately took the elevator down to the lobby. He approached a group of theater employees—the house manager, two box office boys, a press agent and Peter Mason, Frohman's office boy. Ryland excitedly told them that Frohman had returned unexpectedly, and that he was upstairs in his office. The men laughed at Ryland, refusing to believe him, but they finally agreed to accompany him back up to the fifth floor.

When Ryland again unlocked Frohman's office he was met by only darkness. Switching on the overhead light the men saw that Frohman's desk was clear and neat, just as their employer had left it. All the press books, photos, and other material were in their proper files. Now the men really laughed at Ryland, although a couple of them were disturbed by their friend's obvious sincerity and insistence at what he had seen.

The next morning's newspapers carried the story of the sinking of the *Lusitania*. Charles Frohman's name was among those of the lost.

John Ryland continued to work at the Empire Theater for another twenty-odd years, eventually becoming the overseer of the building's maintainance staff. Ryland had a certain idiosyncrasy, though, which was well-known to his fellow workers. Although he could sometimes be persuaded to go to the fifth floor if someone accompanied him, Ryland would not go up there after the sun went down. And he would never go into the offices at the rear of the fifth floor whether anyone accompanied him or not.

For John Ryland to have so drastically altered his behavior following the *Lusitania* disaster, it seems reasonable to assume that he must have seen . . . something?

The next report that we shall examine took place long after the *Lusitania* sank. Although slightly out of sequence in our chronology (and although its reliability might be questioned), the case deserves mention here due to its curious relationship with the account we have just discussed.

Joan Grant (the very Joan who was the eavesdropping daughter of Blanche Marshall, whose premonition we have already examined), was living in London with her husband Charles during the summer of 1944. Grant regarded herself as a "sensitive," being convinced that she had the ability to "see" and be aware of departed spirits who were unable to leave the scenes of their earthly existence. She felt that, by instilling comfort and peace of mind in these troubled spirits, they could be freed to "leave the earthly plane" and "ascend to a higher existence." Charles Grant, sharing many of his wife's beliefs, calmly accepted many conversations and occurrences that would have put off a lesser man.

One evening the Grants entered the crowded grill room of the Savoy Hotel. They were shown to a table, and Joan sat down in a chair that had its back against one of the square pillars. She immediately let out an exclamation and asked her husband to find another table. Grant felt that a disembodied spirit had been sitting in her chair when she took her seat, and she was certain that he was still there.

Charles Grant pointed out to his wife that there were no other tables available, suggesting that she try and ignore the spirit. Joan was unable to do this, however. She told her husband that the spirit was male, and that he had been dead for twenty or thirty years. She sensed, too, that he was *alone,* that he was somehow bound to the earthly plane because he had forgotten his real friends. And so the spirit sat by himself in that chair while the years passed and life flowed on in the restaurant around him.

Joan Grant decided to try and help the unfortunate spirit. Putting herself in the proper frame of mind, she offered thoughts of affection and kindness to the ghost until his loneliness was dissipated and he was free to remember the people he had loved. A departed friend of the spirit then appeared, one whom he had long forgotten, and this friend was soon followed by five more. The earthbound spirit was now free to leave with his friends, released by the current of affection Grant had offered him.

After the Grants finished their dinner and arose to leave, Joan noticed a small brass plaque affixed to the column behind her chair. It read: "This table was regularly used by Charles Frohman for many years up to 1915."

Had Charles Frohman remained earthbound after his apparition was seen by John Ryland in 1915? Or was Joan Grant a victim of self-delusion, "seeing" and "feeling" things that were not really there?

Our next case involves a possible post-death communication with a *Lusitania* victim that occurred just a few days after the loss of the big Cunarder. The sittings at which these communications took place were organized by James Hyslop, a founding member of the American Society for Psychical Research.

Edwin Friend had been appointed under-secretary of the above-mentioned society in the fall of 1914, but resigned his post shortly thereafter due to serious disagreements with Hyslop concerning the editing of the Society's journal. Along with Miss Theodate Pope, Friend decided to found a new psychic journal to compete with the old one, and the two friends sailed for England on May 1 on board the *Lusitania* in order to investigate the feasability of this undertaking.

On May 7 Friend and Pope finished their midday meal before going up to B deck to stand by the ship's railing. Dazzled by the glare of sunlight on the waves, and mindful of the newspaper warning published by the German embassy before the *Lusitania*'s departure, Pope remarked, "How could the officers ever see a periscope there?" The two friends turned and had walked aft just a short distance when the sudden thud of a detonation rent the air. Water and debris flew up past B deck, and Friend struck his fist into his hand, exclaiming, "By Jove, they've got us!" A few moments later the *Lusitania* listed heavily to starboard, and the deck suddenly began to fill with excited passengers.

Friend and Pope watched the crew's efforts to launch one of the port lifeboats, and they were horrified when the boat spilled half its human cargo into the sea while still hanging in the davits. Hurrying to the starboard side, Friend saw that the crew were having an easier time of it there, and he urged Pope to enter a lifeboat. She, however, refused to leave him there alone, so Friend tied lifebelts on the two of them.

The ship was settling rapidly now, and Friend realized that it was time to jump. Pope asked Friend to go first, so he carefully showed her how to get over the railing before he himself dropped into the sea. Surfacing, Friend looked up and encouraged Pope to follow him, which she did. Unlike Friend, however, Pope was swept between two submerged decks of the vessel, immediately after which she received a tremendous blow on the head. Half-conscious, she somehow reached the surface again, where she found herself surrounded by hundreds of frantic, screaming passengers floundering in the water. The *Lusitania* had gone down while Pope was beneath the surface.

Theodate Pope was eventually rescued, but she never saw Edwin Friend again.

It so happens that Hyslop and Friend had both attended sittings with a medium named Mrs. Chenoweth in the fall of 1914, although Friend's identity or relationship with the society had never been revealed to the medium. On May 10, three days after the loss of the *Lusitania*, Hyslop decided to have another sitting with Chenoweth. At this time, due to a misinterpreted cable message, Hyslop was still uncertain whether Friend had survived the tragedy or whether he had gone down with the *Lusitania*. The sitting itself, however, had been arranged without any thought of Friend or his possible fate. In addition, Chenoweth had refrained from reading any newspaper accounts of the *Lusitania* tragedy in case her services might be required as a medium in that connection.

After the sitting began, Chenoweth commenced to groan and show signs of distress. Presently she spoke.

"Oh, my, I don't want to see that terrible thing." When Hyslop asked what was being referred to, the medium seized his hand and squeezed very tightly, still exhibiting signs of distress. "It's the ocean," she groaned. "Oh, oh, I'm dead."

Suspecting that it might be Friend who was attempting to speak through the medium, Hyslop asked for the entity to identify itself. The medium sighed and said, "Went down," paused, then repeated, "down." Hyslop continued to ask for the control's identity, but received the reply, "I have been to my wife." (Hyslop later learned that Friend's widow had already received a message—purportedly from her late husband—during an experiment with automatic writing).

Presently Chenoweth began to show additional signs of distress. "Oh, oh!" she cried. "The boat's filling!" The medium began to groan and make swimming motions before ceasing in apparent exhaustion.

After a long pause Chenoweth became slightly agitated. "Oh, dear!" she exclaimed, leaning forward in her chair. "Oh, I feel so ill." There was a pause, then she whispered what sounded like "Fred." Hyslop hadn't heard her clearly, and he asked for the word to be repeated. The medium whispered, "Fred, Friend, Friend." After again being asked to speak more clearly, the medium said, "I don't know him. F . . . r . . . F . . . r . . . Friend."

Hyslop again asked the medium to repeat what she had just said, and Chenoweth said, "I think your friend is here. I think somebody who calls himself your friend is here." After a pause the medium continued. "I guess, I guess I thought too much on the disaster. I see it all around everywhere. I thought too much about it. It's horrible. It's got on my mind. I tried not to. I didn't read any papers yesterday at all. I kept seeing it all the time."

"Did anyone try to give his name?" asked Hyslop. "Yes," replied Chenoweth, "but I couldn't get it. I could hear something about your friend was here all the time, your friend is here. Friend is here."

"I am sorry that so fateful an end came," said Hyslop.

"The only hope is that out of the tragedy may come some clearer light for the cause we love and which I still . . ." At this point Chenoweth came out of her trance in a slightly confused state, and the sitting ended.

On the following day, May 11, another sitting was held, during which Chenoweth's control asked Hyslop, "Were we going to England?" Hyslop answered in the affirmative and, thinking of Pope, asked whom the control's traveling companion had been. "Yes, yes," was the reply, "but she, where is she? They saved her." Later, the control also made mention of the (unpublicized) ill-feeling between Friend and Hyslop that had been the primary cause of Friend's trip to England.

On May 12, during a session of automatic writing, Chenoweth's control succeeded in spelling out his own name—"Edwin Friend."

Edwin Friend's widow was invited to attend a sitting on June 3, although Chenoweth was kept ignorant of her identity. Using automatic writing, the medium's control manifested himself with the words, "I am here today, and want to say so much to her whom I have left and who is here. I am so excited that I can be so near and in real communication of this sort. . . . I am trying to do all that I can to make myself felt at home and am sure I shall succeed even better than indifferently. . . . Little girl with power to do so much to make a spirit life seem real. I want to come to you. I am not surprised to have you here. I wanted it so. E . . . E . . . You will be a little patient with your boy."

"I will indeed," replied Mrs. Friend, who recognized the pet name—"Boy"—by which she had called her husband.

Later during the sitting Chenoweth's control began using direct voice to communicate with Hyslop and Mrs. Friend. In a possible reference to his experience on the *Lusitania*, the control exclaimed, "He's dead. He's dead. Everybody is crazy. Who are all these people running about?"

After a long pause, the control then asked a question of Hyslop: "Do you know anyone named Theodora?" Hyslop immediately thought of Theodate Pope, with whom Friend had sailed on the *Lusitania*, and he told the control that the name was nearly correct. Although the control then groped around and asked if the names Theodore, Theodora, or Theodosia were correct, he was unable to come up with Pope's proper first name before the sitting ended.

Another sitting was scheduled for June 4, and Hyslop continued his attempt to elicit the girl's name from Chenoweth's control. The medium resorted to automatic writing and, with great difficulty, spelled out a name: "Pope." Later in the sitting, the control asked Hyslop, "Get my notes?" Hyslop immediately recognized the reference to some notes Friend had mailed him immediately before the *Lusitania* sailed. Nobody knew of the existence of these notes except Friend and Hyslop, and the latter was duly impressed when Chenoweth's control alluded to them.

A day or so after the conclusion of the above sittings, Mrs. Friend received a letter that brings to mind the control's statement on June 3 that he was attempting to "make himself felt at home." The letter was written on May 31 by Edwin Friend's sister:

> The other night I had a dream about Edwin in which he appeared to me very well and happy. I said to him, "But Edwin, dear, I thought you were drowned when the *Lusitania* went down," to which he replied, "True enough, dear sister, I did drown, but I am not dead to those whom I love and know me. I live, but to all others I am dead."
>
> It seems that I dream of him so often. I cannot quite tell if they are dreams or not; it seems so real, so vivid, and the next day I feel as if I had really talked with Edwin. Can it be that he really comes to me in spirit?

In addition to attending the above series of sittings with Chenoweth, Mrs. Friend also attended some sittings in the home of a friend, the medium being a young woman named Miss D——. Again, Mrs. Friend was introduced to the medium by her first name only—Marjorie—her actual identity remaining unknown to the medium.

One such sitting took place on June 1, 1915, the medium utilizing her gift of automatic writing in order to relay messages from her control. After some initial difficulty in establishing "contact," Miss D——'s hand began to write a message on the paper in front of her.

"I am looking for Marjorie . . . did you, are you here . . . Dr. X. have you sent my message to Marjorie . . . you know it is Edwin Friend . . . Edwin Friend."

The control exhorted his wife to take care of herself, after which he was asked if any other person could be of assistance in helping him establish contact his wife.

"Yes," was the reply. "Oh, yes, Hyslop, come . . ." When asked to give further names, the medium eventually wrote the names "Chenoweth" and "Soule" (which was Chenowith's true name). Immediately after these names came the words "April . . . first . . . May . . . *Lusitania* . . ."

Later during the same sitting came the words, "I loved to read to Marjorie her voice was so sweet in praise. I can hear her speak now, but I wander . . ." When the sitting finally ended, Mrs. Friend fondly recalled that, before his death, her husband really did enjoy reading to her.

During a sitting on June 11 came the words, "Miss Pope, did you say? Yes, I was thinking of my body. I'm through with it. It's very likely in the wreckage. . . . They never found it." This latter statement was true. The control also recalled the circumstances of a gathering with friends in which he and Mrs. Friend had listened to a recorded song entitled "Till the Sands of the Desert Grow Cold." Mrs. Friend had no personal recollection of this incident until a friend later reminded her of the occasion during which it had taken place.

All in all, Hyslop and Mrs. Friend were greatly impressed by what they had seen and heard during the series of mediumistic sittings, and they felt that there was very persuasive evidence to suggest that they had actually been permitted to speak with the surviving personality of Edwin Friend, a victim of the *Lusitania* disaster.

Our next *Lusitania*-related account was the result of an interesting experiment in hypnotically induced mediumship in which the medium utilized the technique of "psychometry." Psychometry is the (supposed) ability to receive mental impressions of a person or event by the mere touching of an object associated with that person. Although the phenomenon is unproven, striking results have sometimes been obtained that are hard to explain away in conventional terms.

The following experiment in psychometry was conducted in March 1921, yielding results that may have shown a connection with the *Lusitania* tragedy of six years before.

Dr. Gustave Pagenstecher was a German physician who had settled in Mexico in his youth. A patient of his, Maria Reyes de Zierold, suffered from a case of insomnia that was not responding to ordinary treatment. Pagenstecher decided to use hypnosis to ease his patient's symptoms, but he made a curious observation after de Zierold had been put into a trance. It appeared that the hypnotized woman had the ability to accurately describe past events in the history of any object put into her hands.

One day Pagenstecher received a package from a friend who had heard of the woman's gifts. The sender hoped that she would be able to use the contents of the package to help ease the mind of a Cuban widow. The package contained a sealed envelope as well as a folded letter secured with several wax seals. The folded letter was to be given to de Zierold so that she could try to obtain some impressions of its writer. On the evening of March 30, 1921, Dr. Pagenstecher hypnotized de Zierold, handed her the folded letter and then listened as the woman began to put into words the impressions she was receiving.

"I feel cool. . . . It is moving . . . I believe I am on a ship," remarked the sensitive, "because I am seasick."

Now the impressions came faster. "It is night," she continued, "between two and four in the morning." A crowd of frightened people were milling around on the ship's deck, and the hypnotized woman was able to describe a Spanish passenger who was standing right in front of her. The gentleman was rather stout, had a full beard and mustache, and he also had a large scar over his right eyebrow. While the passengers around them screamed and wept, she kept this man under observation.

"Now he tears out a leaf from a little book," said the hypnotized woman. "He turns to write . . . against the wall."

An explosion racked the ship. Now de Zierold began to show some excitement as the scene continued to unfold before her, and she spoke more rapidly. The deck around her was a mass of confusion. Officers were shouting orders in English and attempting to calm the passengers, who were donning lifebelts as quickly as possible.

A second explosion shook the ship, this one much larger than the first. This was followed by a rattling noise like a fusillade of rifle shots. The frightened passengers cried out, but the hypnotized woman kept her eyes on the Spanish gentleman.

"Now he rolls up his paper, " she observed. "He takes a bottle from his pocket and he puts it [the paper] in the bottle and puts a cork in it." Driving the cork into the bottle by pounding it against the wall, the gentleman then threw the bottle into the sea.

Suddenly de Zierold screamed and began gasping for breath. "I'm drowning!" she cried. Pagenstecher immediately took the folded letter from the sensitive's hand and brought her out of the hypnotic trance. Still shaking, the woman cried out, "They have all drowned! It was horrible! Horrible!"

After de Zierold had calmed down a little, Pagenstecher was able to elicit a little more information concerning what she had seen. The ship in her vision had been huge, and hundreds of frightened passengers in various stages of dress were on deck. Officers were supervising the lowering of the lifeboats, and distress rockets were being sent up, bursting into red and blue stars high above the stricken vessel.

After the second big explosion, the rattling noise that followed was so violent that the ship trembled "as though it would go to pieces." As the Spaniard threw his bottle overboard, a man nearby shot himself in the mouth with a pistol, while a second man did the same thing by aiming at his own temple. The ship went down following the rattling explosion, and de Zierold, after her brief sensation of drowning, had found herself floating all alone on a quiet sea. It was at this point that Pagenstecher had taken the letter out of her hand and brought her out of the trance.

Now the doctor put the folded letter aside and took the sealed envelope out of the package. The message inside contained background information on the writer of the folded letter.

The writer of the letter, Ramon —— (whom, for the sake of convenience, we shall call Ramon Juarez) was a Spanish gentleman who had been in New York in 1915. In early April of that year Ramon wrote his wife Luisa (who was in Cuba) and told her that business reasons dictated that he sail to England within a month. He did not, however, specify which ship he would book his passage on or the exact date he would be sailing.

Luisa never heard from Ramon again. She knew that German submarines in 1915 had been torpedoing British ships bound for England, and she suspected that her husband may have been the victim of such a disaster. A check of the passenger lists of torpedoed ships had failed to turn up Ramon's name, but Luisa thought that he may have used a pseudonymn in booking his passage. Since the *Lusitania*'s final voyage had taken place during the period that Ramon planned to sail to England, Luisa felt that her husband might have lost his life on the doomed liner.

Dr. Pagenstecher then read a physical description of Ramon Juarez. It matched that of the Spanish gentleman in de Zierold's vision, even to the thick beard and the prominent scar over the man's right eye.

And finally, the message explained that the folded letter, the one held by de Zierold during her trance, had been found in a bottle on a rocky beach in the Azores. It had been forwarded to Havana and, through several coincidences, had eventually reached the wife of the man who wrote it.

Putting this information aside, Pagenstecher again picked up the folded letter de Zierold had been holding during her hypnotic trance. Breaking the seals on the letter, he opened it and read the message that it contained. Translated from the Spanish, it read, "The ship is sinking. Goodbye, my Luisa, take care that my children do not forget me. Your Ramon. Havana. May God protect you and me also. Goodbye." The message was written in pencil, and the page seemed to have been torn from a notebook.

Pagenstecher was intrigued by the results of this hypnotic session, and he arranged for another session to be held on the following evening, March 31. This time de Zierold went into a different kind of trance, a state of catatonic rigidity. The information she relayed during this session did not come from a vision, but from "Them"—no explanation being given as to who "They" were.

De Zierold was told by "Them" that Ramon was a political refugee who, along with his wife and brother, had been staying in Cuba under the assumed name Ramon P——. "They" requested that the true name not be published, as it would endanger Ramon's brother, who was also a political refugee. The hypnotized woman was also told that the scar over Ramon's eye was the result of a gunshot wound received during a political uprising.

Pagenstecher later wrote to Ramon's widow in an attempt to verify this additional information. Luisa replied on June 26, 1921, expressing her gratitude to the doctor for relieving her uncertainty regarding the fate of her husband. She confirmed the information obtained from the second trance session. Ramon and his brother had both been political refugees, and Ramon had been on his way to Spain to try and gain his inheritance. He had indeed lived in Havana under the assumed name of Ramon P——, and his scar was the result of a gunshot wound from an assassin paid by a political enemy.

Could Ramon have sailed on the *Lusitania* under an assumed name (for political reasons) and lost his life when the great liner went down?

One final mystery stemming from the *Lusitania* tragedy took place five years after the loss of the great vessel. The reader will immediately note its striking resemblance to a puzzle we have already reviewed during our discussion of the *Thresher* disaster, for our mystery involves a piece of flotsam picked up far from the coast of Ireland.

On July 14, 1920, two railroad detectives were on one of Philadelphia's city piers overlooking the Delaware River a hundred miles upriver from the Delaware capes. The men's attention was attracted by something floating in the river close to the pier, and they decided to retrieve it for a closer look. One can imagine their surprise when they found the item to be an old, slime-covered lifebelt. One of its shoulder straps was broken, and the entire belt was draped in seaweed and encrusted with barnacles, as if it had been afloat for a long time. Upon scraping away some of the barnacles the two men were able to discern some lettering, which they read with a shock. Painted on one side of the canvas belt were the words "Life Belt," while the other side, in large black letters, bore the name "*Lusitania*."

The lifebelt seems to have been regarded as authentic by all interested parties, and scientists were interested in the route it must have followed in order to be recovered so far from the coast of Ireland. Hydrographers figured the belt must have floated through the Irish Sea and around the north of Scotland, down through the North Sea and the English Channel, down the coast of France and Spain and Africa. From there the currents carried it across the Atlantic. Entering the Gulf Stream, it was carried north. It escaped from this current and drifted to the Delaware capes. At this point—and greatly reminiscent of Dr. Wolff's theory about the *Thresher* life ring—the *Lusitania* lifebelt was supposed to have become fouled on the propellor of a steamship and carried a hundred miles up the Delaware River to Philadelphia, where it was eventually discovered near the city piers.

Was this lifebelt a genuine relic of the *Lusitania* disaster? At this late date it is unlikely that we shall ever know. The cautious remarks we made about the relics from the *Thresher* and *Waratah* may apply here; either it was yet another case of a belated hoax or, perhaps, another mystery of the sea.

Many innocent lives were extinguished when the *Lusitania* rolled onto her side and sank off the coast of Ireland in 1915. Is it possible that ripples from that disaster made themselves felt in the fabric of time itself, affecting human lives not only *after* the sinking, but *before*?

Having presented a collection of stories suggesting that the death of the *Lusitania* was known to some people before her sailing (or, alternatively, that it was known before the formal notification of her sinking), we have to ask a number of basic questions. Were there any factors that alerted people to the possibility, even the remote possibility, that she would be sunk? If so, given the German declaration that *any* British vessel would be regarded as a legitimate target, is there any implication that the *Lusitania* was specifically singled out, as opposed to any other vessel?

We are asking, of course, whether there were any pre-sailing conditions that might make *this* ship the focus of rumors and/or psychically oriented experiences suggesting that she might be destroyed. If the *Lusitania* had in fact acquired that kind of celebrity, then our interpretation of paranormal incidents recorded after the event will probably alter; prior awareness of the likelihood of that ship's loss might arguably generate a range of anxieties that would find chance confirmation when it *was* lost, but also (and still arguably) it might create the necessary mental atmosphere in which authentic paranormal impressions could be registered. (We dealt with this confusing situation more thoroughly in our chapter on the *Titanic* and will try not to repeat ourselves too much here.)

We could begin by taking a lateral view of the situation. First of all, can we identify any reasons as to why people may have wanted to sail on a British vessel rather than on one belonging to another nation? Factors here include:

1. The preference for fast Cunarders. A speedy crossing was important to many transatlantic passengers, who might prefer to take the risk involved in a fast trip rather than take a slower, "safer" vessel. For example, there is the fact that the American liner *New York* was scheduled to leave New York the same day as the *Lusitania*, arriving in England two days after the *Lusitania*'s scheduled arrival; the *New York* sailed with three hundred vacant cabins.

2. Nationalism. British subjects, who made up the bulk of the *Lusitania*'s passenger list, preferred to sail under their own flag.

3. Observance of social position. "Upper-crust Americans" felt that traveling on a big Cunarder was "the thing to do."

4. Perceived safety of a big Cunarder like the *Lusitania*. At the time of the *Lusitania*'s sailing the U-boat campaign had not yet become truly frightening. The Germans had not yet managed to torpedo a passenger ship anywhere near the size or speed of the *Lusitania*, and many people felt that a German submarine would be unable to waylay or catch her.

These considerations help to explain a little of the charisma surrounding the *Lusitania*. As we speculate elsewhere, it could be hypothesized that the more charismatic a vessel is—the more talismanic her name—so the greater the impact of her loss; at the same time, although it cannot be qualified absolutely, so also the greater likelihood of paranormalistic accounts surrounding her loss.

The reverse side of the coin is that there were cogent reasons to suggest that people may have feared sailing on *any* British ship. The German proclamation of February 4, 1915, declared that the waters around Great Britain and Ireland would be regarded as "an area of war." This meant that German U-boats would destroy all *enemy* vessels, including armed and unarmed merchantmen, that they found within this war zone. Moreover, these merchant vessels would be destroyed "without its always being possible" to avoid endangering the lives of those citizens of neutral countries who might be on board. Germany warned all neutral countries (including America) against "further entrusting crews, passengers and wares to such ships [which included the *Lusitania*]." Basically, this meant that all British ships ran the risk of being torpedoed, while neutral ships (provided they were not carrying contraband to England) did not.

This might account for possible "false premonitions" experienced by people on shore who were awaiting the arrival of a British ship carrying their loved ones. Somehow, though, this doesn't seem to ring true (in our opinion) in the case of Mrs. Holbourn's dream. Nor does it account for the vision of Avis Dolphin experienced by her grandfather. It also fails to explain why Blanche Marshall feared the May 1 voyage of the *Lusitania*, but did not hesitate to book an earlier voyage on the same ship.

More central to the issue is the strong likelihood that there were worries about torpedoing centered specifically on the *Lusitania* rather than upon other major transatlantic liners. There were two possible reasons for this:

1. Along with the *Mauretania, Olympic,* and *Aquitania,* the *Lusitania* had acquired a splendid reputation and attracted much attention during the prewar years. The transatlantic passenger trade, we should remember, was highly competitive—so much so that Anglo-German efforts to outdo one another in terms of size and luxury of their liners was virtually an echo of the two countries' more militaristic antagonisms. However, by May 1915 the *Lusitania* was the only four-funnelled British liner still on the North Atlantic run between England and America, the other three ships having been requisitioned by the British Admiralty for use as troop carriers. Being the largest liner currently traversing the war zone, public attention (naturally attracted to superlatives of all sorts) would inevitably focus on the *Lusitania* and the danger she faced each time she sailed through British waters (which were a "war zone").

2. The German newspaper advertisement (which warned ship passengers about the war zone danger) was situated *right next* to Cunard's *Lusitania* advertisement. Due to this proximity, the average newspaper reader would make a mental connection between the German warning and the sailing of the *Lusitania* (even though the *Lusitania* was not specifically mentioned in the German advertisement). But since the German newspaper warning did not appear until the morning of the *Lusitania*'s sailing, it could not have been responsible (in itself) for any premonitions experienced before May 1.

All this leads us to a survey of reasons people may have experienced false "premonitions of danger" about the *Lusitania* or worried (even unconsciously) about her safety.

1. The German advertisement which appeared on May 1, the day of the *Lusitania*'s sailing, appeared in at least six New York papers. However, it did not appear to alarm many of the *Lusitania*'s passengers, who joked about the possibility of being torpedoed and about the liner's "last trip." Most people thought that the *Lusitania* was too speedy to be caught by a submarine, and that, even if worse came to worst, the great liner would be warned by a U-boat before being torpedoed. Many felt that the great liner would not sink even if she *were* torpedoed. These feelings, needless to say, were encouraged by Cunard.

British newspapers, when informed of the German warning, took much the same view. The *London Daily Telegraph* used such captions as "Berlin's Latest Bluff," "Ridiculed in America," etc. The May 3 *London Times* headlined its account of the incident "The Ineffective Blockade. New Trick To Frighten Americans. *Lusitania* warned."

The British opinion was that, since the German submarine blockade was presently regarded as ineffective, Germany was now instigating a "newspaper blockade" in a further attempt to interfere with transatlantic traffic to England. Even though the German advertisement's effect on British morale was probably minimal, it still might have served to alarm a few people in England who were awaiting the arrival of loved ones on the *Lusitania*. However, Mrs. Holbourn's family had tried to reassure her (following her dream) by saying that the Germans would not dare attack a large passenger ship like the *Lusitania*. Even though it is quite apparent that they did not take the German threat seriously, this does not necessarily mean that Mrs. Holbourn shared her relatives' opinion.

2. Warning telegrams were allegedly received by several of the *Lusitania*'s passengers before the ship sailed. Although newspaper stories exist in which reporters allegedly asked passengers what they thought of these warning telegrams, at least one author claims that the *Lusitania*'s passengers never received these telegrams (which had apparently been sent as a news stunt by certain gentlemen of the press). The telegrams were withheld from the passengers by the direct order of Charles Sumner, manager of Cunard's New York office. Captain Turner himself later testified that "no passenger received a warning telegram."

Even if newsmen did inform several *Lusitania* passengers of these telegrams, the resulting interviews show that passengers dismissed the warnings as the work of cranks. It does not appear that anyone cancelled their passage on the *Lusitania* as a result of receiving one of these anonymous warnings. It appears, however, that reports of these warning telegrams were published in British newspapers on May 2, 1915, the day after the *Lusitania* sailed. Therefore, it seems possible that nervous people in England might have read these reports and begun worrying about *Lusitania*. Any "premonitions of danger" experienced by these people might therefore be due to the newspaper reports about the above warnings.

3. The shutting down of six of *Lusitania*'s boilers reduced her speed from twenty-five to twenty-one knots. Many passengers had booked passage on the *Lusitania* due to her reputation for speed, which, it was felt, would enable the liner to outrun any U-boats that might be encountered. Cunard, however, concealed the fact that, to save coal and labor, almost one-fourth of the *Lusitania*'s boilers had been deactivated, greatly reducing the speed advantage she held over the German submarines. Because it was suppressed by Cunard, it seems unlikely that this news

was the cause of any anxiety the public may have experienced regarding the ship's safety.

It seems, then, that there was a generalized awareness that the *Lusitania might* be a target for a U-boat attack; what the material does not establish is that such an eventuality was believed either inevitable or indeed likely to prove fatal. Not for the first time in these pages we are forced into the unsatisfactory position of saying that many of the fears of disaster were only corroborated—only appear evidential—by virtue of the fact that the disaster occurred to corroborate them. Would we have heard these stories at all if the *Lusitania* had *not* been lost? We focused on this paradox in the chapter on the *Titanic*, though without managing to answer it.

For now let us concentrate on our *Lusitania* stories. Taken together and at face value, they will almost certainly incline some readers to accept that paranormal cognitions of the *Lusitania* sinking—before, during and shortly after (before common knowledge) the event are no less disputable facts than the sinking of the *Lusitania* itself.

But elsewhere in this book, and principally in our chapter on paranormal events surrounding the loss of the *Titanic*, we raised a number of questions about the nature and/or reliability of the material in which these stories appear. We pointed out that, objectively speaking, the evidential status of this database could be open to skeptical protest. As our bibliography will tell you, the present chapter draws upon a variety of sources: on books relating to the *Lusitania* tragedy wherein the paranormal accounts are little more than anecdotal extras (that is, subservient to or arising from the main story), but also upon works written by those with, shall we say, a closer and more dedicated attitude to the psychic world. It could be argued, and frequently is, that the memoirs of mediums, sensitives, and even supposedly cautious parapsychologists must be taken as suspect documents. At best, the theory runs, they are colored by the writer's commitment to the subject, by a desire to impress upon others the legitimacy of the writer's own interest-cum-belief in the "unseen" and perhaps the wish to promote belief in the factually based supernature of the "unseen." At worst, they are pieces of self-advertisement, subjective sensationalism devoid of all real evidential value.

Can a (self-professed) psychic write an autobiography without advertising him- or herself in one way or another? Can *anybody* write an autobiography in a cool, detached fashion that makes the writer seem totally unconnected with the central character of his or her autobiography? We don't ask politicians, war veterans, ballet dancers or paleontologists to remove themselves utterly from their memoirs, but accept an element of bias as natural to involvement in their subject, a direct result of that same commitment to it that makes what they say worth hearing. Surely a psychic who pens his personal account of his adventures should have the same privilege.

However, this does not and cannot remove the suspicion that a writer predisposed towards belief in the paranormal lacks the total objectivity needed to present the case accurately. In what has gone before, the objection may be particularly true of the Joan Grant passages; as author of several best-selling books on her psychic experiences, she plainly displays an unrepentant belief that does indeed color her work—and, let it be said, which gives her books much of their unique appeal. The solution is quite simple: if we find that Joan Grant's commitment to survival issues is too flamboyant—too unscientific—we can ignore what she has to say about the *Lusitania*. The fact that she was the daughter of a person who almost drowned on it (but not quite!) is neither here nor there. The same is true for Nell St. John Montague, the "society clairvoyante," and Geraldine Cummins. Their credentials as practising psychics may disqualify them right away in the minds of some readers: those who believe it is illogical to think that a psychic can write without a wish to impress and convert.

The same might be said for the account written by Alta Piper concerning her heroic effort not to sail on the *Lusitania*. Her expressed reason for writing the account is interesting. By her own statement, Piper was moved to tell her remarkable story due to "circumstances grimly recalling the sinking of the *Lusitania*"—namely, the loss of the liner *Athenia,* also to a German submarine and under conditions that aroused criticism of the U-boat commander's conduct, on September 3, 1939—an event which won *Athenia* the unenvied record of being Britain's first maritime casualty of a war only twelve hours old. Piper is therefore writing about a happening that occurred almost a quarter-century before; a factor that few parapsychologists would applaud.

Again, the account's authoress is patently a believer in spiritualism, which one feels is quite natural and excusable when her mother, Leonora Piper, had acquired the reputation of one of the greatest and least dubious mediums in the history of that subject; even today few responsible researchers will impugn her honesty. It is less than surprising, then, if Alta Piper was disposed to credit "only spirit intervention" for her deliverance. (Some would say that given the fact her mother was who she was, Alta Piper had little choice about the matter.) Whether a predisposition to crediting spirit intervention ruins Piper's credentials as a witness is a matter of opinion; given the nature of her experience, perhaps she had a perfect right to give the spirit intervenors their due.

The experience (graphically described for the consumption of a popular-occult magazine audience) is extremely detailed; it is inevitable that we wonder how much of it has been embroidered to heighten the drama. At the same time, it carries a ring of conviction. The writer's description of the weird, repeated warning perhaps impresses us less than her illogical, intuitive efforts not to board the ship; Piper works as hard to avoid going as she formerly worked to go! Overriding all is the sense that she *knows* she is behaving illogically in turning down that much-in-demand berth—she feels guilty about lying about her passport and generally presents her reactions as wholly unreasonable. The climax of the story is artfully presented to maximize its impact, yet the overall impression is of a personal story rather than a sheerly invented one. "This unforgettable experience convinced me then that the age of miracles is very far indeed from being past," Piper writes in her introduction, "but readers . . . will be able to judge for themselves of this from the . . . narrative." We can't argue with that.

Having pointed out the evidential shortcomings of experiences related by confirmed believers in psychic phenomena, we must now ask the following question: Should we then treat the parapsychologists as more credit-worthy sources? After all, they are (or profess themselves to be) people of scientific and rational bent; their discipline requires objectivity to rise above and beyond subjective impressions. It goes without saying that parapsychologists, being mere humans, sometimes lack this kind of Vulcan detachment. Parapsychologists such as Harry Price or Sir William Barrett may not fall foul of this truism, but nor are they reluctant to back the mundane details of their researches with personal interpretation—statements of where the facts have led them. If this is bias, it is surely of an acceptable kind. And, accidentally or not, some of the more striking material in this chapter comes in the form of mediums' recollections *supported* by what parapsychologists have to say of them. Thus Nell St. John Montague's story impressed Harry Price sufficiently for him to tell it in his *Search for Truth*; we have the Dowden account not merely from her own hand (plus that of fellow spiritualist Geraldine Cummins) but courtesy of the not-easily fooled Sir William Barrett, while Maria Reyes de Zierold's psychometry evidently interested the American Society for Psychical Research.

So the material, while not beyond criticism, seems significant, even if we reject some of it as too anecdotal (the *Lusitania* cat, McFadden, perhaps also Bowen) or dubious on other grounds. It may be harsh to raise the possibility that the personal narratives of Holbourn and Ryland were "processed" in some way for popular consumption in the mass circulation "strange mysteries" magazine *Fate,* but it is necessary; the reliability of *Fate*'s material has been known to fluctuate over the years and some researchers refuse to look at it at all. These researchers are even less enamored of Joan Grant's work, at least as far as taking it as serious evidence of the paranormal is concerned. That aside, Grant episodes seem to waver not so much due to the author's predisposition toward total acceptance of the supernatural but by virtue of over fifty years' lapse between time of alleged occurrence and date of publication. Even then, it is worth repeating that *some* of what you have read appears significant.

One final warning here, relating again to the nature of the material we used, is that selection has a way of highlighting or exaggerating features that do not register as strongly in the original. The absconding cat and John McFadden episodes are not the most dominating aspects of the *Tragedy of the Lusitania* memorial edition; they are quite minor, even supernumerary inclusions within it, but the fact that two writers (Messrs. Behe and Goss) have been looking for that sort of story inevitably gives those anecdotes a certain prominence. Even the Friend communications (abstracted from the ASPR *Journal*) may have suffered here from the way our summary culls a number of haphazard or seemingly irrelevant comments from the "control," with a result that perhaps, though only perhaps, the outcome seems more decisively evidential than it actually was.

Writers on the paranormal have an escape clause written into their contracts, however. It goes something like this: having undertaken the basic research and assessed it to the best of our ability—having conceded also that the said material may provide certain readers with grounds for doubt—we cordially invite the reader to examine the items cited in our bibliography and, on the strength of those original sources, to form his or her own opinion.

Cowardice? Obfuscation? Perhaps so. Stranger things have happened at sea . . .

References

Psychic Material

Edward Bowen case: A. A. Hoehling and Mary Hoehling, *Last Voyage of the* Lusitania (Dell, 1974), pp. 27–28.

Cat mascot case: Frederick Ellis, *Tragedy of the* Lusitania, memorial edition (1915), pp. 174–75; James Croall, *Fourteen Minutes: The Last Voyage of the* Empress of Ireland (Stein & Day, 1979), p. 38.

Hester Dowden case: Geraldine Cummins, *Unseen Adventures* (Rider

& Co., 1951), pp. 24–26; William O. Stevens, *Psychics and Common Sense* (E. P. Dutton, 1953), pp. 188–90; Sir William Barrett, *On the Threshold of the Unseen* (London: Kegan Paul, Trench, Tribner, and New York: E. P. Dutton, 1917), pp. 186–87; see Hester Dowden, *Voices From the Void.*

Edwin Friend case: "Communications from Mr. Friend, Who Was Lost on the *Lusitania,*" *Journal of the American Society for Psychical Research* 10 (January 1916): 148–87; " . . . and then the water closed over me," letter by Theodate Pope, *American Heritage* (April 1975): 98–101.

Joan Grant case: Joan Grant, *Many Lifetimes* (Pocket Books, 1968), pp. 207–209.

Prof. I. B. Holbourn case: *New York Times,* May 12, 1915.

Marion Holbourn case: *Fate* (December 1954): 40–43.

Lifebelt case: *New York Times,* July 16, 1920; *New York Times,* August 23, 1920.

Mrs. Alfred Lyttelton case: J. G. Piddington, "Forecasts in Scripts Concerning the War," *Proceedings of the Society for Psychical Research* 33 (1923). See part 87, March 1923, pp. 439–605; *Journal of the American Society for Psychical Research* 17 (June 1923). (A review of Paddington's "Forecasts," above.)

Blanche Marshall case: Joan Grant, *Far Memory* (Avon, 1969), pp. 43–47.

John McFadden case: Frederick Ellis, *Tragedy of the* Lusitania, memorial edition (1915), p. 174.

Nell St. John Montague case: Harry Price, *Search for Truth* (1942), p. 257; see Nell St. John Montague, *Revelations of a Society Clairvoyante* (London, 1926).

Alta Piper case: *Prediction* (November 1939): 409–411.

John Ryland case: *Fate* (March 1971): 78–82.

Maria Reyes de Zierold case: Gracia Fay Ellwood, *Psychic Visits to the Past* (Signet, 1971), pp. 122–29; "Psychometric Experiments with Maria Reyes de Z," *Journal of the American Society for Psychical Research* 16 (1922): 28–31.

Lusitania *Material*

Thomas Bailey and Paul Ryan, *The* Lusitania *Disaster* (The Free Press, 1975).

Donald Barr Chidsey, *The Day They Sank the* Lusitania (Award, 1967).

C. L. Droste, *The* Lusitania *Case* (7 C's Press, 1972).

Frederick Ellis, *Tragedy of the* Lusitania, memorial edition (1915).

Des Hickey and Gus Smith, *Seven Days to Disaster: The Sinking of the* Lusitania (G. P. Putnam's Sons, 1981).
A. A. Hoehling and Mary Hoehling, *The Last Voyage of the* Lusitania (Dell, 1974).
Charles Lauriat, *The* Lusitania*'s Last Voyage* (Houghton Mifflin, 1915).
Francis Miller, ed. *True Stories of the Great War* (New York: Review of Reviews Company, 1917).
Colin Simpson, *The* Lusitania (Ballantine, 1974).
Lowell Thomas, *Raiders of the Deep* (Doubleday, 1929).

IV

Assorted Tales

8

In Peace and War

By now the reader will be reasonably familiar with the premonitions and other types of psychic phenomena that can be (and have been) reported in connection with ships and the sea. He will have observed the present authors' investigatory approach to these reported phenomena, and will also have learned the importance of examining primary source material in order to minimize the effects of literary "elaborations" by latter-day writers on these subjects.

Most importantly, the reader can see the importance of examining reports of psychic phenomena within their historical context—that is, with reference to the contemporary atmosphere of current events surrounding the percipients of the psychic experiences in question. Even enthusiastic believers in psychic phenomena must admit that current events can sometimes (often?) influence a person's peace of mind and perhaps provide an underlying reason for that person to undergo an experience he believers to be psychic in nature. The honest investigator must first attempt to eliminate all possible "normal" explanations for a "psychic experience" before he makes that vast jump to the conclusion that a "paranormal" explanation is the true one.

This, the final section of our work, will examine reports of psychic phenomena connected with a potpourri of ships that have "gone missing" during the last century and a half. In addition to passenger liners, however, we intend to expand our horizons a bit by examining reports of psi connected with warships that, by their very nature, run a very real risk of meeting with a violent end at sea.

Having reached this point in the book, the reader may find it interesting to compare the cases that follow with some of those cases we have already discussed in earlier chapters. It might also prove instructive to compare psychic cases connected with peacetime ship disasters to those psychic cases connected with the loss of warships in battle.

The authors will—for the most part—keep their own counsel about the cases that follow and will allow the reader to make up his or her own mind about their evidential value.

The *President*—1841

Ocean-going ships were still making the transition from sail to steam power when the London liner *President* left New York on March 11, 1841. A wood-hulled vessel carrying a full spread of canvas on her three masts, the *President* was also equipped with side lever engines and twin paddle wheels that could drive her along at a speed of eight knots. With the ablility to use her engines for propulsion whenever the wind died away, the single-funnelled *President* was regarded as an exceptionally reliable vessel that could keep to her sailing schedule regardless of the whims of the Zephyrs.

Bound for Liverpool with 121 passengers, the *President* was privileged to be carrying some celebrities on this particular voyage. Lord Fitzroy Lennox, son of the Duke of Richmond, was on board, as was Tyrone Power, the celebrated Irish actor (and grandfather of the film star who would later bear the same name), headed for London to fulfill a commitment to appear on the stage there. The *President* was scheduled to make its Atlantic crossing in sixteen days, and no one doubted that she would perform as efficiently on this voyage as she had since going into regular passenger service two years earlier.

One of Tyrone Power's close friends was an elderly man named Benjamin Webster. Webster was the manager and part owner of London's Haymarket Theater, and Power often visited the old gentleman at his home at Blackheath.

During the wee hours of the morning of March 13 a violent wind and heavy rain passed over Blackheath, and Webster was sleeping soundly in his own bed when he was unexpectedly awakened by his butler. This trusted family retainer had been in Webster's employ for many years, and it was unheard of for the man to disturb his master in the middle of the night. The butler was in a highly agitated state, however, and he told Webster, "Someone is knocking at the hall door and is calling out your name."

Irritated at the butler's odd reactions and his seeming lack of common sense, Webster asked his employee, "Don't you know who it is?"

The butler, flustered and momentarily at a loss for words, finally managed to tell his master that it was too dark outside for him to see clearly.

Webster pressed the man further. "Well, who does it sound like?"

"It sounds like Mr. Power's voice, sir," the butler replied. "He keeps calling your name over and over and saying that he is drowned in the rain."

Webster was stunned. He knew that at the present moment his friend Tyrone Power was supposed to be bound for England on board the London liner *President*, and he couldn't understand how the ship could possibly have reached England only two days after leaving New York. Webster sprang out of bed and hurried downstairs to unbolt the front door. Peering outside into the darkness, the old gentleman was unable to see anything except the rain as it poured down onto the surrounding heath.

Puzzled and slightly alarmed, Webster asked his butler to repeat his story once more; the butler did so, and the details of this repetition matched his original story exactly. The strange incident itself did not repeat itself, however, and, still perplexed, Webster tried to put the incident out of his mind until he had the chance to talk with Power when the actor's ship docked at Liverpool.

But Tyrone Power never arrived at Liverpool. Indeed, the *President* herself vanished without a trace after leaving New York, and to this day nobody knows what happened to her. It was thought that she might have foundered in a storm known to have lashed part of her track the day after she sailed, but this is only conjecture. Besides, two smaller ships passed safely through this same storm after suffering only delays. Perhaps one of the *President*'s boilers exploded, disabling her and enabling the storm to finish her off? Perhaps she struck an iceberg? Again, just conjecture.

Some time after the *President*'s name was stricken from the international registry, an Irish newspaper carried a story about the recovery of a bottle purportedly carrying a message that read, "The *President* is sinking. God help us all. Tyrone Power." A hoax? Probably. If Tyrone Power had indeed had time to write a note before the *President* foundered, one might have expected him to address a word of farewell to his wife instead of composing a more general message.

But there were published reports that Tyrone Power's wife (as well as Mrs. Roberts, wife of the *President*'s master) had received letters from their husbands written from Madeira—out in the Atlantic—saying that the *President* was safe in harbor there and was awaiting engine and rudder repairs. Mrs. Roberts denied having received such a letter from her husband, however, and friends of Tyrone Power asserted that the letter received by Mrs. Power was just a cruel hoax.

But even though Mrs. Power never heard from her husband again after the *President* sailed, Benjamin Webster remained convinced that Tyrone Power's surviving personality had somehow succeeded in making his fate known during the wee hours of March 13. Webster never told Power's widow of his eerie experience, however; indeed, the story is said to have remained a Webster family secret for years.

Even though no one knows exactly when the *President* actually went down, the authors feel that the case made for the wee hours of March 13, 1841, may be stronger than most.

References

Robert Stanton, *The Unexplained at Sea* (London: John Clare Books, 1982).

Bill Wisner, *Vanished Without a Trace* (Berkley Medallion, 1977).

The *Mayfly*—1851

The name of the ship, the date at which she is supposed to have joined the spectral fleet of lost vessels haunting the world's waterways, are really quite irrelevant. The *Mayfly*, ghost-wherry of Oulton Broad, never existed. She is another fabricated phantom ship story and we include her here for two reasons. First, the *Mayfly* amplifies points we made in our opening chapters, particularly regarding ghostly craft that celebrate their tragic anniversaries (like the ersatz *Lady Luvibund* and the quasihistorical *Palatine*) but also the processes behind the invention of folklore. Secondly, we wish to pay tribute to the research skills of Mike Burgess, who exposed this "Hoax of the Broads" and "The *Mayfly* Myth" in two articles with those titles in the now-defunct East Anglian mysteries magazine *Lantern,* which he edited and produced until a few years ago.

Burgess wouldn't object to sharing the limelight with Charles Sampson, however. Without him, we surely would not have any *Mayfly* myth to chuckle over and (let's admit!) to enjoy. Born at Sheerness, Kent (England), in 1881 and dying at the age of fifty-nine in 1940, Sampson was a doctor with a string of qualifications and publications meandering from psychotherapy to reminiscences of cruises on his yacht. Arguably, he doctored nothing so well as the ghostly lore and traditions of the Broads, those manmade fens and canals that interlace the coastal region topping the easterly bulge of England and the spiritual heart of what is colloquially called East Anglia.

"Ha-ha, a real succulent ghost-story, and one to make your blood go all gu-ey, and your spinal cord flutter like a flag in high wind," wrote Sampson as he announced one of his tales in *Ghosts of the Broads* (1931), which began life as a series of articles in the *Yachtsman* and which is still selling nicely as a paperback edition. That lip-smacking relish applies to all twenty-six stories as a whole. Despite ingenuous references to emanations, vibrations, and other items from pop occultism—despite also the citations of arcane, heavyweight-sounding parapsychological societies that cannot be traced and probably never existed—we've only ourselves to blame if we take Sampson too seriously. He was and is an entertainer with a sly sense of humor; we suspect he would have been delighted to find his ghostly creations accepted as anything bordering on fact.

Sampson's melodramatic efforts—wordy narratives of beauteous maidens and dastardly villains of bygone times, all presented as authentic history—rarely threaten to make the blood turn "gu-ey"; if anything, they tend to narcotize it. Still less are they genuine folklore; they represent a writer's oversophisticated effort to invent it. The result is what Richard Dorson castigated as *fake*lore, and when locals profess never to have heard the story in question (as our author concedes they sometimes do) the reason is not any reluctance to discuss unhallowed secrets or to expose themselves to ridicule, but simply because Sampson has foisted one of his inventions on some convenient place that looks as though it "deserves" a ghost story.

Judging from Sampson, the Norfolk Broads have so many phantom craft that but for their intangibility they might pose a navigation hazard. Additionally, these gloriously phosphorescent specters follow a strict rota, each scrupulously manifesting only on its own anniversary. "As is well-known, the periodicity of apparitions comes around with extraordinary accuracy," he declares in his introduction, "definite manifestations occurring on certain days, such as St. Mark's Day, 5 March, St. Anthony's Day, 13 June, and All Hallows E'en, 31 October." Well, as a point of interest, they don't—at least, not according to parapsychological critiques more serious than Sampson's, but let that pass. Let go with it the accounts of a flaming Viking burial ship at South Walsham and a veritable armada of Saxon boats at Bredon Water; the writer has witnessed both events, but then—unlike most psychical researchers—Sampson appears to have had spectacular luck: he had only to hear the traditional tale and visit the haunted spot on the appropriate day to rendezvous with any number of ghosts.

The phantasmal *Mayfly* is typical illustration enough of the Sampson style. It was a wherry, a low, barge-like craft with a single sail and a low draught highly favored on the Broads in the nineteenth-century. Her commander was the brutish "Blood" Stevenson, whose mutton-sized fists and vile temper made him "a bruiser of the first order." In 1851 this pugilistic captain sailed down the Waveney River and out onto Oulton Broad, whence he absconded with the *Mayfly*, £400,000 and the lovely Millicent Dormey all at one go. To truncate a drawn-out tale, Millicent was raped by Stevenson, Stevenson was killed by Millicent, and the *Mayfly* stormed out into the Atlantic and vanished. But she was seen again—can still be seen if you visit Oulton Broad on June 24 where and when she appears in ghostly phosphorescent light. You will see a skeleton at the wheel—Sampson is very partial to skeletons, especially ones with burning innards—and also Millicent being pursued toward the deck by Blood Stevenson. For those skeptical readers who have not yet "swallowed the bait," consider the fact that the story is endorsed by parapsychologists! The "British Psychical Phenomena Association" has recorded it in their transactions—see vol. 98, pp. 127–72, 401, 406, and 863. Even better, the "International Society of Metaphysics has tried for the last seven years to make records of this cthonic manifestation by means of the selenic cell and the thermionic valve."

A reader might think Sampson's "cthonic manifestation, selenic cell and thermionic valve" a kind of satire, but that would be taking him too seriously again. And when he vows, "Personally, I wouldn't be on Oulton Broad on the night of June the 24th for anything in the world. I have no desire to see the ghost-wherry, this ship of Hell, with bloody murder on her deck and Death at the helm," there is a temptation to reassure him that he's not in danger of seeing any such thing, not on June 24-nor at any other time.

Ghosts of the Broads came under the critical eye of Mike Burgess in the Spring 1982 issue of *Lantern,* which discouraged any attempt at field-researching Sampson's stories on the grounds that it would be "a waste of time, since we now know that 90 percent of the book is SHEER FICTION!" Sampson's "cases"—the fifth-century Viking burial, for example—usually rely on the assumption that the Norfolk Broads were as we see them today; in truth, they only evolved in the fourteenth and fifteenth centuries. More seriously, none of the alleged witnesses and only a few of the local informants named by Sampson can be identified with real persons (and that tentatively). The sixteen texts he short-titles in his bibliography—without publication dates—are of doubtful relevance. And, most suspicious of all, the phantoms are suspiciously (melo)dramatic; they are a writer's version of what we'd like to believe apparitions are all about, not at all close to what more staid parapsychological records inform us they are or may be.

Sampson, like the unknown craftsman who manufactured the *Lady Luvibund* story (see chapter 1) or the equally uncredited souls who took the observed facts of northeastern America's "ghost lights" and attached thrilling explanatory yarns to them (chapter 2), is creating a species of folklore. Whether or not he was working with genuine oral materials that he then revised and embellished quite drastically to suit his own taste must be a very moot point. In Burgess's view, the central features of *Ghosts of the Broads* are "a conglomeration of twisted history, genuine tradition and sheer fiction": only one solitary ghost story from the book can be found in a version predating it (that is, prior to 1931). As we said of the *Lady Luvibund* affair, the lack of evidence for a supposedly traditional story at any time earlier than the account that informs us it *is* a traditional story cannot be considered a hanging matter, but it certainly raises doubts about the tale's pedigree. How can we be sure that the writer didn't invent it and, in best folk-narrator style, pass it off as a veritable, inherited traditional story?

If you're forging an antique, don't forget the small historical details. When you've made your authentic George III bureau, take a shot gun and blast a few woodworm holes in it (and remember to color them black so as to disguise the fact they're recent). Sampson does not omit the wormholes, but he forgets to darken them; the corroborative and/or historical details in his stories won't stand up to a magnifying glass. In "The *Mayfly* Myth" (*Lantern,* Summer 1982) Burgess exposes the odd illogicality of an anniversary ghost that gets the all-important date of its anniversary wrong: if *Mayfly* sailed out on its last voyage in *September,* as Sampson's opening paragraphs say she did, what business has she to appear on Oulton Broad at just after 12:30 in *June*?

Perhaps we are supposed to think that was the date of the violent scenes—the deaths of Millicent and Blood Stevenson—that condemned the *Mayfly* to a future career as a cyclical ghost ship: Blood stole her in September and took until June to creep round the coast to a point where the wild Atlantic beckoned. This would be slow going even for a nineteenth-century wherry. But how do we excuse the facts that local trade directories of the period reveal no traces of the characters in the story? The patent conclusion is that, like the parapsychological organizations cited by the author—like the *Mayfly* herself—they simply didn't exist.

Just as obviously, Sampson understood the art of the contemporary legend narrator: disguise your own unbelief in what you are saying and persuade the audience to suspend theirs by incorporating authority figures to reassure them—named witnesses, historical personages, dates and reliable-sounding psychical research bodies. All things considered, it is not surprising that Sampson's *Mayfly* outlived its inventor to pass into that ambiguous world of popular ghostcraft that is not (properly speaking) folklore but comes to mimic it thanks to writers' propensities to borrow from one another.

Nearly twenty years after *Ghosts of the Broads* and ten years after Sampson's death, the *Mayfly* hove into view again in an *East Anglian* magazine article by A. E. Regis, who did little more than to paraphrase Sampson's original. Another romantic historian and East Anglian country writer, James Wentworth Day, gave the story another airing in 1951. He claimed he had *his* version from a Bill Solomon, former assistant harbor master at Lowestoft and Oulton Broad and yes! there are a few alterations; for example, the wherry sets out in 1840 to a different destination and there is no mention of deaths among her unnamed crew. Before anyone suspects that Solomon was reciting an earlier version that gave Sampson the idea for his, we should add that subsequently he told the *Eastern Evening News* of June 23, 1972, that he'd taken it from a book. Unshockingly, the book Solomon referred to was *Ghosts of the Broads* by Chas Sampson.

In the space of two decades, then, the *Mayfly* had entered into East Anglian folklore, or into what topographical writers like to call tradition. Whether it contradicts our previous arguments against treating the story as an authentic folk narrative or not, we feel it is only fair to concede that there is at least one piece of evidence to suggest it may have been around before Sampson gave it his own individual treatment. *Black-Sailed Traders,* Roy Clark's affectionate study of the wherry (1961) includes an undated version "from hearsay and gossip" that has Beccles in Suffolk as its setting, with an anonymous but beautiful miller's daughter stabbing a lustful wherryman (cf. "Blood" Stevenson?) and the ship sailing over the horizon in flames; the glowing spectral memento of this exciting event is recreated as before on its anniversary. In Burgess's opinion, this could be the unvarnished original of the tale Sampson adapted to dramatic effect.

Much would depend on whether Clark's story (1961) was a genuine echo from some much older folk tale that was around before Sampson's book appeared (1931). Failing that, we could guess that it was only one more unacknowledged offspring sired by *Ghosts of the Broads.* The point is beyond proof, but in alleging that the fiery phantom has been identified as the thirty-ton Bungay (Suffolk) wherry *May*flower, Clark adds that a craft of this name was certainly owned by a firm called W. D. & A. E. Walker, who operated in Bungay between 1840 and 1860. "Reputed to be the phantom wherry," notes Clark, but without giving any authority to back his statement.

From "*Mayflower*" to "*Mayfly*" is a short trip through the dictionary. As Burgess concluded, Clark's story is either a "corrupted and watered-down version" of Sampson's or the original that inspired the doctor-turned-author. All we can repeat is that no printed version earlier than Sampson's has been located. And it goes without saying that even fewer witnesses of the anniversary-observing phantom wherry of Oulton Broad have been located. None, that is, outside the pages of Sampson's best-known contribution to literature and modern folk legend.

References

Mike D. Burgess, "Hoax of the Broads: An Investigation," *Lantern* 37 (Spring 1982): 4–5 and 7–9.

———, "The *Mayfly* Myth," *Lantern* 38 (Summer 1982): 4–8. Burgess's sources here include, of course, Chas Sampson's *Ghosts of the Broads* (Yachtsman Publishing, 1931; reprinted in paperback by Jarrolds, Norwich: 1973 etc). See the chapter headed "Oulton." His other main materials were: A. E. Regis in *East Anglian* (April 1950); James Wentworth Day, *Broadlands Adventure* (Country Life, 1951), and Roy Clark, *Black-Sailed Traders* (Putnam, 1961). Several repetitive Sampson-indebted summaries appear in gazetteers of British hauntings.

City of Glasgow—1854

In the last decade of the nineteenth century William T. Stead (whom we have already mentioned in our chapter on the *Titanic*) was editor of the *Review of Reviews,* whose 1891 Christmas and New Year's numbers were both devoted to "real ghost stories". The contents were provided by the *Review*'s readers, who sent in their true accounts for Stead's comment and evaluation—he was, after all, a prominent spiritualist. Not long after, these documents formed the basis of a book entitled (unoriginally, but aptly) *Real Ghost Stories.*

The case we are about to discuss, which was sent to Stead by the Rev. Alexander Stewart of Nether Lochaber, had taken place almost forty years previously, in 1854. In spite of the lapse of time separating the event itself from Stewart's retelling of it, the basic facts are so simple and straightforward that the clergyman's report is probably as accurate an account as we could reasonably hope for.

Kenneth Morrison was chief officer of the *City of Manchester,* a liner belonging to the Liverpool & Philadelphia Steamship Co., which sailed regularly between the two cities of its name. In the winter of 1853 Morrison was taking advantage of a brief leave of absence by visiting the Rev. Stewart (his brother-in-law) at the latter's home in Nether Lochaber. During this visit Morrison made the acquaintance of a man named Angus MacMaster, who was in Stewart's service. Morrison and MacMaster struck up an immediate friendship, and when the time came for Morrison to return to his ship he offered MacMaster a position on board as a combination steerage steward and personal valet. MacMaster immediately agreed to this arrangement and accompanied the chief officer back to the *City of Manchester* after his leave of absence expired.

While Morrison and MacMaster spent the ensuing months at sea on the *City of Manchester,* the owners of that steamer were awaiting the newest addition to their fleet of passenger liners. Upon her completion, the 1,087-ton *City of Glasgow* would join other company ships plying the track between Liverpool and Philadelphia. Propelled by steam and carrying auxilliary sail, the *Glasgow* would be able to carry 399 passengers (most of whom would probably be immigrants) in addition to 74 officers and crewmen. As the spring of 1854 approached, work on the *City of Glasgow* neared its completion.

A year after his visit to Nether Lochaber, Chief Officer Morrison took another leave of absence and, along with Angus MacMaster, returned to Lochaber for another visit with Stewart. Morrison had just been appointed master of the brand new *City of Glasgow*, and so pleased had he been with the quality of MacMaster's work that he was resolved to take MacMaster along with him to his new command.

Morrison's leave of absence was only twenty days old when a message arrived stating that the *City of Glasgow* was almost ready to sail; her cabins had been completely booked by prospective passengers, and the loading of her supplies and cargo was just about finished. Morrison's presence would be required to attend to a few last minute details, after which the vessel could begin her maiden voyage to Philadelphia.

Morrison sent word to MacMaster to report to him immediately, as they must leave together for Liverpool in two days. MacMaster dutifully reported to his master that same evening, but Stewart immediately observed that MacMaster was in an unusually grave mood. So noticeable was the latter's gloomy deportment that Stewart took him aside for a private word.

"Angus," said the clergyman, "Captain Morrison leaves the day after tomorrow. You had better get his things packed at once. And, by the way, what a lucky fellow you are! If you did so well on the *City of Manchester,* you will in a year or two make quite a fortune in the *City of Glasgow.*"

"I am not going in the *City of Glasgow*—at least, not on this voyage," replied MacMaster, "and I wish you could persuade Captain Morrison—the best and kindest master ever man had—not to go either."

Stewart was greatly surprised by MacMaster's sudden determination not to sail on the *City of Glasgow*, and he asked what had prompted this decision.

"Well, sir," replied MacMaster, "You must not be angry with me if I tell you that on the last three nights my father, who has been dead nine years, as you know, has appeared to me and warned me not to go on this voyage, for that it will prove disastrous. Whether in dream or waking vision of the night, I cannot say; but I saw him, sir, as distinctly as I now see you; clothed exactly as I remember him in life; and he stood by my bedside, and with uplifted hand and warning finger, and with a most solemn and earnest expression of countenance, he said, "Angus, my beloved son, don't go on this voyage. It will not be a prosperous one." On three nights running has my father appeared to me in this form, and with the same words of warning; and although much against my will, I have made up my mind that in the face of such warning, thrice repeated, it would be wrong in me to go on this voyage."

As Morrison's valet, MacMaster did not feel comfortable in broaching the subject of this "vision" to his master, but he pleaded with Stewart to tell Morrison what had transpired and persuade him to make any possible excuse to the *City of Glasgow*'s owners that would excuse him from taking the vessel on her maiden voyage.

When Morrison was told about MacMaster's nocturnal experience, both he and Stewart tried to reason with the man and convince him to change his mind about staying ashore. MacMaster was adamant, however, and, when the time came for Morrison to leave, the valet wept as he bade his master goodbye.

On Wednesday, March 1, 1854, the *City of Glasgow* sailed from Liverpool with Morrison and nearly five hundred passengers and crewmen on board. After her scheduled date of arrival in Philadelphia—April 8—had come and gone, MacMaster came to Stewart and asked if there was any news of the *City of Glasgow*. Stewart replied in the negative, but said that the vessel's owners had replied to his own inquiries by saying that the ship had probably experienced engine problems and was no doubt proceeding under sail.

"Pray God it may be so," said MacMaster, "but great is my fear that neither to you, sir, nor to me shall word of her safety, or message from her at all ever arrive."

Angus MacMaster was correct; from the day she left Liverpool nothing more was ever heard from Captain Morrison or the *City of Glasgow*.

Directly, that is. On August 18, 1854, the Glasgow-based barque *Mary Morris,* Captain M'Leary was six hundred miles west of Scotland and inching along through heavy seas when she came upon the burned-out hull of a large iron vessel. A boarding party reported that the derelict's hull was compartmented and contained machinery, which seemed to indicate that the vessel had been of a modern, steam-sail design. The next day the *Mary Morris* came upon a seven-foot-tall female figurehead floating in the sea. Although uncertain whether the figurehead was connected with the blackened derelict they had seen the day before, M'Leary knew that no iron-hulled vessel had been reported missing in three years—with the single exception of the *City of Glasgow*—and he felt reasonably certain that he knew what had happened to the newest steamer of the Liverpool & Philadelphia Steamship Co.

The account of MacMaster's dream that Stewart sent to Stead has a rather literary flavor and reads like the sort of ghost story on the "Second Sight in the Highlands" theme, which was popular in Victorian periodicals. However, Stead—not always critical where evidence of the spirit survival issue was concerned—appears to have taken it at face value and without more information we may have to do the same. Perhaps we should recall that Stead's *Real Ghost Stories* was intended (a) to entertain—ghost stories were expected of a Victorian periodical at Christmas!—but also (b) to present evidence of the spirit world in which Stead believed.

The *City of Glasgow* tragedy falls into a class of Victorian stories based around well-known disasters; in the same style are all the ghost stories (fictional or allegedly otherwise) that focused on the "Franklin expedition," the "Indian mutiny," etc. None of this, however, provides grounds for supposing that Stewart was trying to "sell" Stead a piece of fiction; even though Stewart may have "polished" his account a bit in order to maximize its dramatic effect, the basic story of MacMaster's dream warning is so similar to multitudes of other "authenticated" accounts of "precognitive dream warnings" that we cannot just cast it aside as a piece of fiction.

Judging from appearances, at least, it would seem that MacMaster's dream warning somehow made him privy to the knowledge that death would soon overtake the *City of Glasgow* and everyone on board. One interesting aspect of this "paranormal warning" about the doomed vessel is the fact that the identical warning was repeated on three separate occasions. We are struck by the similarity between this episode and three other cases discussed in this book: Prof. I. B. S. Holbourn's three dreams about the sinking of the *Lusitania,* an unnamed steward's three dreams about the impending loss of the *Empress of Ireland* (which we discuss in a later section of this chapter), and Claude Sawyer's three identical dreams, which influenced him to leave the *Waratah* before her final, fatal voyage. Assuming that there really is such a phenomenon as precognition, might repetition of a "precognitive warning" sometimes be the only way for the human subconscious to emphasize to the conscious mind the importance of such a warning?

Another interesting facet of the "warning" about the impending loss of the *City of Glasgow* is the fact that it was relayed by a "dream image" of MacMaster's deceased father. Three possible explanations for this come to mind.

The first and most "obvious" is that the surviving personality of MacMaster's deceased father had returned from the "other side" to warn his son about the danger of sailing on the *City of Glasgow*. If we are to accept this explanation as the true one, we are acknowledging the reality of "life after death" as well as conceding that "surviving spirits" are able to make use of their own precognitive abilities.

A second possible origin of the above dream warning might be that Angus MacMaster *subconsciously* received a precognitive insight concerning the danger of sailing on the *City of Glasgow*; after receiving this information, MacMaster's subconscious mind was faced with the task of making him consciously aware of the information in its possession. It chose a dramatic way of presenting that information; it created a dream image of MacMaster's deceased father and had *him* relay the warning about the doomed vessel. Interestingly, this explanation fits well with our above speculation about the subconscious mind repeating the same "dream warning" several times as a way of "gaining the attention" of the conscious mind.

A third possible explanation, of course, is that MacMaster's "vision" was actually just a hallucination, which, coupled with the coincidental loss of the *City of Glasgow*, produced the appearance of MacMaster having received a paranormal forewarning of the loss of the vessel.

Which, if any, of the above explanations have any merit is something the reader must decide for himself.

References

A. A. Hoehling, *They Sailed Into Oblivion* (Ace, 1959).

W. T. Stead, *Borderland: A Casebook of True Supernatural Stories* (University Books, 1970), pp. 85–88. Originally published in 1897 under the title *Real Ghost Stories*.

The *Arctic*—1854

The Collins liner *Arctic* sailed from Liverpool on September 20, 1854, with 281 passengers and 153 crewmen on board. She was a wooden vessel of roughly 2,800 tons and was powered by twin steam engines that each turned a twenty-five-foot side paddlewheel. The *Arctic* and her sister vessels were faster than some of the Cunard Line's steamers, and the American Collins liners had begun to make a dent in their British rival's passenger trade.

As popular as the *Arctic* was, however, several people whose passage had been booked on her for the September 20 voyage had undergone experiences that undermined their faith in the vessel. Caroline Mitchell, for instance, had been travelling through Europe with her brother Charles, a cotton broker from Charleston, South Carolina. The two Mitchells had booked their passage back to the United States on the *Arctic*, but Caroline cancelled her own booking at the last minute. The night before the *Arctic*'s departure, Caroline had a dream that led her to believe that something tragic was going to happen if she sailed on the *Arctic*. Although Charles probably tried to convince her otherwise, Caroline was apparently convinced that her fear was justified. Charles Mitchell was forced to sail for America without his sister. As it happened, Charles was one of the lucky ones who survived what fate had in store for the big paddle-wheeler.

John Fryer, a young man from Cincinnnati, Ohio, had been visiting relatives in Bath before he finally headed for Liverpool and booked his passage home on the *Arctic*. Friends later recalled that Fryer had often told them of a presentiment he once had that he would lose his life in a shipwreck. The memory of this portent did not prevent Fryer from wanting to sail for home, but perhaps it should have—on this ship, at least—for Fryer was destined never to see Cincinnati again.

Another *Arctic* passenger had once been warned about the grave danger he would face one day if he insisted on traveling by sea. The passenger was William Brown, and the warning was witnessed by his friend Howard Potter. Potter recounted the story to his friend Charles Nott, who in turn recorded it in 1912 in a letter to Mrs. John Crosby Brown. Even though the account was recorded at third hand over fifty-eight years after the event, it is worth repeating here.

One Thanksgiving day prior to the *Arctic*'s September 20 voyage, Brown, Nott, and James Lord decided to visit P. T. Barnum's wondrous museum. A little old woman in the museum was telling fortunes, and the three gentlemen decided to have her peer into the future on their behalf. What the fates predicted for Nott and Lord is unknown, but the seeress seemed startled by what she saw in William Brown's hand and raised her eyes to gaze intently into his.

"I see an awful wreck in your hand, sir," the old woman said earnestly. Both Potter and Lord were chilled by what they heard, but Brown didn't seem at all perturbed by the message, and he asked the woman for more details. None were forthcoming, however. The old woman merely gazed at Brown with great solemnity and repeated her message:

"I can only say that I see an awful shipwreck in your hand."

If Brown recalled the old woman's warning, it did not prevent him from sailing for home on the *Arctic*. Brown's fate and that of the *Arctic* were identical.

On September 27 the *Arctic* was only three days out of New York and was some forty or fifty miles off Cape Race, Newfoundland. This area had long been known as a region of dense fog—always hazardous to safe navigation—and it was while running through such a fog that the *Arctic* collided with the *Vesta,* an outbound French steamer. The *Vesta*'s bows were crushed in, but she had a steel hull divided into watertight compartments. In spite of the extensive damage she suffered, the French vessel was never in any real danger of sinking.

The *Arctic*'s situation was far different, however. Her wooden hull was not divided into watertight compartments, and the sea was flooding into her vitals so quickly that the pumps could not keep up with it. The *Arctic*'s master, Captain Luce, tried to run his vessel toward the nearest landfall and safety, but the great paddle-wheeler had only covered fifteen miles before the sea reached her furnaces and brought her to a halt.

Like other ships in much later years, the *Arctic* did not have enough lifeboats to accomodate everyone on board. Panicky crewmen and a few male passengers defied Luce's attempts to maintain order and fought with one another to scramble into what few lifeboats were available. Even though other crewmen and passengers behaved heroically, the end was inevitable. The *Arctic*'s stern rose slowly into the air as her bows sank deeper until, finally, the great vessel disappeared beneath the frigid water. Those of her people who went into the water grasped at any piece of floating wreckage they could find in order to stay afloat until help came.

But help was days in coming. By the time several liners and fishing boats happened upon the scene of the disaster, only 23 passengers—out of 281—were rescued. The crew fared a little better, with 61 surviving out of a total of 153.

Despite the rather threadbare nature of the above paranormal anecdotes concerning the *Arctic*, the reader will immediately note their similarity to several other cases discussed in this book. By itself, this similarity by no means forces us to accept these present cases as being genuinely precognitive in nature. The resemblance might just as easily mean that people with similar superstitious fears of approaching misfortune are always with us, and that, eventually—a few of these people will encounter a misfortune that coincides with their inner fears. However, even though this statement might seem like a logical explanation for seemingly precognitive experiences, the reader should ask himself the following question: Assuming that such a phenomenon might actually exist, how would a *genuine* case of precognition differ from cases the reader believes to have stemmed from simple coincidence?

But whatever criteria the reader might decide to rely upon, there is no question that the loss of the *Arctic* was truly a tragedy in which forewarnings, psychic or otherwise, would have been a blessing.

References

Alexander Crosby Brown, *Women and Children Last: The Loss of the Steamship* Arctic (G. P. Putnam's & Sons, 1961).

Bill Wisner, *Vanished Without a Trace!* (Berkley Medallion Books, 1977).

The *Oomaru* and the Vanishing Ship—1883?

This story, brief as it is mysterious, almost crept into our chapter on the *Flying Dutchman.* R. L. Hadfield felt no scruple about presenting it in that eerie light when he wrote his *The Phantom Ship* (1937), where it occurs between the 1835 logging of "le volant Hollandais" and the adventure of the *Orkney Belle* in 1911. The latter ends with the venerable sea-phantom heeling off into the fog; our present account has it (or something similar) disappear into patchy mist.

It is one of the many incidents crammed into the tough, romantic sailor's life of Captain D. J. Munro, whose formative sea years were spent with the Albion Shipping Co. on the last of the old Eastern trade clippers. At the age of seventeen Munro had risen to be third mate on the 1,350-ton *Ooamaru* and at a date Hadfield estimates as 1883—two years after a couple of royal princes ran across the *Flying Dutchman* off Australia—this ship was emerging from a spell of brisk weather near the Snares on the southern coast of New Zealand:

> To windward we saw a large ship standing on the same course, evidently a "Blue Nose" packet (Nova Scotia or Yankee). The mist was in patches and when it cleared off nothing could be seen of the ship. What became of her was much discussed on board. Every man in the watch saw her repeatedly, so there was no doubt as to her being there. The weather was not bad and there was no visible reason why she should have foundered. She might have altered course, but there was no apparent reason why she should do this. Another mystery of the sea.

While we feel that Hadfield may have forced the pace a little in calling this a *Flying Dutchman* account—why no traditional bad luck sequel, for instance?—we have no wish to dispute Captain Munro's final verdict.

References

R. L. Hadfield, *The Phantom Ship* (1937). Originally in Cpt. D. J. Munro's *The Roaring Forties and After* (1929). See pp. 84–85.

Shannon—1885

In the same issue of the *Review of Reviews* that formed the basis of our *City of Glasgow* section there appeared a second account with a nautical/paranormal flavor, this one concerning a vessel named the *Shannon*. This account was sent to W. T. Stead by the Rev. T. E. Lord, vicar of Escomb, whose son Jack had been a crewman on the above-named vessel.

Jack's grandmother, Mrs. Bowness, lived in the vicarage as Lord's housekeeper, and Jack visited his family as often as his sailing schedule allowed. Upon the completion of one of the *Shannon*'s voyages to Australia the young sailor came home to the vicarage bringing with him a painting of his ship; he gave this painting to his grandmother, who hung it in her bedroom.

On January 17, 1885, Jack boarded the *Shannon* as she lay in London's East India docks, from which point the vessel set sail for Calcutta. The *Shannon* was carrying a crew of twenty-eight men along with a cargo of about 2,200 tons of general merchandise, including 5 tons of gunpowder. On February 28 (as determined later by the Board of Trade Wreck Commission) the *Shannon* was spoken by a vessel called the *Senator,* the two vessels sailing along in company for the next five or six days.

At this point the *Senator* and *Shannon* parted company; it was the last time the *Shannon* was ever seen by mortal man.

This brings us to the event at Escomb Vicarage that so impressed Lord and two members of his family. On May 2 Mrs. Bowness was sitting in her bedroom with Lord's seventeen-year-old daughter Kattie when, suddenly, the two women noticed a sudden change in the painting of the *Shannon,* which was hanging on the wall. According to Bowness, the painting "became enveloped in a bright cloud, and for a moment the vessel was lost to sight." Kattie became alarmed and ran out of the room in search of her father, but Lord happened to be out at the time; by the time he returned the painting of the *Shannon* had lost its eerie glow and regained its normal appearance.

Bowness was a remarkably calm woman, and she related to Lord everything that she had observed about the unearthly glow that had enveloped the painting of the *Shannon*. She seemed to feel that the event might prove to be of major significance.

"If Jack's ship is lost, it is lost today," Bowness told the clergyman; so certain was she of the truth of her statement that she made one of her granddaughters write a memorandum of the event on a slip of paper: "Light on ship, May 2nd, 1885, Saturday evening, between six and seven p.m. Seen by Grannie and Kattie." Despite Lord's confident assertions that the *Shannon* was undoubtedly safe, Bowness put the memorandum inside her prayer book, where it could be referred back to if the need arose.

Unfortunately, the complete disappearance of the *Shannon* precluded any determination of the exact date upon which the vessel met her fate. We will never know if she went down on May 2, 1885, the day that Jack's grandmother and sister saw the painted image of his ship become "lost to sight" in a "bright cloud" of unknown origin.

It is interesting to note that the mysterious "bright cloud" surrounding the painting could not have been a purely subjective mental phenomenon (in the ordinary sense, that is). In other words, the "bright cloud" does not seem to have been a mere hallucination; the fact that *both* women saw the same manifestation makes it reasonably clear that the glow had some type of objective existence.

But this does not necessarily mean that the painting was actually glowing in a *physical* sense, that is, in a way that could be captured on film by a camera. It is still possible that the two women were mentally *perceiving* the painting to be glowing, even though it was not physically doing so. This implies that some unknown external force was influencing the mental processes of both women in an identical way at the same time; in other words, something was *causing* the two women to "see" a supernatural glow surrounding the painted image of the *Shannon*.

In later years Lord felt that the *Shannon*'s cargo of gunpowder might accidentally have been ignited, with the resulting explosion being the cause of the vessel's loss. Could the "bright cloud" Bowness saw obscuring the painted image of the *Shannon* somehow have been telepathically induced by the last thoughts of young Jack Lord as his vessel was destroyed by the explosion of her gunpowder cargo? In a later section of this chapter we have postulated a similar explanation for the metallic grating noise heard by relatives of a crewman who had been lost on HMS *Aboukir* several hours earlier. In the present case, however, the unknown date of the *Shannon*'s sinking makes it impossible for us to authoritatively connect the vessel's loss with the odd "vision" experienced by Bowness and her granddaughter.

In our opinion, though, the date May 2, 1885, has a reasonably strong claim for being the actual date on which the *Shannon* took Jack Lord and his twenty-seven mates to Davy Jones's Locker.

References

W. T. Stead, *Borderland: A Casebook of True Supernatural Stories* (University Books, 1970), pp. 208–209. Originally published in 1897 under the title *Real Ghost Stories.*

Volturno—1913

It was what spiritualists call a "home circle": a small gathering of psychically attuned persons, none of them professional mediums but committed in varying degrees to belief in the possibility of communicating with the Next World and sufficiently so to meet regularly in each other's homes to hold séances.

On this occasion—Thursday, October 9, 1913—the home in question was a sixteenth-century farmhouse known as "Botches" at Wivelsfield Green, England, and its owners were Claude Askew and his wife Alice. Not all present were out-and-out believers in psychism; Askew himself appears to have been inclined towards rational, even deflating explorations for the phenomena he encountered during their table-tilting sessions. Nor were all of them experienced sitters like Josephine Scott or Mildred Watson; it was to be the first experience of spiritualism in action for Beryl Gibbons. If the account that came to be forwarded to the Society for Psychical Research is credited, her Thursday night initiation was an extraordinary one.

The friends spent a light-hearted evening, their talk centered on a fundraising entertainment they had staged at the village hall the night before; in her subsequent letter to the SPR Mrs. Askew was careful to stress that "our thoughts had been directed the whole of that evening far from shipwrecks or any sort of calamity." At about 11 p.m. they adjourned to Mrs. Askew's bedroom, where a low fire burned in the grate and a small table was in readiness. The experimenters had opted to try the time-honored table-tilting mode of communication in which sitters rested their hands lightly on the table top while one of them (in this case Mr. Askew) called out the letters of the alphabet; the invisible spirit-communicants would relay their messages by causing the table to tilt significantly at each appropriate letter. It was a slightly cumbersome style of procedure and a time-consuming one, but it frequently brought results.

Indeed, the sitting opened briskly, only to stall when the table lapsed into disappointing unintelligibility. Mr. Askew stopped reciting his alphabet. Fifteen, perhaps thirty minutes slid by, when the ladies became aware of a marked odor of burning: "not an ordinary burning smell," as Watson qualified, "but very strong and disagreeable." Who noticed it first was a moot point, both Watson and Mrs. Askew vying for that honor, but all agreed that it was notably, powerfully unpleasant. All, that is, except Mr. Askew—but he, in his wife's words, "has no nose and can't even smell a lamp when it is turned up too high." The aroma filled the room, creating the uncomfortable impression that something downstairs was on fire. Scott thought she had smelled something like it once before when a stable and cottage had gone up in flames: a blend of burning paint, burning wood, and "burning human belongings."

Next the four women believed they could hear a liquid sound. The solitary male, Mr. Askew, again registered nothing unusual and his suggestion that it was only the gas jet was unanimously rejected. However, no two of the participants heard the sound "in the same way." It was like water dripping—a rushing river—or (in Scott's more graphic words) "the sea, very stormy, beating against something ceaselessly . . . I think I said it was a ship on fire in a storm." The full significance of that comment—and the desirability of corroborating whether Scott made it or didn't—would become apparent in the next twenty-four hours.

For the immediate present, the sitters' attention was captured by a number of puzzling lights near or across the door. Watson's testimony (in some ways the most comprehensive, though whether she remembered the order of events correctly or more accurately than her friends is not certain) described them as flashes, "as if a candle or match with a very long flame had suddenly been lit," about two feet long and traversing the surface of the door horizontally. She was sure they had nothing to do with the fire in the grate, which had sunk into embers. And once again there was a hint that each person may have seen something different; at least, she added that, "I do not think we all saw the same lights, or at the same time, as we exclaimed at different times and did not describe what we were seeing in exactly the same way."

There is a strong inference, too, that either the phenomena were diversifying or that the séance-goers were becoming increasingly sensitive—increasingly impressionable?—with each passing minute. The smell of burning seemed to grow stronger: like burnt leather, suggested but Scott disagreed: "It's nothing of the sort, it is burning flesh, it is a ship on fire at sea; I can see the whole thing, and the people holding up their hands trying to be saved."

Scott urged Mrs. Askew to look. Whether or not she shared this dramatic vision is unclear, but most certainly there is Watson's confirmation that:, "She said she was certain we would hear of a liner being on fire. At last I begged her to desist, it was becoming so horrible."

At this point Mr. Askew asked the spiritual forces controlling the table whether they could expect further manifestations, and it tilted out the reply that if their hands were removed from the surface, they could. Hands duly removed, the circle was rewarded by an assortment of sounds resembling the loud bang of a champagne bottle being uncorked from somewhere outside the window, a whistle, rappings, and stumbling or falling noises from a distant part of the house.

It is worth recalling that Botches was an old house—a very old house—and that, like any old house it was inevitably subject to strange creakings, groanings and other nocturnal auditory effects. Doubtless the Askews were well aware of this and the fact they tended to regard the sounds they had just heard as other than those familiar to them may be worth noticing. Nonetheless, Mr. Askew was astute enough to leave the room in order to check on the source of the cork-like detonation and of course on the possibility that something was on fire downstairs. He found nothing, but it is only fair to say that his wife discovered later that a bottle in her bedroom was shattered, and that she accepted that this may have been the cause of the noise they'd heard.

But while Mr. Askew was absent the ladies had further adventures of their own. On hearing someone in the passage and apparently entering Mr. Askew's dressing room, they confidently expected that the husband had returned from completing his check; Gibbons investigated and found it was not so—no Mr. Askew and the room was empty. The stumbling or falling noise might have been caused by another guest currently staying in the house or by servants. Mrs. Askew went to find out: she found the guest fast asleep and, as she believed, the servants accounted for. That was not all she had to report. Coming back along the passage to the séance room, she had been *followed* by something. Gibbons, the novice sitter, was quite excited by that—as her hostess reentered, she said, she'd thought a tall, dark, female figure had come into the room behind her.

There appears to be no harm in estimating that a cumulative sense of expectancy and its near-relative suggestibility had gripped the circle. The intense concentration on the table-tilting, the gradual all-embracing onset of strange sensory impressions, had overcome the sitters, encouraging them to anticipate more of the same, and it would not be surprising if their heightened awareness led them into misinterpretations or even into delusions. Gibbons's shadowy figure (which she could only say she *thought* she saw) may have been an honest product of a situation where the critical faculties were hampered and reduced by the moment; it might also have been a tacit conformity, an unconscious effort to gain acceptance from the more seasoned sitters. Whatever else is true or may be true, the lights were turned out, the séance continued, and the phenomena along with it.

Again the smell of burning, the sound of water. Mrs. Askew drew the group's attention to the strip of light beneath the door; a visual effect of feet passing back and forth could be seen. Scott dominated the latter stages of the séance with her persistent, insistent references to having an impression of a ship; she elected to go into a mediumistic trance (and did so) but apparently came out of it with nothing fresh to add. Or, as she wrote later: "I had a vivid impression of a burning ship in a storm, and a great crowd of people, all stretching out their hands for help. And I knew that there was help there, though for some reason or other it could not reach them."

By now the odor of burning was so vivid, as Watson said, that the sitters decided it was time to leave off. The circle broke up at around 1 a.m. with Scott prophetically saying, "I am quite certain that we shall hear of a burning ship, and a great loss of life during the next few days."

Take the Greenwich Mean Time of 11 p.m. (which was when the Wivelsfield Green home circle sat down at their tiltable table) and deduct two hours twenty minutes. As a result you will have an approximate idea of the time in mid-Atlantic latitude 48°25′ longitude 34°33′ west, which on Thursday, October 9, 1913, was where the 3,600-ton steamer *Volturno* was fighting for her life. And losing.

British-owned and on charter to the Uranium Steamship Co., the *Volturno* had left Rotterdam for New York via Halifax, Nova Scotia, the previous week. She carried 93 crew commanded by Captain Inch and 564 passengers, most of them Balkan, Levantine, and Polish immigrants, bringing the total to 657; more to the point, she also carried a potentially inflammable cargo of oils, rags, wines, straw mats, gin, peat moss, and chemicals. At some time close to 6:55 a.m. on the stormy morning of October 9, Second Officer Lloyd made a discovery that boded no good for anyone on board; with a terrific gale raging, smoke was pouring from the forward hold.

There was no time to debate whether the conflagration was owing to an ill-placed cigarette butt, to some kind of spontaneous combustion among the oil-saturated rags, or to any third alternative. Seeing the fire too powerful for the crewmen to control, Inch acknowledged that the *Volturno* was doomed and ordered SOS calls sent out. Hardly had the wireless telegraph begun to rasp out its distress message when a series of explosions hit the ship. Several passengers, also acknowledging the hopelessness of the situation, are said to have leapt overboard and drowned; those who waited for the launching of the lifeboats fared little better. Quite simply, no Edwardian lifeboat could survive in the seas with which *Volturno* had to contend. The first to be lowered promptly snagged, turned turtle, and came up minus its passengers. The second got clear of the vessel and vanished forever from human ken. Worse if possible, the third was crushed as the plunging stern of the *Volturno* descended on it in the rolling waves. There was a fourth and unofficial or unsanctioned launch made by the desperate passengers: the boat went down overloaded aft and spilled its occupants into the sea. Estimates of how many died in these abortive attempts to sail or row away from the inferno are not entirely reliable; some put the figure as high as 100, representing a terrible proportion of the lives lost in the disaster as a whole (about 136).

Seventy-eight miles away, the Cunard liner *Carmania* picked up the SOS at about 10 a.m. and was with *Volturno* in several hours. Among her passengers was the journalist Arthur Spurgeon, whose dramatic account of the rescue bid has been a great help to us; it is largely thanks to his writing that we can appreciate how dire the situation was, not merely for the victims but for those who wanted to help them. The same churning seas that turned the *Volturno*'s efforts to launch her boats into another phase of the tragedy defeated *Carmania*'s efforts to reach the incandescent vessel; with the fire raging fore and the passengers plainly visible as they clustered towards the stern in blistering heat, the *Carmania* lifeboat found it impossible to bridge the gap between the steamer and liner; in fact, it only managed to get back to the *Carmania* with extreme difficulty. The nine men who made the attempt and defied the odds by returning were rightly treated as heroes.

The SOS had brought other ships, too. As the afternoon light thickened a small flotilla circled the unreachable ship: the *Gar,* the *Rappahannock, Kroonland, Minneapolis, Devonian, Grosser Kurfurst, Seydlitz, La Touraine,* and *Narragansett.* Some tried to launch lifeboats; none managed to reach the *Volturno.* Although later Second Officer Lloyd and three others miraculously managed to get off in a boat and to reach *Grosser Kurfurst* before it was smashed to pieces, no large-scale evacuation was feasible. On board *Carmania,* the heat from the burning ship was palpable, but there was nothing they could do but watch. "Can something be done to help us?" wired Captain Inch. All too obviously, nothing could. "They must have felt," wrote Spurgeon, "as if they were inside a ring of spectators who had come to watch them fight to the death."

Around 9:30 p.m.—or around the time that Mr. and Mrs. Askew and their friends were settling down at the small table to hold their séance—flames burst through the middle sections of the *Volturno* and a large explosion occurred. The fire worked its way gradually toward the stern over the next few hours, incinerating the ship's magazine and bridge, not to mention three crew members. Before wireless contact was severed, Captain Inch had time to issue one last, futile appeal: "For God's sake send us boats or do something."

As Spurgeon remarked apologetically, "The Captain was too absorbed with other things to consider niceties of phraseology."

Just before dawn on Friday, October 10, survivors were seen jumping into the sea. With the tanker *Narragansett* literally pouring oil on troubled waters, the rescue boats began to move in and this time successfully. At 10:44 a.m. Captain Inch formally abandoned the *Volturno.* Circumstances had precluded the opening of her sea valves and she became a derelict, a charred hulk that drifted at the direction of the waves until on the October 17, when she was boarded by the Dutch oil steamer *Charlois* and scuttled.

Spurgeon's account declares that no written messages were received or dispatched during the twenty-four hours covered (in his reckoning) by the tragedy. Another source tells us that the first information on that event reached England via the Fishguard coastal wireless station at 5:50 a.m. on Saturday, October 11, passing thence inland to the general post office and so to the press in time for it to be mentioned in the early afternoon editions of the newspapers. Logically, no one in England could have known about it before this time and (equally logically) few could have expected anything of the kind; the *Volturno,* after all, was not a well-known or highly profiled vessel. The importance of this emerges as we return to the Wivelsfield home circle and particularly to Josephine Scott.

"I am quite certain that we shall hear of a burning ship and a great loss of life during the next few days," she had predicted at the end of the séance. Scott left for London the next day (Friday) and on the following Saturday at Baron's Court Station she found herself fulfilling her own prediction. "Liner on Fire, Great Loss of Life" she read on an *Evening News* placard. When she reached Waterloo Station she rushed off a telegram to Mrs. Askew: "Fire on liner with loss of life just reported remember séance. Jose." What the telegraph operator made of that isn't recorded.

This telegram was preserved and soon passed into the keeping of the Society for Psychical Research. The idea of placing all the evidence before the SPR appears to have been Mrs. Askew's inspiration; on the same Saturday that Scott's telegram arrived and presumably not too many hours afterwards she had written to the Hon. Everard Feilding, the society's investigating officer, to report their "most interesting séance," giving especial emphasis to:

> the sound of dripping water, followed by the smell of burning. We can all swear to this, and Miss Scott suddenly exclaimed that a ship was burning on the sea, and the passengers getting burnt and drowned. This we can all testify to . . . the smell was horrible and now we learn that the poor *Volturno* must have been on fire at that time. . . . The coincidence was extraordinary, if it was only a coincidence.

Or was it more than extraordinary coincidence? Predictably and correctly, the SPR needed more evidence before venturing an opinion, not least of all that Scott's prophetic impressions had been uttered before, practically or theoretically, she could have heard about the disaster from so mundane a source as a Saturday afternoon paper. Had her predictions been made public to anyone outside the Wivelsfield home circle, for instance? Mrs. Askew claimed that she had mentioned the séance to some friends, the Pentons, while motoring down to the Kempton races and that she had excitedly insisted upon buying a newspaper on the way home, wherein the blazing *Volturno* was described. Unluckily, Mrs. Penton recalled it somewhat differently. According to her, Mrs. Askew had not mentioned the Thursday séance until *after* they arrived at Kempton Park and *after* she had bought her paper. Only after reading the news of the *Volturno* (with evident astonishment) had she told them of the séance, Miss Scott's visions and all, and even then the Pentons had been too preoccupied with the horse racing to pay much heed to what she said. On the drive home, though, they got from her a thorough account of her psychic adventure.

Then there was Watson. She had stayed with her friend Dorothy Dymond on the weekend of October 11 to 13; she heard the news of the *Volturno* on the latter date. It was confirmed that she had spoken of a séance with flashing lights, footsteps, and the sound of running water. Dymond could not recall precisely whether Watson had related the incident of the burning-flesh aroma or Scott's vision of the outstretched hands, etc. before she read the newspaper account. *After* reading and having been patently distressed by it, she evidently did so.

In a second letter to Feilding, Mrs. Askew described the séance as "profoundly interesting at the time, but now it seems quite extraordinary, for just at the time that Miss Scott was exclaiming that a ship was on fire and people being drowned, the unfortunate people must have been flinging themselves into the water." It was an assumption, perhaps, or an imaginative correlation, but not necessarily an outrageous one. What the SPR had to decide was whether the testimony of a small group of mutually supporting but arguably excited witnesses was reliable.

In its constitutionally cautious way, the society felt it was "not improbable" that what the sitters had taken to be abnormal or paranormal sounds were ordinary ones misinterpreted—all too easy, "especially as the house was an old one." It was "also possible" that the burning smell was a "natural" or real (but not *super*natural) one of undiscovered origin; the report's authors saw no reason for inevitably connecting it with a ship on fire rather than, say, something in the house. There remained the more important putative connection between the phenomenal occurrences and the "contemporary external event" of the *Volturno* tragedy. If the case represented an illusion of memory inflamed by hindsight—"No doubt there are people who sometimes imagine, after an event has happened, that they had some supernormal impression about it beforehand"—it had been remarkably uniform in its effect.

Read hypercritically, the evidence supports the view that at least two of the sitters may not have associated the burning smell and dripping/running water with the *Volturno* until many hours after the news appeared in the papers. And yet that part of the evidence relating to the séance—Mrs. Askew's account—firmly suggests that the newspapers provided only a confirmation and a name—that of the ship—missing from the actual incidents at Botches. Askew herself was certain that the phenomena were connected with the distant disaster and that hindsight or retrospective interpretation did not enter into the story.

If Scott's rather dramatized narrative be taken as a true record of events, even allowing for the possibility of verbal embellishment that strengthened the correspondence between her psychic impressions and what she read of the *Volturno* affair subsequently, we are left with the fact that the seer seems to have made an instinctive connection between a smell of burning, sounds of running water, and a ship at sea at a time when, far, far away, a seagoing ship *was* on fire. The visionary episode itself may have been a focusing of Scott's clairvoyant powers; those perceptive abilities may have been lubricated by the auditory, olfactory effects (of which at least three other persons were aware) and refined into a quasivisual one which, however, remained unique to Scott. Other parapsychological accounts imply that mediums sometimes need a period of practice or exercise, a kind of "sensitivity warm-up," before producing their more striking results. Perhaps Scott demonstrated that pattern here.

But although her impressions may have pointed to the fact of the *Volturno*'s distress—surely the only ship ablaze at or about this time—Scott did not specify the name of the ship. "We shall hear of a burning ship and a great loss of life," she had predicted. Sure enough, they did. But how much more wonderful her vision would have been had she gleaned that the ship in prospect was the *Volturno* and none other!

As we remark elsewhere, complaining because a paranormal experience falls fractionally short of tying up all the loose ends smacks of ingratitude. Some readers may find it sufficient that Scott was allowed to glean as much as she did, while others will feel that her failure to name the burning vessel scarcely offsets the fact she received *any* information relative to some burning vessel. We may regret the absence of a name for her visionary ship—we may regret that the sitters didn't consult their spirit-animated table in the hope of supplying that detail. Regardless of all this, are we justified in putting Scott's impressions and the coterminous event of the *Volturno* down to mere "extraordinary coincidence"?

Even with the help of Spurgeon's eyewitness account or newspaper reports of the *Volturno*'s last days, it is difficult to correlate features of the Scott vision with corroborated facts. Rather, it is difficult to do so with a certainty that prevents skeptics from claiming that the various details depicted by the sensitive lady were of a generalized, even predictable nature given the situation she visualized. There are problems about treating Scott's vision as a literal outside broadcast of the distant tragedy. As a symbolic image of that event—a translation of the emotions of the sufferers—it works quite well, however. This concession says no more than reinstating our previously rendered idea that telepathic transferences of tragic information may not be photographic but metaphorical.

It is worth pondering whether the séance would have taken the turn it did ("a liner on fire . . . great loss of life") had not the sitters been aware of a previous marine tragedy notable for its sheer direness. The deathless story of the *Titanic* (as one author calls it) was less than a year old. Ignoring the detail that the great ship suffered from ice, not fire, it is impossible to ignore the fact that the Wivelsfield home circle would have had vestiges of that epoch-making disaster on their minds; with the world's consciousness still fixed upon *Titanic*, sea disasters were highly topical in 1913. Whether that contributed to the events of Thursday, October 9, is yet another unanswerable question.

Referring to Spurgeon's small book, though, it is curiously patent that reporting of the *Volturno* contained certain echoes of the *Titanic* story. Either that, or both disasters contained elements common to any ship that finds herself in grievous difficulties. Compare Spurgeon with one of the early *Titanic* accounts like Logan Marshall's. There are the same interludes of panic among the passengers (most obviously, those classifiable as lower-class emigrants), of mob disorders quelled by officers at gunpoint, and cowardly males trying to usurp the places of females in the lifeboats and being righteously pummelled (again, by the officers). Spurgeon even mentions a "phantom vessel" (hitherto nicknamed "The Vulture") that stood off and did not go to *Volturno*'s assistance, paralleling those unidentified lights assumed to be those of the *Californian*, which failed to move to the help of the *Titanic* in several survivors' memoirs. There is even an intriguing analogue that connects the wireless officers of both ships by way of psychic premonitions.

The forewarning of *Titanic*'s Jack Phillips must be regarded as flimsy evidence; he is supposed to have told a friend some months before sailing that he was afraid of icebergs, and that is the kind of remark that only takes on a menacing meaning when we have the luxury of hindsight. An awful lot of transatlantic sailors must have shared Phillips's anxiety without finding it come true, simply because *they* weren't on the *Titanic*.

The *Volturno*'s Christopher Pennington could boast a premonition far more substantial, though whether he did so or not we can't say. The story (which may have come via Mrs. F. W. Alexander of New York, who spoke to Pennington on the night preceding the disaster) was that the junior wireless operator had put in a written request for reassignment following a recurrent dream of a ship on fire and himself at the Morse key calling for help. This sounds to us a more specific set of details than Phillips's iceberg fear and of course there is the corollary that the young man suddenly found himself going through the very motions he'd dreamed of. If you accept this brief story, you may believe that there is more than one way to receive a distress signal—more than one way to send one—and the alternative utilizes apparatus far more mysterious than anything invented by Mr. Marconi.

References

General background for this section comes from Arthur Spurgeon's *The Burning of the* Volturno (Cassel, 1913) plus newspapers and journals contemporary with the disaster (*Times, Daily Mail, New York Times, Illustrated London News*). "A Telepathic Impression of the *Volturno* Disaster," in the SPR *Journal* 16, no. 306 (February 1914): 177–92, provides functional background summarized from daily newspapers of October 11 to 17, 1913, and the subsequent Board of Trade inquiry, and the Askew et al. documentation. Pennington's dream is a brief episode in A. A. Hoehling's chapter on the same sea tragedy for his *They Sailed Into Oblivion* (Thomas Yoseloff, 1959, and Ace paperback), pp. 136–43.

The *Empress of Ireland*—1914

On May 28, 1914, the Canadian Pacific liner *Empress of Ireland* was ready to cast off her lines and begin her first transatlantic crossing of the season from Quebec to Liverpool. Weighing in at 14,000 tons and measuring 550 feet in length, the *Empress* was booked to carry a total of 1,057 passengers and 420 crewmen, her voyage to England being scheduled to take about six days. The first two days of this journey would be passed in the St. Lawrence River, down which the twin-funnelled liner had to steam before reaching the open sea. Indeed, the *Empress*'s owners took advantage of this fact by promoting the smooth sailing that the Liverpool-bound passengers could expect for fully one third of their voyage, a feature which was a boon to poor sailors. The *Empress of Ireland* had been safely plying this same route for the past eight years, and there was no reason to think that her present voyage would end any differently than had dozens of others.

This time, however, fate was destined to step in and alter the final destination of the *Empress of Ireland*, a fact that was unknown to all except, seemingly, a privileged few.

After leaving her home port of Quebec, the *Empress* steamed majestically down the St. Lawrence during the afternoon of May 28 and on into the evening hours. Midnight came and went, and the ship grew silent as her passengers headed for their staterooms for a well-deserved rest after an active day. At 1:30 a.m. the *Empress* stopped momentarily to put off the pilot who had guided her past Father Point; then, her engines throbbing steadily, she resumed her voyage to the sea.

A few minutes later the lights of another ship appeared in the distance ahead of the *Empress*, but, at almost the same time, a fog bank rolled across the St. Lawrence and obscured the view of this rapidly approaching vessel. Captain Kendall ordered the *Empress*'s engines reversed, bringing her to a halt in order to allow sufficient room for the approaching ship to pass by in safety. It was a futile gesture, however. Two minutes later the stranger—the Norwegian collier *Storstad*—loomed out of the fog on a collision course with the *Empress of Ireland*. Horrified crewmen on both vessels watched helplessly as the *Storstad*'s bow plunged through the *Empress*'s side at a point between her two funnels. Then, finally reacting to her reversed engines, the *Storstad* backed slowly out of the gaping hole in the *Empress*'s side and drifted away to be lost again in the darkness and fog.

Sixty thousand gallons of water per second were pouring through the cavernous opening in the shattered hull of the stricken *Empress*. Her crew performed gallantly, but the situation was hopeless from the very beginning. Fourteen minutes after being rammed by the Norwegian vessel, the *Empress of Ireland* rolled onto her side and vanished beneath the swirling waters of the St. Lawrence River. Of the 1,477 people who had boarded her at Quebec, only 465 survived to see the dawn of another day.

As we implied a moment ago, there are accounts on record that suggest that the tragic fate of the *Empress of Ireland* did not come as a complete surprise to everyone connected with the doomed ship. If these reports are to be given credence, a small handful of people seemed to be aware that the *Empress*'s first voyage of 1914 to Liverpool would end in tragedy. The reader will want to carefully consider each of the following accounts of seemingly psychic phenomena, whether those phenomena were experienced by man or beast.

Like a similar event mentioned in our coverage of the *Lusitania* disaster, the mascot of the *Empress of Ireland*—a yellowish cat that the ship's crew had adopted two years before—raced down the ship's gangway to the docks just moments before the *Empress* was scheduled to cast off on her voyage to Liverpool. A steward pursued the fugitive feline and succeeded in capturing her, and the cat was then carried back up the gangway and onto the deck of the *Empress*. No sooner had the steward put her down, however, than the cat once again fled down the gangway and away from the ship, this time taking refuge in a freight shed until the *Empress of Ireland* eased away from the dock to begin her voyage. Only then did the cat emerge to squall her own farewell to the departing vessel.

Did the *Empress of Ireland*'s mascot somehow become aware that Death was stalking her seagoing home of the past two years? We will never know. But one can only wonder if some of the *Empress*'s stokers—had they known of the desertion of their mascot—might have fled the doomed *Empress* as did several *Lusitania* stokers who deserted their own vessel when faced with the strategic withdrawal of their mascot.

But right now we are more interested in possible paranormal forewarnings of disaster experienced by human beings connected with the *Empress*'s last voyage. As will quickly be seen, however, the documentation for several of these cases is pretty sketchy and leaves much to be desired.

Our first case was undoubtedly the result of pure coincidence rather than of paranormal activity, but we shall relate it here merely for the sake of comparison. Our account concerns a young Englishman named F. P. Godson, who was a second-year engineering student at the Kingston (Ontario) School of Mining. In mid-May of 1914 the school term ended and Godson gravitated toward Quebec with the intention of sailing to England on the *Empress of Ireland*. Before leaving Kingston he laughingly told his friends, "If I don't drown on the way over, I will be back to college in the fall."

In reading this account, the reader should consider how its entire meaning might be altered if an unscrupulous writer were to omit the word "laughingly" from his description of Godson's mood: the tale would thereby be changed into a dramatic story of unconscious precognition. The student of psychic phenomena should be aware that the use of precise language is of paramount importance in the accurate relation of anecdotal accounts.

At any rate, our first case of *possibly* genuine psychic phenomena comes from an interview with the wife of one of the *Empress of Ireland*'s stewards. This woman related how her husband had recently dreamed three times that the *Empress* was sinking, and she added that he had been reluctant to sail in the vessel again. The newspapers did not identify either the steward or his wife, so we do not know how reliable the report is or whether the crewman survived the sinking of the *Empress*. It is worth noting, however, that precognitive-type dreams of approaching tragedy often seem to be repeated two or even three times. (We are thinking specifically of Prof. Holbourn's three dreams that the *Lusitania* would be torpedoed, Sawyer's thricefold dream on the *Waratah*, and MacMaster's triple-dream of his father that predicted the disappearance of the *City of Glasgow*.) Indeed, it is often the repetitive nature of such dreams which makes the percipient pause and reflect on whether the dream is somehow more than "just a dream."

The newspapers also told of two unnamed women who were reported to have booked their passage on the *Empress of Ireland*. One of the ladies then consulted a gypsy fortune-teller, who advised her not to travel during the month of May. The woman cancelled her passage on the *Empress* even though her traveling companion retained her own booking on the vessel. The companion perished when the ship foundered.

An interesting account about which we wish we knew more involved a young Regina woman named Mary Wood. Wood had booked her passage on the *Empress*, but she apparently felt certain that some calamity was about to befall her. Before leaving home she told her relatives, "I am sure I will never land in England." Wood's fears proved to be well-founded—she lost her life in the tragedy.

Our next account concerns Ab Tapping, stage manager of London's Kingsway Theater. Tapping told reporters of a complicated and highly allegorical dream he had experienced at "about the time of the *Empress of Ireland* sinking," a dream that had led him to believe that something tragic had befallen Laurence Irving, a famous actor and personal friend of Tapping.

In Tapping's dream he found himself in a handsomely appointed room among a large gathering of people. A solemn procession of these people was passing before Sir Henry Irving (the deceased father of Laurence Irving). Sir Henry was seated and looked as if he was dying, and each person who passed before him shook his hand sadly in a last farewell.

When everyone had passed by and shaken his hand, Sir Henry said, "I can endure it no longer." He then placed his hand on his forehead and disappeared, the inference being that Death had claimed him.

Then Tapping noticed Sir Henry's son, Laurence Irving, standing alone at the far end of the room. Walking toward him and stretching out his hands appealingly, Tapping addressed the young actor. "Don't you see what is happening?" he exclaimed. "You're father is dying; he has left us forever."

Laurence Irving looked amazed and appeared as if he would collapse, but he suddenly drew himself up and "followed his father with unfaltering step."

Tapping described to reporters his own reaction to his dream about Laurence Irving following his father into death. "It was a most dramatic departure and made a deep impression on me," he said. "There was no farewell on the part of the son whose call to go seemed to come suddenly and unexpectedly."

Tapping later saw a photograph of the *Empress of Ireland*'s salon and recognized it as the room he had seen in his dream. Tapping had not known that Laurence Irving was on board the *Empress* until he saw the actor's name in the lists of victims, and the stage manager was certain that—in some unknown manner—his dream had "told" him of his friend's death.

The allegorical quality of Tapping's dream is quite interesting, and it calls to mind the symbolic dream experienced by *Titanic* passenger Bert John the night before his own vessel went down.

One of the more dramatic accounts recounted in the newspapers concerned a man named Charles Hirxheimer, apparently a regular First-Class passenger on the *Empress.* Hirxheimer was said to have attended a small farewell party shortly before the *Empress* sailed at which several other passengers and some of the ship's officers were present. Oddly, however, Hirxheimer refused to join the toast that was offered—he solemnly pronounced his belief that the *Empress of Ireland* was going to sink. The ship's officers didn't think much of this "jest," but Hirxheimer maintained that his grim statement would come true and that they would all drown.

The party broke up on this depressing note, but Hirxheimer's fears continued unabated. After the *Empress* sailed from Quebec, Hirxheimer was said to have wandered around the vessel trying to give away $500 in cash, explaining that he would have no further use for it. He even tried to throw in the small change he had in his pocket. It is unknown whether Hirxheimer's desperate attempts at philanthropy met with any success, but (if the above story is true) his fears were well-founded. Charles Hirxheimer perished with the *Empress of Ireland.*

A group of Canadian Salvation Army bandsmen were booked to sail on the *Empress.* Their bandmaster was a thirty-five year old Londoner named Edward Hanagan, whose wife, Edith, and seven-year-old daughter, Gracie, were to accompany him on the voyage to Liverpool. The little family spent the evening before their departure at a little farewell gathering with Edward's brother John and his wife Annie.

John Hanagan took his niece on his knee and told her how lucky she was to be looking forward to such an exciting journey. Normally a cheerful child, Gracie nevertheless reacted in an unexpected manner. "I don't want to go!" she said quietly. The other adults ceased their conversation, Gracie's unexpected remark having suddenly made her the center of everyone's puzzled attention. Edith Hanagan asked her daughter why she didn't want to take a trip in the "big boat," and Gracie replied with an unsettling question of her own.

"Suppose we all get drowned?" the little girl asked.

The adults forced smiles and tried to make Gracie see how silly her fears were, but Edward Hanagan may have taken her statement more seriously than he let on. Later in the evening he took his brother John aside and pressed a folded paper into his hand.

"That's my will, John," he said. "If anything happens to Edith and me, I want you and Annie to look after Gracie."

John Hanagan attempted to laugh away his brother's fears, pointing out that there were no icebergs in the shipping lanes at this time of year and stressing that since the *Titanic* disaster ships were required to carry enough lifeboats for everyone on board. Edward Hanagan was not to be put off, however.

"I can't explain it, John," he said, "but I feel I'm doing the right thing."

John pointed out how unlikely it would be for both Edward and Edith to be lost at sea while little Gracie was saved; Edward was adamant, however, and John finally accepted his brother's will, promising to care for Gracie should anything happen to her parents.

It was fortunate that he did; little Gracie later described what happened after she and her parents had been flung overboard by the capsizing *Empress*.

"I went down deep. Then I hung onto a black rope. When I came up, after a long time, I looked around and saw a light in front of me. Then when I looked a second time I saw my Mama and Papa. They were swimming." Later a man pulled Gracie into a lifeboat, but by this time she had lost track of her parents.

Gracie told this story to John and Annie Hanagan on the train platform after she returned to Toronto. The little girl still did not know that her parents were dead, though.

"They are not on the train now," Gracie assured her aunt and uncle. "They are coming on the next one." But Gracie was wrong, and she was raised by John and Annie Hanagan just as her father had specified in his will.

At first glance, Edward Hanagan's insistence on leaving his will with his brother *appears* to have resulted from his uneasiness caused by Gracie's remark about drowning. Upon reflection, however, it seems clear that Edward Hanagan already had his will made out before he visited his brother, and that he intended all along to leave it with his relatives. However, the possibility remains that Edward Hanagan made out his will as the result of his own earlier premonition of danger regarding his upcoming trip, and that Gracie's remark only reinforced his own misgivings. "I can't explain it, John," he told his brother, "but I feel I'm doing the right thing." We'll probably never know what caused Edward Hanagan to feel he was "doing the right thing."

A very similar account occurred at the Toronto home of Sarah Rigby. The woman planned to sail to England with her nine-year-old daughter, Win, to visit with relatives, and she had already booked their passages on the *Empress of Britain*. Rigby's sister, Flo Gibson, was also traveling to England, although her own passage had been booked on the *Empress of Ireland*. Gibson was trying to convince her sister to transfer her two bookings to the *Empress of Ireland* so that the three relatives could all travel together.

Rigby considered her sister's suggestion, but then looked doubtfully at her daughter.

"Well, I'm a bit dubious about Win here," Mrs. Rigby said. "She says she doesn't want to go at all."

"I don't like the water!" exclaimed little Win insistently.

Rigby was at a loss as to what to do with the extra ticket she had purchased for her daughter, but Gibson looked at her own daughter Mary and had a sudden inspiration.

"If Win won't go, why not let Mary go in her place?"

And it was so arranged. Sarah Rigby sailed with Flo Gibson and her daughter Mary on the *Empress of Ireland.*

It seems reasonably clear that little Win Rigby's fear of the water was a general fear that probably had nothing to do with the *Empress of Ireland*'s upcoming voyage. Unlike Edward Hanagan in the previous case, however, neither Rigby or Gibson were influenced by Win Rigby's reluctance to cross the ocean, for neither woman had any presentiments of danger when they boarded the *Empress* on sailing day.

Edward Gray was a talented Toronto artist who was invited to England by the Salvation Army to take part in the army congress being held there. Two days before he sailed on the *Empress*, Gray went to see his fiancée, Sadie Bilham. The young woman embraced him and he returned her hug, but he held her so long that she broke away and looked into his eyes.

"Why, Ted," she exclaimed. "You look so solemn. What's wrong?"

Gray didn't reply, but he asked Bilham's parents if he could see their daughter alone for a moment. The elder Bilhams laughingly agreed, thinking that the two young people wanted to make the most of their last evening together before Gray left on his trip.

But Sadie suddenly felt uneasy, and she asked Edward what was wrong. She then noticed some papers he had in his hand, and, suspecting what they might be, she began to banter with him to cheer him up.

"Surely, you don't expect anything to happen to the *Empress*!" she exclaimed. "Ocean travel's as safe as the 'Old Gray Mare' these days."

But Edward looked at her earnestly. "Don't joke, Sadie," he said. "Don't think I haven't prayed about this. I'm leaving you my will . . . forgive my silly feelings . . . I felt led to do this . . . leaving my little all to you." Embarrassed and flustered, the young man handed his fiance the papers.

Sadie paled and tried to refuse, but she eventually accepted Edward's will and put it into a nearby drawer. Then, forcing an outwardly cheerful appearance, the two young people rejoined Sadie's parents, who nevertheless observed their daughter's unusual pallor. Later, when the two young people were saying goodbye to each other, Sadie again tried to cheer Edward up, reminding him of their approaching wedding date. They embraced with unusual intensity, and then Edward was gone. Sadie never saw him again, for something did indeed happen to the *Empress*.

Another future *Empress* passenger, Ernest Evans of Toronto, had an insistent feeling that some kind of serious misfortune was in his immediate future. Even today his relatives recall Evans' absolute certainty of approaching trouble and how he insisted on taking out last-minute life and accident insurance policies on both himself and his wife. It turned out to be a prudent precaution, even though it could not provide any safety to the policy holders themselves. Mr. and Mrs. Evans both perished on the *Empress of Ireland*.

Our final *Empress*-related paranormal account is also one of the most compelling we have come across. It involves Maj. Nettie Simcoe, an officer in the Vancouver Corps of the Salvation Army who was booked to sail on the *Empress* with the rest of the army contingent. Simcoe had arranged to stay overnight with some friends in Montreal before traveling on to Quebec the next morning to board the *Empress*. She did not spend a very restful night, however, for she experienced a dream that jolted her awake, her heart pounding in fright. The next morning she described her experience to her friends at the breakfast table.

"I saw a huge procession of corpses, crossing a stream of water," Simcoe said. "In the water itself, people were struggling. Some broke through the procession. Their faces were horrible, frantic with fear and pain, distorted with frenzy. Some had torn flesh; others, twisted limbs. It was ghastly!"

So impressed were Simcoe's friends with her dream that one of them repeated it to other members of the party with whom Simcoe was to sail. Several of these people were so impressed with so graphic a portrayal of possible disaster that they actually cancelled their bookings on the *Empress of Ireland*. Simcoe's friends entreated with her to transfer her own booking to another vessel, but the loyal Salvationist decided to go through with her original plans and sail on the *Empress*.

After the *Storstad* plunged into the side of the *Empress of Ireland*, another Salvationist, Ensign Pugmire, was hurrying past Simcoe's stateroom door and paused to ask if she was coming to the upper deck. Simcoe asked Pugmire to go up and find out what had happened to the ship, and Pugmire continued on his way in an attempt to do so. He was the last person to see Simcoe alive. Her body was one of the first to be picked up on the shore of the St. Lawrence River.

Might Nettie Simcoe's dream have actually been a fleeting glimpse of her own future? Who can say?

Since the magnitude of the *Empress of Ireland* tragedy proved comparable (in number of lives lost) to both the *Titanic* and *Lusitania* disasters, an objective researcher might expect an equivalent number of "premonition stories" to have been made public following the loss of all three of the above vessels. To a great extent this expectation seems false in the case of the *Empress of Ireland.* Admittedly, the present authors have not conducted the exhaustive search for *Empress* cases that we did while researching the *Lusitania* and the *Titanic*; to a certain extent we have relied on the research of other authors who have made a specialty of investigating the *Empress of Ireland* tragedy.

Even though most accounts of "disaster premonitions" surface after the disaster in question has taken place, the reader may have noted how few truly compelling cases have been connected with the sinking of the *Empress of Ireland.* Indeed, in spite of the magnitude of the tragedy, the very name of the Canadian liner is practically unknown to the general public of today.

Might the authors be allowed to speculate for a moment on possible reasons for this? Indeed, might we wonder if there is some mysterious connection between modern-day unfamiliarity with the *Empress*'s name and the dearth of paranormal accounts connected with that vessel? In a nutshell, the authors wonder if these two facts might somehow be explained by the following statement of opinion: The concept of "The Romance of the Sea" was missing from the public's *perception* of the *Empress of Ireland* disaster.

Let us explain our premise more fully. Both the *Titanic* and *Lusitania* disasters took place on the open sea. "The sea" . . . Mankind's very concept of that entity is inextricably bound together with countless tales of human bravery, suffering, and nobility that reach back through the aeons to the days when our species made its first attempts to challenge and conquer the "vasty deep." "The Sea": what images the very words conjure up in our mind's eye! The ocean has a mystique unlike anything else in human experience. A maritime tragedy unfolding on its broad surface, therefore, might be expected to command our attention and capture our imagination more fully than a disaster unfolding in some other location.

Unlike the *Titanic* and *Lusitania,* both of which went down in the ocean proper, the *Empress of Ireland* met her tragic end in a *Canadian waterway.* In effect, even though the loss of life in the latter disaster was heartshaking, the "romance of the sea" was nevertheless missing from the public's perception of the disaster. This might account for the relatively short-lived public interest in the *Empress*'s loss; in a sense, the *Empress of Ireland* tragedy might even be regarded as a "local disaster" that took place on a Canadian waterway instead of out on the "universal" high seas.

A case in point. The *Eastland* was a passenger excursion steamer that plied the waters of the Great Lakes in the early years of the twentieth century. On July 24, 1915, the vessel capsized at her Chicago pier while overloaded with 2,500 passengers who had crowded aboard her. The official death toll was finally set at 812, and America was shocked at the magnitude of the tragedy. Yet in the late 1980s the *Chicago Herald* reported that officials of the Illinois Historical Society, which is based in Chicago, had never even *heard* of the *Eastland* disaster!

If even local historians are capable of forgetting a "local disaster" of the magnitude of the *Eastland* tragedy, should we be surprised that today's general public is unfamiliar with another "local disaster"—the *Empress of Ireland*?

As terrible as the *Eastland* disaster was—and despite of all the contemporary publicity given that tragedy by American newspapers—the present authors are currently unaware of any paranormal accounts connected with the capsizing of that excursion steamer. In a similar vein, there seem to be very few well-documented cases connected with the *Empress of Ireland* that are striking enough to be regarded as evidential of paranormal activity. This raises an interesting question: does public perception of a disaster—as well as the amount of publicity that the disaster receives later—somehow have a bearing on the number of people who later claim to have had paranormal forewarnings of the tragedy? Does a "local disaster" somehow fail to grip the imagination of people who do not reside in the immediate vicinity of that disaster? If so, we would expect few "fake" stories of disaster-related psychic activity to spring into existence far distant from the disaster site, since few people would bother to fabricate a story concerning a distant event in which nobody was interested. Should we assume that this is the reason for the relative scarcity of *Empress* cases?

On a related topic, does the length of time a tragedy remains newsworthy influence the number of people who feel moved to report their own paranormal experiences connected with the tragedy? In other words, does prolonged newspaper coverage of a disaster increase the number of people who publicly describe their own disaster-related paranormal accounts? If so, then lengthy (and far-ranging) newspaper coverage of a disaster might conceivably inspire a certain number of publicity-hungry persons to fabricate tales of "psychic" activity connected with that disaster. On the other hand, such prolonged coverage would no doubt also inspire honest people to report their own accounts of apparently genuine psychic activity relating to the disaster. Newspaper publicity concerning a maritime disaster undoubtedly has definite effects (both good and bad!) on the number of spurious—and genuine—paranormal accounts are brought to public notice.

But should we look at this thorny issue from another vantage point? Perhaps "local disasters" generate as much psychic activity as do "international disasters," but shortlived newspaper coverage of them makes it difficult for accounts of paranormal activity to elbow their way into print alongside "hard" news stories. After all, the (peacetime) *Titanic* disaster was newsworthy for weeks, allowing ample time for stories of related paranormal activity to find their way into print. The sinking of the *Lusitania,* on the other hand, occurred during wartime; even though it was an "international disaster" (as opposed to a "local disaster"), most editors couldn't spare valuable space in their newspapers to print "trivial" psychic stories when there were world-shaking events to be covered on the Western Front. This might explain why there are fewer *Lusitania* psychic cases extant than *Titanic* ones, and might also explain why most *Lusitania*-related accounts did not appear in print until after the war.

As for the *Empress of Ireland*, her loss was covered by the world press, of course, but for a much shorter period of time than was devoted to either of the above two tragedies. Even though Canadian attention remained focused on the *Empress* for awhile, the world at large soon shrugged off this "local Canadian disaster" and got on with the business of living. Of course, this meant that—even if there *had* been a large number of psychic forewarnings of the *Empress* tragedy—the international press was no longer interested. This would explain why most *Empress*-related psychic experiences, if they occurred in the first place, never found their way into print.

Of course, there is another possibility. Perhaps few *Empress of Ireland* psychic accounts were made public because most of the people who underwent such experiences went to the bottom of the St. Lawrence with the doomed liner.

References

Historical Information

Thomas Bonsall, *Shipwrecks* (Bookman Dan, 1988). For information on the *Eastland* disaster.

James Croall, *Fourteen Minutes: The Last Voyage of the* Empress of Ireland (Stein & Day, 1979).

Logan Marshall, *The Tragic Story of the* Empress of Ireland (L. T. Myers, 1914).
New York Times, May 29–June 4, 1914.
Herbert P. Wood, *Till We Meet Again: The Sinking of the* Empress of Ireland (Toronto: Image Publishing, 1982).

Paranormal Accounts

Anonymous steward account: James Croall, *Fourteen Minutes: The Last Voyage of the* Empress of Ireland (Stein & Day, 1979).
Cat mascot account: Croall, *Fourteen Minutes*; *New York Times,* July 16, 1914, p. 4. The story was told in London (England or Ontario?) at a meeting of the "Occult Club."
Evans account: Herbert P. Wood, *Till We Meet Again: The Sinking of the* Empress of Ireland (Toronto: Image Publishing, 1982).
Godson account: *New York Times,* May 30, 1914.
Gray account: Wood, *Till We Meet Again.*
Gypsy fortune teller account: Croall, *Fourteen Minutes.*
Hanagan account: Wood, *Till We Meet Again*; *New York Times,* May 31, 1914.
Hirxheimer account: Croall, *Fourteen Minutes.*
Rigby account: Wood, *Till We Meet Again.*
Simcoe account: Wood, *Till We Meet Again*; Logan Marshall, *The Tragic Story of the* Empress of Ireland (L. T. Myers, 1914).
Tapping account: *New York Times,* June 3, 1914, p. 4.
Wood account: *New York Times,* May 30, 1914.

HMS *Amphion* and *Pathfinder*—1914

Thursday, August 6, 1914: "Had a bad dream of a ship sunk," wrote Ann Jones in her diary. That bare statement of fact concealed more than it revealed. She might also have written about the strange sensation of "great depression and fatigue" that the dream brought along with it, a sensation as inconvenient as it was peculiar, since at the time (between 8:30 and 9 p.m.) Jones was expecting friends at any minute. She could have made more of the irresistible impulse to stretch out on the sofa where she "sank into a kind of swoon, a state between sleeping and waking" unlike anything she'd ever experienced before. In due course Jones—a pseudonym, incidentally—*would* have more to tell of these things, but only when the Society for Psychical Research pressed her for further details, whereupon she produced not only her diary entry but her friends' corroboration as proof she had both recorded and spoken of her experience right after it had happened. For the moment, though, it seemed enough to note down that she had suffered a strikingly bad dream: why should she go into extra detail?

The answer to that question came with next morning's papers. Here, with the war against Germany only seventy-two hours old, the Admiralty was announcing Britain's first naval loss: the 3,440-ton *Amphion.*

On August 5 the newly built £280,000 light cruiser had helped to chase and sink the converted German minelayer *Konigen Luise* off Antwerp. Next morning at 6:35 a.m., or some fourteen hours before Jones's dream vision, cruel irony and even crueller luck overtook *Amphion* as she reconnoitered the East Coast; a mine detonated under her forebridge, causing heavy casualties among her seamen as well as setting the entire forecastle area on fire. The destroyer *Linnet* managed to get *Amphion* in tow, but the stricken vessel, her back broken and her forward decks burning out of control, began to settle at the bows. Concerned that the flames would soon reach the forward magazine, Captain Fox ordered his crew to abandon ship. The captain's own lifeboat had moved scarcely fifty yards from the burning cruiser when there was a "terrific roar" resembling the explosion of a volcano. The forward half of the ship erupted in a huge ball of flame; wreckage was thrown high into the sky, and one of the *Amphion*'s four-inch guns went cartwheeling through the air and barely missed landing on the *Linnet. Amphion*'s shattered bow sank beneath the waves and touched bottom while her stern still jutted above the surface of the shallow coastal waters. At 7:30 a.m.—fifteen minutes after the second explosion—*Amphion* vanished completely, taking with her 132 out of her total complement of 283 officers and men.

Placed beside Jones's impressions of a ship sinking, these facts seemed to conform with an age-old paranormal pattern in which impressions of some distant events are perceived by random persons who have made no special efforts to obtain them. A time lag or lapse evidently took place between the foundering of the *Amphion* at 7:30 a.m. and Jones's dream at 8:30 to 9 p.m. As the event in question here was long past—thirteen hours or more past—Jones was not experiencing a coterminous form of precognition, obviously. It was not clairvoyance in the usual application of the term, since in these episodes the seer is supposed to receive the impressions at the exact time of the geographically remote occurrence.

More important than the timing, however, was the Admiralty's release of the story, which did not reach the general public before the arrival of the next morning's newspapers. Jones—and her friends—firmly denied having heard about the *Amphion* sinking before the papers announced it. Since it seems unlikely (if not impossible) that she could have done so at any earlier time (as there was also the existence of her diary entry and the friends' confirmation that she had spoken of her dream the night before the news media reported the loss of the cruiser) it is easy to see why psychical researchers were inclined to believe that her channels of information were not orthodox ones.

Even then, the case remained annoyingly deficient. It fell short of being totally convincing. Jones had described via her dream vision the sinking of *a* ship; she doesn't appear to have described it as a warship and she certainly did not say it was the *Amphion.* Even at this early stage in the conflict at sea, deep concern had been voiced over the Germans' mine-laying tactics. It was clearly only a matter of time before one British vessel or another fell victim to the practice; crudely speaking, the likelihood grew with every passing hour. So Jones's dream may have been simply a dramatized expression of that common apprehension. (We used the same argument to put many of the *Titanic* forewarnings into a tighter perspective.) That Jones should have dreamed her dream so close to the dreadful fact of a British ship realizing the fears of so many people could have been a great coincidence, but skeptics rule that coincidence can be ever so great and still remain . . . coincidence. By the most stringent canons of parapsychology the case was suggestive but unproven. It would have stayed that way had Jones not succumbed to a second dream vision coincident with Britain's second naval loss of the war the following month.

Saturday, September 5, 1914: Allowing for the minor difference that on this occasion the vision came after Jones had been out paying a visit rather than at home waiting to receive one, the incident was almost a repeat of the previous event. Arriving home at around 2 p.m., Jones was flooded by the same sense of enervating depression and thirty minutes later lay down in the same quasiswoon; at 5 p.m. she made an unavailing effort to rouse herself, but remained in her trancelike state for a further two hours. And again there was a dream-cum-vision of a disaster in the North Sea: a ship sinking.

This time, however, Jones was alert to the desirability of providing strong evidence to support her claims. The September 5 diary entry was a trifle more evocative than descriptive—"Had a dreadful drowning sleep"—but she not only made a point of expanding on this when she mentioned the affair to a friend with whom she dined at 7:30 the same evening, but asked her to memorize both the date and the substance of their talk. Thus the friend was able to confirm in writing that Jones had spoken about "a strong impression . . . of the sinking of a ship" and that the visionary had anticipated hearing bad news that might justify the feeling—as, in a manner of speaking, she did less than twenty-four hours later.

The Admiralty announced the loss of the cruiser *Pathfinder* at 11:15 p.m. on September 5, when it was erroneously stated that she had struck a mine some twenty miles off the East Coast at 4:30 that afternoon. Subsequently, the time of the catastrophe and its cause were corrected to 3:50 p.m. and torpedo damage. *Pathfinder* had been the victim of a single torpedo fired by the U-21 from a range of 1,500 yards; the resulting explosion detonated the cruiser's forward magazine and simultaneously broke her back. *Pathfinder* foundered within four minutes, the first British warship to fall victim to a submarine in the Great War.

The 3:50 p.m. time of *Pathfinder*'s sinking places the incident well within the duration of Jones's dream, though the rest of Britain would have to wait until the next morning's papers to learn of it.

Two dreams or visions: one a possible but debatable hit and the second, precognitive in character, apparently close on the center of the target. A professional clairvoyant might have been pleased with that rating. Jones was not a professional clairvoyant, although it is worth mentioning that she went on to record two or three unpublished impressions of the land war and to prophecy an eventual Allied victory (but under circumstances that did not overexcite Mrs. Henry Sidgewick of the Society for Psychical Research). Confirmed skeptics, we suppose, would protest that even hit no. 2 fails to make plain the useful detail that the sinking ship of Jones's dream was the *Pathfinder*.

As it turned out, neither Jones nor investigators for the Society for Psychical Research could be entirely sure which ship had been featured in her latest vision; Britain lost two during the four and a half hours of her mental adventure. At 3:50 p.m. on September 5 off May Island in the Firth of Forth the 2,940-ton light cruiser *Pathfinder* with her 268 officers and men became an early casualty of one of the dreaded U-boats—a menacing new form of warfare that, alongside the use of mines, had loomed large in the popular imagination. Next to this event, the mining of the Wilson liner *Bruno* forty-five minutes later may have seemed paltry, though presumably not to anyone connected with the twenty or so Russian emigrants who went down with her. Theoretically, either could have been the ship of Jones's dream vision.

The implications of the *Pathfinder* sinking and its possible effects on a psi-sensitive mind intrigued Mrs. Eleanor Sidgwick, a founder-member of the SPR and one of its most active researchers. Could the horrific novelty of sea mines and submarine warfare have stimulated the woman's psychic powers? Had it contributed to Jones's swoonlike state and might she have lapsed into her strange condition at the very moment when the Germans were preparing to bring home the full meaning of U-boat warfare? Put another way: Had Jones received a clairvoyant demonstration of the terrors of modern armaments—mines and U-boats—at the precise instant they actually arrived in this new, high-technology war?

Perhaps there was no need to ask such esoteric questions at all. Wartime anxieties, as a skeptic might protest with some justice, are bound to produce a crop of "impressions" and the ones that are coincidentally borne out are the ones that tend to be remembered, unlike those that come to nothing, which are politely forgotten. But on balance, the SPR was prepared to believe that something more substantial—something less explicable—may have underpinned Jones's visionary episodes. She had enjoyed or suffered both at a juncture when naval losses seemed likely, if not imminent, yet they corresponded closely in time with two actual disasters, the first that had overtaken the British fleet. This factor made them appear more specific than a random cast would have. Had British ships been sinking daily or even weekly up until September 5, there would have been a strong statistical likelihood of Jones "seeing" something of the sort by sheer coincidence; the feat of having her dreams synchronize with the then-unique circumstance of the only two naval losses to date plays havoc with the mathematics of the thing.

Then there were the marked physico-mental effects—the out-of-the-blue sensation of depression, the prostrating fatigue—that accompanied the experiences. Jones, we are told, was a woman of good health and not abandoned to psychic impressions or visions. This might not give much comfort to skeptical readers, nor will the assertion that the same unpleasant symptoms have been described vis-a-vis other clairvoyant perceptions and that some researchers would categorize them as a typical (even necessary) fugue state in which ordinary conscious mechanisms recede in order for images of remote events to surface in the percipient's subconscious. In the final analysis—and as always—the interpretation of Jones's visions comes down to the reception that these dark matters find in *our* conscious and subconscious minds.

Intriguingly, Jones's precognitive warning of the death of the *Pathfinder* may have been preempted by a less direct or allusive but no less ominous impression received by another psychic lady as early as April 25, 1914. In our chapter on the *Lusitania,* we mentioned the arduous work that J. G. Piddington undertook on the automatic scripts of Mrs. King and others; it was King and her otherworldly sources again who produced a staccato message that Piddington found highly significant. Sandwiched between and unconnected with something that the researcher took to be a near-quote from Ruskin's *Modern Painters* and what he regarded as "one of the clearest predictions of the War" was the phrase: "The Pathfinder Die Pfadfinderin cut out a new way for the spirit."

As usual, the psychic's highly literate consciousness appeared to have intruded into the (putative) paranormal content. Piddington felt that, unless a product of accidental coincidence, the relationship between the statement and the event it seemed to fulfill was evidential. That King should connect the name "Pathfinder" with the Germanic "Die Pfadfinderin" did not surprise him. The latter was the title of a Paul Heyse story that King had previously translated. Its convention-defying heroine could be said to have "cut out a new way for the spirit," but Piddington argued this was a case of supersensory ingenuity; King's normal consciousness had resorted to the Heyse allusion in order to express an idea perceived by her *sub*consciousness, reinforcing the informational content (the ship *Pathfinder*) and obliquely, through use of German language of the Hayse title, implying the danger to that ship *from* German enemies. It is, to say the least, a clever piece of deconstruction.

References

Amphion: "Case L. 1201. Impressions," *Journal of the Society for Psychical Research* 16, no. 314 (December 1914): 306–310. Cf. Mrs. Henry Sidgwick, "Phantasms of the Living" in *Proceedings of the Society for Psychical Research* 33, part 86 (October 1922): 353–53.

Pathfinder: Sidgwick, "Phantasms," and J. G. Piddington, "Forecasts in Scripts Concerning The War," *Proceedings Society for Psychical Research* 33, part 87 (March 1923): 502.

Historical information: James Goldrick, *The King's Ships Were At Sea* (Naval Institute Press, 1984).

HMS *Aboukir, Cressy,* and *Hogue*—1914

If Jones or, come to that, King, also foresaw the triple disaster that hit the British Navy a little over two weeks after the *Pathfinder* went down, she, they, and/or the Society for Psychical Research do not seem to have publicized the fact. To compensate for that, however, there is the precognitive experience of yet another unseeking seer whose ostensibly true dream captured what marked a somber first month of Britain's war at sea.

In the early morning hours of September 20, 1914, the British cruisers *Euryalus, Hogue, Cressy,* and *Aboukir* assembled in the North Sea near the Maass Light Vessel to begin their scheduled patrol off the coast of Holland. Heavy weather soon damaged the wireless aerial of the *Euryalus,* which, coupled with the necessity for recoaling, forced this vessel to leave the patrol and return to Harwich.

All through September 20 and 21 the *Hogue, Cressy,* and *Aboukir* continued their cruise, the muzzles of their broadside six-inch guns dipping underwater as the vessels rolled in the heavy seas. Lightly armored and without offensive weapons for use against submerged German U-boats, the three old cruisers were relics of a bygone era in sea warfare. Dubbed the "live bait squadron," the outmoded vessels nevertheless went bravely about fulfilling their mission of watching for enemy warships.

At sunset on the September 21 the weather finally began to moderate, and by midnight the wind had died away altogether. The three cruisers had a fairly easy time of it for the next several hours, but at 5 a.m. on the morning of September 22 they were spotted by Lt. Cmdr. Otto Weddigen of the submarine U-9. Weddigen at first thought the vessels were the advance screen of a major British fleet, but he soon realized that the three old cruisers were utterly alone. Taking advantage of this, U-9 moved in for a submerged attack.

Aboukir, Cressy, and *Hogue* were strung out at three mile intervals and were steaming at ten knots, and they were not zigzagging. Weddigen could not believe his good fortune as he approached his first victim—the *Aboukir*—from fine on her port bow.

One torpedo was enough; it struck the *Aboukir* amidships on her port side, causing immediate heavy flooding that heeled the old cruiser twenty degrees to port within minutes of the explosion. With her boilers and engines crippled, *Aboukir* lost way, and Captain Drummond ordered his injured crewmen to be put into the one available lifeboat and lowered away. Believing that his ship had struck a mine, Drummond hoisted a flag warning *Cressy* and *Hogue* of the mine danger and ordered them to close with *Aboukir* to pick up survivors. Within minutes, however, the captain realized that his ship had been struck by a torpedo, and he warned his two escort cruisers away from the scene to prevent their own destruction. He then assembled his crew on deck in preparation for abandoning ship.

Hogue and *Cressy* kept coming on to pick up survivors, however; the *Hogue*'s Captain Nicholson felt that his own vessel would be safe if he kept *Aboukir* between himself and the point from which the submarine had fired its torpedo. *Hogue* came to a stop a mile from the stricken *Aboukir* and began putting her boats into the water; her captain, however, did not know that the U-9 had altered course and was now only three hundred yards off *Hogue*'s port beam. At 6:55 a.m., as *Aboukir* finally rolled onto her side and then capsized completely, two torpedoes struck the *Hogue* amidships. With her engine room flooded and her watertight doors partially open, the old cruiser rapidly filled with water, turned slowly over on her side and, at 7:05 a.m., followed *Aboukir* to the bottom.

Unwilling to leave fifteen hundred British seamen to perish in the icy water of the North Sea, Captain Johnson of the *Cressy* launched his own vessel's lifeboats and lingered in the area to pick up survivors. When a periscope was reported, *Cressy* got under way at full speed and made an attempt to ram. Unsuccessful at this, *Cressy* slowed again, her guns at the ready, and attempted to pick up her small boats, which were now loaded with survivors from the *Hogue* and *Aboukir*.

It was what Weddigen was waiting for. At 7:20 a.m. two torpedoes streaked toward the *Cressy*, one of them exploding in her starboard bow. The damage was light, however, and *Cressy* made an attempt to escape. The U-9 closed to within five hundred yards of the crippled cruiser and fired its last torpedo. It struck home, and *Cressy* followed her two sisters to the bottom of the North Sea. The U-boat, meanwhile, turned her own course homeward for Germany and a hero's welcome.

Two Dutch merchantmen and two British trawlers had observed the sinking of the three cruisers and, despite the danger they thought existed from mines, steamed to the rescue of the sailors in the water. At 10:30 a.m. British warships arrived on the scene and picked up the few men in the water who remained alive. A total of 837 men survived the sinking of the *Aboukir, Cressy,* and *Hogue*, while 1,459 men either went down with their vessels or died of exposure in the icy waters of the North Sea. The losses were announced in the morning papers the next day.

Some ninety-six hours before this, on Friday, September 18, Mr. F. Harcourt Page of East Preston, Sussex, had a dream. "With remarkable clarity of vision" he saw a large British warship "suddenly, by means of an instrument not clearly revealed," burst into flames. Two similar ships hastened to its aid, but somehow the dreamer knew the first attack "was but a lure to the others" and he could see among "small German ships that hovered in the vicinity, intense gratification at the approaching success of their stratagem. I was possessed of a fierce desire to do something, to warn those oncoming vessels. . . . But with that utter sense of helplessness experienced in dreams I could merely watch and avail nothing." Both went the same way as the first vessel.

Page knew that when he awoke he must warn the Admiralty in the hope of averting the catastrophe, but in the cold light of next day he was sure they would not listen. "Now, unhappily, it has come all too true," he concluded in a letter printed by the *Evening Standard and St. James's Gazette* for September 24.

To Page's mind, there was no question that he had dreamed true. By way of actual evidence, as the SPR found, Page's wife could confirm that he'd awakened her at 7 a.m. on the nineteenth and described his dream, "But being essentially an unbeliever in such things, and, further, only half awake, I paid slight heed to what he said." All she could recall was that he had said he'd seen "three large British warships sunk in the North Sea by a German stratagem, and that they had become a mass of flame before they sank." Mrs. Page knew he was thinking of warning the Admiralty next day, and that he'd decided not to. Page's father remembered him saying, "I've had a beastly dream about our ships," but being a skeptic he cut the revelation short by a studied lack of sympathy.

The dream-premonition may seem valid, though its most decisive features (the German stratagem, the ships in flames) cannot be corroborated. Also, Page does not refer to torpedoes, but to "an instrument not clearly revealed—though his father had an uncertain memory that his son had referred to torpedoes or submarines"—the "small German ships" he saw?

The SPR admitted that there was a resemblance between the loss of the three cruisers and Page's dream. "Too much stress, however, should not be laid upon the coincidence, for when we consider what a large place the war occupies in the public mind, and the likelihood, therefore, of war incidents figuring in dreams, the scope for the occurrence of chance-coincidences is very great, especially in the case of an event so probable as that represented in Mr. Page's dream."

In November 1926 the London *Daily News* issued a call to its readers to step forward and contribute (for possible publication) their own first-hand accounts involving what might be considered "paranormal" events. Reader response was gratifying, and reports describing a wide variety of phenomena were contributed to the newspaper. The best of these accounts were later published in a series of four books so that, according to the publisher, "this important body of evidence on a subject of continual controversy should not be lost."

By saying "the best of these accounts" we do not mean to imply that they were horrific or spine-chilling; far from it. Most of the above accounts were not very frightening at all, at least, to *read* about. (It is difficult to say just how unfailing one's own courage might be when personally experiencing uncanny events like those described by the readers of the *Daily News*.)

In any case, one of the accounts contributed to the newspaper came from the mother of a woman whose husband had been a sailor on HMS *Aboukir* during the Great War. The unnamed mother and daughter had together undergone an experience which, they felt, was connected with the loss of the sailor and his ship.

After reading about the horror and heroism connected with the sinking of HMS *Aboukir* and her sisters, the following account of possibly paranormal activity connected with *Aboukir*'s loss might seem quite tame and, perhaps, unconvincing. Nevertheless, it was striking enough in the minds of the percipients for them to connect the two events in their own minds.

On the night of September 22, 1914—presumably, about eighteen hours after the *Aboukir* went down—the wife of the *Aboukir* crewman was sleeping in the same room as her mother when both women were awakened by a noise "such as would be caused by the dragging of heavy chains." Both ladies sat up with a start, and the crewman's wife cried out, "Oh, mother! What is it?" The mother got up and summoned the only man in the house, who searched the house and yard without finding anything that might have caused the noise. Everyone went back to bed, but a few minutes later the noise was repeated, a "dreadful clanking—weird and unmistakable." Again the house and grounds were searched without result.

The next morning the newspapers announced the loss of the *Aboukir*; the husband/son-in-law of the two women in question was among the crewmen who perished in the tragedy. At least one of the women—the mother-in-law—made a mental connection between the loss of her daughter's husband and the strange noises heard during the night.

Was the nocturnal sound of "chains dragging" really paranormal in nature, and was it connected with the loss of the *Aboukir*? And, if so, what kind of paranormal experience was it? The noise occurred many hours after the disaster itself took place, so the two women were clearly not "mentally tuning in" to the disaster as it happened. Indeed, at the time they heard the odd noise, the two women did not even associate it with their relative on the *Aboukir* or feel that the noise signified any danger he might have encountered. It was only after reading newspaper reports of *Aboukir*'s loss that they seem to have made a connection between the two events. Clearly, it was only with the advantage of hindsight that they were able to make such a connection.

And yet, the very fact that the women were unaware of *Aboukir*'s loss at the time they heard the "dragging of heavy chains" gives one pause for thought. Assuming that the noise really did have a paranormal origin, is it possible that that "dreadful clanking—weird and unmistakable" might have been the last sound heard by their loved one on the *Aboukir* as the great vessel rolled onto her side and went down? It is interesting to note that the two women heard this strange noise a *second* time shortly after they had returned to bed. We can't help but point out that the *Hogue* sank only ten minutes after the *Aboukir* went down; could this second occurrence of the strange, metallic noise have been connected somehow with the destruction of U-9's second victim?

It is unlikely that we will ever know. But taking these cases together with the sinkings of *Amphion* and *Pathfinder*, we might be forced to concede that although these allegedly paranormal cognitions might be reduced to mere expressions of generalized concern about the onset of a long-awaited and putatively crucial contest for supremacy at sea, they might represent much more than that. The fact remains that within weeks of the outbreak of World War I, the Allied fleet sustained five medium-to-major losses, all of which were accompanied by suggestions that the events had been apprehended before, during, or shortly after they took place, in ways not easily explained by the notion of coincidence—and not by Allied war leaders, but by ordinary citizens aided by some seemingly extraordinary power.

References

S. Louis Giraud, ed. *Ghosts in the Great War, and True Tales of Haunted Houses* (London: Fleetgate Publications *Daily News* Books Department, 1927?).

James Goldrick, *The King's Ships Were at Sea* (U.S. Naval Institute, 1984).

A. A. Hoehling, *The Great War at Sea* (Thomas Crowell Co., 1965.)

Journal of the Society for Psychical Research 16, nos. 312/313 (October/November 1914): 301–303.

HMS *Queen Mary*—1916

On May 31, 1916, Florence Baxter was lying ill in her Peterborough home, having been stricken with facial erysipelas five days previously. The young woman was suffering from a spreading inflammation of the facial skin and underlying tissues, symptoms accompanied by a very high temperature, toxemia, vomiting, and occasional delirium. Baxter was a very sick young woman, and her mother, Hannah Malpress, was staying in the daughter's home and looking after her during her illness.

Baxter's acute illness caused her mind to cloud over during nighttime hours, and her mother noticed that she seemed to ramble and say "queer things" during these periods of nocturnal delirium. During the daylight hours, however, Baxter's mind seemed to be clear and alert, a fact vouched for by her physician, Dr. H. Latham of Peterborough.

At about 5 p.m. on the afternoon of May 31 Malpress checked on her daughter only to find that Baxter seemed "listless and blank."

Realizing that these symptoms had never manifested themselves in her daughter during the daytime, Malpress felt certain that Baxter was dying; the frantic mother hurried downstairs and sent someone to fetch the doctor before it was too late. But, although Baxter may have looked "listless and blank" to an observer at her bedside, in reality the young woman was undergoing an unusual mental experience, the timing of which makes it worthy of consideration.

While lying in her sickbed, Baxter had "felt something snap" inside her and experienced the sensation that part of herself had left her physical body. The young woman felt certain that she was now in the process of dying, but a moment later she experienced a vision—suddenly seeming to be "on a ship, or very near it." Baxter could see sailors moving about on the vessel, many of them singing and all of them appearing to be very happy. The young woman saw her brother—Seaman George William Malpress—standing on the deck singing with his mates, and she spoke to him; for some reason, however, he wouldn't answer her. Remembering that she was disfigured by her illness, Baxter asked her brother for a scarf so that she could hide the marks on her face.

Suddenly the scene changed, and Baxter again found herself in her bedroom, only her brother was now standing beside her sickbed. Again the young woman spoke to her brother, but once again the sailor would not answer her. Baxter began to cry, thinking that her brother refused to speak to her because of her facial disfigurement. The vision of her brother faded, but Baxter continued crying and was still very upset when her mother returned to the bedroom a moment later. Malpress asked what was the matter, and Baxter replied that her brother Will had been to see her, but that he wouldn't speak to her. She asked her mother if Will had returned to his duty station, and Malpress replied that Will had not been home. Baxter was certain that her brother had been with her, though, because the experience had seemed so real to her.

The following morning Malpress asked her daughter how Will had looked, and Baxter said he looked the same as always; he had been wearing his uniform and looked very happy. Baxter had thought that he was home on leave. When Dr. Latham arrived to check on his patient, the ladies told him about the odd vision; neither woman seemed overly interested in the subject, however, apparently now regarding the experience as being a side-effect of Baxter's illness.

Baxter's "vision" occurred at about 5 p.m. on the afternoon of May 31. Twelve minutes earlier, at 4:48 p.m., an incident had occurred elsewhere that might have a strong bearing on the vision experienced by the young woman.

Unknown to the general public, the British Grand Fleet had for the last two hours had been locked in a furious engagement with the German High Seas Fleet in the North Sea. This engagement would eventually see the loss of six thousand British lives and fourteen British warships, and it came to be known as the Battle of Jutland; among the British vessels taking part in this engagement was the battle cruiser HMS *Queen Mary*.

At 30,000 tons and mounting 13.5-inch guns, the 32-knot *Queen Mary* was the newest and fastest of England's battle cruisers. The *Queen Mary* was presently in the thick of the battle, and was hotly engaging the German battle cruiser *Von der Tann*. The British warship had found her range and was beginning to make some telling shots at her enemy when disaster struck. At 4:48 p.m. the *Queen Mary* was hit simultaneously by two salvoes from the *Derfflinger* and *Seydlitz*, the explosions shattering the British warship and stunning those crewmen left alive on board her. A few sailors jumped overboard and managed to swim fifty yards or so from the stricken vessel when, with a blinding flash, the *Queen Mary* blew up. A huge, black mushroom cloud hurled itself into the sky from the spot where the *Queen* had been only a moment before, and a steady rain of wreckage fell from the sky for the next minute or two. The *Queen Mary* was no more. Only eighteen crewmen out of her total complement of 1,266 officers and men survived to tell of the manner in which their ship had met her death.

Among the British sailors who died with the *Queen Mary* was Seaman George William Malpress, the son of Mrs. Hannah Malpress and brother of Mrs. Florence Baxter. Although she didn't know it at the time, Mrs. Baxter's odd vision of her seafaring brother had taken place only about twelve minutes after he had met his death in the North Sea.

The general public did not learn about the Jutland naval battle for three more days; on Saturday, June 3, the Admiralty finally informed the newspapers of what had transpired between the German and British fleets in the North Sea. It was then that Malpress first learned what had befallen the *Queen Mary*, but she still had no idea if her son Will had been saved or was among the lost. In any case, Dr. Latham ordered Malpress to refrain from telling Mrs. Baxter about the loss of her brother's ship for fear of worsening her condition. It was only by accident that, around June 8, Baxter picked up a newspaper within her reach and noticed the published list of the lost *Queen Mary*'s crewmen. Among the names on the list was that of G. W. Malpress, A.B.

Was Baxter's vision of her brother—only minutes after his death at sea—merely a hallucination, a result of the intermittent delirium induced by her illness? Possibly. Baxter's vision clearly did not convey to her any literal information about what her brother had been going through on the North Sea for the last couple of hours. Seaman Malpress had been happily singing with his mates when his sister first "saw" him in her vision, but we can be reasonably certain that Malpress was not in reality raising his voice in song during his vessel's engagement with the *Von der Tann, Derfflinger,* and *Seydlitz.*

The chief points of interest concerning Baxter's vision are: (1) It occurred almost simultaneously with the death of her brother, (2) it was the only "hallucination" that took a specific, memorable form during her illness, (3) it was the only "hallucination" described by the percipient during her illness, and (4) the percipient had never had another experience like it.

In spite of the proximity in time between Baxter's vision and the death of her brother, it is still possible that the odd occurrence might have been the result of simple coincidence. Also, since Baxter had apparently never suffered from facial erysipelas before, it is possible that the disease's "novelty" (and severity) might explain the vividness of her hallucination (as well as the fact that she had never experienced a hallucination before).

But perhaps we should ask the following question: Was Seaman Malpress's appearance in his sister's vision a form of "crisis apparition"?

Many cases are on record where far-distant relatives of a sick, injured, or dying person suddenly become aware that that person is presently undergoing a life-threatening crisis. Many times this awareness comes in the form of a "vision" (or an "apparition") of that loved one at the same time the loved one is facing critical danger (or death). It is as if a "mental link" somehow forms between the percipient and the endangered person, enabling the former to become aware of the latter's danger.

Assuming that Baxter's vision was indeed a "crisis apparition," it is interesting to speculate about the atypical form it took. Baxter's "encounter" with Seaman Malpress was distinctly upbeat and nonalarming (except for his odd reluctance to speak to his sister). Baxter had seen her brother singing and smiling, and there was nothing in her vision to suggest that he had just suffered a violent death along with most of his shipmates. If Baxter had indeed seen a "crisis apparition" of her brother, it was in stark contrast to the type of crisis apparition we have just touched on. The percipients of the aforementioned type of crisis apparition somehow know that their distant loved one is facing danger; indeed, the apparition itself often gives the appearance of being injured or in distress, an appearance that usually inspires fear or anxiety on the part of the percipient.

Baxter's vision, however, had just the opposite effect. She was pleased to see her brother, who appeared to be happy and carefree. Her only concern was that he would not talk to her. This last concern *did* leave

Mrs. Baxter upset, but this upset was caused mainly by hurt feelings—a much milder form of anxiety than that of a sudden mortal fear for her brother's safety. If Baxter had indeed undergone a sudden, shocked concern for her brother's welfare, it is conceivable that the anxiety might have proven too much for the sick woman to handle.

Might this have been the reason Baxter's vision took such a basically pleasing form? Was George William Malpress somehow permitted to "say goodbye" to his sister, but in such a way that, in her weakened state, she would not become unduly alarmed and thereby endanger her own health? Or was Baxter's vision of her brother merely a a product of her illness, and its odd timing merely a coincidence? It is much simpler to ask these questions than to answer them.

References

C. R. M. F. Cruttwell, *History of the Great War* (Oxford at the Clarendon Press, 1940).

A. A. Hoehling, *The Great War at Sea* (Thomas Crowell Co., 1965).

Norman Hoerr, M.D., and Arthur Osol, M.D., ed. *Blakiston's Illustrated Pocket Medical Dictionary* (New York: McGraw-Hill, 1960).

Eleanor Mildred Sidgwick, "Case L. 1204," *Phantasms of the Living* (University Books, 1962), pp. 190–93.

SS *Athenia*—1939

At noon on September 1, 1939, the 13,500-ton Donaldson liner *Athenia* cast off from her dock in Glasgow and steamed down the Clyde River on the first leg of her voyage to the Canadian ports of Montreal and Quebec. There were 420 passengers on board the vessel, mostly American and Canadian, as well as a few British emigrants. Although there was nothing unusual about the mixture of nationalities, there was an additional group of passengers whose mere presence on the ship bespoke major events taking place in Europe even as the liner sailed. A busload of European refugees had taken passage on the *Athenia*, their sole purpose in sailing to Canada being to escape the oppression of Nazi rule in their native country, Germany.

Everyone on board the *Athenia* that day was in a state of nervous unease, being not quite sure what experiences they might expect to undergo during the next few days. Adolf Hitler's Wehrmacht had invaded Poland that very morning, and everyone on the *Athenia,* passengers and crewmen alike, realized that England would very soon find herself in a state of war with Germany. Naturally enough, the American and Canadian passengers on board felt lucky to be returning to their respective homelands, while many of the *Athenia*'s crewmen felt that German bombs might wreak many changes in the city of Glasgow by the time their ship returned. But, for the moment at least, England was still at peace with Germany and many of the *Athenia*'s passengers felt that their vessel would be far from any potential danger by the time hostilities erupted between the two countries.

And even if war *was* declared sooner than expected, the *Athenia* was, after all, only a passenger liner. Surely the Germans would not consider her a threat and would allow her to go her way in peace.

Late on the evening of September 1 an additional 136 passengers boarded the *Athenia* when she arrived at Belfast, Ireland. At 7 a.m. on the morning of September 2 the great vessel dropped anchor at Liverpool, her last port of call, where 546 additional travelers boarded her, all anxious to leave the anticipated future war zone and avoid any possible unpleasantness that might occur there. At 4:30 p.m. on September 2 the *Athenia* weighed anchor for the last time and steamed down the Mersey toward the open sea.

At 11 a.m. on the morning of September 3 England declared war on Germany. Eight hours later the German submarine U-30 was lying on the surface 250 miles northwest of Rathlin Island when her captain saw a blacked-out ship approaching his position through the dusk. The unknown vessel was clearly attempting to avoid detection, and so, shortly after 7 p.m., the U-boat fired a spread of four torpedoes at her. One torpedo misfired and jammed in its launch tube, while two others missed their target. The fourth torpedo, however, slammed into the *Athenia*'s side and detonated in one of her holds, throwing up a shower of wreckage and splinters that killed or maimed many of the liner's passengers before they even knew what had happened. The stricken liner began to go down by the stern, and her crewmen spent the next few hours loading her lifeboats with passengers and lowering them away into the darkness, this being accomplished with reasonable success. Only one lifeboat was mishandled during launching; the boat's stern fell the last eight feet to the ocean's surface while its bow remained suspended in the falls. Many of the boat's passengers fell into the sea and drifted away into the darkness, never to be seen again. Additional passengers lost their lives when a couple of lifeboats were accidentally smashed and sunk by two rescue ships, the *Knute Nelson* and the *Southern Cross,* which had responded to the *Athenia*'s distress calls and arrived during the night.

Athenia lay wallowing in the sea until 10:35 a.m. the next morning, when her bows suddenly rose up into the air and she went down stern first; *Athenia*'s awe-stricken survivors watched her passing from their vantage points on the rescue ships which had arrived during the night.

The German U-30 had fired the first shots of World War II in the West, and 112 people, half of them women and children, lost their lives as a result.

It will undoubtedly occur to the reader that he has read an account in this very book that is uncannily similar to this story. Of course, we are referring to the torpedoing of the *Lusitania* during World War I. Indeed, the international diplomatic tensions preceding the sailings of both the *Lusitania* and *Athenia* were very similar: in both instances Germany had already commenced hostilities against England or one of her allies, causing much uncertainty about whether passengers should brave the U-boat menace and sail to or from England on the liners in question. As in the case of the *Lusitania,* the question that concerns us here is whether the commencement of hostilities between Germany and Britain might have alarmed certain people so much as to cause them to experience dreams or "feelings" that the *Athenia* would definitely fall victim to a German torpedo before reaching its destination.

Certainly there is evidence that several *Athenia* passengers made (or received) comments that make it clear they thought there was a possible danger of their vessel being torpedoed. Before she boarded the *Athenia*, Meg Jamieson's brother Donald had bade her goodbye and then added a last word of advice: "Look out for subs, Meg."

"Oh, they won't be out yet," she replied.

"Don't be too sure," replied her brother.

Once the *Athenia* was out on the Atlantic on September 2, Barbara Bailey was seated at dinner with Chief Radio Operator Don when she offered the opinion that the vessel was far too crowded with passengers. "Don't worry," laughed the radioman. "There'll be a lifebelt for you."

Late that evening in the smoking room the passengers' conversation turned to the likelihood that tomorrow would see England's declaration of war against Germany. One woman became greatly agitated and exclaimed that there were "submarines all around us." Her outburst was immediately quashed by other passengers, but everyone there knew that the woman could well be right. The next morning Jocelyn Pick was lying in her cabin when she began counting the number of lifebelts on top of the closet. She wondered if there would be enough for everyone on board should the need arise.

Late on the afternoon of September 3 Stewardess Rogerson was going to her cabin to iron a uniform for the next day when she ran into the chief stewardess, Miss English, who asked, "Well, Rodgie, have you left all your affairs in order?"

"No; why?" was the reply.

"You should, you know," said English. "You can never tell."

In spite of the generally gloomy outlook of the people who made these comments, their pessimistic frame of mind was clearly caused by information they received through *normal* means—the news that Germany had invaded Poland and the probability that England would declare war on the morrow. The tone of the comments they made is completely understandable given the circumstances of the time.

Other passengers on the *Athenia* were experiencing presentiments which, although undoubtedly stemming from the same news of impending war, were more specifically focused on the *Athenia* herself. Belle Maranov had developed a bad feeling about the *Athenia*, although this might have stemmed from her depression over leaving her family in Glasgow. Mrs. Maranov was convinced she would never see her loved ones again—she felt certain they would be killed by German bombs in the coming air raids. (As it turned out, Maranov *did* see her family again; she returned to Glasgow after the *Athenia* went down).

At 11 a.m. on the morning of September 3 England declared herself in a state of war with Germany. Upon hearing this news over the ship's radio, *Athenia*'s captain, James Cook, ordered his vessel's lifeboats to be uncovered and swung out so as to be more easily launched should the need arise. Judith Evelyn and her fiancé, Andrew Allen, stood on the boat deck watching the crewmen work on the lifeboats. All day long Evelyn had been conscious of a "dull, oppressive sense of disaster," but now she experienced a sudden feeling of certainty: no matter what anybody said, the *Athenia*'s lifeboats would have to be used—something was going to happen to the ship.

So certain was Alta Magoon that disaster was near that she found herself unable to eat lunch that day; her tenseness affected her stomach to the point where she had no desire to eat. Normally a friendly and outgoing person, Magoon was glad the ship's dining room was so empty. She had no desire to talk with anyone.

That afternoon Meg Jamieson was sitting in a deck chair watching her little son playing nearby. Several women sat next to Jamieson, and their conversation was so alarming that one of them became slightly hysterical. "I'm sure something's going to happen," the woman repeated over and over, and her fear began to affect the other women. Jamieson got up and walked away from her alarmist neighbors, realizing that, for her son's sake, she must remain calm just in case something *should* happen to the ship.

That evening, after the *Athenia* was torpedoed, Alta Magoon and other passengers were lowered away from the ship in a lifeboat. The boat leaked badly and was soon half-full of water, and Magoon and her fellow passengers were busy bailing out the water using only their shoes. In spite of her precarious position, however, Magoon felt oddly secure; she *knew* she was not going to drown, and that all she had to do was help bail water until the rescue ships arrived.

Although Magoon's certainty that she would remain safe suggests that some precognitive ability of hers might have come into play, a similar feeling of certainty experienced by another *Athenia* passenger failed to come true. George Gray kissed his daughter, Ella Flowers, goodbye and put her into a lifeboat. "I believe I'll drown, but that you'll be saved," the elderly gentleman told his daughter. Although giving the general appearance of being precognitive in nature, Gray's "prediction" was actually a fairly realistic assessment of what might be expected to befall both himself and his daughter. Flowers was leaving the *Athenia* in a lifeboat; thus, she would be saved. Gray, elderly and by no means sure of getting into a lifeboat before the ship sank, ran a very real risk of dying. Gray's last words to his daughter stood a very good chance of coming true.

But they didn't. Gray eventually left the *Athenia* in another lifeboat and was saved. It wasn't until three days later that he received word that Flowers was indeed safe and among the *Athenia* survivors who had been landed back in Glasgow. It is important to ask ourselves how prophetic George Gray's last words might have appeared if he had indeed lost his life on the *Athenia* while the life of his daughter was spared. Certainly his statement would have had all the earmarks of a precognitive insight that had come true. The fact that it did *not* come true is instructive, for it makes us look more critically at other, similar statements made by other *Athenia* passengers that *did* come true—for instance, Miss Magoon's certainty that she would not lose her life in her half-swamped lifeboat. As it happened, Magoon's conviction was borne out, but we should ask ourselves if there were other *Athenia* passengers just as certain as Magoon that they would be saved, only to later lose their lives because their lifeboats were the ones accidentally smashed when the two rescue ships arrived. Indeed, this dilemma is the whole crux of the problem concerning the possible reality of precognition: is a seemingly precognitive feeling or dream the result of actual foreknowledge or is it instead the result of a simple coincidence? It is a critical question, but one not easily answered.

The two most convincing paranormal incidents connected with the *Athenia* disaster both occurred *before* Germany's attack on Poland and England's resulting declaration of war. The two accounts have one interesting thread in common: both took place because the percipients did their best to ensure they would *not* take place.

In 1939 Mr. and Mrs. A. Lennon and their nine-year-old daughter were living in a comfortable home in Toronto. When the child's school closed for the summer, Mr. Lennon's mother took the child to England for a short holiday while the parents remained behind in Toronto. In late August, however, Mrs. Lennon had a disturbing dream; she saw her daughter being pulled into a lifeboat from the cold, black waters all around it. Lennon was so disturbed by this dream that she insisted that her husband wire his mother in England telling her to bring their daughter home to Canada at once. The grandmother did as she was asked, and booked their passage home on the *Athenia.*

We'll never know if Lennon's dream might have been caused by anxiety for her daughter's safety; considering the world-shaking events taking place in Europe at the time, such anxiety would be understandable. Still, it is interesting that Lennon did not dream of her daughter facing some war-related danger on dry land in England; instead, she pictured her daughter facing life-threatening danger at sea.

Since there was no way for the little girl to return to Canada other than to sail on a passenger liner, it was a risk that eventually had to be taken if Lennon ever wanted to see her daughter again. In 1939 there were any number of vessels plying the steamer track between England and Canada upon which the little girl and her grandmother could have sailed. As it turned out, however, it was due *entirely* to Lennon's dream that her daughter and mother-in-law were on the *Athenia* at all. In trying to ensure that the alarming scene in her dream would never take place, Lennon was actually the instrument that *caused* it to take place.

We mentioned a moment ago that one of the *Athenia*'s lifeboats was wrecked when the sea dashed it against the stern of the Swedish yacht *Southern Cross.* Just as Lennon's daughter owed her own presence on the *Athenia* to her mother's dream, the *Southern Cross* owed *her* presence at the disaster site to a "vision" experienced by the wife of her owner.

Fifty-eight-year-old Axel Wenner-Gren, millionaire industrialist and owner of the 320-foot *Southern Cross,* lived in a mansion in Stockholm with his American-born wife, Marguerite. Late one night Mrs. Wenner-Gren was on her way upstairs to retire, the house behind her in darkness while the hall lights illuminated the staircase ahead of her.

Suddenly, at the top of the stairs, two human figures appeared out of thin air. One figure was of a man whose clothing was soaking wet and hair all plastered down, giving every appearance of someone who had just climbed out of the water somewhere. In his arms the man carried a child either unconscious or dead whose forehead had a jagged laceration. Both figures appeared so real that the startled Wenner-Gren screamed in fright, whereupon both figures vanished as quickly as they had appeared.

Wenner-Gren was terribly upset but was unsure if she should mention the uncanny incident to her husband. Finally she did so, but Axel patiently assured her that her nerves had merely been playing tricks on her. He told Marguerite that she needed a period of complete relaxation. Since the Wenner-Grens had already been planning a vacation cruise to Bermuda on the *Southern Cross,* Marguerite suggested that they leave immediately—two days earlier than they had originally intended. Axel agreed, and the *Southern Cross* was readied for sea.

At 9:22 p.m. on September 3 the *Southern Cross* received the *Athenia*'s distress call and turned her bows toward the position she had been given. Five hours later the yacht arrived at the sinking liner's position and began criss-crossing the moonlit sea toward the red flares being burned in the *Athenia*'s lifeboats. One by one, 380 survivors climbed out of the lifeboats onto the deck of the *Southern Cross*; among the first to be welcomed aboard by Mr. and Mrs. Wenner-Gren was a sea-soaked man carrying a dying child whose forehead was bleeding from a deep gash.

As far as we know, there was no apparent reason for Marguerite Wenner-Gren to suddenly experience a hallucination in which the figures of a water-soaked man carrying a dying child should appear at the head of her staircase. At the time she underwent her odd experience the two figures held no significance for her at all—they were just frightening because of their unexpectedness and because, obviously, they didn't belong in the house. It was only later, when Marguerite's nocturnal "vision" was duplicated at the scene of the *Athenia* tragedy, that the significance of the vision became clear.

Precognition? Or coincidence . . . ?

References

Max Caulfield, *Tomorrow Never Came: The Story of the S.S.* Athenia (W. W. Norton, 1959).

New York Times, September 7, 1939. This article stated that Ella Flowers had been reported safe in Glasgow the day before. Caulfield's book says she perished in the disaster.

C. R. Vernon Gibbs, *British Passenger Liners of the Five Oceans* (London: Putnam, 1963).

Bill Wisner, *Strange Sea Stories and Legends* (Signet Books, 1981).

RMS *Queen Mary*—1967 and After

Thus far, our accounts of ship-related psychic phenomena have involved just about every type of paranormal occurrence except one: "hauntings." Granted we have discussed the alleged haunting of the German submarine UB-65, but the absence of documentation regarding that incident indicates, to the authors, at least, that there is no reason for us to believe it took place at all. We have shown readers ghosts that haunted living rooms, séance rooms and bedrooms, and even Southsea Beach, but none of them took up permanent residence in these places, which is what the term "haunting" implies.

If a house is said to be haunted we tend to suppose it is so permanently. The ghost is in twenty-four-hour residency; it doesn't come and go like some casual visitor. And permanently haunted ships seem to be rare. However, there *is* a vessel still in existence that is reputed to be the site of various types of paranormal activity, including unexplained noises, apparitions and other related phenomena.

What is a haunted house, anyway? For that matter, what is a haunted ship? Whatever the correct answer may be, the RMS *Queen Mary* has gained a reputation of being the latter. Tied up at her moorings in Long Beach, California, the *Queen Mary* today is a hollow shell of what she once was: her staterooms are utilized as hotel rooms for the convention center that operates on board, and four restaurants cater to the palettes of hungry tourists who flock aboard her every day. The old passenger liner's upper decks—the ones open to the public—are spic and span, giving the appearance of being thoroughly modern and completely unmysterious.

When one descends to her lower decks, however, a different atmosphere envelopes the visitor. The *Queen Mary*'s cavernous engine rooms, stripped of their machinery, are rusting away in silence; pools of water lie here and there on the floors of the lowest decks, and stacks of old furniture—remnants of happier days—lie in jumbled piles wherever adequate storage space is available. It is here, on the lower decks, that people have reported seeing and hearing things that they have been unable to explain to their own satisfaction (in "normal" terms, that is).

How long have these paranormal events been happening on board the *Queen Mary*? We don't know for certain, but the old liner's present master, Captain John Gregory, has spoken about it with former passengers and crew members, including John Treasure Jones, the master who commanded the *Queen Mary* on her last voyage from England to Long Beach. These people told Gregory that they either had undergone shipboard paranormal experiences themselves or else had heard about the experiences of others in such a way as to believe that they had happened. But, however long ago such phenomena may have originated, various people who today work on board the vessel in Long Beach will testify that mysterious goings-on are still taking place.

In 1984 one of the lieutenants in charge of security, Fred McMullin, experienced considerable difficulty in keeping several doors closed and locked in various parts of the ship. In the middle of the night alarm lights would glow on a panel in the ship's security office, indicating that locked doors had just been opened down in the lower regions of the ship. Doors in the swimming pool area were found unlocked for several nights in a row, two of the doors even being found propped open. At first McMullin thought that security people from the previous shift were not checking the doors, but these people claimed that the doors were locked when their shifts ended. Then McMullin thought that somebody was deliberately tampering with the lock mechanisms in the doors; he and several other security officers spent several months trying (unsuccessfully) to determine just how the alarms were being triggered. Many times McMullin would lock doors himself and go away on his rounds only to return a short time later to find the doors open again.

Another security guard, Bill Thompson, reported similar occurrences on G deck, where the ship's original morgue was believed to have been located. Lights that had been left on would be turned off, and vice versa; doors would slam without any seeming cause; motion sensors in the padlocked artifacts section would go off, indicating that a moving body was inside the locked room.

A secretary named Cheryl Zalfini reported hearing noises in the engine room, clanging noises like those that might be made by someone working down there. The only catch was that, at 6 p.m. nobody was supposed to be in the engine room.

Although the precise reasons for these occurrences remain unknown, one cannot help but notice that many of the events we are discussing are similar to nuisance-type occurrences typical of poltergeist activity. Nevertheless, it is still possible that the "mysterious origins" of some of these events were not so mysterious after all. Might not some unauthorized person have been roaming the *Queen Mary*'s lower decks unlocking various doors after the security teams had locked them? Unlikely, but not impossible. Could a fastidiously correct security guard have been responsible for the extinguished lights and slamming doors on G deck? Again, it is possible, although each security guard probably should have known whether any of his comrades were patrolling those parts of the ship in which the lights were blinking and the doors slamming. As for the sensor set off inside the locked artifact room, could a wandering rat have been responsible for the movement picked up by the sensor? Undoubtedly. But *was* it a rat?

In 1983 a reporter from the *Long Beach Press-Telegram* named Tom Hennessy had been talking with Captain Gregory about the *Queen Mary* when Gregory happened to mention the uncanny occurrences being reported aboard his vessel. A confirmed skeptic, Hennessy ridiculed the stories and Captain Gregory threw out a challenge of sorts: he invited Hennessy to spend a night aboard the *Queen Mary* with permission to visit any part of the ship he wished. Hennessy took up the gauntlet and reported to the ship at sundown, planning to pass the night in the various areas of the vessel Captain Gregory said had been the sites of unexplained happenings.

Hennessy spent half an hour alone near the ship's empty swimming pool in the wee hours of the morning; although he saw nothing out of the ordinary, he later reported that the eerie shadows in the dimly lighted room made this "the second-longest half hour of my life."

The *longest* half hour of his life occurred shortly thereafter, when Fred McMullin locked Hennessy in "shaft alley" (housing the ship's propellor shafts), promising to return in thirty-five minutes. No sooner did the security officer depart when a clanging noise shattered the silence, the noise coming from the forward end of the alley and sounding like someone banging on pipes with a wrench. When Hennessy walked forward to investigate, the noise stopped, only to begin again when he retreated aft. But that wasn't all. . . . When Hennessy retreated aft, his way was blocked by an oil drum which, as far as he could recall, had not been there before. Hennessy walked forward again, then returned a few moments later to find *two* oil drums blocking his path. He reasoned that he must have somehow missed seeing the second drum when he encountered the first one, although that still didn't explain where the *first* drum had come from.

Next Hennessy climbed to a metal catwalk and started walking along it when, suddenly, he felt vibrations in the metal like someone was walking along the catwalk toward him. The reporter turned and beat a hasty retreat, soon getting out of the range of the vibrations. Now, however, a sudden breeze blew by him, an event that was "impossible" due to the fact that shaft alley is in the very bottom of the ship, far from any openings to the outside.

Then, at 3:33 a.m., alone in shaft alley, the reporter heard voices. They sounded like two or three men talking together, the words muffled and indistinct. The voices finally trailed off until only a single voice could be heard, and Hennessy was able to understand the last phrase spoken by this voice: ". . . turning the lights off."

Even though Hennessy knew that he was supposed to be alone in this part of the ship, he felt that the voices had probably been carried to shaft alley through a ventilator from another part of the vessel. Security guard Bill Thompson denied that this was so, however, claiming that the closest person to shaft alley had been another security officer two decks away. Besides, said Thompson, Hennessy wasn't the only person to have heard voices in shaft alley.

Hennessy made a point of interviewing as many people as he could who claimed to have had eerie experiences on board the *Queen Mary*. A tour guide named Patricia Salcido told him that she once heard a metallic clanking noise coming from a wall; at the same time, she saw two circles of light—perfectly round, like portholes—moving along the wall. Two other tour guides claimed to have heard the sound of someone clearing his throat, after which a chain across an entryway in the engine room started whipping up and down. Other people reported hearing such noises as keys jangling, chains dragging, and shouts and splashing in the (empty) pool area.

Other reports of odd occurrences came from the *Queen Mary*'s kitchens, where pots and pans disappeared and reappeared, dishes moved and lights went on and off without apparent reason. Hennessy's research uncovered a reported death in the kitchen that he felt might be linked to the odd goings-on. Around 1943, when the *Queen Mary* was being used to transport American troops to Europe, a certain cook had been so bad and so unpopular that a brawl developed in the ship's kitchen. Before it ended the unfortunate cook was somehow pushed into an oven, his burns eventually proving fatal. Apparently decidely less skeptical than when be began investigating the *Queen Mary,* Hennessy felt that the poltergeist-like activity in the ship's kitchen might be linked to the sudden death of this wartime cook.

Hennessy also interviewed a security guard who had once been patrolling D deck with his guard dog when, without any apparent reason, the dog stopped near a hatchway and began to snarl. Its hair bristled as it stared ahead at something which the guard could not see. The dog refused to move and began whining when the guard attempted to force it to move forward. Suddenly a noise attracted the guard's attention, a noise which sounded like a heavy metal object rolling toward where he was standing. Both man and dog turned and ran from the noise, whatever it was, and nothing further happened. A possible sidelight on this incident was discovered later, however; records show that, in the early days of World War II, a crewman had been crushed to death by heavy metal objects in the very hatchway where the guard's dog reacted so strangely.

One can't help but note that the above event is suggestive of what we might term an "auditory replay" of an event from the *Queen Mary*'s past. Is it possible for a specific location to be a "memory storehouse" that somehow "records" traumatic events that have taken place there? Can these "recordings" be "played back" under certain unusual circumstances long after the events themselves have faded from human memory? Although the exact circumstances of the wartime crewman's death are unknown, it seems at least possible that a heavy metal object may have shifted in the *Queen Mary*'s cargo hold and rolled on top of the unfortunate victim. If this is indeed what happened, perhaps the aforementioned security guard and his dog were somehow privileged to "listen in" to a tragedy that had taken place a generation earlier.

A similar case to the one we have just discussed took place in August 1988 in the *Queen Mary*'s forepeak, at the opposite end of the ship from shaft alley. Security guard Thompson had taken parapsychologist William Roll into this area of the vessel to investigate the paranormal events said to have taken place there. As Roll peered down a ladder leading into the depths of the bow, both he and Thompson heard the voices of two men talking together somewhere below. Roll called out to the owners of the voices, asking who they were and what they were doing down there, but his only answer was silence. Thompson told Roll that nobody was supposed to be in any of the three compartments below them; deciding to investigate, Roll climbed down the ladder toward the very bottom of the ship. On his way down he examined each of the three compartments he passed through, but there was nobody there. This was interesting, because the three compartments were watertight, and the only means of entry or egress was by the ladder Roll was using. When Roll climbed back up to where Thompson was waiting for him, the security guard said that he had heard the two men resume their conversation while Roll was down below looking for the source of the voices. Roll had heard nothing, however, and now the voices were silent.

Roll came back to the *Queen Mary* the next day armed with a voice-activated tape recorder, that is, one that begins recording only when some sound activates it. He placed the recorder in the ship's bow on the second deck from the bottom, feeling that this may have been the place where the unknown voices had come from. He left the recorder there overnight on September 4–5, 1988, hoping to tape any noises occurring inside the ship during the night. The bow area was then sealed off to prevent the entry of any unauthorized persons during the night.

Roll's experiment was successful. For two minutes during the wee hours of the morning his tape recorder picked up noises that should not have been occurring on board the *Queen Mary*. These were the sounds of several booming metallic blows. They sounded much like what an enormous dungeon door might sound like if slammed shut inside an echo chamber. (This is our own description, having heard a copy of the tape.) There was also a noise like the sound of rushing water, while in the background a gravelly male voice, almost intelligible, could be heard speaking.

The reason Roll had decided to concentrate his investigation in the *Queen Mary*'s bow area was that he had previously spoken to John Smith, the *Queen Mary*'s chief engineer during her final voyage. Smith's duties on the great vessel had carried him to many different parts of the ship. One of Smith's duties had been to keep an eye out for leaks in the hull, and one February night in 1988 found him on the top deck of the *Queen Mary*. Pointing his flashlight down into the bow compartments, the engineer heard the sound of rushing water. Thinking that a pipe might have burst or that the vessel's hull had sprung a leak, Smith hurried down the ladder to see how much water had accumulated inside the hull. As he approached the forepeak the sounds of rushing water faded away, only to be replaced by metallic tapping sounds, the odd sensation of a "shuddering tremor," and the sound of voices—a gravelly one in the distance, but also others crying, laughing, moaning, and shrieking.

Over the next few years Smith heard these same eerie sounds seven or eight additional times—always in the *Queen Mary*'s forepeak—but he was at a loss to explain how the sounds might have originated. Then he read a history of the ship and discovered something that might have a bearing on the unexplained noises in her bow.

During the use of the *Queen Mary* as a troop transport in World War II, on October 2, 1942, the great vessel, fully loaded with ten thousand American soldiers, was approaching the Clyde River when the old British cruiser *Curacao* steamed out to escort her into port, as was her custom. The 81,000-ton *Queen Mary* and her 4,200-ton consort zigzagged their way toward home, but then one or both of the captains made a misjudgment as the two vessels' courses converged on each other. The *Queen Mary* brushed against the *Curacao*'s stern and swung the smaller vessel broadside into her own path. The great liner's bows cut the cruiser in half and left the two sections wallowing in her wake; under orders never to stop (because of the U-boat menace), the *Queen Mary* was forced to steam on, leaving the *Curacao*'s surviving crew to be picked up by destroyers visible seven miles in the distance. By the time the destroyers arrived, however, only 102 of the cruiser's 440-man crew were still alive. By contrast, the *Queen Mary*'s bow had been crushed in only six or eight feet by the collision, and there were no fatalities on board her.

This wartime tragedy was kept from the public at the time, and Smith had never heard of the incident before reading about it in the ship's biography.

Could the disembodied sounds heard by Smith in the *Queen Mary*'s forepeak have been an "auditory replay" of her wartime collision with the *Curacao*? Were the sounds tape recorded by William Roll the same sounds that had echoed through the liner's bow when she cut the cruiser in half? Smith's description of what he had heard on the ship was so similar to the sounds Roll had recorded himself that the parapsychologist played his recording for Smith, but without saying where or under what circumstances it had been made. The *Queen Mary*'s former chief engineer became visibly emotional; his eyes filled with tears, and he chokingly told Roll that the sounds on the tape were exactly like those he had heard in the *Queen Mary*'s forepeak.

The fact that no casualties occurred on the *Queen Mary* at the time of the collision might make one wonder why Smith should have heard screams among the unexplained sounds in the ship's forepeak. Perhaps they stemmed from screams originating in the *Curacao,* which was right outside the *Queen Mary*'s bows during the collision. But, according to Smith, he also heard sounds of *laughter* among the unexplained moans and shrieks in the forepeak. It is unlikely that anyone, whether on the *Queen Mary* or the *Curacao,* would have been laughing while the huge liner cut her escort in half. Could the unexplained sounds emanating from the forepeak be a sort of collage of sounds from different points in the *Queen Mary*'s career? If the sounds really are "recordings" that are being "replayed" for us from our hypothesized "memory storehouse," perhaps it is not really important for us to know exactly *which* recordings are being replayed. The possibility that their origin might truly be paranormal is enough of a challenge for the present.

In addition to the variety of unexplained phenomena just discussed, apparitions have occasionally been reported in various parts of the *Queen Mary*. Records show that at least forty-nine deaths occurred on board the big Cunarder during her many years of active service. Assuming that apparitions really do exist—a big assumption, but a possibility the authors are unwilling to dismiss out of hand—perhaps a few of the people who met their demise on the *Queen Mary* have continued to hold forth on the liner even though she no longer plies the steamer track between the Old and New Worlds.

Official records show that a woman once drowned in the big Cunarder's swimming pool, and a nice-looking female apparition (clad in a miniskirt) has occasionally been seen walking toward the pool only to vanish behind a pillar. Another female apparition is the "Woman in White," who is said to drape herself over the piano in the ship's salon. The "Poisoned Officer" is sometimes observed in an area near the bridge where one of the *Queen Mary*'s officers once died from accidental poisoning.

The swimming pool is one part of the ship that seems to have more than its share of apparitions. In addition to the miniskirted wraith already mentioned, a second has also been seen in the area, this one by a witness who, before her sighting, had been an admitted skeptic toward all things psychic. Our witness, a former security sergeant named Nancy Wazny, had been standing alone on a stairway overlooking the empty swimming pool when she saw something out of the corner of her right eye. It was a woman, described by Wazny as being forty or fifty years old (or, according to another interview, sixty or seventy years old) and dressed in an old-style, black-and-white striped bathing suit. The woman stood at the edge of the empty pool and appeared to be poised to dive into it. Wazny went down the stairway and stepped around a pillar to get a better look at the woman, but, even though only a few seconds had elapsed, the woman was no longer there. There had not been enough time for the woman to reach an exit, nor was she lying crumpled at the bottom of the empty swimming pool. She was simply . . . gone.

Wazny also sighted a much more typical apparition. This incident took place in shaft alley, where reporter Tom Hennessy had his eerie experiences in 1983. Perhaps it is worth noting that a tragedy once occurred in shaft alley that might have a bearing on both of the above incidents. In 1966 a crewman named John Pedder was crushed to death in that location when a watertight door descended on him before he was able to get clear; since that time, at least two tour groups have reported seeing an apparition of a bearded man in blue coveralls in shaft alley.

At any rate, on the evening in question Wazny was working as a "lead guide" on the *Queen Mary*; at 6 p.m. she was engaged in closing down the tour route and making sure that no straggling tourists were still wandering around in the bowels of the ship. Wazny got on an escalator and was ascending to the upper decks when she got the sudden feeling that she wasn't alone. Turning around, she was startled to find a bearded man in dirty blue coveralls standing immediately behind her on the escalator. Thinking that he wanted to pass by her, Wazny stepped aside and turned around to face forward again. When the man didn't climb past her, she looked around once again. There was nobody behind her—she was alone on the escalator.

Another odd incident—one the authors will refrain from commenting on—is reported to have occurred in the pool area late one night. Maintenance supervisor Cathy Lund and a coworker were walking into the pool room (the pool being filled with water at this time) when they heard the sound of giggling, as if a child was playing in the area. They then saw splashing in the pool, even though nothing could be seen in the water that might cause such a disturbance. The activity in the water ceased, and once again the two coworkers heard the sound of a child giggling. Then, amazingly, the wet footprints of a child appeared one after another along the side of the pool, the trail of prints leading into a nearby locker room.

Our last apparitional encounter was also reported by a crew-woman engaged in her normal workday activity. Carol Leyden was a waitress whose career on the *Queen Mary* had spanned the previous fourteen years, so we must assume she was by this time completely accustomed to her shipboard surroundings. (Might we wonder, however, if the longevity of her shipboard career might also have thoroughly exposed her to other crewmens' tales of uncanny goings-on on board the vessel?) Whatever the case, on this December morning Leyden picked up a cup of coffee from her work area and walked into the dining room and past a table at which a lady wearing a cocktail dress like those from the 1940s was sitting. The waitress noticed that the woman's face was without makeup and was very pale, while her dark hair was rolled up at the sides in an outdated fashion. The woman just sat there, absolutely motionless, as Leyden walked past her. When she was about ten feet beyond the table, Leyden turned and looked back at where the woman was sitting—but there was nobody there.

On the face of it, these sightings of apparitions on the *Queen Mary* would seem to support the contention that ghosts walk the corridors of the old passenger liner. For most people, however, the word "ghost" implies that the actual *personality* of a deceased human being has, in a manner of speaking, "survived" the death experience while retaining the intellect it possessed in life. Even though cases are on record that suggest the possible survival of human personality after death, we must ask ourselves if the apparitions on the *Queen Mary* have given any indication that they are conscious of, and able to interact with, the people who observed them.

Decidedly not. The shadowy figures on board the *Queen Mary* do not appear to have made eye contact with their observers or shown any real awareness that living people were anywhere in the vicinity. Rather, the apparitions seem to have been observed while "going about their business"—that is, while doing something appropriate to both their location on the ship and to the time period in which they seem to have originated. The woman in the 1940s cocktail dress was sitting at a table in the dining room; the bearded crewman was ascending an escalator from his duty station in shaft alley; the elderly woman in the striped bathing suit was preparing to dive into a (now empty) swimming pool; the giggling and splashing accompanied by wet footprints leaving the swimming pool would be typical of a child who once enjoyed playing there. In other words, the activities of the apparitions seem to be "replays" of events that once took place.

Might our postulated "memory storehouse" theory explain the apparitions described above? Might several areas of the *Queen Mary* have somehow "recorded" certain occurrences that took place during the great vessel's active career? Might modern-day observers, through some process we do not yet understand, have somehow triggered a visual "replay" of these events? After all, there would be no point for an apparition clad in a bathing suit to dive into an empty swimming pool. However, if the apparition was merely the image of a past *event* (as opposed to an actual intelligent entity), the actions of the apparition would not change no matter how many alterations might have occurred to the "scenery" surrounding the location of that past event. Thus, even if the swimming pool no longer existed at all, the elderly bather might still stand in the same location and prepare to dive into the spot where the pool *used* to exist.

A crude analogy: imagine a movie projector throwing the filmed image of a diver onto a screen—not onto a blank screen, but onto the photograph of a filled swimming pool. The combined scene of diver and filled swimming pool will represent an actual event that took place in a certain location. Now, let us represent the passage of time by removing the photograph of the filled swimming pool and replacing it with a photograph of the same pool, only empty. When the film of the diver is projected onto this empty pool, the diver's actions do not vary one iota. The empty pool is in the same physical location as the filled pool, and so the diver dives into the pool no matter what its current condition. If we simulate the passage of eons of time by removing the photo of the empty pool and replacing it with the photograph of a desert, the filmed diver obligingly leaps into the desert, because the location of this desert is identical to the *location* of the original swimming pool.

Might this explain why an elderly apparition was seen preparing to leap into an empty swimming pool? Might this account for the feminine wraith seen sitting at a dining room table, or the phantasm of a crewman apparently still making the rounds of his duty station? Did these events once actually take place on the *Queen Mary*, and were they somehow "recorded" at that time for periodic "playback" to receptive observers?

These are questions to which we do not yet have answers.

References

Tom Hennessy, *Long Beach Press-Telegram,* March 6, 1983.
The Liners (Time-Life Books, 1978).
Arthur Myers, *The Ghostly Register* (Dorset Press, 1990).
William Roll, "Journey to the Grey Ghost," *Fate* (May 1991).
"Unsolved Mysteries," NBC-TV, broadcast October 1989.
James Crenshaw, "Ghosts on the *Queen Mary*," *Fate* (April 1984).